Comparative Effectiveness Research

Evidence, Medicine, and Policy

CAROL M. ASHTON, MD, MPH

NELDA P. WRAY, MD, MPH

OXFORD
UNIVERSITY PRESS

OXFORD
UNIVERSITY PRESS

Oxford University Press is a department of the University of Oxford.
It furthers the University's objective of excellence in research, scholarship,
and education by publishing worldwide.

Oxford   New York
Auckland   Cape Town   Dar es Salaam   Hong Kong   Karachi
Kuala Lumpur   Madrid   Melbourne   Mexico City   Nairobi
New Delhi   Shanghai   Taipei   Toronto

With offices in
Argentina   Austria   Brazil   Chile   Czech Republic   France   Greece
Guatemala   Hungary   Italy   Japan   Poland   Portugal   Singapore
South Korea   Switzerland   Thailand   Turkey   Ukraine   Vietnam

Oxford is a registered trademark of Oxford University Press in the UK
and certain other countries.

Published in the United States of America by
Oxford University Press
198 Madison Avenue, New York, NY 10016

Library of Congress Cataloging-in-Publication Data
Ashton, Carol M.
Comparative effectiveness research : evidence, medicine, and
policy / Carol M. Ashton, Nelda P. Wray.
p. ; cm.
Includes bibliographical references and index.
ISBN 978–0–19–996856–5 (hardback : alk. paper)—ISBN 978–0–19–996957–9 (e-book)
I. Wray, Nelda P.   II. Title.
[DNLM: 1. Comparative Effectiveness Research—history—United States.   2. Health Care
Costs–legislation & jurisprudence—United States.   3. Comparative Effectiveness Research—
legislation & jurisprudence—United States.   4. Evidence-Based Medicine—
United States.   5. Government Regulation—United States.   6. History, 21st Century—United
States. W 74 AA1]
RA440.85
362.1072—dc23
2013006780

1 3 5 7 9 8 6 4 2
Printed in the United States of America
on acid-free paper

To our mothers and fathers, and to the person
who for more than 30 years has made all
good things possible, including this book.

CONTENTS

PART THREE   INTERESTS

ACKNOWLEDGMENTS

We have been privileged to have had excellent resources and the help of many exceptional people in doing the research for this book and preparing the manuscript. An Investigator Award in Health Policy Research from the Robert Wood Johnson Foundation made the work possible. Our colleagues in that program shared their expertise, insights, and wisdom and made this book better than it would have been without them. David Mechanic, program director, encouraged us and gave us excellent advice on the book proposal. Lynn Rogut advised us on the framing of the book; her comments on drafts of Part III of the book were invaluable.

As we designed the project, John Lavis led us to the work of John Kingdon, whom we were later privileged to meet in person. Kingdon's seminal work on how problems, policy alternatives, and politics move an issue onto the public policy agenda informed our approach to the research for this book.

Over 100 individuals inside and outside government granted us interviews (some, several times) and shared with us their knowledge of comparative effectiveness research as a policy option, their interpretation of the legislative process and the politics, and their understanding of how events were unfolding as the policy evolved. We promised each of them that their comments would not be associated with their names, and so they remain anonymous.

Susan Lexer and Emily Rowe Holubowich introduced us to many people directly involved in the crafting of federal policy of comparative effectiveness research. Their enthusiasm reinforced our beliefs about the importance of the project.

Grants from the National Institutes of Health (R01CA134995) and the Agency for Healthcare Research and Quality (R13HS016863) supported work that enabled us to understand the special challenges of comparative effectiveness research involving surgical procedures.

Anna F. Jarman, research assistant par excellence, participated in the analyses of interview transcripts, managed the databases of thematic fragments from the transcripts, helped us track the chronology of legislative events, retrieved and handled hundreds of documents, and provided valuable insights and interpretations.

Lorraine Laird and Donna Herrick provided excellent transcriptions of the recordings of often-lengthy, complex, and acronym-filled interviews. We are grateful to the other individuals who provided assistance during the project, including Marie Ashton, Michael Ashton, Heaven Chee, Tracy Moore, Roseann Packer, Elizabeth Russell, Matthew Viscuso, and Stephanie Yi.

AcademyHealth kindly provided us with temporary office space for some of the interviews we conducted in Washington, DC. Janet Arsenault and Marie Grodde of Fifty Point Conservation Area in Winona, Ontario arranged for research space for us in Ingledale House (built c. 1815) during the summer of 2010.

We are indebted to Barbara L. Bass, MD, chairman of the Department of Surgery at The Methodist Hospital in Houston, Texas, for the material help for the completion of our manuscript that she has provided to us as members of her department.

The opinions and interpretations in this book are ours and do not necessarily represent the views of our research sponsors. We are responsible for any errors, omissions, or misinterpretations.

LIST OF ABBREVIATIONS

ACO	accountable care organization
ADOPT	A Diabetes Outcome Progression Trial
AHCPR	Agency for Health Care Policy and Research
AHRQ	Agency for Healthcare Research and Quality
ALLHAT	Anti-hypertensive and Lipid-Lowering Treatment to Prevent Heart Attack Trial
CBO	Congressional Budget Office
CDER	Center for Drug Evaluation and Research (FDA)
CER	comparative effectiveness research
CHAMP	Children's Health and Medicare Protection Act of 2007
CMS	Centers for Medicare and Medicaid Services
CRO	contract research organization
DHHS	Department of Health and Human Services
DREAM	Diabetes Reduction Assessment trial
DTC	direct-to-consumer
FDA	Food and Drug Administration
FFRDC	federally funded research and development center
FY	fiscal year
GAO	Government Accountability Office
GSK	GlaxoSmithKline
HELP	Health, Education, Labor, and Pensions Committee (of the U.S. Senate)
HHS	Health and Human Services (department of)
IDE	investigational device exemption
IND	investigational new drug
IOM	Institute of Medicine
LCD	local coverage determination
LDL	low-density lipoprotein
MMA	Medicare Modernization Act of 2003

NCD	national coverage determination
NDA	new drug application
NIH	National Institutes of Health
OND	Office of New Drugs (part of the FDA)
OSE	Office of Surveillance and Epidemiology (part of the FDA)
PBM	pharmacy benefits manager/management
PCOR	Patient-Centered Outcomes Research
PCORI	Patient-Centered Outcomes Research Institute
PhRMA	Pharmaceutical Research and Manufacturers of America
PIO	pioglitazone
PIPC	Partnership to Improve Patient Care
PMA	pre-market application
PPS	prospective payment system
PSA	prostate-specific antigen
PTCA	percutaneous transluminal coronary angioplasty
RECORD	Rosiglitazone Evaluated for Cardiac Outcomes and Regulation of glycemia in Diabetes trial
REMS	risk evaluation and mitigation strategy
RSG	rosiglitazone
TIDE	TZD (thiazolidinedione) with vitamin D Evaluation trial
USPSTF	U.S. Preventive Services Task Force
VA	(Department of) Veterans Affairs, or Veterans Health Administration

INTRODUCTION

Many things are remarkable about the comprehensive health care reform bill signed into law by President Barack Obama in March 2010. This book explores one of them: the inclusion of provisions in the Patient Protection and Affordable Care Act (P.L. 111–148, hereafter the Affordable Care Act) that mandate research into the comparative effectiveness of health care interventions. The Act creates a Patient-Centered Outcomes Research Institute as the nexus for this research, places the Institute outside of the usual government oversight of federal research programs, and funds its activities principally through a levy on health insurers.

Most people outside of the medical profession would wonder about the need for such an institute. We Americans like to believe that the medical care we get from our doctors is backed up by solid scientific evidence and that American medical care and medical research are the best in the world. Why, then, does the federal government need to mandate and fund a new structure to evaluate the effectiveness of health care interventions? Aren't the facts already known?

In this book, we examine federal policy on comparative effectiveness research and its implications from the perspective of evidence in medicine: how evidence is generated through research and how evidence is used—or not—in various aspects of medical care. We show where comparative effectiveness research fits in the schema of the generation and application of evidence about the net benefits and harms of treatments for human diseases and conditions, and explain the importance of this kind of research to all who have a stake in American health care in the 21st century. We also tell the story of how and why the federal government decided to make comparative effectiveness research an important feature of health care reform. We have written this book from our perspectives as insiders in the health care system and observers of what happens to patients as they use the system. During our respective 30+ year careers as physicians, we have cared for patients, served on medical school faculties and taught medicine to students and trainees, conducted numerous research projects, built and led medical research programs, and served in many local and national leadership positions in the health care sector.

A Brief Account of Our Research Methods

Our analyses of comparative effectiveness research as federal policy are based on five lines of research. First, we conducted three waves of interviews of policy influentials and stakeholders inside and outside government. The waves corresponded to the run-up to the 2008 presidential elections, the period between the election of Barack Obama and the passage of comprehensive health reform in March 2010, and the months after the March 2010 passage of the legislation. We conducted 117 interviews, transcribed them, systematically coded their contents, and cross-checked and verified all information. Second, we tracked the events, their chronology, and the actors using the daily electronic briefs in *Congressional Quarterly, Roll Call, The Hill*, and other specialized electronic media. Third, by following the daily newspapers of major cities we tracked how events were being interpreted by analysts, reporters, and the public. Fourth, we read and analyzed information about comparative effectiveness research presented in the peer-reviewed medical and health-policy literature. Fifth, we analyzed the notes and transcripts from a national workshop that we planned and hosted in Washington, DC in 2008. At this workshop, "Surgical and Minimally Invasive Procedures: Incentive-Based Approaches to Improving the Evidence Base," we convened 100 representatives of major stakeholders in comparative effectiveness research focusing on surgical procedures.

A Preview of the Book

Although comparative effectiveness research can apply to diagnostic as well as therapeutic interventions, in this book we focus mostly on therapeutics. For patients the stakes are higher with therapeutics because such interventions are intended to change the natural history of a disease or condition for the better.

Part I of the book—"Evidence"—is devoted to the concepts of scientific evidence in clinical medicine: how evidence is generated by research, how it is used in the regulation of medical therapies, and how it influences clinical decision making in everyday practice. We discuss the ideals of evidence in medicine as well as the reality that medical decision making is plagued by evidence that is nonexistent, faulty, subverted, or ignored. Part I positions the reader to understand the medical-evidence context into which comparative effectiveness research falls.

In Part II—"Politics and Policy"—we provide a journalistic account of how comparative effectiveness research became federal law. Our research indicates that the roughly 10-year legislative odyssey of this federal policy was marked by six inflection points at which it gained political traction. The positions taken by various stakeholders became clear during this process.

Part III—"Interests"—examines the implications of federal policy on comparative effectiveness research for key sectors: those who pay for medical care (patients and third-party payers), doctors and hospitals, and the clinical research enterprise. In the Epilogue we take a look at how the statutory provisions for comparative effectiveness research provisions were implemented between 2010 and 2012 and anticipate some of the challenges that will arise.

"Looking for Daylight"

In 2002 and again in 2003 Representative Thomas Allen (D-ME) introduced bills on comparative effectiveness research. A version of his 2003 bill, which was co-sponsored by JoAnn Emerson (R-MO), eventually became part of the 2003 Medicare Modernization Act. It was Representative Allen who deserves the credit for launching the journey of federal policy on comparative effectiveness research. Mr. Allen had heard repeatedly from his Maine constituents about unaffordable prescription drugs and medical services and was looking for solutions. When we asked Mr. Allen about the genesis of his legislative proposal, he told us, "Legislating is a lot like being a running back. I was one once, and you look for an opening. You run to daylight. And comparative effectiveness research was an area we came across that seemed to have enormous potential and was not being covered by anyone else."

Federally mandated comparative effectiveness research is indeed an area of enormous potential, an endeavor that could shed daylight on what does and does not work in health care and lead to substantial improvements in health outcomes. Will the potential for daylight be realized? This is the story behind this book.

PART ONE

EVIDENCE

The Generation of Evidence in Medicine

Evaluating the Benefits and Harms of Treatment

The goal of every treatment is to make the patient's outcome better than it would have been without any intervention. Because of advances in research in the past six or so decades, clinical scientists are able to estimate with considerable precision whether a particular intervention will lead to net benefit over harm in groups of individuals possessing certain characteristics. That said, much of clinical practice lacks a supporting evidence base, and what research evidence exists is predominantly of poor quality. Federally mandated comparative effectiveness research is to increase the amount of high-quality research that focuses on the benefits and harms of treatments. In this chapter, we provide a brief overview of the clinical research methods that are used to evaluate the benefits and harms of therapeutic interventions and what it is about experimental methods that enable them to yield results that are more valid and reliable than those of non-experimental methods.

Methods for Determining the Benefits and Harms of Treatments

A wide range of design choices is available for comparative effectiveness research: experimental designs, that is, clinical trials; specially designed observational studies; analyses of data collected for a different purpose; and syntheses of already-published studies and trials for systematic reviews, meta-analyses, individual patient meta-analyses, or decision analyses.

Over the past 60 years, experimental approaches—clinical trials—have assumed primacy in the evaluation of the effects of a putative therapeutic intervention.[1] Advances in the methods of clinical trials, particularly methods to reduce bias, have made possible ever more valid and precise estimates of a treatment's effects. (Bias is the extent to which research results and/or inferences drawn from them differ systematically from the "truth.") A clinical trial is a prospective (forward-looking) research design—an experiment—in which a putative therapeutic intervention is delivered to human subjects. In a clinical trial, a priori hypotheses are posed about the intervention's possible effects on subjects, and all aspects of the study architecture, data collection, and data analysis are set out beforehand by the investigators. In contrast, in non-experimental studies involving human responses to therapeutic interventions, the investigators observe phenomena but do not have control over which treatments are given to which people or how the treatments are administered and followed up, and they often must use existing data that are of uncertain accuracy and completeness—all factors that can potentially bias the study results.

Non-experimental studies are thus weaker than well-designed and conducted clinical trials in the ability to assess cause-effect relationships between treatments and outcomes, and, for most therapeutic interventions, they may lead to wrong conclusions. Some sensational failures illustrate this point. For example, for decades hundreds of thousands of post-menopausal women were prescribed hormone replacement therapy based on the findings of observational studies that suggested a myriad of benefits on cardiovascular, bone, and brain health, and little risk of harm.[2] Then, in 1998 and 2002, the results of two large randomized trials demonstrated the opposite—that such treatment causes women more harm than good. Having peaked in 1999 and 2000, hormone replacement use by American women fell sharply after the trial results appeared, and the incidence of breast cancer in the United States fell with it.[3]

The clinical trial versus observational study debate is a constant companion of comparative effectiveness research. To contrast the two and review contemporary research methods for evaluating the benefits and harms of a putative therapeutic intervention, we will use an example from our own experience, the "Knee Study."

Arthroscopic Interventions to Relieve Knee Pain due to Osteoarthritis

Knee pain is extremely common in the adult population. Treatment options range from oral analgesics, injections of corticosteroids or other agents into the joint space, physical therapy, and interventions delivered via an arthroscope to the surfaces of the joint or the fluid inside. When these measures fail, the knee joint may be replaced, a major surgical procedure.

In 1990, J. Bruce Moseley, MD, then the chief of orthopedics at the Houston Veterans Affairs (VA) Medical Center and later the team physician for the U.S. men's and women's basketball "dream teams" of the 1996 Summer Olympics, came to see one of us (Nelda Wray). Moseley said that though arthroscopic surgery for relief of knee pain due to osteoarthritis was one of the high-volume procedures performed by his service, he had serious reservations about its effectiveness. He wanted to design a study to test it. The arthroscopic procedure was lavage, that is, washing out the knee joint with large volumes of fluid in the operating room, with or without débridement, that is, the use of arthroscopic instruments to shave roughened cartilage on the joint's surfaces and to snip off loose pieces of cartilage.

At the time, arthroscopic surgery for relief of knee pain attributed to osteoarthritis was widely performed in the United States and had been for years.[4] In the mid-1990s, more than 650,000 procedures were performed each year in the United States at an estimated cost of $5,000 each. Obviously, people believed that it worked. But how? Moseley said that the physiologic mechanism for why osteoarthritis causes knee pain was unknown. (It still is.) The arthroscopic interventions did not appear to arrest the progression of the arthritis as seen on postoperative radiographs of the knees.

Ignorance about the basic mechanism of a disease or condition makes it difficult to design an intervention that will be effective in improving its natural history. Yet when we reviewed the existing literature in 1990–1991, which consisted of 27 articles reporting primary data on the effects of arthroscopic lavage with or without débridement of the knee for relief of pain due to osteoarthritis, we found that the reports claimed that at least half of the people undergoing the procedure reported symptomatic improvement.

But the literature had serious limitations. Inferences that the intervention was effective were based on weak study designs. Twenty-one of the 27 studies described case series, which are retrospective looks at the experience of a series of patients, in this case, patients treated with arthroscopic surgery. For a number of reasons, a case series is considered to be the weakest study design on which to base inferences about a treatment's effectiveness. It is the design most prone to lead to spurious conclusions. The six other studies of knee arthroscopic procedures were prospective and included comparison groups, but they had serious deficiencies in the choice of the comparator, the method by which subjects were allocated to test and comparison groups, and failure to mask treatment assignment to subjects and other assessors of outcome.

Taken together, the 27 studies available in 1990–1991 did not exclude the possibility that something other than the operation explained the apparent pain relief. These competing explanations included a priori notions of patients and doctors that the operation would work, the fact that pain is very difficult to measure, and that surgical interventions are known to be associated with a substantial placebo effect.

Moseley was surprised when Wray told him that to put arthroscopic lavage with or without débridement to a fair test would require a comparison against a placebo arthroscopic procedure, that is, a procedure that appeared to patients and other observers to be the real thing but that did not include the key element of the intervention. Testing surgical interventions against sham procedures was then, and is still, very uncommon. The reasoning behind the need for testing against a placebo or sham procedure was that the efficacy of neither arthroscopic lavage alone nor lavage plus débridement had been established. The results of testing one unproven intervention against another could never rule out the possibility that any observed benefit was simply due to the placebo effect or to spontaneous resolution of the primary problem.

Wray put in a call to her colleague Baruch A. Brody, PhD, an internationally renowned research ethicist who was at that time director of the Center for Ethics at Baylor, to ask for his help in designing a placebo-controlled trial of arthroscopic surgery for relief of knee pain due to osteoarthritis. The research team for the project was born. Moseley served as the project's lead orthopedist, Wray as the lead scientist, and Brody as the project's ethicist. Other key experts, including statisticians and measurement experts, were brought onto the team.

Controlled clinical trials pose methodological as well as ethical challenges for the investigative team. The goal is to field and complete a trial that is of high methodological quality and at the same time of high ethical quality. The methodological quality of a trial is the extent to which its initiation, design, conduct, analysis, and reporting minimize or avoid biases in estimating the benefits and harms of the treatment being evaluated. In other words, a clinical trial of high methodological quality comes as close as possible to a true estimate—not an over-estimate or an under-estimate—of the test treatment's benefits. The ethical quality of a trial is the extent to which trial initiation, design, conduct, analysis, and reporting protect the moral commitments to respect for persons (treating individuals as autonomous agents and protecting persons with diminished capacity), beneficence (minimizing harms and maximizing benefits), and justice (fairness in the distribution of the benefits and burdens of research). The methodological rigor and ethical quality of a trial are inextricably linked. To use the words of one international body, "scientifically unsound research on human subjects is unethical in that it exposes research subjects to risks without possible benefits."[5]

The challenge facing us on the Knee Study team was to design a trial that would yield reliable and bias-free estimates of the amount of benefit that arthroscopic surgery conferred on its recipients while at the same time protecting the rights of the trial's participants.

We planned a three-arm trial comparing arthroscopic lavage, lavage plus débridement, and placebo arthroscopy in which every participant would have a 33% likelihood of being randomized to any of the three arms. The most challenging aspect of the design was the placebo-surgery control. We carefully considered whether existing conditions justified the use of a placebo-surgery control. We thought they did. First, at the time many Americans were undergoing arthroscopic procedures for osteoarthritic knee pain without adequate evidence that the procedure is beneficial. Second, it was feasible to minimize the risk to participants allocated to the placebo arm by using intravenous sedation rather than general endotracheal anesthesia, and by making superficial skin incisions over the knee mimicking the arthroscopy ports but not placing any instruments into the joint. Third, the risk to a placebo participant would be less than if that individual were to undergo standard arthroscopic surgery for knee pain outside the trial. Fourth, the risk: benefit ratio of the trial was favorable given the minimized risk and the real possibility that the whole benefit of the procedure comes from a placebo effect. Finally, it was feasible to establish procedures to ensure that all prospective participants were fully informed about the placebo-surgery arm and about the possibility that they would be randomized to it.

Because the clinical intent behind the arthroscopic intervention was to relieve pain and improve the function in the operated knee, we decided that those should be the outcomes measured in the trial. A reliable questionnaire for knee pain did not exist, so we developed one and tested its reliability, validity, and responsiveness to a subject's change in symptoms over time.[6] To boost confidence that any effects detected were real, we selected supplementary outcome measures, including other self-reported measures of pain and function as well as objective tests of walking and stair-climbing.

We calculated that 180 participants, or 60 per group, would be needed in order to measure the effects of the procedures with acceptable precision and to minimize the chance of drawing erroneous conclusions, and that we could recruit that many from our own hospital. We developed a multi-faceted approach to keeping all parties except the operating surgeon blinded to the treatment assignment of the participants—and even the surgeon was kept blinded until after the participant had arrived in the operating room. We explored every aspect of the placebo procedure so that participants' well-being would not be threatened but they could be kept blinded to their treatment group assignment.[7] We developed a procedure by which participants would not be randomized to their study arm until they arrived in the operating suite, to eliminate the possibility of dropouts and crossovers. Once the patient was wheeled into the room, the surgeon was handed an envelope to open, inside of which was the treatment assignment. The assignment was not revealed to the subject. We set up the postoperative follow-up examinations so that the operating orthopedist (Moseley) would have no responsibility for seeing the participants after they left the operating room and evaluating their outcomes. Instead, a different orthopedist provided postoperative care; he and the other personnel who assessed outcomes were kept blinded to the intervention the participant had had.

Because the trial included the possibility of being randomized to a placebo-surgery arm, we devised safeguards to ensure that persons eligible to enter the trial were making fully informed decisions about whether to enroll. At the end of the informational dialogue, enrollees were required to write in their own handwriting that they understood they had a 33% chance of being allocated to a placebo procedure that had no way of affecting their knee arthritis. The other safeguard was a monitoring of refusal rates among persons eligible to enroll. Reasoning that, because of the placebo-surgery arm, this trial should have a higher-than-average refusal rate, we set a threshold and planned to stop enrollment if the refusal rate sank below it.

After we designed the trial, the next step was to secure external grant funding to support it. We were challenging an operative procedure firmly entrenched in clinical practice and were employing a sham procedure control group in the design. We anticipated some difficulties in obtaining funding. We were right. The first application, submitted in 1991 to the Veterans Health Administration Health Services Research and Development Service, did not get funded, and neither did a second application to the National Institutes of Health (NIH). (One reviewer of the NIH application wrote, "This is ridiculous. We know this procedure works.") Then we dropped back. With oversight by the hospital research and development committee, and the institutional review board of Baylor College of Medicine, the Houston VA Medical Center's academic affiliate, we designed a pilot study with 10 participants to evaluate formally the trial's feasibility and test and refine some of the trial methods. The pilot study began in June 1992.[8] Some of the reviewers of our first two applications were skeptical that people would volunteer for a trial that included a 33% chance of their being assigned to a placebo procedure (the pilot study confirmed they would), and they doubted that the proposed tactics for keeping them blinded to their treatment-group assignment would work (they did).

Armed with the findings of the pilot study, we submitted another grant application in June 1993, this one to the Veterans Health Administration Medical Research Service. It was funded, and the trial began in October 1994.

The results of the trial were reported in the *New England Journal of Medicine* in July 2002.[9] The abstract is provided in Box 1.1. All three groups reported less knee pain over the 2-year postoperative follow-up period compared with their baseline preoperative knee pain scores. Participants who got the placebo procedure got "just as better" as those who got arthroscopic lavage and those who got lavage plus débridement. At no point during the 2-year follow-up period did either arthroscopic group report greater pain relief or greater improvement in function than the placebo group. On objective tests of walking and stair-climbing, knee function actually deteriorated over the 2-year follow-up in all three groups—in the face of less self-reported pain.

Box 1.1 **Abstract of the Knee Study**

Background Many patients report symptomatic relief after undergoing arthroscopy of the knee for osteoarthritis, but it is unclear how the procedure achieves this result. We conducted a randomized, placebo-controlled trial to evaluate the efficacy of arthroscopy for osteoarthritis of the knee.

Methods A total of 180 patients with osteoarthritis of the knee were randomly assigned to receive arthroscopic débridement, arthroscopic lavage, or placebo surgery. Patients in the placebo group received skin incisions and underwent a simulated débridement without insertion of the arthroscope. Patients and assessors of outcome were blinded to the treatment group assignment. Outcomes were assessed at multiple points over a 24-month period with the use of five self-reported scores—three on scales for pain and two on scales for function—and one objective test of walking and stair-climbing. A total of 165 patients completed the trial.

Results At no point did either of the intervention groups report less pain or better function than the placebo group. For example, mean (+SD) scores on the Knee-Specific Pain Scale (range, 0 to 100, with higher scores indicating more severe pain) were similar in the placebo, lavage, and débridement groups: 48.9 + 21.9, 54.8 + 19.8, and 51.7 + 22.4, respectively, at 1 year ($p = 0.14$ for the comparison between placebo and lavage; $p = 0.51$ for the comparison between placebo and débridement) and 51.6 + 23.7, 53.7 + 23.7, and 51.4 + 23.2, respectively, at 2 years ($p = 0.64$ and $p = 0.96$, respectively). Furthermore, the 95% confidence intervals for the differences between the placebo group and the intervention groups exclude any clinically meaningful difference.

Conclusions In this controlled trial involving patients with osteoarthritis of the knee, the outcomes after arthroscopic lavage or arthroscopic débridement were no better than those after a placebo procedure.

Source: The New England Journal of Medicine. Moseley JB, O'Malley K, Petersen NJ, Menke TJ, Brody BA, Kuykendall DH, Hollingsworth JC, Ashton CM, Wray NP. A controlled trial of arthroscopic surgery for osteoarthritis of the knee. Volume 347, pages 81–8. Copyright © 2002 Massachussetts Medical Society. Reprinted with permission.

The conclusion is not that lavage with or without débridement does not "work"—it is just that they do not work any better than placebo in lessening knee pain. The benefit of these arthroscopic procedures, when used in people like those who entered this trial, is ascribable to the placebo effect associated with surgery. A subsequent Canadian randomized trial of arthroscopic lavage and débridement of the knee together with optimized physical and medical therapy showed no incremental benefit of surgery.[10]

The Knee Study was featured on the front pages of the major U.S. newspapers and on many national and some international TV news shows. The trial report has been cited hundreds of times in the medical literature and has been mentioned in several books. Its broad appeal seems to reside in the fact that it addressed a very common clinical problem in U.S. adults, knee pain; that it debunked a very popular operation; that it tested real surgical procedures against the benchmark of a placebo procedure; and that it documented that surgical procedures for relief of self-reported symptoms are associated with substantial placebo effects.

How did the publication of the Knee Study affect clinical practice? In the Veterans Health Administration, the number of arthroscopic procedures performed for relief of knee pain due to osteoarthritis trial declined by 25%.[11] In June 2004 the Centers for Medicare and Medicaid Services issued a national coverage determination on arthroscopic lavage and arthroscopic débridement for the osteoarthritic knee; it specified three indications for which Medicare would no longer cover the procedures. These were largely based on the results of the Knee Study.[12] But the procedure is still widely performed for pain relief for osteoarthritic knees. For example, the Canadian Institute for Health Information reported that in 2008–2009, more than 3,600 knee arthroscopies were performed in Canadian hospitals "despite mounting evidence from randomised controlled trials that the procedure is of little benefit."[13]

The Knee Study sparked a debate about the circumstances under which a sham procedure is ethical to use in trials evaluating the effectiveness of a surgical procedure. It also has led to a deeper understanding of the consequences of the way in which surgical innovations enter into widespread use without prior systematic evaluation of their benefits and harms in trials designed to yield valid and useful results, which is a topic of Chapter 4. But now we will return to the issue at hand, which is to review the features of clinical trials that enable valid and reasonably precise estimates to be made of a treatment's effects.

Key Design Features of Clinical Trials

For the foreseeable future in comparative effectiveness research, the clinical trial will continue to be the gold-standard study design, simply because it is the design that provides the least biased estimates of a treatment's real effects.

The Concept of the Disease "Model" and the Design of an Appropriate Intervention

Medical scientists and practitioners develop theoretical models for the cause of the disease or condition in question and for how the disease undermines human longevity, functional status, quality of life, or other outcomes. These models or conceptions reflect contemporary beliefs about "how things work,"[14] beliefs based on the findings and interpretations—and limitations—of research in the area of interest. Always imperfect (if not completely wrong), the models are not static but are revised to incorporate new evidence as it becomes available. These models are fundamentally important in clinical research because scientists use them as the basis for developing testable hypotheses; in the case of therapeutics research, testable hypotheses about interventions that should change the natural history of the disease for the better. If the model that has been posed to justify the intervention is wrong, the intervention, when put to a fair test, may be ineffective or harmful. Such "negative" trials can be useful for prompting a re-evaluation of the disease model itself.

To return to the Knee Study as an example, one source of Moseley's reservations about the value of arthroscopic lavage with or without débridement was that he knew of no pathophysiological reason why it *should* work. Scientists had not elucidated the chemical or biophysical etiology of the knee pain. No "bad humours" explaining the pain had been isolated from the synovial fluid. Radiographs of the knees of older adults with pain-free knees were indistinguishable—showed just as many arthritic changes—from those of similarly aged adults with chronic knee pain.[15] Without a plausible theoretical model for the cause of the knee pain, what was the basis for thinking that the intervention should work? Perhaps it was a technology (a fairly lucrative one) in search of a problem instead of the other way around. One of the people we interviewed for this book put it like this: "Every age believes that it knows how the body works and that it has the answer to what ails humans. Physicians who were bleeding their patients believed they were doing them good. How else could you cut people's veins open and watch them blanch and faint, unless you really believed you were doing them good? The other problem, now in particular, is that belief and money are aligned. It is very easy to fool yourself that you're doing good if you're making a lot of money doing it."

The Superiority of the Experimental Approach over Observational Approaches

In the experimental approach, the investigator exerts as much control as possible over all the extraneous as well as manipulable factors that may conceivably bias the estimate of the outcome of interest. This control allows for the true effect of the intervention being tested, if such an effect does exist, to be detected. Comparative clinical trials in which participants are randomly allocated across the trial's arms and which incorporate all other measures to limit bias are considered to be the "gold standard" for determining the effects of therapeutic interventions.

If we partition out clinical trials from all therapeutics research on humans, what is left are observational studies. Obviously, observation is a fundamental activity in a clinical trial, so a more accurate term for studies that are not clinical trials is "non-experimental." However, the term "observational" has come to denote studies in which the investigators do not manipulate or control the interventions performed on the subjects. They only observe.

Observational studies can be planned before any data are collected and can involve the enrollment and subsequent follow-up of consenting subjects. An example is the ongoing Framingham Heart Study, which began in 1948. The data collected in this kind of observational study, also called a prospective cohort study, are called primary data, because they are being collected for the primary purpose of research. The research team has control over the nature of the data collected as well as the data's accuracy and completeness, even though the investigators do not control the interventions the subjects receive.

Other kinds of observational studies are based on look-backs to data collected at a past time. The data might have been collected for a different research project or recorded for a non-research purpose, for example, clinical care or workload reporting. For this reason, this kind of observational study is called a secondary-analysis study. The investigative team has no control over the variables for which data were collected or the completeness or accuracy of those data. They must make do with whatever their data source(s) provides.

In trying to determine whether the intervention being tested benefits the persons who are treated with it, the major goal is to be able to anticipate and minimize, if not eliminate, alternative explanations for any changes observed in the intervention group other than the intrinsic action of the intervention itself. That research designs are more or less successful in this regard is the principle underlying the idea of the "hierarchy of research designs" (example in Table 1.1). Confidence in the inferences drawn from a study about a treatment's effectiveness, in direction as well as magnitude, is directly related to where the study design falls in the hierarchy and the extent to which its design meets specific criteria for methodological quality.

While there is a hierarchy of research designs, it does not follow that observational studies, because they include more "noise," just detect a weaker signal about the benefits of an intervention, but in the same direction, as clinical trials. Studies have shown that observational studies may underestimate or overestimate the treatment effect of an intervention compared with clinical trials of the same intervention, or come up with results that are in the opposite direction of the trials. The hormone replacement research mentioned earlier is an example of the latter.

Table 1.1 **Research Designs in the Hierarchy of Internal Validity Endorsed by the U.S. Preventive Services Task Force**

I: Properly powered and conducted randomized controlled trial (RCT); well-conducted systematic review or meta-analysis of homogeneous RCTs

II-1: Well-designed controlled trial without randomization

II-2: Well-designed cohort or case-control analytic study

II-3: Multiple time series with or without the intervention; dramatic results from uncontrolled experiments

III: Opinions of respected authorities, based on clinical experience; descriptive studies or case reports; reports of expert committees

Note: Not all studies within a research design have equal internal validity ("quality"). To assess more carefully the internal validity of individual studies within research designs, the Task Force has developed design-specific criteria for categorizing individual studies as "good," "fair," and "poor." (Accessed January 28, 2011, at http://www.uspreventiveservicestaskforce.org/uspstf08/methods/procmanual4.htm)

The Importance of the Comparison Group

After preclinical studies and single-group clinical trials indicate that a new therapeutic intervention shows promise for changing the natural history of a disease for the better, the effects of the intervention are evaluated in comparative clinical trials.[16] The comparison group in a clinical trial or observational study consists of individuals who are supposed to be like those in the intervention group in every aspect except for the intervention itself. The direction and magnitude of the intervention's effects in the two groups can then be compared and conclusions drawn about the extent to which the intervention is beneficial. In clinical trials parlance, this ratio is called the "treatment effect."

Comparison groups can be internal (part of the study) or external (composed of persons not enrolled in the current study) and can be concurrent (studied at the same time as the intervention group) or historical (drawn from past trials or past observational studies).

But why do we need comparison groups? Why is it not possible to treat a group of people with a new intervention and base our conclusions about its effectiveness simply on their experience alone? In rare instances, it is. For example, in the 1800s, wound infections after surgery were the rule rather then the exception, and what caused them was not known. In 1870 Joseph Lister published his case series of patients undergoing amputation of a limb. He showed that, in the pre-antiseptic period, 16 of 35 amputation cases died from postoperative pyemia (literally, "pus in the bloodstream") compared with only 6 of 40 in the antiseptic period. A trial involving a concurrent comparison group was not needed to demonstrate the benefits of carbolic acid sprays in the operating room.

On a lighter note, in 2003 the *British Medical Journal* published a paper spoofing those who demand that all therapeutic interventions be subjected to clinical trials. In a paper titled "Parachute use to prevent death and major trauma related to gravitational challenge: systematic review of randomised controlled trials," Gordon Smith and Jill Pell concluded: "As with many interventions intended to prevent ill health, the effectiveness of parachutes has not been subjected to rigorous evaluation by using randomised controlled trials. . . . Everyone might benefit if the most radical proponents of evidence-based medicine organized and participated in a double-blind, randomised, cross-over trial of the parachute."[17]

The common denominator of these two interventions is the very high frequency of bad outcomes in the absence of the intervention and the extremely large reduction in the frequency of bad outcomes when the intervention is used. The de facto comparison group consists of past experience. In contemporary medicine, new interventions with this magnitude of "treatment effect" are rarely, if ever, seen. The benefits of most therapeutic innovations are modest, making their valid and reliable detection a challenge, and making the inclusion of comparison groups a necessity for the estimation of the size of the treatment effect.

Had a sham-procedure control group not been included in the Knee Study, we would have spuriously concluded that arthroscopic lavage and arthroscopic lavage plus débridement possessed the intrinsic ability to reduce the severity of knee pain at the 2-year mark by about 20%. The inclusion of a placebo procedure control group allowed us to identify a competing explanation for the observed reduction in knee pain: participants allocated to the placebo procedure also showed a roughly 20% decrease in the severity of knee pain.

Comparison groups in observational studies are more challenging to constitute than in trials. It is not possible to know, in observational studies, why a certain individual received or did not receive the therapeutic intervention of interest. It is therefore impossible to ensure that the persons in the comparison group share all the characteristics of those in the intervention group (except for the intervention), and such imbalances can substantially bias the results. Several statistical approaches are used to adjust for imbalances of known influential factors between treatment and comparison groups in observational studies. (Renowned statistician Peter Armitage disdainfully referred to these as "rescue operations on non-randomized data sets."[18]) Nevertheless, inferences about treatment effects drawn from observational studies are less secure and more likely to be wrong than those drawn from comparative clinical trials.

Goals of Clinical Trials: Demonstration of Superiority, Equivalence, or Non-Inferiority

A clinical trial of a therapeutic intervention may be undertaken to demonstrate whether the new intervention is better than the control, as good as the control, or not worse than the control to an unacceptable extent. The goal of a trial—demonstration of superiority, equivalence, or non-inferiority to an alternative—is set out explicitly beforehand and drives other design features such as the choice of the control intervention, the size of the sample of participants that will be needed, and the statistical analysis plan.

Although the term "comparative effectiveness research" conjures up tests of superiority in most minds, the truth is that trials testing equivalence or non-inferiority are also types of comparative effectiveness research. The concept that one therapeutic intervention may be superior or roughly equivalent[19] to another in terms of its effectiveness or safety is easy to grasp. But what is "non-inferiority"?

Non-inferiority trials always use an active control—an intervention of known effectiveness—instead of a placebo in a two-arm trial or along with a placebo in a three-arm trial. In a non-inferiority trial, the intention is to determine whether the test intervention is, to use the words of the Food and Drug Administration (FDA), "not materially worse" than the control, that it "has at least some effect, or, in many cases, an effect that is not too much smaller than the active control."[20] If the effect of the test intervention falls within a preset margin, which is always one sided in that its upper bound is the point estimate of the active control's effectiveness, the test intervention will be rated as non-inferior. Non-inferiority trials are justified when the inclusion of a placebo group is not ethically defensible (if, for example, an intervention known to be effective exists and not treating individuals with it would place them at serious risk).

Random Allocation of Subjects to Intervention and Control Arms of a Trial

The goal with any allocation strategy is to ensure that known and unknown factors that influence the response to the new therapeutic intervention are balanced in the intervention group and control group. Several allocation strategies can be used: deterministic allocation, random allocation, and minimization.

In a deterministic scheme, the investigators determine which individuals will receive the intervention and which will not. This approach virtually guarantees spurious conclusions. Because investigators often have well-founded hunches about whether a given subject will respond to the treatment under study, allowing them to assign individual subjects to study arms will bias upward the estimate of the treatment effect and make the effect size larger than it really is. The same holds for allowing individual subjects to choose the arm of a trial in which they will participate, which have been called preference trials.

Even if trialists plan to use a non-deterministic allocation scheme, a failure to conceal the allocation scheme from those who might subvert it in effect makes the design deterministic.

The most commonly used method of allocating participants among the arms of clinical trials is random allocation, in which the subject's assignment is determined by a process over which the investigator (and the participant) has no control and no way to manipulate.[21] In random allocation, each individual subject has the same likelihood of being assigned to either (or any, if there are more than two) of the study arms. In general, random allocation balances between the study arms the levels of factors, known and as yet unknown, that affect the probability of response to the intervention. It mitigates selection bias and also satisfies assumptions for the validity of statistical tests of the difference in effects observed between the arms of the trial.

In the field of clinical therapeutics, the first use of random allocation of human subjects to the treatment and control arms of clinical trials is attributed to Austin Bradford Hill (1897–1991). It was first used in two trials undertaken by the Medical Research Council of Great Britain during the 1940s, one of a vaccine against whooping cough, reported in 1951, and the other of streptomycin against pulmonary tuberculosis, launched in 1946 and reported in 1948.[22]

The third allocation option, minimization, is infrequently used. Minimization keeps the study groups balanced as to known confounders. Because the allocation of an individual to an arm is determined by a preset algorithm and is not under the control of the investigator, minimization does control selection bias.

The Importance of Blinding or Masking: "I Wouldn't Have Seen It If I Hadn't Believed It"

Individuals who care for patients or subjects and assess the outcome of a therapeutic intervention, be they the treating physicians, members of the clinical research team, or patients or trial participants themselves, have preconceived notions of the treatment's benefits and harms. These notions influence interpersonal interactions between providers and patients/subjects and their assessments of the treatment's effects. Masking the outcome assessors as to trial arm mitigates the influence of this bias, often referred to as expectancy bias. The importance of blinding or masking in clinical trials was recognized as early as 1800.[23]

Blinding in a trial of an orally ingested medication is generally achieved by the use of placebo pills or capsules that look, smell, and taste the same as the active drug but do not contain the drug. In a placebo-controlled drug trial, the participant, persons dispensing the drug, and observers assessing clinical outcomes of participants, are all kept unaware of whether the participant is receiving the active drug or the placebo. Estimation of the magnitudes of benefits and harms is therefore as free as possible from preconceived notions of the outcome assessors.

The attributes of some interventions such as surgery make it challenging or impossible to blind one or more of the three sets of outcome assessors (practitioners administering the treatment, trial participants, and research team members assessing post-intervention outcomes). But it is always possible to identify an outcome measure that can be assessed by observers kept blinded to treatment assignments. In the previously mentioned 1948 streptomycin trial, the drug was administered to the participants in the intervention group by painful intramuscular injection four times a day over a 4-month study period. For obvious reasons it was thought unreasonable to plan to administer placebo injections to the participants randomized to the control condition (bed rest). This means that trial participants and those caring for them were not blinded to the group assignment. However, the research team considered the extent of tubercular disease on the chest radiograph to be "the most important single factor to consider" in judging the response to treatment. Three radiologists, working separately and without knowledge of the group to which participants had been assigned, read and interpreted the radiographs.

Blinding or masking confers another important advantage. It takes into account what is known as the placebo effect, "the nonspecific, psychological, or psycho-physiological therapeutic effect produced by a placebo, or the effect of spontaneous improvement attributed to the placebo."[24] All treatments, whether intrinsically effective or ineffective, whether medical, surgical, or of another sort, are associated with placebo effects. The magnitude of a placebo effect correlates with the patient's perception of the potency of the treatment, in the following increasing order: pills, capsules (the number and color of the pills and capsules also matters), injections, injections of substances that sting, and surgery.[25]

The placebo effects associated with therapeutic interventions, whether non-operative or operative, are of particular importance when the clinical intent of the intervention is to restore function or relieve symptoms, endpoints that are necessarily subjective rather than objectively measurable. A recent study of 746 clinical trials found that lack of blinding was associated with overly optimistic estimates of treatment effects in trials evaluating subjective outcomes; the bias was less in trials assessing all-cause mortality or other objective outcomes.[26] The findings of the Knee Study demonstrate this: participants in all three arms, including the placebo-surgery arm, reported less pain and better function on the self-report scales. However, deterioration rather than improvement was observed on the objective tests of walking and stair-climbing.

When the primary outcome of a trial is an endpoint that can be objectively determined, for example, the development of cancer, the occurrence of stroke, or death, the influence of expectancy bias is less but may still be present. For example, the behavior of participants or trial staff may be influenced. A participant in an unblinded trial who is assigned to the treatment arm he finds less desirable may be less compliant in taking the study medication or fail to keep his follow-up visits. An endoscopist who knows that the individual she is evaluating was allocated to a new ablation treatment for Barrett's esophagus may take more biopsies—or fewer—at the follow-up visits, depending on what she believes about the new treatment's effectiveness in reducing cancer risk. Also, the judgments of those assessing outcomes may be influenced by their knowledge of treatment arm. It is easy to determine the vital status of a trial participant, but assigning cause of death is a matter of judgment. For many non-fatal endpoints used in clinical trials, including stroke and acute heart attack, diagnostic criteria can be inconsistently applied.

Sample Size and Statistical Power

In the 1970s it became clear that a relationship exists between the number of participants in a controlled clinical trial and the likelihood of drawing a false conclusion about the effectiveness or lack of effectiveness of a new therapeutic intervention.[27] This relationship is mediated by the size of the effect expected from the new intervention and the variability around measurements of the effect. Controlled clinical trials test hypotheses; conventionally, the null hypothesis in a superiority trial is that the test intervention has no effect, while the working, or alternative hypothesis, is that it does. When the null hypothesis of "no effect" is erroneously rejected, this is a type I or α error. When the null hypothesis of "no effect" is erroneously accepted, this is a type II or β error. Alpha and beta represent the probabilities of drawing incorrect conclusions; acceptable levels are set out in the planning phase of a trial. The "statistical power" of a trial is the probability of correctly rejecting the null hypothesis.

The concern raised in the 1970s was that the small sample sizes of some controlled clinical trials were leading to spurious conclusions that the interventions being tested were ineffective. These trials were "under-powered," that is, they did not possess enough statistical power to detect an effect, if such an effect was actually present.

Over the last decades it has become widely accepted that a priori sample size and power calculations are necessary if controlled clinical trials are to be designed, analyzed, and interpreted correctly. Standards for reporting clinical trials require that the components and assumptions that figured in the power calculations are provided for readers. However, the problem with under-powered trials continues.[28] Under-powered trials not only lead to mistaken impressions about a treatment's effects. They are ethically suspect because they are methodologically unsound.

Best Methods for Detecting a Treatment's Harms

While the clinical trial is the research design that yields the least biased estimate of the benefit conferred by a putative therapeutic intervention, it is generally not the best method for estimating harms. Harms are generally low-frequency events with interventions that make it to the comparative clinical trial stage. Individual clinical trials may have short follow-up periods and/or may include too few participants to detect low-frequency events.

Meta-analyses, study designs in which individual trials that meet inclusion criteria constitute the "subjects" of the mathematical and statistical analyses, are better than single trials at estimating the risks of these infrequent harms. Also, large prospective or retrospective observational studies have much to offer in the way of detecting harms associated with therapeutic interventions. They can track large numbers of people over long periods of time and, to the extent the harms of interest are reliably recorded in the database, estimate their frequency. Electronic medical records hold tremendous promise for detecting harms associated with treatments. In May 2008 the U.S. Food and Drug Administration launched the Sentinel Initiative to monitor the safety of prescription drugs, biologics, and medical devices after these products reach the market. As of January 2011, the FDA had the capacity to query the electronic health information of more than 60 million Americans to monitor the safety of the products it approves; the ultimate goal is a minimum of 100 million.[29]

The Problem of Under-Reporting and Poor Reporting of Trials

We turn now to another source of inaccurate conclusions about treatment effects: the body of literature published about a particular intervention. Judgments about the extent to which a given intervention causes net benefit over harm are never based on a single study, but rather on the body of published empirical work on the intervention.

Trials that failed to demonstrate a benefit for the intervention, or demonstrated that it was in fact harmful, are less likely to be written up for publication by the investigators; and if the results are written up, they are less likely to be accepted by medical journal editors for publication in the broadly accessible peer-reviewed press. This publication bias means that the body of published work on any given intervention is likely to offer a rosier view than is accurate. How much rosier is generally impossible to know, but a recent analysis gives some hints.

A recent evaluation of Phase 2 and 3 clinical-trial programs of 12 antidepressant agents approved by the FDA between 1987 and 2004 found 74 trials that had been registered with the FDA. These trials involved over 12,000 participants. The FDA had deemed 38 of the 74 trials to be "positive" (results supporting that the drug provided net benefit over harm). All but one of these 38 positive trials were eventually reported in the peer-reviewed literature. Of the remaining 36 studies, the FDA had deemed 24 to be "negative" and 12 "questionable." Three of the 36 were reported in the literature as negative, 22 were never published, and 11 were reported as positive, conflicting with the FDA's judgment. The end result of this publication bias was to inflate the effect size for these antidepressant drugs—to overestimate their benefit—by more than 30%.[30] Much rosier, indeed.

The under-reporting of negative trials is considered such a liability for medical decision making that the 2007 Food and Drug Administration Amendments Act included provisions expanding the requirements for trial sponsors and investigators to post information about clinical trials, including some trial results, on http://www.clinicaltrials.gov, a publicly accessible Web site.[31]

Poor reporting on the aspects of individual trials is another factor leading to mistaken impressions about a treatment's value. Concerted efforts began in the mid-1990s to improve the quality of reporting, led by a group that formulated reporting standards (the Consolidated Standards of Reporting Trials, or CONSORT statements).[32] The editors of the leading medical journals require authors to comply. However, reporting continues to be substandard.

Poor reporting makes it impossible for a reader to judge the extent to which the trial's results are valid and believable (internal validity), and whether they should be considered applicable to real patients who are like those who participated in the trial (external validity or generalizability). Moreover, poor trial reporting undermines the value of the individual trials included in research syntheses and meta-analyses.

How Good Is the Evidence?

The body of work about a given intervention carries more information about its benefits and harms than the results of a single trial. Methods have been developed over the past 40 years that formalize how a body of work may be fairly and reliably synthesized or viewed as a whole, including systematic reviews of primary research, meta-analyses, and individual patient meta-analyses, in which data from individual subjects from multiple trials are combined in a pooled analysis. These research syntheses serve many important functions. For example, for a clinician posing a specific question, a systematic review or meta-analysis can point to the best clinical course forward for the patient at hand. These research syntheses also help to resolve what appear to be conflicting results between trials addressing the same clinical question.

Research syntheses not only provide direction on specific clinical issues: they tell us how good our evidence is. And clinical practice can only be as good as the evidence on which it rests.

To take a reading on the quality of empirical therapeutics research, let us examine the conclusions from four recent systematic reviews of therapeutic interventions for common ailments (Table 1.2). Note the similarities among

Table 1.2 **Assessments of the Strength of Evidence on Selected Therapeutic Interventions, as Determined by Systematic Reviews**

Intervention of Interest	Question Motivating the Review	N Potentially Relevant Studies Uncovered by Search	N (%) Studies Meeting Inclusion Criteria	N(%) of Included Studies That Were Randomized Controlled Trials	Review Authors' Qualitative Assessment of State of Evidence
Non-operative and operative treatments for rotator cuff tears[a]	Compare benefits and harms of non-operative and operative interventions on clinically important outcomes in adults	5,766	137/5,766 (2.4%)	21/137 (15.3%)	"Limited evidence, which was often of low quality, precluded conclusions for most comparisons. Selective outcome reporting may have introduced bias."
Radiofrequency catheter ablation for atrial fibrillation[b]	Compare benefits and harms of medical therapy vs. catheter ablation in adults	2,169	108/2,169 (5.0%)	32/108 (29.6%)	"Study follow-up was generally 12 months or less. Large heterogeneity of applied techniques and reporting of outcomes precluded many definitive conclusions."
Statin therapy for lipid disorders[c]	Compare benefits and harms of high-dose monotherapy with those of combination therapy in adults at high risk for coronary disease	9,735	102/9,735 (1.1%)	98/102 (96.0%)	"Studies were generally short, focused on surrogate outcomes, and were heterogeneous in the sample's risk for coronary disease. Few studies examined treatment combinations other than statin-ezetimibe."

(continued)

Table 1.2 Continued

Intervention of Interest	Question Motivating the Review	N Potentially Relevant Studies Uncovered by Search	N (%) Studies Meeting Inclusion Criteria	N(%) of Included Studies That Were Randomized Controlled Trials	Review Authors' Qualitative Assessment of State of Evidence
Charged-particle radiation therapy for cancer[d]	Review evidence about benefits and harms of charged-particle radiation for patients with cancer	4,747	243/4,747 (5.1%)	8/243 (3.3%)	"Few studies directly compared treatments with or without particle irradiation. Evidence on the comparative effectiveness and safety of charged-particle radiation in cancer is needed to assess the benefits, risks, and costs of treatment alternatives."

[a] Seida JC, LeBlanc C, Schouten JR, Mousavi SS, Hartling L, Vandermeer B, Tjosvold L, Sheps DM. Systematic review: nonoperative and operative treatments for rotator cuff tears. Ann Intern Med 2010;153(4):246–55.

[b] Terasawa T, Balk EM, Chung M, Garlitski AC, Alsheikh-Ali AA, Lau J, Ip S. Systematic review: comparative effectiveness of radiofrequency catheter ablation for atrial fibrillation. Ann Intern Med 2009;151(3):191–202.

[c] Sharma M, Ansari MT, Abou-Setta AM, Soares-Weiser K, Ooi TC, Sears M, Yazdi F, Tsertsvadze A, Moher D. Systematic review: comparative effectiveness and harms of combination therapy and monotherapy for dyslipidemia. Ann Intern Med 2009;151(9):622–30.

[d] Terasawa T, Dvorak T, Ip S, Raman G, Lau J, Trikalinos TA. Systematic review: charged-particle radiation therapy for cancer. Ann Intern Med 2009;151(8):556–65.

the findings of these reviews. First, algorithm-directed systematic searches of the indexed medical literature recover massive numbers of seemingly relevant papers. Second, closer reading of the recovered papers reveals that only a small fraction employed research designs that yield least biased estimates of the treatment effect. (Substantial differences in methodological quality are found even among the papers whose methods earned them inclusion in the review, but we do not include these data in the table.) Finally, there is the invariable conclusion by the authors of the reviews that the collective evidence suffers from serious limitations that undermine its usefulness in providing direction to doctors and patients. These four reviews typify what systematic reviews always find.

If we look at poor evidence from the patient's perspective, it becomes clear that this is not just a theoretical problem. Take the case of prostate cancer, the most common cancer of men in the United States, excluding skin cancer, and the second most common cause of cancer deaths in men. According to the Centers for Disease Control and Prevention, nearly a million American men received a diagnosis of prostate cancer between 2001 and 2005. From a smorgasbord of 10 different interventions, these men selected what they hoped was their best treatment choice. What was the state of the evidence upon which their doctors' recommendations and their own decisions were based? A March 2008 systematic review of treatments for clinically localized prostate cancer (the stage at which most men are diagnosed) found that 14,045 potentially relevant articles had been published up through 2007.[33] Only 18 of them were reports of randomized controlled trials of a prostate cancer treatment in men with clinically localized disease. Moreover, no randomized controlled trials were discovered for the following commonly used treatment modalities: cryotherapy, laparoscopic or robotically assisted radical prostatectomy, primary androgen deprivation, high-intensity focused ultrasonography, proton-beam radiation, or intensity-modulated radiation therapy. The authors concluded, "[there is] little high-quality evidence establishing the superiority of one therapy over another...all caused urinary, bowel, or sexual dysfunction; the frequency, duration, and severity of these adverse events varied among treatments. Available data insufficiently characterize their relative benefits."

One would think that with the high frequency of the condition, it would be easy enough to conduct definitive randomized trials to determine which treatment for prostate cancer leads to the best outcomes for men. But once doctors (and patients) believe they know what treatment is best, trials are impossible to perform no matter how bad the existing evidence. Dr. Timothy Wilt, the senior author of the systematic review, spear-headed the development and fielding of a randomized trial of radical prostatectomy versus watchful waiting for men with clinically localized prostate cancer with funding from the Veterans Affairs Cooperative Studies Program and the National Institutes of Health.

The trial involved 52 U.S. centers and began enrolling men in 1994. Only about 15% of potentially eligible men agreed to participate. Because of recruitment difficulties, by the time enrollment closed in 2002 the trial included fewer than half of the number of men in the original sample-size estimates.[34] It was not because there were too few eligible men. Most men declined to enter because they wanted the surgery and did not want to face the chance of being assigned to watchful waiting. In other words, recruitment targets could not be achieved because of the large proportion of men eligible to enroll in the trial who had decided that they and their doctor already knew what was best.

But did they? The trial results, which became available in July 2012,[35] showed that radical prostatectomy did not significantly reduce all-cause or prostate-cancer-specific mortality through at least 12 years of follow-up. However, it did double the prevalence of erectile dysfunction (to 81%), and it tripled the incidence of urinary incontinence (to 17%).

Conclusions

From the preceding pages we can draw two conclusions. The first is that research methods have advanced to the point that it is possible to design and conduct studies that yield valid evidence, with a fair amount of precision, on the probability that a given intervention will lead to net benefit over harm under certain circumstances. The second conclusion is that clinical research often falls far short of the attainable ideal. Clinical practice can only be as good as the evidence on which it rests.

Notes

1. This chapter does not provide an in-depth account of the architecture or history of the controlled clinical trial. For a highly readable description of methods in clinical trials, see Friedman LM, Furberg CD, DeMets DL. Fundamentals of clinical trials. 3rd ed. New York: Springer, 1998. For a history of clinical research in the United States, see Marks HM. The progress of experiment: science and therapeutic reform in the United States, 1900–1990. Cambridge, UK: Cambridge University Press, 1997. For a lively account of why it is necessary to put putative treatments to fair tests, see Evans I, Thornton H, Chalmers I. Testing treatments: better research for better healthcare. London: Printer & Martin, 2010.
2. To estimate the risks and benefits associated with hormone replacement therapy, Grady et al. conducted a meta-analysis of epidemiologic studies that had been published between 1970 and 1992. (Their systematic literature search uncovered only one controlled clinical trial conducted during that period.) They concluded that the evidence to date indicated that "estrogen therapy decreases risk for coronary heart disease and for hip fracture, but long-term estrogen therapy increases risk for endometrial cancer and may be associated with a small increase in breast cancer" (Grady D, Rubin SM, Petitti DB, et al. Hormone therapy to prevent disease and prolong life in postmenopausal women. Ann Intern Med 1992;117:1016–37). Two large randomized trials, the

Heart and Estrogen/Progestin Replacement Study (HERS) and the Women's Health Initiative (WHI), were subsequently conducted. HERS, which studied 2,673 women who had established coronary heart disease, showed that hormone replacement therapy does not reduce the overall rate of coronary heart disease events, increases the risk for venous thromboembolism and biliary surgery, shows unfavorable trends for cancer and fractures, and does not improve cognitive function (Hulley S, Grady D, Bush T, et al. Randomized trial of estrogen plus progestin for secondary prevention of coronary heart disease in postmenopausal women. JAMA 1998;280:605–13). The WHI trial included 16,608 women aged 50–79 years. It was stopped early because interim data analysis showed that risks of hormone therapy exceeded benefits. It showed that hormone replacement therapy increases risks for coronary heart disease events, strokes, pulmonary embolic events, invasive breast cancer, and ovarian cancer; these risks exceed the smaller benefit from increased bone mineral density and lower fracture risk (Risks and benefits of estrogen plus progestin in health menopausal women: principal results from the Women's Health Initiative randomized controlled trial. JAMA 2002;288:321–33).

3. Kreiger N, Chen JT, Waterman PD. Decline in US breast cancer rates after the Women's Health Initiative: socioeconomic and racial/ethnic differences. Am J Public Health 2010;100:S132–9.

4. Arthroscopic surgery to repair acute traumatic injuries to the knee joint sustained by athletes (e.g., anterior cruciate ligament rupture) is a very different procedure than arthroscopic lavage with or without débridement for arthritis pain.

5. Council for International Organizations of Medical Sciences (CIOMS) in collaboration with the World Health Organization (WHO). International ethical guidelines for biomedical research involving human subjects. Geneva, 2002. (Available at http://www.cioms.ch/publications/layout_guide2002.pdf.)

6. O'Malley KJ, Suarez-Almazor M, Aniol J, Richardson P, Kuykendall DH, Moseley JB, Wray NP. Joint-specific multidimensional assessment of pain (J-MAP): factor structure, reliability, validity, and responsiveness in patients with knee osteoarthritis. J Rheumatol 2003;30:534–43.

7. Because placebo-surgery participants were given intravenous sedation rather than general anesthesia, we simulated an actual arthroscopic procedure in the operating room to maintain the blind in case they did not have total amnesia. Placebo-surgery participants were kept in the operating room as long as they would have been with the actual arthroscopic procedures. The knee was prepped, draped, and manipulated as if arthroscopy were being performed. Skin incisions were made in the usual places and the surgeon asked for all the usual instruments though none were placed into the joint. A video of a real arthroscopic procedure was played on a screen in the operating room, mimicking what is seen through the "buddy scope." Fluids were splashed into containers to mimic the sounds heard during lavage. The operative report stated only that the individual had undergone "an experimental procedure" and provided a telephone number to call in case the clinical situation required that the nature of the procedure be divulged.

8. The results of the pilot study were published in 1996. See Moseley JB, Wray NP, Kuykendall D, Willis K, Landon G. Arthroscopic treatment of osteoarthritis of the knee: a prospective, randomized, placebo-controlled trial. Results of a pilot study. Am J Sports Med 1996;24:28–34.

9. Moseley JB, O'Malley K, Petersen NJ, Menke TJ, Brody BA, Kuykendall DH, Hollingsworth JC, Ashton CM, Wray NP. A controlled trial of arthroscopic surgery for osteoarthritis of the knee. N Engl J Med 2002;347:81–8. Two editorials accompanied the report: Felson DT, Buckwalter J. Débridement and lavage for osteoarthritis of the knee. N Engl J Med 2002;347:132–3; Horng S, Miller FG. Is placebo surgery unethical? N Engl J Med 2002;347:137–9.

10. Kirkley A, Birmingham TB, Litchfield R, et al. A randomized trial of arthroscopic surgery for osteoarthritis of the knee. N Engl J Med 2008;359:1097–107. This trial did not include a sham procedure arm.

11. Analyses of VA databases performed by Nancy J. Petersen, PhD.

12. Effective June 11, 2004, Medicare's three new "Nationally Noncovered Indications" were arthroscopic lavage used alone for the osteoarthritic knee, arthroscopic débridement for osteoarthritic patients presenting with knee pain only, or arthroscopic débridement and lavage with or without débridement for patients presenting with severe osteoarthritis. U.S. Department of Health and Human Services; Centers for Medicare and Medicaid Services. National coverage determination (NCD) for arthoscopic lavage and arthroscopic débridement for the osteoarthritic knee (150.9). (Accessed January 28, 2011, at http://www.cms.gov/medicare-coverage-database/details/ncd-details.aspx?NC DId=285&ncdver=1&NCAId=7&ver=12&NcaName=Arthroscopy+for+the+Osteoarthrit ic+Knee&CoverageSelection=National&KeyWord=Arthroscopy&KeyWordLookUp=Title &KeyWordSearchType=And&bc=gAAAACAAEAAA&.)

13. Kermode-Scott B. Ineffective surgical procedures are used to treat Canadians with osteoarthritis. BMJ 2010;341:c7436.

14. For a superb discussion of this issue in cardiovascular disease, see Jones DS. Visions of a cure. Visualization, clinical trials, and controversies in cardiac therapeutics, 1968–1998. Isis 2000;91:504–41.

15. Englund M, Guermazi A, Gale D, et al. Incidental meniscal findings on knee MRI in middle-aged and elderly persons. N Engl J Med 2008;359:1108–15.

16. This progression from animal and preclinical studies to single group prospective trials and then to comparative clinical trials is the path taken by prescription drugs and biologics, but not necessarily by other therapeutic interventions such as surgery, as will be seen later in Chapter 4.

17. Smith GC, Pell JP. Parachute use to prevent death and major trauma related to gravitational challenge: systematic review of randomised controlled trials. BMJ 2003;327:1459–61.

18. Armitage P. Fisher, Bradford Hill, and randomization. Int J Epidem 2003;32:925–8.

19. Equivalence clinical trials are intended to demonstrate that there is no clinically significant difference between a standard and an experimental treatment. It is impossible to determine whether the effects of one intervention are identical to another because an infinite sample size would be required. Therefore, equivalence trials instead test for a specified difference (equivalence range) between the effects of two treatments of no more than some value delta, d (generally a clinically predefined value). They are out of favor at present because of problematic ethics and methods.

20. To read the FDA's guidance on non-inferiority trials, see Guidance for industry on non-inferiority clinical trials (March 2010). (Accessed September 12, 2012, at http://www.fda.gov/downloads/Drugs/GuidanceComplianceRegulatoryInformation/ Guidances/UCM202140.pdf.)

21. Random allocation is a method that uses the play of chance to assign participants to comparison groups in a trial, for example, by using a random numbers table or a computer-generated random sequence. Random allocation implies that each individual or unit being entered into a trial has the same chance of receiving each of the possible interventions. It also implies that the probability that an individual will receive a particular intervention is independent of the probability that any other individual will receive the same intervention.

22. Though the pertussis vaccine trial began before the streptomycin for tuberculosis trial, because the streptomycin trial results were reported earliest it is usually labeled as the first clinical trial in which random allocation was used. See Medical Research Council. The prevention of whooping-cough by vaccination. Br Med J 1951;i:1463–71, and Streptomycin treatment of pulmonary tuberculosis: a Medical Research Council investigation. Br Med J 1948;1:769–82. Bradford Hill wanted to be a physician but his medical education was forestalled by World War I and his enlistment in 1916 into the Royal Naval Air Service. He contracted tuberculosis during his military service and had to be discharged from the service in 1917. His lengthy convalescence put a medical education out of reach for him. Though he took a degree in economics, he quickly found his

way into statistics. His contributions over a career spanning roughly 40 years made him the greatest medical statistician of the 20th century. See Doll R. Sir Austin Bradford Hill and the progress of medical science. BMJ 1992;305:1521–6.

23. Differences in the way treatment outcomes are assessed [editorial commentary]. The James Lind Library, 2007. (Accessed January 31, 2011, at http://www.jameslindlibrary.org.)

24. Shapiro AK, Shapiro E. The placebo: is it much ado about nothing? In: Harrington A. The placebo effect: an interdisciplinary exploration. Boston: Harvard University Press, 1997: 12–36.

25. Brody H. The doctor as therapeutic agent: a placebo effect research agenda. In: Harrington A. The placebo effect: an interdisciplinary exploration. Boston: Harvard University Press, 1997: 77–92.

26. Wood L, Egger M, Gluud LL, et al. Empirical evidence of bias in treatment effect estimates in controlled trials with different interventions and outcomes: meta-epidemiological study. BMJ 2008;336:601–5.

27. Freiman JA, Chalmers TC, Smith H Jr, Kuebler RR. The importance of beta, the type II error and sample size in the design and interpretation of the randomized control trial. N Engl J Med 1978:299:690–4.

28. See Halpern SD, Karlawish JH, Berlin JA. The continuing unethical conduct of under-powered clinical trials. JAMA 2002;288:358–62, and Wenner DM, Brody BA, Jarman AF, Kolman JM, Wray NP, Ashton CM. Do surgical trials meet the scientific standards for clinical trials? J Am Coll Surg 2012;215:722–30.

29. Information on FDA's Sentinel Initiative. (Accessed January 31, 2011, at http://www.fda.gov/Safety/FDAsSentinelInitiative/default.htm.) See also Behrman RE, Benner JS, Brown JS, McClellan M, Woodcock J, Platt R. Developing the Sentinel System—a national resource for evidence development. N Engl J Med 2011;364:498–9.

30. Turner EH, Matthews AM, Linardatos E, Tell RA, Rosenthal R. Selective publica-tion of anti-depressant trials and its influence on apparent efficacy. N Engl J Med 2008;358:252–60. A comprehensive review of reporting bias can be found in: McGauran N, Wieseler B, Kreis J, Schuler YB, Kolsch H, Kaiser T. Reporting bias in medical research—a narrative review. Trials 2010 Apr 13;11:37.

31. Wood AJ. Progress and deficiencies in the registration of clinical trials. N Engl J Med 2009;360:824–30.

32. The reporting standards are available from http://www.consort-statement.org.

33. Wilt TJ, MacDonald R, Rutks I, Shamllyn TA, Taylor BC, Kane RL. Systematic review: comparative effectiveness and harms of treatments for clinically localized prostate cancer. Ann Intern Med 2008;148:435–48.

34. Wilt TJ, Brawer MK, Barry MJ, et al. The prostate cancer intervention vs. observa-tion trial: VA/NCI/AHRQ Cooperative Studies Program #407 (PIVOT): design and baseline results of a randomized controlled trial comparing radical prostatectomy to watchful waiting for men with clinically localized prostate cancer. Contemp Clin Trials 2009;30:81–7.

35. Wilt TJ, Brawer MK, Jones KM, et al. Radical prostatectomy versus observation for localized prostate cancer. N Eng J Med 2012;367:202–13.

2

The Use of Evidence

Federal Regulation of Prescription Drugs and Medical Devices

In this chapter we focus on how evidence is used to regulate prescription drugs and medical devices in the United States and, once approved, the forces that drive their adoption. Current law does not require that, in order to be approved for marketing, a drug or device be shown to be superior or even equivalent for its proposed clinical indications to a product already on the market. It just must be safe and effective. Similarly, in post-approval uptake and dissemination of new products, the major force is marketing rather than evidence of comparative advantage.

The U.S. Food and Drug Administration

The U.S. Food and Drug Administration (FDA) is the federal agency charged with regulating medical products and devices. The agency works under congressional oversight in the center of a nexus of patients, providers, industry, payers, and other governmental agencies concerned with health care. These constituencies sometimes have very different priorities. The FDA's regulatory purview includes prescription drugs, biologics, and devices.[1] The evidential standards that devices must meet before they can be marketed are substantially lower than those for prescription drugs and biologics. The FDA does not regulate surgical procedures, behavioral therapies, or rehabilitation programs; consequently, they take different paths from development to dissemination. Paradoxically, surgical innovations, generally costlier and riskier than pharmaceutical agents,[2] can enter clinical practice with a much weaker evidential base than drugs and devices, an issue that we will examine in Chapter 4.

A Brief History of "Safety" and "Effectiveness" at the Food and Drug Administration

Safe and effective pharmacotherapy is taken for granted now, but it was not until the 20th century that drugs were discovered and put into clinical use that had notable intrinsic activity against some of the major scourges of humankind.[3] Such drugs include the first effective agent against *Treponema pallidum*, the bacterium that causes syphilis (the arsenic-containing compound arsphenamine, marketed as Salvarsan, in 1910), antibiotics against the most common bacterial causes of pneumonia, puerperal fever (childbed fever), and serious skin and wound infections (sulfonamides in 1936, penicillin in 1941, chloramphenicol in 1949), the first antibiotic against *Mycobacterium tuberculosis* (streptomycin in 1943), and the first effective anti-psychotic agent (chlorpromazine for schizophrenia in 1952).

However, the late 19th and early 20th century also showed the dark side of drugs, and of the makers and prescribers of drugs. Views of the dark side persuaded the nation of the need for federal authority in the oversight of remedies purported to treat the ills of humans. As it evolved during the 20th century, this oversight progressively raised the pre-marketing evidential bar for prescription drugs—a bar first of safety, and then of effectiveness as well as safety. And now, in the 21st century, post-marketing surveillance undertaken via the Sentinel Initiative (mentioned in Chapter 1) will raise the safety bar for drugs and devices, and the federal mandates of the 2000s for comparative effectiveness research are likely to raise the post-marketing effectiveness bar.

The Pure Food and Drug Act, enacted in 1906 during the Administration of President Theodore Roosevelt, required that medicines be accurately labeled and free of ingredients injurious to health. This law was passed in response to concerns about adulterated food products and patent medicines containing secret ingredients that were often addictive. The Act also established the Bureau that was the forerunner to today's Food and Drug Administration.

In 1938, during the Administration of Franklin D. Roosevelt, Congress passed the Federal Food, Drug, and Cosmetic Act, which required drug manufacturers to demonstrate the safety of their products before they could be approved for marketing. The need for stronger regulation of drugs had been apparent to many for some time, but what finally led to the passage of the 1938 law was the tragedy caused by the Massengill Company's elixir of sulfanilamide.

Sulfanilamide, introduced in 1935, was the first antibiotic found to be effective against bacterial infections in humans. Sulfanilamide pills tasted bad, and so the manufacturer decided to create a pleasant-tasting elixir. The drug is difficult to solubilize, but the company's chemist found it would dissolve

in diethylene glycol, a colorless, odorless, sweet-tasting liquid. Cherry fla-
voring and red colorant made a palatable product and the elixir sold well.
Unfortunately, diethylene glycol is poisonous. (Products in the glycol family are
used in antifreeze, among other things.) Within weeks of the initial shipments
of the elixir from the factory, the first deaths were reported. Many poisonings
and at least 107 deaths, many of them children, occurred. Under the limits of
the law then in force, the FDA could fine the manufacturer only for "misbrand-
ing:" no requirement existed for pre-market demonstration of safety.

From 1938 to 1962, to gain approval for marketing a drug, the manufacturer
had to prove the drug was safe. After 1962, drug manufacturers had to prove
effectiveness[4] as well as safety. The 1962 Federal Food, Drug, and Cosmetic Act
passed during the Kennedy Administration put into place a requirement that,
to gain FDA approval to market a drug, the manufacturer had to present "substantial evidence" of its effectiveness.[5] What finally made the passage of the
1962 law possible—it had been subjected to 2 years of congressional hearings—
was the thalidomide tragedy.[6] Section 505(d) of the Act defined substantial evidence as "evidence consisting of adequate and well-controlled investigations,
including clinical investigations, by experts qualified by scientific training and
experience to evaluate the effectiveness of the drug involved, on the basis of
which it could be fairly and responsibly concluded by such experts that the
drug will have the effect it purports or is represented to have under the conditions of use prescribed, recommended, or suggested in the labeling or proposed
labeling thereof."

Since the passage of the 1962 law, the dimensions of safety and effectiveness
have been considered together. In the words of the FDA, "It is recognized that
no drug is safe in the sense of being entirely free of adverse effects. Reference
in the Federal Food, Drug, and Cosmetic Act to the safety of a drug for the uses
recommended in labeling has been interpreted as meaning that the benefits of
a drug outweigh its risks for those uses."[7]

In effect, the 1962 law redefined the evidential standard for prescription
drugs. No longer would the opinions of knowledgeable experts serve as proof
enough of effectiveness. Proof would now reside in the findings of "adequate
and well-controlled investigations"—a shift from impressions based on personal experience and professional judgment to external, objective data arising
from systematic, documented observations. The shift embodied in the 1962
law reflected and in turn accelerated a shift in medical epistemology, in "how
we know" in clinical medicine.

Just as the sulfanilamide and thalidomide tragedies precipitated the
strengthening of oversight and regulation of prescription drugs, tragedies
related to devices such as the Dalkon Shield precipitated the passage of the
Device Amendments to the Federal Food, Drug, and Cosmetic Act in 1976
during the Administration of President Gerald Ford. Before then, the FDA's

authority was restricted to trying to keep fraudulent or harmful devices out of the market. The 1976 Amendments established a classification system for devices and required the agency to set and enforce standards that devices had to meet before they could be marketed.

An unforeseen consequence of the 20th-century legislation establishing pre-marketing evidential requirements for the safety and effectiveness of prescription drugs was an evolving understanding of the need for and power of controlled clinical trials. The paradigm shift in clinical trial methodology had begun in the 1940s when, in two British studies, random allocation of trial participants was first used with humans. But in many ways, the proof-of-effectiveness requirements placed on drug manufacturers by the 1962 Federal Food, Drug, and Cosmetic Act created the favorable conditions for the advances in clinical research methods and the formalization of clinical trials methodology that have occurred over the past 60 years. The FDA's policies, procedures, and monographs called "guidance for industry" describing how the safety and efficacy of new drugs are to be tested reflect the state of the science in clinical trial methodology. Continual improvement in the methods of clinical trials has occurred on an international basis as well, led by the International Conference on Harmonisation of Technical Requirements for Registration of Pharmaceuticals for Human Use (ICH), launched in 1990.[8]

The Regulatory Approval Process for Drugs and Biologics in the United States: What Is Known about Safety, Effectiveness, and Comparative Effectiveness at Approval for Marketing?

The FDA issues the decision about whether a drug or biologic agent[9] is approved for marketing based upon the evidence for the agent's safety and effectiveness that emerges from a portfolio of preclinical studies (laboratory and animal studies) and clinical trials (trials in human subjects). The first step is the submission to the FDA, by the sponsor and/or investigator, of an Investigational New Drug (IND) application.[10] The IND is not an application for marketing, but rather an application for permission to conduct human research on the drug. The IND application is a packet of information about the agent to be investigated (chemistry, manufacturing, pharmacology, toxicology) and the study protocols by which the safety and efficacy of the agent will be evaluated prospectively in humans. The contents and format of an IND are governed by statutory regulations. Within 30 days of receiving an IND application, FDA staff assigns it to an appropriate review team. The review team evaluates the IND application in order to ensure that the safety and ethical rights of human subjects will be protected in the proposed trials and to ensure that the proposed safety and efficacy studies and trials will provide adequate evidence for subsequent regulatory decision making. If the IND application passes the review, the FDA notifies the sponsor and/or investigator that it is "safe to proceed" with the proposed studies.

That "the clinical (that is, in humans) testing of a previously untested drug generally follows three phases" is spelled out in Section 312.21 of Chapter 1 (Food and Drug Administration), Title 21 of the Code of Federal Regulations (21CFR312.21). An IND application can be submitted for one or more phases of the investigation of a new drug. This section of the Code also describes the nature of the three phases of investigation, specifically the goals, the kinds and numbers of human subjects, and whether control subjects are to be included. The descriptions of Phase 1, 2, and 3 studies are summarized in Box 2.1.

Box 2.1 The Three Phases of Investigations of New Drugs for Human Use

An investigational new drug application (IND) may be submitted for one or more phases of an investigation. The clinical investigation of a previously untested drug is generally divided into three phases. Although in general the phases are conducted sequentially, they may overlap.

(a) *Phase 1*. Phase 1 includes the initial introduction of an investigational new drug into humans. Phase 1 studies are typically closely monitored and may be conducted in patients or normal volunteer subjects. These studies are designed to determine the metabolism and pharmacologic actions of the drug in humans, the side effects associated with increasing doses, and, if possible, to gain early evidence on effectiveness. During Phase 1, sufficient information about the drug's pharmacokinetics and pharmacological effects should be obtained to permit the design of well-controlled, scientifically valid, Phase 2 studies. The total number of subjects and patients included in Phase 1 studies varies with the drug but is generally in the range of 20 to 80.

(b) *Phase 2*. Phase 2 includes the controlled clinical studies conducted to evaluate the effectiveness of the drug for a particular indication or indications in patients with the disease or condition under study and to determine the common short-term side effects and risks associated with the drug. Phase 2 studies are typically well controlled, closely monitored, and conducted in a relatively small number of patients, usually involving no more than several hundred subjects.

(c) *Phase 3*. Phase 3 studies are expanded controlled and uncontrolled trials. They are performed after preliminary evidence suggesting effectiveness of the drug has been obtained, and they are intended to gather the additional information about effectiveness and safety needed to evaluate the overall benefit–risk relationship of the drug and to provide an adequate basis for labeling. Phase 3 studies usually include from several hundred to several thousand subjects.

Source: From Title 21, section 312.21, of the Code of Federal Regulations. Available from http://www.gpo.gov/fdsys/granule/CFR-2011-title21-vol5/CFR-2011-title21-vol5-sec312-21/content-detail.html.

Once the Phase 1, 2, and 3 studies proposed in the IND application(s) have been completed and appear to support the sponsor's and/or investigators' hypotheses about the safety and efficacy of the drug, the next step for the sponsor is to prepare a New Drug Application (NDA) for submission to the FDA (or a Biologics License Application, if the agent is a biotechnology product). Just as the contents and format of the IND application are governed by statute, so are those of the NDA. The NDA is in essence an application to be able to market and sell the new drug for a set of specific clinical indications proposed by the sponsor/investigator. The NDA presents the results and an integrated summary of all the clinical trials of the drug, as well as the results of animal studies, other laboratory studies, and manufacturing processes. It provides the empirical evidence of the safety and effectiveness of the drug when used in humans for the indications proposed, and also provides the data on the drug's pharmacodynamic and pharmacokinetic profiles in humans.

A team of internal FDA reviewers examines the NDA to determine whether the agent's benefits outweigh its risks; external advisory committees composed of outside experts may be consulted. This benefits and risks assessment is circumscribed by the drug's proposed "label," that is, the statements of the instructions specifying the clinical condition(s) for which the drug is intended for use, restrictions as to the types of people who should use it, and known side effects. FDA officials then come to a decision about whether to approve the drug for marketing in the U.S. If the drug is not approved—common reasons involve failure to show a drug's effectiveness, safety concerns, or manufacturing issues—the FDA issues a response letter outlining the problems and deficiencies that need to be corrected. If the drug is approved by the FDA for marketing, the FDA grants the sponsor a period of "exclusivity"—exclusive marketing rights for the drug—that varies in length based on the type of the drug.[11]

A Closer Look at Phase 1, 2, and 3 Clinical Trials
in the Drug Approval Process

Because our focus is on what is known about effectiveness, safety, and comparative effectiveness at the time a new drug is approved by the FDA for clinical use, we will now more closely examine the clinical trials the agency requires for the investigation of a new drug and the support of a marketing application.

The NDA for a new molecular entity (a drug containing an active ingredient never before marketed in the United States) must describe the findings of preclinical studies and Phase 1, 2 and 3 trials in humans. This incremental evaluation of an agent allows the manufacturer, at each step, to make a data-based decision about whether the agent shows enough promise to warrant proceeding on to the next evaluative step. The highly formalized sequence of studies also allows for refinement of the agent or the mode of its administration. Each phase of evaluation leads to a deeper understanding of the various effects of the agent—adverse effects, beneficial effects, and effects of a biochemical nature that are imperceptible to the subject but detectable, for example, on laboratory tests of liver or kidney function. Taken together, the steps in the evaluative process give some information about possible harms, and they confirm or disprove the clinical benefit of the agent. The steps allow a reasonably firm estimate to be made of the magnitude of the clinical benefit of the agent. In most cases, however, the magnitude of the clinical benefit is estimated by comparing the agent against a placebo rather than a different active agent of established effectiveness.

The preclinical studies performed in vitro on laboratory benches and in vivo in animals establish the time course of drug distribution in tissues and organs, and show the effects of the agent on the structure and functions of cells, organs, and tissues. Preclinical studies also inform about how the agent is metabolized and excreted. If the manufacturer believes that the preclinical studies are promising, the next step is the phased trials in humans described in Box 2.1.

As a result of these incremental preclinical studies and clinical trials, a substantial amount of information is known about the clinical effects of a drug or biologic agent by the time the Phase 3 trials are completed and the full integrated data are presented to the FDA in the NDA (or BLA, for a new biologic agent). But even for drugs that meet FDA approval standards under the standard or priority review designation, many uncertainties remain. The portfolio of clinical trials in the NDA on which FDA bases its marketing approval decision may include fewer than 2,000 individual human subjects. This may be too few subjects to observe rare or uncommon adverse effects.[12] Also, the study populations used in Phase 2 and 3 trials, though composed of persons with the target condition of interest, are very homogeneous: the samples are restricted in age, generally not including the very young or the very old, and they include only individuals who have few or no co-existing medical conditions and whose health habits differ from those of the general population. These factors generally magnify the clinical benefits seen with the agent: when it is used in routine clinical practice, less clinical benefit and more harm can be anticipated. Recognizing the limitations of the evidence on which it bases its drug approval decisions, FDA can require sponsors and/or investigators to conduct post-marketing studies to gather additional information about product safety, efficacy, or optimal use and report the data to the FDA. Manufacturers may in other cases agree with the FDA that one or more post-marketing studies should be conducted to gain additional information, or to address a safety concern identified after the drug was approved for use, and commit to the agency to conduct them.

At any time during the drug development process a drug manufacturer may request that its product be designated by the FDA for a "Fast Track" development and review process, if the drug is intended to treat a serious disease and fills an unmet medical need. Another designation that may be sought by a manufacturer is that of "Accelerated Approval," in which the FDA allows the use of surrogate endpoints as outcomes in clinical trials rather than the usual clinical endpoints. The goal of this designation is to get potentially valuable drugs for serious conditions out into the market more quickly. A surrogate or substitute endpoint is a measurable element such as a change in the size of a malignant tumor or in the level of hemoglobin A1c (a measure of blood sugar control) which it is hoped correlates, but which may not, with a clinical outcome such as increased survival time in a patient with cancer or a reduction in the risk for cardiovascular death in a person with diabetes. Surrogate outcomes are chosen because they are achieved more quickly than clinical outcomes, thereby reducing the size or length of trials and their cost. FDA requires post-marketing studies or confirmatory clinical trials of drugs approved under Fast Track and Accelerated Approval designations. Obviously, at the time of FDA approval, less is known about the safety and effectiveness of Fast Track and Accelerated Approval drugs than about drugs approved under the standard or priority review tracks.

Generation of Comparative Effectiveness Information during the Drug Approval Process

The FDA has no statutory mandate at this time to require that the controlled clinical trials that comprise an NDA contain valid and useful information on the drug's comparative clinical effectiveness. Current law does not require that, in order to be approved for marketing in the United States, a new drug or biologic agent be shown to be superior for the proposed clinical indications to an agent already on the market. It just must be shown to be safe and effective for the indications proposed. Where, then, does an evaluation of the comparative effectiveness of a new drug or biologic agent come into the picture?

In a large proportion of Phase 2 and 3 trials, placebo comparators are used. But in certain instances the inclusion of a placebo control group would not be ethical,[13] and an active comparator must be used instead. An active comparator is a drug or biologic agent that has met the FDA's standards for safety and effectiveness and is approved for marketing. Trials using an active comparator would meet the definition of "comparative effectiveness research" that evolved during the debates of the 2000s; placebo-controlled trials would not (more on this definitional evolution in Chapter 6). The sponsor or manufacturer submitting the IND application for submission to the FDA may elect to propose one or more trials comparing the new agent against an active comparator, or it may be required by the FDA to do so.

The goal of a clinical trial using an active comparator may be to demonstrate that the new agent is better (more efficacious and/or safer) than the active comparator (superiority trial), or it may be to demonstrate that the new agent is not worse than the active comparator by a preset margin (non-inferiority trial). The reasoning behind the latter is that, since the active control has already been proven to be effective, if the new drug is almost as good, then it too has met a threshold of effectiveness. But the ethics of non-inferiority trials are not completely worked out.[14] Valid non-inferiority trials are challenging to design. Moreover, the concept of non-inferiority, which does not mean "the same as or equivalent to," but rather "not more than x% worse than," is much harder to grasp and to explain than that of superiority.

It is easy to see how a series of non-inferiority trials in which successive drugs aimed at the same clinical condition were found to be "not much worse" than their predecessors could constitute a race to the bottom, eventually culminating in an approved drug that could be called "not much better than nothing." In response to a congressional request, the Government Accountability Office (GAO) examined the FDA's use of evidence from non-inferiority trials in the drug approval process.[15] Reviewing the 175 NDAs for new molecular entities intended to prevent or treat diseases or other conditions submitted to the FDA between 2002 and 2009 on which a decision was made by the FDA before December 31, 2009, the GAO found that 43 of the NDAs (25%) included evidence from at least one non-inferiority trial. Poorly designed non-inferiority trials were an issue in 9 of the 43 NDAs. Since 2002 the FDA has issued over 20 guidance documents for industry that include information on expectations for non-inferiority trials in various therapeutic classes, including one devoted completely to design and statistical analysis issues in non-inferiority trials.[16]

Findings from non-inferiority trials performed as part of NDAs may be of dubious usefulness for guiding choices between alternative drugs in the patient care setting. However, NDAs submitted to the FDA that include the findings from superiority trials against active comparators often contain valuable information on a drug's effectiveness and safety relative to an alternative. Unfortunately, the relative inaccessibility of many trials conducted for regulatory purposes undermines their clinical usefulness. Such trials must be registered on clinicaltrials.gov, and summary results are presented on the FDA's Web pages, but manufacturers are not required to post full reports because trial designs and other details are considered proprietary. Many of these trials are never reported (or are poorly reported) in the peer-reviewed literature. The resulting publication bias inflates the estimates of clinical benefit.

Factors Driving the Post-Approval Uptake and Dissemination of New Drugs and Biologics

From the preceding section it should be clear that it is not scientific evidence of *relative* superiority that drives post-approval uptake of a new drug. Such data are simply not generated in the pre-market approval process. The major drivers are marketing and the mitigation of financial barriers through prescription drug insurance coverage.

Marketing by Pharmaceutical Companies

Once the FDA approves a prescription drug or biologic for marketing, the manufacturer is free to market it to users for the indications and population listed on the label. Those users include the doctors who prescribe it and the patients for whom it is prescribed. Manufacturers of prescription drugs and biologics devote a substantial amount of resources to marketing their products. Strategies include hard-copy advertisements in professional or lay magazine, television ads, one-on-one detailing of physicians, the provision of free samples to doctors' offices, and other activities whose promotional intent is not as explicit, such as support for conferences, research grants to physicians, direct-to-consumer advertising, and providing free or reduced-cost brand name medications for patients unable to afford them. Estimates of annual U.S. pharmaceutical marketing expenditures (2004 data) range from $27.7 billion to $57.5 billion.[17]

Physicians have long wanted to believe that their interactions with the pharmaceutical companies do not sway their prescribing behaviors, that when faced with a choice of several drug options for treating a condition, they choose the one that best suits the characteristics of the patient at hand rather than the one most recently or vigorously promoted by the pharmaceutical representative. But over the past 15 years, research has proven otherwise. Drug company gifts and personal interactions with physicians do indeed increase the likelihood that the physician will write more prescriptions for the agent(s) being promoted. The 2000s saw some corrective actions on conflicts of interest. Most recently, the 2010 Affordable Care Act includes provisions that require medical industry firms to disclose the names of physicians to whom they provided any gifts or payments exceeding $10 (food, entertainment, consulting fees, honoraria, etc.). The data will be posted on a public Web site searchable by physician name beginning in 2013.

Marketing to physicians is important for pharmaceutical companies, but so is marketing to patients. In 1999, the FDA issued guidance for industry on consumer-directed broadcast advertising, in effect, telling pharmaceutical manufacturers what they needed to include in broadcast advertisements of prescription drugs in order to be in compliance with existing FDA regulations on consumer-directed ads. Television ads for prescription drugs proliferated, and spending by the pharmaceutical industry on direct-to-consumer advertising skyrocketed from about $300 million in 1994 to $2.5 billion by 2000.[18] Using subtle and not-so-subtle "patients like me" approaches, the ads are intended to stimulate individuals to consider whether they might benefit from the drug, and if so, to go to their doctor and request it. Does it work? Every $1 the industry spends on DTC advertising yields an additional $4.20 in sales (2000 data).[19]

The creation of demand for the product is key, of course—necessary but not sufficient. The party who wants to consume the product must have the means to procure it. The Medicare Modernization Act of 2003 extended prescription drug benefits to Medicare beneficiaries, and an increasing number of nonelderly Americans have some form of prescription drug coverage.

Marketing and the lessening of financial barriers have been very successful. Americans have increased their use of prescription drugs over the past decade.[20] Nearly 50% take at least one prescription drug, and 1 out of 10 take five or more. U.S. spending for prescription drugs between 1999 and 2008 more than doubled to $234.1 billion. H. L. Mencken was right when he claimed, "What distinguishes man from animals is the desire to take medicine."

FDA-Approved "Labels," Off-Label-Marketing, and Off-Label Prescribing

The FDA approves a prescription drug or biologic agent for marketing under an explicit "label." The FDA-approved label is the official description of a product, which includes the indication (what the drug is used for); who should take it; instructions for use during pregnancy, in children, and in other populations; and safety information. The contents of the label are based directly on the results of the clinical trials conducted in the pre-market testing of the drug.

Once a product has FDA approval, the law allows doctors to prescribe it for any clinical indication and to any individual they believe to be medically justifiable, including for indications and to populations not listed on the label.[21] In other words, the law allows physicians to prescribe an approved drug for conditions and types of patients in which it has not been formally tested in clinical trials. However, the makers and vendors of an FDA-approved drug or device are prohibited by law from marketing it for any indication other than those listed on the label.

It is easy to see why off-label marketing, while illegal, is so tempting to drug makers and sellers. Getting physicians to prescribe a drug for an off-label indication and/or to expanded patient populations can greatly expand the clinical market for a given agent. Sales volume goes up without the manufacturer having to invest the time and resources to establish the safety and efficacy of the agent for its expanded use in another set of phased trials and applying to the FDA for a new label. Off-label marketing is common, insidious, and difficult to detect.[22]

The Pharmaceutical Supply Chain

Between the prescribing physician and the patients for whom she writes prescriptions exists the pharmaceutical supply chain, which consists of drug manufacturers, distributers, pharmacy benefit managers, retailers (brick-and-mortar chain and independent pharmacies and pharmacies within other retailers such as grocery stores), mail-order dispensers, and hospitals and other sites where direct care is delivered.

An extremely complicated web of financial and nonfinancial incentives and arrangements motivates the behavior of entities within the supply chain. For example, pharmacy benefits management (PBM) companies administer prescription drug insurance programs; many work under contract with managed care companies, large employers who self-insure for health care, and state and local government providers of health care. Because pharmacy benefit management companies can buy drugs in large volumes, they are in a position to negotiate with drug manufacturers for discounted prices. Most PBM companies utilize what is called a formulary, which is a list of "preferred" medications. The medications may be preferred because of their effectiveness or safety profiles, or, more often, their lower costs compared to agents considered therapeutically equivalent. For many conditions, several drug classes and many drugs within a given class exist as treatment choices; often the only substantive difference among alternatives is cost. While doctors can prescribe and patients obtain any FDA-approved drug, even those not listed on the formulary, non-formulary drugs will come at a higher cost to the patient and/or require extra paperwork and more hassle for doctor and patient. By incentivizing doctors and patients to use the formulary, the managed care company under contract to the PBM exerts some control over the cost of prescription drugs, and the PBM can realize a profit on the drug procurement side. Of the players in the pharmaceutical supply chain, PBMs are likely to be the most avid users of the findings of comparative effectiveness research on prescription drugs.

The Regulatory Approval Process for Medical Devices: What Is Known about Safety, Effectiveness, and Comparative Effectiveness at the Time of Market Approval?

For medical devices, the law sets the evidential bar to market entry quite low. Almost all medical devices can enter the market on the strength of bench testing alone, that is, without any confirmation in human studies that they are effective and safe. Consequently, much less is known about the effectiveness and safety of a new device at the time of market entry than is known about a newly approved prescription drug.

Medical devices are assuming ever greater importance in the treatment of human diseases. From a clinical standpoint, a useful way of thinking about medical devices is that some are tools that assist the operator to perform a certain action, while others are actually the treatment for the condition in question. Examples of the former range from tongue depressors used in examinations of the oropharynx to the da Vinci® Surgical System of Intuitive Surgical, Inc.—the "robot"—that assists a surgeon to perform minimally invasive procedures. The da Vinci system consists of a console at which the surgeon sits to control the surgical maneuvers; a cart including three or four robotic arms that is positioned by the side of the patient; a vision system for the surgeon and others to view the operative field; robotic instruments for cutting, suturing, and so on; a range of disposable instruments and supplies; and the supportive computer software. Examples of the devices that can be considered actual treatments include the implantable stents used to prop open blocked arteries or ducts, heart valves made out of artificial materials or biologic tissue, implantable defibrillators used to shock a heart out of lethal rhythm, penile implants, and prosthetic joints used to replace irreversibly damaged native knees and hips. All these are designed and manufactured to remain in the body permanently.

Through its Center for Devices and Radiologic Health, the FDA is responsible for "protecting and promoting the public health by assuring the safety, effectiveness and quality of medical devices...fostering innovation, and providing the public with accurate, science-based information about the products [the agency] oversees, throughout the total product life cycle."[23] The FDA has classified and described over 1,700 types of devices—within these types hundreds of thousands of devices are "cleared" by the FDA for sale—and organized them into 16 medical specialty areas such as cardiovascular (21CFR 862-892).

The 1976 Medical Device Amendments to the Federal Food, Drug, and Cosmetic Act established a regulatory classification system for devices and imposed pre-marketing requirements on manufacturers that vary by the device class. The definition of a medical device is given in Box 2.2. The classification of the device is based on its intended use and the risk the device poses to the patients in whom it is used. Briefly, class I devices pose the lowest risk to patients; class II, moderate risk; and class III, the highest risk. The FDA clears class I and II products for marketing on the basis of a pre-market notification [501(k)] submitted by the manufacturer. Class III products cannot be marketed until the agency approves a pre-market approval application (PMA) that provides information on the safety and effectiveness of the device when used in humans.

Box 2.2 **FDA Definition of a Medical Device**

Medical devices range from simple tongue depressors and bedpans to complex programmable pacemakers with microchip technology and laser surgical devices. In addition, medical devices include in vitro diagnostic products, such as general purpose lab equipment, reagents, and test kits, which may include monoclonal antibody technology. Certain electronic radiation-emitting products with medical application and claims meet the definition of medical device. Examples include diagnostic ultrasound products, X-ray machines, and medical lasers. If a product is labeled, promoted, or used in a manner that meets the following definition in section 201(h) of the Federal Food, Drug, and Cosmetic (FD&C) Act, it will be regulated by the Food and Drug Administration as a medical device and is subject to premarketing and postmarketing regulatory controls. A device is an instrument, apparatus, implement, machine, contrivance, implant, in vitro reagent, or other similar or related article, including a component part, or accessory which is:

- recognized in the official National Formulary, or the United States Pharmacopoeia, or any supplement to them,
- intended for use in the diagnosis of disease or other conditions, or in the cure, mitigation, treatment, or prevention of disease, in man or other animals, or
- intended to affect the structure or any function of the body of man or other animals, and which does not achieve any of its primary intended

purposes through chemical action within or on the body of man or other animals and which is not dependent upon being metabolized for the achievement of any of its primary intended purposes.

Source: From the FDA Web site. Available from http://www.fda.gov/medicaldevices/deviceregulationandguidance/overview/classifyyourdevice/ucm051512.htm

All classes of medical devices, before they can be marketed, are subject to the "General Controls" of the FDA, including registration of manufacturers, distributors, and other involved companies; listing of the device with the FDA; compliance with good manufacturing practices in the making of the product; compliance with requirements for labeling; and submission of a pre-market notification [510(k)] before marketing the device.[24] Class II devices are subject to Special Controls in addition to General Controls. Special Controls may include expanded labeling requirements, construction requirements, requirements for resistance to chemicals, and mandatory performance standards. Mandatory performance standards include technical specifications such as biocompatibility and non-pyrogenicity for devices that come in contact with body tissue and fluids and functional specifications such as ultrafiltration coefficients for hemodialyzers. Class III devices are the most stringently regulated. They are subject to General Controls and the approval by the FDA of a PMA that includes human studies of the device. The PMA contains the results of the manufacturer's preclinical and clinical studies evaluating the safety and effectiveness of the device. The PMA includes information on laboratory studies of the device, including information on such elements as microbiology, stress, and wear, as well as the results of the human studies of the device, including study protocols, safety data, effectiveness data, device failures, and so on.

The 1976 Amendments had to handle existing devices already in clinical use at the time the amendments were passed ("pre-Amendments devices") as well as new devices that manufacturers wanted to market after the new law was passed (post-Amendments devices). The statute required FDA officials to go through and classify all devices already in use at the time the new law was enacted. Class I and II pre-Amendments devices were allowed to remain on the market; their manufacturers were not required to present any formal evidence of safety and effectiveness. Class III pre-Amendments devices could continue to be marketed until the FDA required their makers to submit a PMA in which evidence of the device's safety and effectiveness had to be presented. At the time the 1976 Device Amendments were enacted, relatively few class III devices were on the market.

With regard to post-Amendments devices, the 1976 Amendments authorized the FDA to clear any device in class I or II for marketing if the manufacturer marshaled convincing evidence, in a pre-market notification [510(k)] submission that the device is "substantially equivalent" to an existing, already-marketed class I or II device. The FDA reviews the pre-market notification submitted by the manufacturer and determines whether the device is "substantially equivalent" to a class I or II device already in commercial distribution.[25] In other words, the manufacturer does not have to provide empirical evidence for the safety and effectiveness of the new device as used in humans, but only documentation that it has the same intended use, has no important technological differences (accompanied, for some devices, with data from performance tests), and therefore is expected to pose the same risk as a comparable or predicate device already on the market. Of course, what is expected and what is shown through rigorous clinical research are two different things.

To gain FDA clearance to market a new post-Amendments class III device classified as high risk,[26] the sponsor or manufacturer must submit a pre-market application (PMA) that includes "valid scientific evidence" that the device is safe and effective in humans.[27] Such human studies of an investigational (i.e., not cleared for marketing by the FDA) device can be legally conducted only under an approved investigational device exemption (IDE). The IDE must be approved by the FDA if the device involved is considered to be "significant risk" or if the human subject will need to undergo a potentially risky additional procedure, for example, surgery, as part of device testing. Otherwise, the IDE must be approved only by an institutional review board.

The FDA's Office of Device Evaluation receives many more requests for clearance for devices via the pre-market notification [510(k)] path than the PMA process. In a given year, PMA approvals of devices account for <1% of all applications. For example, in 2009, the Office of Device Evaluation received 3,597 pre-market notifications [510(k)] but only 20 original PMA applications.[28] Some find it astonishing that human studies are required for 100% of new drugs but for <1% of medical devices.

Like prescription drugs and biologics, devices are approved by the FDA for uses specified on a "label." Device manufacturers and sellers are prohibited by law from promoting the device for indications not listed on the label. Doctors by law can use approved devices for any indication they deem justifiable, even if it is not listed on the label. As in the drug approval process, the FDA may approve a device conditional upon the manufacturer's compliance with requirements such as the conduct and reporting of post-approval studies.

A Closer Look at the Role of Scientific Evidence
in Medical Device Regulation in the United States

The standard for what constitutes "valid scientific evidence" of safety and effectiveness established by the 1976 Device Amendments is broader and weaker than that for prescription drugs and biologics.[29] Whereas the drug regulations require a drug manufacturer to present "substantial evidence" of effectiveness, defined as "evidence consisting of adequate and well-controlled investigations" (see earlier in this chapter), "valid scientific evidence" as defined in the device regulations (21 CFR §860.7) can include "well-controlled investigations, partially controlled investigations, studies and objective trials without matched controls, well-documented case histories conducted by experts and reports of significant human experience with a marketed device, from which it can fairly and responsibly be concluded by qualified experts that there is reasonable assurance of the safety and effectiveness of a device under its conditions of use."

In other words, significant risk devices can be judged as safe and effective and be approved for marketing based upon weak study designs—even "case histories"—that, as we saw in Chapter 1, may lead to erroneous inferences about the effects of a therapeutic intervention.

Even when the stronger design of "controlled" investigations is intended for the testing of the device in humans, device trials pose unique challenges with regard to the choice of control group (concurrent, historical, or self?), nature of the control condition (placebo, surgical therapy, or medical therapy?), method of allocation (randomization or deterministic?), rapid technological change in the design or components of the device itself, and the influence of the operator—the person using or implanting the device—on the apparent safety and effectiveness of the device. The extent of operator-dependent poor outcomes may vary within and across operators as they gain additional experience with the device and progress through their learning curves.

The Regulatory Framework for Medical Devices:
Time for an Overhaul?

Contemporary clinical medicine grows more device dependent by the day. The roughly 35 years following the passage of the Medical Device Amendments have been a period in which advances in materials and technology have enabled the development of ever more sophisticated assistive and implantable devices. Development has been matched by demand, as techniques for minimally invasive therapeutic and diagnostic procedures—first used in the early 1980s —continue to advance. At the same time, the "substantial equivalence" regulatory approval standard for moderate risk (class II) devices via the pre-market notification [501(k)] process appears to be increasingly insufficient, as does the weak scientific evidence standard on which the approval of some high-risk (class III) devices is based. Taken together, these regulatory standards have allowed the marketing and clinical use of devices that have caused significant and sometimes fatal harms to patients. Increasing concerns stemming from high-profile device failures and inadequacies have fueled calls for legislative action to strengthen the standards.

The deficiencies of the 510(k) approval pathway have justifiably gotten more attention than problems in the PMA pathway. Concerns raised about the safety and effectiveness of the devices approved under this program—concerns from inside the FDA as well as physicians, patients, and the press—were joined with the device industry's complaints that the vagaries of the review process were retarding innovation and the pace of device development. In September 2009, the FDA's Center for Devices and Radiological Health launched a comprehensive evaluation of its 510(k) program. This evaluation included an internal review by two working groups of FDA staff[30] and an external review that the FDA commissioned from the Institute of Medicine. Attempting to meet three objectives—foster device innovation, enhance regulatory predictability, and improve patient safety—the agency released its 510(k) Plan of Action in January 2011;[31] its Medical Device Innovation Initiative, which focuses on transformative innovative devices, in February 2011;[32] and created a Science Council in the Center for Device and Radiological Health in March 2011.[33]

The Institute of Medicine's (IOM) report was released on July 29, 2011.[34] Even before its contents were known, members of the device industry criticized the IOM's process and the makeup of the Committee, which some interpreted as a way to undermine the recommendations (which are non-binding) even before they were issued. The IOM Committee found the current 510(k) process to be flawed and recommended that an integrated pre-market and post-market regulatory framework be developed that provides a reasonable assurance of safety and effectiveness throughout the device life cycle. This recommendation was immediately and vociferously rejected by the industry[35] and many politicians. Unfortunately for the device industry, the IOM report and the industry's reaction to it coincided with national publicity about a surge in reports of serious and sometimes crippling problems with metal-on-metal hip prostheses. This kind of prosthesis, which is cleared under the 510(k) pre-market notification program, is used in about a third of the 250,000 hip replacements performed in the United States each year. On August 22, 2011, just 3 weeks after the release of the IOM report, the *New York Times* reported that the FDA had received over 5,000 reports of failures of metal-on-metal hip prostheses between January and mid-August 2011.[36]

Problems with metal-on-metal hip prostheses are happening at the same time as widely publicized problems with other devices such as bone-graft implants for spinal fusion operations and implantable cardioverter defibrillator leads, which were cleared for marketing under the PMA pathway, and surgical mesh implanted in vaginal walls to treat incontinence and pelvic organ prolapse, class II devices approved via the pre-market notification 510(k) pathway. Since 2005, the FDA has received over 3,874 adverse events with the latter, such as mesh erosion through the vagina leading to pain, infection, bleeding, pain during sexual intercourse (and not only for the woman—men have reported penile irritation and pain), organ perforation, and urinary problems. Vaginal mesh problems often require multiple surgical procedures and many cannot be corrected. Moreover, evidence is mounting that surgical repair for incontinence and pelvic organ prolapse can be achieved without the mesh implantation. Many women and their families are questioning why these problems with an FDA-regulated device were not known before it was cleared for marketing.

Information on Comparative Clinical Effectiveness at the Time of Device Approval

As is the case with drugs and biologics, the FDA has no statutory authority to require the makers of medical devices to compare the safety and effectiveness of their devices with those of competitors or with alternative therapies.

The pre-market notification 501(k) pathway for FDA clearance is not one in which comparative clinical effectiveness information on devices is generated or used. Over 90% of the medical devices currently on the market were cleared by the FDA via this path. Moreover, a large proportion of class II (moderate risk) 501(k) devices were cleared on the basis that they were "substantially equivalent" to a predecessor device already in commercial distribution. But, as presented earlier in this chapter, the determination of "substantial equivalence" is not made on the basis of head-to-head tests in humans.

One of the effects of clearance based on "substantial equivalence," a relatively low-cost pathway for device makers, is the proliferation of me-too devices with the same "intended use." For example, according to the FDA Web site as of late August 28, 2012, 805 different prosthetic knee joint systems or components have been cleared by the FDA and are on the market. How can doctors and hospitals know which device works best for a given patient? Whatever they do know, it is not based on evidence generated as part of the device clearance process.

Class III devices, which are approved via the PMA process that requires clinical data on safety and effectiveness, may come onto the market with some comparative clinical effectiveness data. The maker of a class III device may compare its safety and effectiveness with an alternative device or therapeutic intervention.

Factors Driving the Post-Approval Uptake and Dissemination of Medical Devices

Marketing to doctors and hospitals as well as to patients is the primary driver for the uptake and dissemination of new devices. Because of the dearth of comparative effectiveness evidence that is required in the FDA clearance process, evidence of relative value can play little if any role. The medical device supply chain is maturing but is less well developed that the pharmaceutical supply chain. Recent signs indicate that cost containment efforts by hospitals and payers are exerting downward pressure on device prices. In a crowded device category, absent evidence of comparative clinical effectiveness and safety, the only decisional factors left for purchasers and payers are price and clinicians' preference for certain brands and models. For example, large device companies can protect and increase their market share by entering into contracts with large hospitals or hospital chains under which, in return for lower-than-list prices, the hospital or chain promises to purchase a pre-set amount, say 80%, of its assistive devices (such as staplers, endoluminal devices such as graspers and dissectors) from that company instead of a competing company. Such contracts only work for the hospital or chain if their staff surgeons agree to and actually use the "preferred" products at least 80% of the time.

Off-Label Use of Medical Devices

After a device is cleared by the FDA, it is legal for doctors to use the device in any way they feel is clinically justifiable, though it is illegal for device makers to promote the device for indications not listed on the FDA-approved label. As with the off-label uses of prescription drugs and biologics, off-label uses of devices expand sales volumes for device makers without requiring their outlay of time and resources for testing and application to the FDA, but they also subject patients in whom they are used to unknown risks.

The extent of off-label use of medical devices is surprisingly high. For example, a 2010 randomized trial comparing two different brands of drug-eluting coronary artery stents enrolled 2,292 human subjects from over 15 European hospitals.[37] The interventional cardiologists participating in the study were free to use the stents as they saw fit with the subjects who enrolled in the study. In two-thirds of the study population, one or more stents were implanted for indications not listed on the FDA-approved label. Another example is a 2011 observational study of 111,707 people receiving implantable defibrillators at 1,227 U.S. hospitals. This study found that nearly one-fourth of the patients had none of the clinical indications for which the device is FDA approved or for which professional societies recommend it.[38]

An Unintended Effect of the Pre-Market
Notification 510(k) Pathway

The FDA's pre-market notification [510(k)] pathway for medical devices has an unintended, and, we might say, perverse effect. It inadvertently encourages the rapid and wide uptake of invasive therapeutic procedures that have not been put to fair tests of clinical effectiveness and safety. For example, in May 2009, the FDA cleared the LARIAT II Suture Delivery Device (SentreHEART, Inc.) under a 510(k) pre-market notification as a class II device. Its approved intended use (label) is to "facilitate suture placement and knot tying for use in surgical applications where soft tissues are being approximated and/or ligated with a pre-tied polyester suture." In the 510(k) notification to the FDA (available on the FDA Web site), the manufacturer stated that the device was similar to four predicate devices, that functional testing had been performed, and that the materials used in the device are commonly used in other medical devices and are biocompatible. Testing in human subjects was not described.

On February 14, 2011, a front-page article published in the *Houston Chronicle* described in glowing terms and with many cowboy allusions[39] how surgeons at a prominent Houston hospital, one of whom is the developer of the device, are using the LARIAT in people to reduce the risk of stroke from blood clots traveling to the brain from an origin in the heart. The surgeon uses the LARIAT device to deliver a loop of suture with which to snare the left atrial appendage of the heart and pull closed its opening. The left atrial appendage is a small pocket ("about the size of a jalapeno," according to the article) attached to the left atrium, that, in people with a normal cardiac rhythm, contracts to eject blood and help fill the left atrium. In people with an abnormal rhythm called atrial fibrillation, it is thought that blood pools and clots in the lax left atrial appendage. These clots, if they find their way into the left atrium and thence to the left ventricle, can be ejected into the arterial circulation and cause strokes and problems in other tissues and organs. As early as 1949, this etiologic model led physicians to postulate that obliteration or removal of the left atrial appendage should reduce the risk of cardioembolic stroke in people with atrial fibrillation. Since then surgical (open) and percutaneous (catheter-based) approaches have been used to remove, obliterate, occlude, or otherwise attack the left atrial appendage. One catheter-based device, the Watchman® Left Atrial Appendage Closure Technology (Atritech, Inc.), has been approved for that use in certain patients by the FDA via the PMA application pathway.[40] Of all the methods used to remove or obliterate the left atrial appendage over the past 60 years, closure with this device is the only one to have ever been tested in a randomized clinical trial for its ability to reduce stroke risk.[41]

The *Houston Chronicle* article about the LARIAT stated that "There now have been about 140 cases done in humans, and the device has FDA approval."

The reporter, like most people, did not grasp that all the LARIAT device has FDA approval for is "use in surgical applications where soft tissues are being approximated and/or ligated with a pre-tied polyester suture," not for the reduction of embolic strokes from clots originating in the left atrial appendage of individuals with atrial fibrillation. The surgeon featured in the article said, "Now we can't definitely say this reduces strokes yet. But I believe we're removing, arguably, the most important source of stroke in patients with atrial fibrillation. We're going to save some lives, hopefully tens of thousands." The LARIAT procedure's ability to reduce stroke risk in people with atrial fibrillation is not yet being tested in clinical trials.[42] But it is easy to see why plenty of patients would sign up to have the procedure. After all, "it's FDA approved," and "we're going to save some lives." This kind of language conjures up in physicians as well as patients the erroneous belief that the FDA has cleared the device on the evidence it improves patients' outcomes. It creates the circumstances ripe for wide dissemination of an unproven intervention, dissemination unaccompanied by systematic observation that can teach us how well it really works and whether it causes net benefit over harm.

The Role of Patients in the Uptake of New Medical Devices

While the most important market for most devices consists of physicians, proceduralists, surgeons, and hospitals, device companies also market their products directly to consumers. Billboards along highways for "Lap banding" procedures for obesity (a procedure discovered, after wide use, to be ineffective) and TV ads presenting former ice-skaters touting artificial knee joints are cases in point. But the story of "the robot" shows how patients can be captivated by certain new technologies, regardless of whether evidence of their effectiveness or comparative effectiveness exists. Earlier in this chapter we mentioned the da Vinci Surgical System® of Intuitive Surgical, Inc.—the robot—and described its components. The FDA cleared this system for marketing in 2000. By 2011, less than a dozen years from its introduction, four of every five radical prostatectomies for prostate cancer were performed using the robot, and robotic assistance is now being extended to many other procedures. The company estimates that over 1,000 of their robotic systems are in use in the United States.[43]

To what can this amazing rate of diffusion and market penetration be attributed? It certainly cannot be attributed to scientific evidence that radical prostatectomy performed with robotic assistance was superior to the open or laparoscopically assisted procedure in terms of cancer control, cure, or preservation of continence or sexual function. There was a lot of hope but no actual data. According to what a urologist told us (Box 2.3), patients played a major role.

Box 2.3 **A Urologist Describes How "the Robot" Took
Hold in American Medicine**

How did the patients know about this [*the robot*]? Largely from other
patients. Private practitioners who were using it were having some good
results with it and they mentioned it to as many people as they could.
It was a tremendous marketing ploy for them, not so much to compete
with academic centers but with Doctor X down the street. "Well, I can do
robotic surgery." Private-practice doctors who were doing a lot of it [were]
talking to their patients out in the community. [*Those patients*] talk to
other patients.

And then the word "robot" had a lot of cachet. "Robot" connotes a lot of
different things to different people. I think it drew people to the fact that
somehow a robot was mechanical, that it was computerized, that it was
perhaps not subject to human flaws as doctors might be, that somehow it
was better. They didn't really know that this [*the prostatectomy*] is not robot
driven. Doctors do the surgery with the robot mimicking what you do. But
patients didn't know that. Many of them assumed that the robot does it
and the doctor kind of sips coffee, hangs out. You tell the robot what to do
but the robot does it magically. And it's certainly not what happens.

So there was a combination of that connotation of what a robot is and
private-practice doctors who were adopting it rapidly and were aggressively marketing it. Patients did not know there was no data. [*At that time*]
there were not even quality of life studies, certainly no cancer efficacy
studies. But there was tremendous energy in the community of patients:
people with the disease [*prostate cancer*] talking to other people with the
disease, and marketing to some degree by the company. In the city where I
was practicing when you would fly into their airport the two major hospitals had, in their advertising, pictures of robots next to doctors... Patients
got the sense that this was what "big, bad hospitals" do.

When I got my first job after residency and fellowship, my first encoun-
ter at that institution was with a patient [*with prostate cancer*] who I spent a
lot of time with and going over not only my thoughts about his disease but
my qualifications. The long and short of it was, "That sounds great, Doctor,
but do you do robotic surgery?" And the answer of course was at that time
"No, but I do this other surgery." And the patient said, "Well, that sounds
really nice and you seem very nice, but can you recommend to me someone
who does robotic surgery?" Then it dawned on me that to practice where
I was, and I was in an academic environment, that I had to rapidly adopt
and change to the landscape of what was taking place currently.

Because of the competitive and revenue-generating nature of American medicine, and the fact that evidence of clinical effectiveness is not, for most devices, required in pre-market phases of device development, hospitals often find themselves having to make sizable investments in devices not yet proven to be a true clinical advance in the treatment of a disease. A major driver in the uptake of new devices is hospitals that decide to invest in expensive new technology—which earns them points on the *U.S. News and World Report* "Best Hospitals" rankings—and then must make sure the volume of use ensures a return on the investment. Hospitals in dense medical markets such as New York or Philadelphia often strive to be the first to acquire new high-profile technology so that they can use it to attract patients and gain market share. For example, on June 24, 2007, shortly after they acquired their new surgical robot, Mount Sinai Hospital in New York City ran a full page ad in the *New York Times* Sunday magazine promising "Prostate cancer surgery so good, even women can feel the difference." There was no evidence at that time that robotically assisted prostatectomy was associated with lower rates of postoperative sexual dysfunction, and there still is no such evidence.[44]

Conclusions

The assessment of comparative effectiveness of FDA-regulated drugs and devices is not a statutory requirement for marketing approval. Consequently, little evidence about comparative effectiveness is generated as part of the regulatory process. It is easy to understand why the medical products industry was and is by far the strongest opponent of federally mandated comparative effectiveness research. They have the most to lose. While the mandates enacted in the 2000s do not increase the amount or type of evidence that is required as part of the statutory regulatory process for drugs and devices, they change the forces acting on medical products once they enter the market. Comparative effectiveness research can make a drug or a device a winner or a loser, and losers lose market share.

Notes

1. The FDA defines a prescription drug product as a specific strength or potency of a drug in final dosage form for which a human drug application has been approved by the FDA and which may by law be dispensed only by prescription. Biologicals include a wide range of products, including vaccines, blood and blood components, allergenics, cellular and gene therapy products, tissue and tissue products from humans or animals such as corneas and heart valves, and recombinant therapeutic proteins. Medical devices regulated by the FDA range from simple tongue depressors and bedpans to complex programmable pacemakers with microchip technology and laser surgical devices; also included are in vitro diagnostic products and electronic radiation-emitting products such as X-ray machines.

2. The price of some FDA-approved biologic products exceeds that of many surgical procedures. For example, Genentech's Avastin (bevacizumab), a recombinant humanized monoclonal antibody approved for the treatment of patients with certain kinds of metastatic carcinomas, is administered every 2 or 3 weeks in a dose based on body weight (5 to 15 mg/kg body weight). The average adult weighs 70 kg; at 10 mg/kg, the dose would be 700 mg. In December 2010, the wholesale price for 100 mg of Avastin was about $600. Therefore, the wholesale price of one dose for the average adult—not counting acquisition, dispensing, administration, and physician charges—would be $4,200, and the wholesale cost of the drug for a 3-month course of therapy could range from $16,800 to $25,200.

3. The few effective drugs and biologics available before the 20th century included digitalis, aspirin, morphine, inoculations with matter from the pustules of cow-pox (vaccinia) to immunize against smallpox, and diphtheria antitoxin.

4. The FDA uses the term "efficacy" to refer to the findings on a human drug or biologic product in an adequate and well-controlled trial, and the term "effectiveness" to refer to the agency's regulatory determination made on the basis of clinical efficacy and other data.

5. 21CFR314.50 specifies the content and format of applications for FDA approval to market a new drug. In the technical sections describing the clinical investigations of the drug that are required as part of such application, the applicant must provide data on effectiveness (see 314.50(d)(5)(v)) and safety (see 314.50(d)(5)(vi)): "An integrated summary of the data demonstrating substantial evidence of effectiveness for the claimed indications...the effectiveness data shall be presented by gender, age, and racial subgroups and shall identify any modifications of dose or dose interval needed for specific subgroups. Effectiveness data from other subgroups of the population of patients treated, when appropriate, such as patients with renal failure or patients with different levels of severity of the disease, shall also be presented.... The applicant shall submit an integrated summary of all available information about the safety of the drug product, including pertinent animal data, demonstrated or potential adverse effects of the drug, clinical significant drug/drug interactions, and other safety considerations.... The safety data shall be presented by gender, age and racial subgroups." The applicant must also provide (see 314.50(d)(5)(viii)) "An integrated summary of the benefits and risks of the drug, including a discussion of why the benefits exceed the risks under the conditions stated in the labeling." In some cases the applicant must submit to the FDA as part of the application (see 314.50(f)(2)) "the case report forms from each patient who died during a clinical study or who did not complete the study because of an adverse event, whether believed to be drug-related or not, including patients receiving reference drugs or placebo."

6. Thalidomide was widely prescribed in Europe for morning sickness in pregnancy. Though unapproved for sale in the United States (the FDA was reviewing the application), the company distributed free "investigational" samples to American physicians, who passed them along to their patients. Thalidomide was soon found to be a teratogen that caused a developmental abnormality called phocomelia. Affected babies are born without limbs or with stumps resembling the fins of a seal. Frances Kelsey was the FDA medical officer assigned to review the drug application for thalidomide; suspecting it was an unsafe drug, she continued to request more safety data from the Richardson-Merrell Company. In the meantime, the link between thalidomide and phocomelia became clear. Ten thousand cases of phocomelia occurred in 46 countries, but only 17 in the United States, due to Kelsey's diligence. See Bren L. Frances Oldham Kelsey. FDA medical reviewer leaves her mark on history. FDA Consumer Magazine; March-April 2001:24–9.

7. FDA Guidance (Drugs): Attachment B: Clinical safety study review of an NDA or BLA of the good review practice: clinical review template (MAPP 6010.3Rev 1) p. B-1 (footnote).

8. ICH grew out of the European Union's need to harmonize regulatory requirements pertaining to prescription medications across its member nations. ICH brings together the drug regulatory agencies and pharmaceutical industry of Europe, the United States,

and Japan. The ICH devotes its energies to the furtherance of clinical trial methods and publishes guidelines in four topic areas for the evaluation of new pharmaceutical agents: quality, safety, efficacy, and cross-cutting topics. (See the ICH Web site at http://www.ich.org/home.html.)

9. Drugs are chemically synthesized (most drugs) and their chemical structure is known. Biological products (biologics) are isolated from natural sources (human, animal, or microorganism) or may be produced in the laboratory by biotechnology processes; their structures are complex and often incompletely characterized.

10. Agents are classified by FDA as follows: 1—new molecular entity; 2—new ester, salt, or other noncovalent derivative; 3—new formulation; 4—new combination; 5—new manufacturer; 6—new indication; and 7—drug already marketed but within an approved NDA. In addition, based on the drug's "therapeutic potential," it is targeted either for priority review (the drug appears to offer significant improvement compared to marketed products in the treatment, diagnosis, or prevention of a disease) or standard review (the drug appears to have therapeutic qualities similar to those of one or more already-marketed drugs). FDA's goal for completing the review of drugs with standard-review designation is within 10 months; for drugs with a priority review designation it is within 6 months. The scientific standards for approval, and the quality of evidence necessary, does not differ between standard-review and priority-review drugs.

11. A "new chemical entity," defined in 21CFR314.108, means a drug that contains no active moiety that has been approved by the FDA in any other application. When FDA approves a new chemical entity for marketing, a 5-year period of exclusivity is granted. An orphan drug is granted a 7-year period. Other exclusivity periods exist. Patents differ from exclusivity and can be granted anywhere along the development cycle of a drug; patents and exclusivity may or may not run concomitantly and may be based on different claims. Exclusivity is a statutory provision (see 21CFR314.108). Its goal is to balance economic incentives between drug innovation and the production and sale of generic versions of already-approved drugs.

12. For example, imagine a drug that causes a certain kind of serious adverse event in 1 out of 1,000 users. To be 95% sure of detecting even one such event, 3,000 users would have to be observed. Sackett et al call the statistical explanation for this the "inverse rule of 3" that is, to be 95% sure of observing an event that occurs once per x-subjects, you have to observe $3x$ subjects. See Sackett DL, Haynes RB, Gent M, Taylor DW. Compliance. In: Inman WHW, ed. Monitoring for drug safety. Lancaster, CA: MTP Press, 1980: 427–438.

13. Placebo-controlled drug trials are precluded in persons with serious clinical conditions for which an effective treatment is known to exist and for which foregoing such effective treatment even for a short time would place individuals at undue risk of harm.

14. See Garratini S, Bertele V. Non-inferiority trials are unethical because they disregard patients' interest. Lancet 2007;370:1875–77.

15. Report to Congressional Requesters: new drug approval: FDA's consideration of evidence from certain clinical trials. United States Government Accountability Office (GAO-10-798), July 30, 2010. (Available at http://www.gao.gov/new.items/d10798.pdf.)

16. Food and Drug Administration. Guidance for industry: Non-inferiority clinical trials [draft guidance]. March 2010. (Available at http://www.fda.gov/downloads/Drugs/GuidanceComplianceRegulatoryInformation/Guidances/UCM202140.pdf.)

17. Gagnon MA, Lexchin J. The cost of pushing pills: a new estimate of pharmaceutical promotion expenditures in the United States. PLoS Med 2008 5(1):e1. doi:10.1371/journal.pmed.0050001.

18. Rosenthal MB, Berndt ER, Donohue JM, Epstein AM, Frank RG. Demand effects of recent changes in prescription drug promotion. 2003. (Accessed September 17, 2012, at the Kaiser Family Foundation Web site: http://www.kff.org/rxdrugs/upload/Demand-Effects-of-Recent-Changes-in-Prescription-Drug-Promotion-Report.pdf.)

19. Kaiser Family Foundation. Impact of direct-to-consumer advertising on prescription drug spending. June 2003. (Accessed September 17, 2012, at http://www.kff.org/

rxdrugs/upload/Impact-of-Direct-to-Consumer-Advertising-on-Prescription-Drug-Spending-Summary-of-Findings.pdf.)

20. Gu Q, Dillon CF, Burt VL. Prescription drug use continues to increase: U.S. prescription drug data for 2007–2008. NCHS Data Brief No. 42, September 2010. (Accessed October 23, 2012, at http://www.cdc.gov/nchs/data/databriefs/db42.pdf.)

21. The so-called practice of medicine exemption was reiterated and extended to medical devices in 1997 with P.L.105–115: "Nothing in this chapter shall be construed to limit or interfere with the authority of a health care practitioner to prescribe or administer any legally marketed device to a patient for any condition or disease with a legitimate health care practitioner-patient relationship" (21USC.396).

22. The practices employed include internal company policies that encourage pharmaceutical representatives to engage in off-label marketing to prescribers, strategies aimed at getting payers to reimburse for drugs prescribed off label, and various incentives directed at patients, including inducements for requesting their physicians to prescribe medications for off-label indications. Allegations, lawsuits, and findings against drug manufacturers for illegal "off-label marketing" are very common. Off-label marketing schemes are intended to expand the market for, and therefore the sales of, a drug; the expansions fall into three general categories, namely expansion to unapproved diseases, to unapproved disease subtypes, and unapproved drug doses. See Kesselhein AS, Mello MM, Studdert DM. Strategies and practices in off-label marketing of pharmaceuticals: a retrospective analysis of whistleblower complaints. PLoS 2011;8:e1000431.

23 "CDRH FY 2010 Strategic Priorities" available at http://www.fda.gov/AboutFDA/CentersOffices/OfficeofMedicalProductsandTobacco/CDRH/CDRHVisionandMission/ucm197647.htm

24. Most devices in class I and some in class II are exempt from one or more General Controls.

25. For the FDA's guidance on the its pre-market notification review, the definition it uses, such as "substantially equivalent," "predicate device," "intended use," and so on, and flowcharts depicting its assessment and decisional processes, see Guidance on the CDRH pre-market notification review program. (Available from http://www.fda.gov/MedicalDevices/DeviceRegulationandGuidance/GuidanceDocuments/ucm081383.htm.)

26. All post-Amendments devices that are assessed by the FDA to be not "substantially equivalent" to already-marketed class I or II devices are automatically placed in class III and must have an approved PMA from the FDA before they can be marketed. However, not all such class III devices meet the FDA definition of "high risk," that is, "supports or sustains human life, is of substantial importance in preventing impairment if human health, or presents a potential, unreasonable risk of illness or injury." Class III devices not high risk may be eligible for the FDA's de novo approval process as a class I or II device. Human studies of effectiveness are also waived in the case of a device intended to benefit patients by treating or diagnosing a disease or condition afflicting fewer than 4,000 people in the United States each year. In that case the manufacturer may apply for a Humanitarian Device Exemption (HDE). An HDE is similar in format and content to a PMA, but without the effectiveness component. That is, an HDE application need not contain the results of valid clinical investigations demonstrating that the device is effective for its intended purpose.

27. Not all class III devices require a PMA for approval. For class III devices, a PMA is required, unless it is a post-Amendments device substantially equivalent to a pre-Amendments device for which the FDA has not called for pre-market approvals. The pre-market Notification 510(k) is the route to the market for such a device.

28. The 2009 annual report of the Office of Device Evaluation is available from http://www.fda.gov/downloads/AboutFDA/CentersOffices/CDRH/CDRHReports/UCM223893.pdf.

29. For this section we were informed by a 2008 unpublished manuscript prepared by former FDA official Miriam Provost titled, "The role of the Food and Drug Administration in the dissemination of new medical device technology."

30. The 510(k) and science report is available from http://www.fda.gov/downloads/AboutFDA/CentersOffices/CDRH/CDRHReports/UCM239449.pdf.

31. The action plan for implementation of the 25 recommendations regarding the 510(k) program is available from http://www.fda.gov/downloads/AboutFDA/CentersOffices/CDRH/CDRHReports/UCM239450.pdf.

32. Information on the Medical Device Innovation Initiative is available from http://www.fda.gov/AboutFDA/CentersOffices/CDRH/CDRHInnovation/ucm242067.htm and http://www.fda.gov/AboutFDA/CentersOffices/CDRH/CDRHInnovation/ucm242068.htm.

33. Information on the CDRH Center Science Council is available from http://www.fda.gov/AboutFDA/CentersOffices/CDRH/CDRHReports/ucm249249.htm.

34. IOM (Institute of Medicine). Medical devices and the public's health: The FDA 510(k) clearance process at 35 years. Washington, DC: National Academies Press, 2011.

35. The Advanced Medical Technology Association's statement said, "The report's conclusions do not deserve serious consideration from Congress or the Administration. It proposes abandoning efforts to address problems with the administration of the current program by replacing it at some unknown date with an untried, unproven, and unspecified new legal structure. This would be a disservice to patients and the public health."

36. Meier B, Roberts J. Hip implant complaints surge, even as the dangers are studied. New York Times 2011 Aug 22. (Accessed September 17, 2012, at http://www.nytimes.com/2011/08/23/business/complaints-soar-on-hip-implants-as-dangers-are-studied.html)

37. Serruys PW, Silber S, Garg S, et al. Comparison of zotarolimus-eluting and everolimus-eluting coronary stents. N Engl J Med 2010;363:136–46.

38. Al-Khatib S, Helkamp A, Curtis J, et al. Non-evidence-based ICD implantations in the United States. JAMA 2011;305:43–9.

39. Berger E. This Lariat is designed to rope piece of the heart. Houston Chronicle Feb 14, 2011. Phrases used in the article included "the surgeon stands straight up in his cowboy boots," "put the bridle around the horse's neck," "lasso," and so forth. (Accessed September 17, 2012, at http://www.chron.com/disp/story.mpl/metropolitan/7426069.htm.)

40. This device was "approved with conditions" by the FDA on April 23, 2009, on the basis of a randomized clinical trial of the device versus warfarin in persons with atrial fibrillation. (Information available from http://www.fda.gov/AdvisoryCommittees/CommitteesMeetingMaterials/MedicalDevices/MedicalDevicesAdvisoryCommittee/CirculatorySystemDevicesPanel/ucm142895.htm.)

41. The Watchman® LAA Closure Technology was tested in a randomized controlled trial called PROTECT-AF, and in accordance with the FDA's conditions for the approval of the device, a follow-on registry study is continuing after the trial. Holmes DR, Reddy VY, Turi ZG, Doshi SK, Sivert H et al. Percutaneous closure of the left atrial appendage (LAA) versus warfarin therapy for the prevention of stroke in patients with atrial fibrillation: a randomised non-inferiority trial. Lancet 2009;374:534–42. The trial showed that LAA closure with the device was no worse than ("noninferior to") warfarin in reducing the risk of stroke but was associated with a significantly greater risk of adverse events than warfarin (bleeding, pericardial effusion, device embolization, and procedure-related stroke). The conclusion was that the device may play a role in stroke-risk reduction for selected patients unable to take warfarin.

42. A study of stroke risk reduction was anticipated for the future, according to a personal communication from William Cohn to Carol Ashton on May 11, 2011.

43. Tracking the rise of robotic surgery for prostate cancer. NCI Cancer Bulletin, August 9, 2011. (Accessed September 17, 2012 at http://www.cancer.gov/ncicancerbulletin/080911/page4/.)

44. Orvieto MA, Coelho RF, Chauhan S, Mathe M, Palmer K, Patel VR. Erectile dysfunction after robot-assisted radical prostatectomy. Expert Rev Anticancer Ther 2010;10:747–54.

3

The Subversion of Evidence

The Rosiglitazone Story

The last chapter describes a very systematic, sequential approach to the evaluation of a new drug, an approach that yields evidence sufficiently firm to support a federal regulatory agency's decision about whether the product is safe enough, and effective enough, to be allowed to be marketed to Americans. But the truth is, even when clinical studies are well designed and carefully conducted, the evidence they yield can be ambiguous or equivocal. Add the "winners-and-losers" element to that reality, and you have a perfect opportunity for powerful stakeholders to manipulate the process by which scientific evidence is generated and interpreted so as to get the answers they want. We offer the rosiglitazone story as an example. Our principal sources for this story are the Senate Finance Committee's investigative report (see later) and all the publicly available materials about rosiglitazone that are posted on the Food and Drug Administration (FDA) Web site.

The FDA's Approval of Rosiglitazone (Avandia) in 1999

On November 3, 2011, the *New York Times* reported that the pharmaceutical company GlaxoSmithKline (GSK) had agreed to pay $3 billion to settle U.S. government civil and criminal investigations into its sales practices for numerous drugs, among them the anti-diabetes drug rosiglitazone (RSG), marketed by GSK under the name Avandia.[1] The federal cases against GSK followed the Senate Finance Committee's intensive review of the company's behavior regarding RSG, the results of which were made public on February 20, 2010.[2] Under the leadership of Chairman Max Baucus (D-MT) and Ranking Member Chuck Grassley (R-IA), the Senate Finance Committee had been investigating the practices of pharmaceutical companies for several years, following up on allegations that pharmaceutical companies had attempted, as stated in the report, "to manipulate science to improve the marketability of drugs, potentially at the expense of public safety" as well as "intimidating scientists . . . suppressing studies that may show that a drug could be dangerous, and selecting data to publish results that favor one product over another."

GSK had substantial financial reasons to try to protect the share of the diabetes market it captured with RSG. Diabetes affects 25.8 million Americans (2010 data),[3] and 2 million new adult cases are diagnosed every year. The prevalence of Type 2 diabetes (previously called adult-onset), which accounts for 90%–95% of all adult cases, is rising exponentially due to the epidemic of overweight and obesity. Diabetes is the nation's seventh leading cause of death. It is the leading cause of blindness and kidney failure, the leading cause of lower limb amputation, and a major cause of heart attack and stroke. The last three are called macrovascular complications.

Weight loss and physical exercise can improve glycemic control in persons with Type 2 diabetes, but most eventually require drug therapy. Anti-diabetic drugs are directed at reducing hyperglycemia, that is, abnormally high blood glucose levels. Why treat hyperglycemia in diabetics? First, extremely high levels of blood glucose can produce coma and death. Second, pharmacologic "tight control" (achieving and maintaining normal levels of blood glucose) has been shown to reduce the rate of diabetes-associated blindness and kidney failure in Type 2 as well as Type 1 diabetics. The situation is different with macrovascular complications, including myocardial ischemia. Tight control reduces the rate of macrovascular complications in Type 1 diabetes, but it does not do so in Type 2 diabetes. Given that Type 2 accounts for 90%–95% of diabetes, this lack of effect between glycemic control and risk for macrovascular complications is a matter of great concern. Cardiovascular events, ischemic cardiac events in particular, remain the leading cause of death in these individuals, accounting for over 65% of deaths.

Several classes of drugs with different mechanisms of action have been developed to treat hyperglycemia in Type 2 diabetes. RSG is a member of the thiazolidinedione class. In its medical review for the approval of RSG in 1999, FDA officials noted that "The durability of the thiazolidinediones in controlling hyperglycemia appears to be greater than that of other classes of oral anti-diabetic medications."[4] At the same time, all members of this drug class cause weight gain, fluid retention, and edema, and they increase the risk of congestive heart failure—serious issues in people with an already-elevated cardiovascular risk. In addition, specific drugs in the class have been associated with specific complications.

The first drug in this class to receive FDA approval was troglitazone, in 1997. As use widened, the FDA began to receive reports of severe cases of hepatotoxicity leading to liver transplant or death. In 2000 the drug was removed from the market. However, because this class of drugs is so effective in controlling blood glucose in people with Type 2 diabetes, the FDA decided to give a priority review[5] to RSG, which was at that time a product of SmithKline Beecham. (SmithKline Beecham and Glaxo Wellcome merged in late 1999 to form GSK.)

RSG received FDA approval in 1999 on the basis of the findings of three placebo-controlled dose-finding trials and five trials aimed at demonstrating the efficacy of RSG in controlling blood sugar. Across all eight studies, the total number of subjects who received RSG for 6 months or more was only 2,664; of these, only 1,005 took it for at least 1 year. All five efficacy trials demonstrated that RSG was highly effective in controlling blood glucose. Cardiac ischemic events (angina pectoris, chest pain, coronary artery disorders, and heart attack) occurred in more subjects taking RSG than those on placebo (0.3%–0.4% vs. 0.0%–0.2%), but the trials included too few subjects and were too short to determine whether RSG truly increased cardiac risk. Because of the experience with troglitazone, the major focus of the FDA's safety review was liver toxicity. No hepatotoxicity was observed with RSG in the premarket trials, to the delight of the company and the FDA. In retrospect, the focus on liver problems distracted attention from early warning signs of other problems.

Fluid retention and edema had been a problem with troglitazone, and, in the efficacy trials of RSG, edema was two or three times as frequent in subjects randomized to RSG than in controls, a similar frequency as with troglitazone. The mechanism by which these drugs caused edema was not understood. Animal studies showed that some animals receiving RSG developed cardiac hypertrophy, and some FDA officials were concerned that the fluid retention might be a manifestation of reduced cardiac function. If this were true in humans, it would have serious implications for using the drug in people with diabetes, who are already at elevated risk for cardiac problems. However, the portfolio of premarket human trials of RSG did little to elucidate the mechanism of the edema. In two of the efficacy trials, subjects taking RSG were evaluated to see if their heart size changed while on the drug. No change was demonstrated. FDA officials criticized the company for using echocardiography in these studies, because this test could have detected only "gross changes," and argued that the company should have tried harder to understand the mechanism of edema and its relation to cardiac function in subjects taking RSG.

The behavior of SmithKline Beecham in these premarket trials—using insensitive tests to detect problems or insensitive study designs to detect poor outcomes—was a harbinger of how its successor company GSK would behave after the merger in its post-market evaluations of RSG. Insensitive methods allowed the company to claim that they had tested and found no problems, when in fact a more sensitive test might have discovered them.

Of greater concern than fluid retention were the effects of RSG on body weight and serum lipids. In the premarket trials, almost one out of five subjects taking RSG had an increase in body weight of 5% to 10%; moreover, weight gain continued throughout the time subjects took the drug. In addition, total and low-density lipoprotein (LDL) cholesterol increased by a statistically significant amount, and the ratio of LDL ("bad") cholesterol to high-density lipoprotein ("good") cholesterol consistently increased. In people with diabetes, increased body weight and lipid abnormalities increase the risk for poor outcomes.

The FDA approval letter of May 25, 1999 for RSG reflects agency concerns about the drug's effects on the heart, body weight, and serum lipids and their potential for causing undesirable outcomes: "Regardless of the cause, these findings alone [the lipid abnormalities] or in combination with weight increments are not welcome in the treatment of Type 2 diabetics." Accordingly, as a condition of approval, the FDA required the drug maker to conduct a post-marketing (also called Phase 4) study under a mutually agreed-upon protocol design, and the FDA described its main features in the approval letter.

In fact, as approved by the FDA, the product label for RSG (marketed as Avandia) warns that ingestion of the drug could be associated with an 18.6% increase in LDL cholesterol. A meta-analysis involving 14 trials and over 18,000 people with diabetes showed that *lowering* LDL cholesterol by that amount was associated with a 17% reduction in major cardiovascular events.[6] Moreover, the FDA has approved lipid-lowering agents achieving that level of reduction of LDL cholesterol under the presumption that that amount of reduction confers a cardiovascular benefit. If the evidence demonstrates that reducing LDL cholesterol by a certain amount leads to a predictable reduction of cardiovascular events, isn't it likely the opposite is also true?

The same year that the FDA approved RSG (1999), it approved another drug from this class, pioglitazone (PIO), marketed under the name Actos by Takeda Pharmaceuticals, Japan's largest pharmaceutical company. PIO did not appear to cause liver toxicity, but like troglitazone and RSG, caused fluid retention and edema and increased the risk of heart failure. Because these three effects were seen with all the drugs in the class, they are called "class effects" related to a direct pharmacologic effect. However, unlike RSG, PIO did not cause a worsening of the serum lipid profile. If the worsening lipid profile seen with RSG did in fact increase patients' risk for cardiovascular events, then Takeda's PIO would have a distinct marketing advantage over RSG.

GSK Intimidates Individual Physicians

As early as 1999, Dr. John Buse, a diabetologist and professor of medicine at the University of North Carolina, began to point out publicly at conferences and letters to the FDA and GSK that patients taking RSG had increased cardiac risk because of the abnormalities in the lipid profile that the drug caused, and that this effect on lipids was not seen with the other drug in this class on the market, PIO. The unfavorable comparison between RSG and PIO had the potential to greatly undermine RSG's market share. The means by which GSK intimidated Dr. Buse in order to silence him are described in the previously mentioned Senate Finance Committee staff report on GSK and Avandia, which includes internal GSK documents and testimony from Dr. Buse and others. Internal GSK company documents refer to Dr. Buse as the "Avandia Renegade" and suggest that he should receive a threatening letter warning him about making such statements or be punished by the company calling his University superiors. In fact, GSK's head of research did contact Dr. Buse's department chairman. The chairman made clear to Dr. Buse that a lawsuit had been threatened. Dr. Buse ultimately signed a "clarification" letter composed by GSK in which he agreed not to discuss the issue in public, and he wrote a personal letter to GSK asking that they "call off the dogs." Two other academic physicians, reporting a case of liver failure associated with RSG, were similarly intimidated by GSK.

GSK and the Phase 4 Study Required as a Condition of FDA Approval of RSG

To satisfy the condition of a post-approval study, GSK designed "A Diabetes Outcome Progression Trial" (ADOPT). But instead of focusing on cardiovascular or other adverse outcomes, the primary outcome for ADOPT was time-to-monotherapy failure. (The FDA agreed to this protocol design, even though it was considerably less rigorous than the one laid out in the medical review of the FDA drug approval package for RSG.) Subjects would be randomized to RSG, metformin, or glyburide, the latter two anti-diabetes drugs from other classes, and followed until glycemic control was inadequate and another drug had to be added. From the pre-marketing trials GSK already knew that RSG outperformed metformin and glyburide in this regard. The results of ADOPT posed no risk to GSK: they would position the company to continue to stress superior glucose control as a marketing advantage, and avoid the prospect of uncovering adverse effects of RSG.

Warning Flags from Other Sources: 2003 and 2005

In December 2003, the World Health Organization reported that a data-mining analysis of adverse drug reactions from its database had detected a signal for cardiac disease overall from the class of drugs that contained RSG and PIO. This resulted in the FDA asking GSK to conduct a meta-analysis of all the trials of RSG that they (GSK) had conducted. It took the company almost 2 years to submit to the FDA what it called "a preliminary report." In October of 2005, GSK provided the FDA with summary slides of its preliminary meta-analysis of 42 Phase 2 and 3 controlled trials of RSG, which showed that the drug was associated with an increase in ischemic cardiac events. GSK at the time proposed a "more formal analysis" of the data; one wonders why they did not conduct "a more formal analysis" in the first place.

But in October 2005 GSK had another thing to worry about. Results were published on a Takeda-sponsored randomized, placebo-controlled trial of PIO's effects on cardiovascular outcomes in people with pre-existing cardiovascular disease.[7] Subjects taking PIO had fewer events, favoring PIO, though the trend in the primary outcome did not achieve statistical significance (the secondary outcome did). This news came to GSK at the same time they were seeing the results from their own 52-week trial of RSG versus placebo in patients with pre-existing heart disease.[8] Though there was no difference between the groups in echocardiographically-assessed cardiac function, the RSG group had higher rates of heart failure and ischemic events. GSK submitted the trial results to the FDA. Because of the trial findings, in April 2006 the FDA posted in the Avandia label a warning about adverse cardiac events.

In August 2006, GSK submitted to the FDA the final results of the meta-analysis of the 42 trials. It showed that patients taking RSG were 31% more likely to experience a cardiovascular ischemic event than patients not taking it. But at the same time, GSK presented to the FDA conflicting results from an observational study, an analysis of a proprietary database containing pharmacy and hospital use data of U.S. managed care enrollees. The only outcomes analyzed were hospitalizations for heart attack and/or cardiac revascularization. The analysis, which GSK paid a contract research organization to conduct, showed no differences in hospitalization rates between patients taking RSG and those not taking it. FDA requested all GSK's data from both studies and conducted its own meta-analysis and analysis of the database.

At this time, the most damning information about RSG's potential to increase the risk for cardiovascular events—the GSK meta-analysis showing a 31% increase—was not available to the public. Only the company and the FDA had it. But now things began to move more rapidly.

GSK's Post-Approval Study "ADOPT": Results (2006) and Flaws

In December 2006, the results of the post-marketing study GSK undertook to satisfy FDA's condition of approval for RSG, ADOPT, were published.[9] The trial demonstrated what GSK designed it to demonstrate: that RSG was superior to metformin and glyburide in achieving glycemic control. Regarding cardiovascular outcomes, the authors of the paper state, "Our study was not designed to evaluate cardiovascular disease outcomes." This is an innocuous statement for most readers of trial reports, who know that no study can test all things. But in view of what motivated the FDA to require a post-marketing study—concerns including but not limited to RSG's cardiovascular safety profile—it shows that GSK designed the study to protect its market-share interests rather than those of patients. The tally provided in the paper showed that heart failure and heart attack were more common in subjects taking RSG; the numbers are small, but even so, the increased hazard ratio for heart failure with RSG versus glyburide reached statistical significance. And despite the fact that GSK had for months had in hand the results of the meta-analysis showing that RSG increased the risk of ischemic cardiovascular events by 31% over placebo, the authors of the ADOPT report devoted very little discussion to the ischemic events (or to any cardiovascular outcomes) observed in ADOPT subjects.

The company forwarded the ADOPT data to the FDA in February 2007. Some FDA officials strongly criticized the trial design, pointing out that ADOPT's design flaws undermined its ability to generate accurate evidence on the relationship of RSG to cardiovascular complications.[10] We discuss some of those flaws to show how easy it is to design a trial that avoids yielding evidence that would be damaging to commercial interests.

Defining Safety Endpoints and Setting Out Methods for Ascertaining Their Occurrence

ADOPT's study protocol (the written document that sets out the research plan and "procedure manual" for the study) did not predefine or set out diagnostic criteria for any specific cardiovascular events that should be identified and reported in trial subjects while on study. As with all trials, investigators were told to report any and all adverse events, but such events are often in the eye of the beholder and recognition and reporting varies across co-investigators and trial sites. Without a priori definitions and criteria for adverse events, the only way to proceed is to analyze reports of adverse events post hoc. In doing so, GSK used the broadest possible definition of cardiovascular events, including such things as venous thrombosis, hematoma, hypertension, and varicose veins—a definition flooded with irrelevancies. GSK's motivation for this is obvious: it is a ploy that makes it less likely to identify any true differences in the safety outcomes, myocardial ischemia in this case, between groups in the trial. When trying to establish whether a drug or other intervention causes certain adverse events, the events counted in the trial should be those that have a plausible relationship to the biological nature and actions of the drug or intervention. This affords the greatest possibility of detecting a difference between the groups, if one actually exists. Flooding the adverse event rate with irrelevancies boosts the rate of total events in both groups, and the noise insures that the signal for events of interest, if present, will not be detected.

Choice of Comparator

In ADOPT, subjects were allocated to RSG or the active controls glyburide or metformin. A placebo control was not used. This is another way of dampening any signal that RSG subjects are experiencing a greater rate of certain adverse events. Active-control subjects may suffer higher adverse event rates than placebo controls, narrowing differences between the groups.

Eligibility Criteria and Withdrawal after Randomization

Two features of ADOPT would have ensured a very low baseline rate of cardiovascular adverse events in trial subjects, making any spike associated with RSG harder to identify with confidence. First, only newly diagnosed people with Type 2 diabetes were eligible to enroll in ADOPT, at a time when most individuals do not yet have disease-related macrovascular complications. Second, the higher-than-expected withdrawal rate of ADOPT trial subjects kept follow-up to only 3 years. Consequently, the statistical power of the trial to exclude the probability that RSG increased cardiovascular risk by 20% over the comparator drugs was less than 10%. In other words, if a true difference existed between adverse event rates in RSG and comparator groups, there was a 9 out of 10 chance that ADOPT would be unable to detect it.

The Public Finally Hears about RSG's Cardiovascular Effects: The Nissen Meta-Analysis

The bomb regarding RSG's adverse effects was dropped in May with the publication of the report of a meta-analysis[11] led by Dr. Steven Nissen, a Cleveland Clinic cardiologist. The meta-analysis included data from 42 trials of RSG with a minimum follow-up of 24 weeks. Compared to controls, subjects receiving RSG had a 43% increase in risk for myocardial infarction (heart attack), which was statistically significant, and a 64% increase in the risk of death from cardiovascular causes, which approached but did not reach statistical significance ($p = 0.06$). The authors noted that they were unable to obtain the individual patient-level data, and therefore had based their analyses on summary data from the trials. They had made several requests to GSK for the original data, but GSK refused to grant access unless Nissen agreed to use a GSK statistician for the analysis, a condition Nissen understandably refused. In fact, it was serendipity that Nissen got access to the summary trial data (most of the 42 trials were unpublished). As a result of a New York State court case, GSK was required to post on its Web site summary results of all its trials involving RSG; Nissen found some of the data he used there.

FDA's Response to the Nissen Meta-Analysis

The FDA was on the hot seat—how could they have known about the cardiovascular risks associated with RSG and not informed the public? Moreover, Wall Street wanted guidance about the potential fallout. U.S. sales of Avandia in 2006 were approximately $2.2 billion, and the drug was a major contributor to GSK's revenue.

The FDA called a press conference the same day the Nissen paper was published online, May 21, 2007.[12] Most of the questions put to agency officials focused on what the Nissen findings meant, and why the FDA had not acted on the data contained in the meta-analysis GSK submitted to it in August 2006, when the findings were similar to what Nissen had found. The FDA's strategy in responding consisted of expressing caution about the significance of Nissen's findings, emphasizing the ambiguity of findings across multiple studies evaluating RSG (to justify their caution), and describing steps the agency had taken and planned to take.

The FDA also called for an advisory committee meeting[13] so that the agency could obtain guidance. The joint meeting of the Metabolic & Endocrine Advisory Committee and the Drug Safety & Risk Management Advisory Committee was scheduled for July 30, 2007.

GSK's Reaction to the Nissen Meta-Analysis

On the very day the Nissen meta-analysis was published online by the *New England Journal of Medicine*, May 21, 2007, GSK issued a statement: "GSK strongly disagrees with the conclusions reached in the *NEJM* article, which are based on incomplete evidence and a methodology that the author admits has significant limitations." Never mind that the company's own meta-analysis, never publicly released, showed similar findings, and that 2 months earlier, an expert panel GSK convened to review its own meta-analysis strongly endorsed that it demonstrated a link between RSG and cardiovascular complications.

It turns out that GSK had had time to plan its attack on the Nissen findings. A confidential draft of the pre-publication manuscript had been leaked to GSK management. Nissen had submitted his manuscript to the *Journal* on May 2, 2007. The editors, recognizing the importance of the findings, immediately sent the paper out for peer review. External peer review of submitted manuscripts is standard practice for medical journals, and it is understood by all that all elements of the process—including the manuscript—are confidential. One of the reviewers who received Nissen's paper was Dr. Steve Heffner, then a professor of medicine at the University of Texas Health Science Center in San Antonio and a consultant for GSK. Heffner faxed a copy of Nissen's manuscript to a GSK executive on May 3, 2007, marking the article as "confidential" and the fax as "urgent." Internal GSK documents show that over 40 GSK executives received a copy of this "confidential" manuscript or heard of its contents, including the GSK chief executive officer.

The first move GSK made to refute Nissen's findings was to send the paper to their internal statisticians. These statisticians reanalyzed the data using a different method, one they thought would be more accurate than Nissen's. But they told their superiors, "These results are very similar to the conclusion from the [Nissen] paper using the Peto method. As such there is no statistical reason for disregarding the findings as presented."

GSK executives then turned to the findings of several individual large trials to see if they could be used to refute Nissen. The findings of ADOPT and the Diabetes Reduction Assessment (DREAM) trial had already been published. (DREAM was funded in part by RSG and conducted by investigators at McMaster University: it showed that RSG but not ramipril, compared with placebo, reduced progression to diabetes, but as acknowledged by the authors, if not GSK, the trial lacked statistical power to detect differences in cardiovascular outcomes.[14]) Both trials showed that RSG was associated with an increased risk, though not statistically significant, of cardiac ischemic events. Besides, Nissen had included the ADOPT and DREAM trials in his meta-analysis—and even in the face of including these two large "negative" trials, his results showed a 43% increase in risk of myocardial infarction with RSG. GSK had one trial left—one whose results had yet to be reported—to use to defend against Nissen's findings, "RECORD" (Rosiglitazone Evaluated for Cardiac Outcomes and Regulation of glycemia in Diabetes).

RECORD was a post-marketing trial required by the European Medicines Evaluation Agency, which had granted GSK authorization to market RSG in 2000. The Agency directed GSK to "conduct a large, long-term clinical trial evaluating the effects of rosiglitazone on cardiovascular (CV) risk." Exhibiting its typical behavior, GSK designed a trial that would have little chance of detecting an increased cardiovascular risk of RSG, if one indeed existed. First, they designed RECORD as a non-inferiority trial and set the non-inferiority margin at 20%. This meant that RSG could cause as much as a 20% increase in risk for cardiovascular complications compared with controls and still be considered to be "non-inferior" to those controls. Second, as in the ADOPT, GSK configured RECORD's primary outcome variable to be very broad and to flood it with events that either had no plausible relationship with RSG or were subject to serious misclassification bias. Third, GSK over-estimated the event rate; the a priori power calculations were based on a prediction of 11 primary outcome events per year. The actual rate was far below that, which eroded the statistical power of the trial. (The FDA later estimated that RECORD had a power of less than 10% to detect any association between RSG and ischemic cardiovascular events.) Fourth, RECORD was an open-label, unblinded trial. Subjects and investigators knew what agent they were taking, which inflates or deflates outcome rates based on the observer's expectations about the agent in question. RECORD had other design flaws besides these.[15]

The trial design issues described earlier are elementary, and it is implausible that GSK statisticians and trialists did not know exactly what they were doing when they designed RECORD. Internal GSK documents show that the company was aware at least as early as 2004 that RECORD was statistically inadequate to answer questions regarding RSG's cardiovascular safety. Yet in the May 21, 2007 "strongly disagree" statement GSK issued in response to the Nissen paper, GSK went on to emphasize the findings of RECORD, holding RECORD up as "the most scientifically rigorous way to examine the safety and benefits of a medicine."

But GSK had a problem: the RECORD trial had not been completed. There were no data that doctors and others could review and evaluate for themselves. By May 23, 2007, GSK executives decided to publish interim results from RECORD, and by May 29, manuscript drafts were being circulated among some of RECORD's steering committee. One noted, "The hazard ratio (and 95% confidence interval) for myocardial infarction in RECORD is not inconsistent with Nissen's—and he had more events; what's to stop him adding the events from RECORD to his meta-analysis and reinforcing his view?" This individual went on to express concern about the validity of the draft's message, noting "manuscript looks to downplay the 239% INCREASE [sic] in heart failure. I have taken the liberty of doing some rewording."

The manuscript reporting RECORD's interim results was submitted for publication to the *New England Journal of Medicine*. The editors sent it out for peer review to eight experts. All eight were highly critical of the trial design and conclusions unsupported by the data. The letter from the *Journal* editors to the manuscript's corresponding author summarizes the many design faults of the study and states, "[I]n the opinion of all the readers, the data that you present are completely compatible with the results of the meta-analysis by Nissen and the meta-analysis for myocardial ischemic events posted on the GSK Web site...The editors feel strongly that your data do not support the statement that the RECORD results for myocardial infarction contradict the Nissen meta-analysis; this statement must be removed or modified."

The *New England Journal* published the revised report of RECORD's interim findings on July 5, 2007, with an accompanying editorial by two giants of pharmacoepidemiology, Bruce Psaty and Curt Furberg.[16] Psaty and Furberg pointed out, "Although the limitations in design and conduct of the RECORD trial argue for a cautious interpretation of its findings, the results for risk of myocardial infarction (hazard ratio, 1.16; 95% CI, 0.75 to 1.81) are nonetheless compatible with those of the meta-analysis." They went on to say, "even with the findings from the RECORD trial included [in the meta-analysis]...there is still significant evidence of harm with a hazard ratio [for myocardial infarction] of

1.33." Psaty and Furberg castigated GSK for failing to make a serious effort in DREAM and ADOPT to assess the effects of RSG in a timely fashion and focusing instead on marketing questions, and said, "These industry-sponsored trials do not represent compelling science."

Psaty and Furberg also had harsh criticism for the FDA. Noting that the agency had received GSK's meta-analysis in August 2006 and that it showed results very similar to Nissen's but had not yet (10 months later) revised Avandia's product label to include ischemic cardiovascular events as potential adverse effects of the drug, Psaty and Furberg stated, "The primary measure of regulatory success is the timeliness of information, warnings, and withdrawals. With rosiglitazone, the FDA failed to warn or inform in a timely fashion."

FDA Advisory Committee Meeting, July 30, 2007

Most FDA advisory committee meetings attract little notice, but not this one, with the fate of a $2.6 billion money-maker riding on it. The topic of the meeting was "cardiovascular ischemic/thrombotic risks of the thiazolidinediones, with focus on rosiglitazone." Before the meeting committee members were provided with briefing books: a 196-page book from GSK and a 436-page book from the FDA. (All briefing materials, presentations, complete meeting transcripts, and minutes are available online for all FDA advisory committee meetings.)

At the meeting GSK executives spoke first. The strategy that the first speaker used to undermine the Nissen findings was to attack the ability of meta-analysis—any meta-analysis—to come up with valid answers to a research question and to tout the superiority of single, large trials (such as ADOPT, DREAM, and RECORD) to meta-analysis in coming up with valid results. The second GSK speaker re-emphasized the shortcomings of meta-analysis and then presented the results of the ADOPT, DREAM, and RECORD trials. Flaws in trial design were not mentioned. On his slides, the first line of data for a specific cardiovascular outcome gave the data from GSK's meta-analysis (data from the non-GSK meta-analyses were not presented). The next lines gave the data from each of the three trials. The pictorial representation of one line of data showing there was a relationship followed by three lines showing there was not must have made an impression in the minds of the audience. Next he presented the results of three observational studies (analyses of managed care databases), again not mentioning any limitations. The conclusions were stated dramatically: "the three studies contained over 1.35 million diabetic patients" and "the risk of myocardial infarction is similar for RSG compared to other anti-diabetic agents." Summarizing the findings from their three trials and the three database analyses (and ignoring the findings from their own meta-analysis), GSK concluded with their take-home message: "There was no increase in myocardial ischemia in the long term comparator study (ADOPT); for myocardial infarction, the data are inconsistent and there is no overall evidence that RSG is different from other oral anti-diabetic drugs...Rosiglitazone is not associated with an increase in cardiovascular or all-cause mortality."

The FDA took a more rigorous approach to presenting and discussing the data. Three presentations on the evidence were made: first, an in-depth discussion of the FDA meta-analysis, the GSK meta-analysis, and a comparison of these results to the Nissen meta-analysis; second, an in-depth discussion of ADOPT, DREAM, and RECORD; and third, an in-depth discussion of the three database analyses. The fourth and final presentation summarized where things were. In contrast to the GSK speakers, the FDA speakers did not simply present the findings from the three trials and the three database analyses but methodically and thoroughly discussed their value as well as their limitations. In addition, FDA speakers discussed the findings of trials of PIO, the other approved drug from RSG's class, and contrasted the data on PIO's cardiovascular risk with that of RSG.

However, tone, emphasis, and interpretations differed among the first three FDA speakers. This was a sign of the substantial internal disagreement that had developed within the agency over RSG and foretold the struggles to come. Within FDA's Center for Drug Evaluation and Research (CDER), disagreement had developed between the Division of Metabolism and Endocrinology Products (part of CDER's Office of New Drugs), which believed that the evidence regarding the ischemic cardiovascular risk of RSG was inconclusive, and the Office of Epidemiology and Surveillance, which took what it called "a public health perspective" and believed no justification existed for leaving Avandia on the market. These two statements are not contradictory, and both can be simultaneously true. But which of the two was accepted by the Committee would exert substantial effects on people with diabetes—the management of it and potentially their cardiovascular health—and on sales of Avandia.

The podium was then turned over to two final presentations by the FDA, one by Robert Meyer, director of the Office of Drug Evaluation II (part of CDER's Office of New Drugs), and the next by Gerald Dal Pan, director of CDER's Office of Surveillance and Epidemiology. Meyer opened by admitting the dissension within the FDA, saying, "I think it is important that the committee understand there is a fundamental disagreement within CDER on the scientific conclusions that should be drawn from the information available." He then drew a line in the sand as to how the data should be evaluated, noting that "If the evidence does reasonably establish an elevated cardiovascular ischemic risk for Avandia, and the evidence reasonably establishes that this risk is not found with comparator drugs, that would raise a profound concern for us, irrespective of any statistical significance." Laying out his arguments for why he thought the evidence was not straightforward, he strongly implied that his line in the sand had not been met and said he had no "particular opinion at this moment of the correct regulatory action that should be taken." Taking the podium, Pan conceded that there was "uncertainty in the data…concerning the myocardial ischemic risk of rosiglitazone." "However," he went on to say, "the available data do point to an increased risk and, moreover, don't point to any convincing evidence that such a risk does not exist." Concluding, "Given this information, I believe that the balance of benefits and risks do not favor rosiglitazone," Pan expressed his Office's opinion that RSG should be removed from the market.

The Committee then adjourned for lunch. The afternoon session was filled with presentations by the NIH and the public, including Public Citizen, whose representative answered a resounding "No" to the question, "Does the overall risk-benefit profile of Avandia support its continued marketing in the United States?"

The next morning, the Committee was asked to comment on the contributions of the various RSG studies to the understanding of its cardiovascular risk. The minutes reflect concerns of the Committee about the limitations of the studies but state, "Though there is evidence of increased cardiovascular risk with Avandia, the committee identified the need for more long-term data." Then the Committee had to vote. The first question the committee was asked was, "Do the available data support a conclusion that Avandia increases cardiac ischemic risk in Type 2 diabetes mellitus?" The vote was 20 Yes and 3 No. When asked, "Does the overall risk-benefit profile of Avandia support its continued marketing in the United States?" the vote was 22 Yes and 1 No. The meeting adjourned.

During the ensuing months the disagreements continued within the FDA's Center for Drug Evaluation and Research (CDER) between the Office of New Drugs and the Office of Surveillance and Epidemiology, with the latter recommending RSG be taken off the market and the former claiming insufficient evidence for withdrawal and recommending "strengthened labeling for cardiovascular risk." On October 13, 2007, the CDER issued a decision to keep RSG on the market, but with a Boxed Warning on its label about increased cardiovascular risk.

In the formal letter to GSK communicating CDER's decision, dated January 2, 2008, CDER's Director states, "The firm should be required to begin and promptly execute a study comparing their drug to pioglitazone." GSK responded in its customary fashion.

More of the Same: GSK's TIDE Study

GSK called the study it designed to comply with FDA/CDER's directive "TZD (for thiazolidinedione, the drug class into which RSG and PIO falls) with vitamin D Evaluation" or TIDE. The reader must be wondering where "Vitamin D" came from, given that the FDA's and the public's interest was in cardiovascular risk. The company justified this on the basis that, in ADOPT, women taking RSG had significantly more bone fractures than women taking metformin or glyburide. But just as they did with ADOPT, DREAM, and RECORD, GSK designed TIDE to suit its marketing purposes, building in design features that would ensure TIDE would yield ambiguous evidence about RSG's cardiovascular risk. Instead of designing a head-to-head trial of RSG and PIO (recall that evidence up to this point suggested that, in contrast to RSG, PIO did not increase the risk of cardiovascular complications), GSK designed a trial comparing cardiovascular risk in subjects taking a TZD—*either* RSG or PIO—to subjects taking a placebo. Combining subjects taking PIO and subjects taking RSG into one group would surely dampen RSG's cardiovascular risk signal. Further dampening any signal was the fact that eligibility criteria allowed persons taking other anti-diabetes drugs (metformin or glyburide) to enter the trial. The overlay of the long-term evaluation of supplemental vitamin D injected another source of noise into the trial. GSK submitted the TIDE protocol to FDA in July 2008. Over the vigorous opposition of the Office of Surveillance and Epidemiology, it was approved by FDA's CDER. The first subjects were entered into TIDE in February 2009.

The Tide Starts to Turn

Meanwhile the FDA undertook its own research to shed light on the cardiovascular safety of RSG, with four studies conducted by the Office of Surveillance and Epidemiology (Table 3.1). All showed RSG to be associated with increased cardiovascular risks. In the fourth study, which was an analysis of Medicare databases, the authors calculated that in Medicare beneficiaries between 1999 and 2009, there were 48,000 excess episodes of acute myocardial infarction, stroke, heart failure, or death in patients taking RSG than would have occurred had they been taking PIO instead.[17]

While these studies were under way, in December 2008, the consumer watchdog group Public Citizen submitted to the FDA a Citizen Petition to ban RSG from the market. Professional societies began to take a public stance against RSG. In January 2009, the American Diabetes Association and the European Association for the Study of Diabetes published a consensus statement containing their recommendations for managing the hyperglycemia of Type 2 diabetes. After discussing the meta-analytic evidence for RSG's cardiovascular risk, "the consensus group members unanimously advised against using RSG."[18]

In October 2009, after reviewing the results of the FDA's own studies and the data from the completed RECORD trial that GSK had forwarded to the

Table 3.1 **Four Studies of Rosiglitazone's Safety Conducted by the FDA's Office of Surveillance and Epidemiology in Late 2008**

Study Description	Findings
Systematic review of epidemiologic studies; comparison of cardiovascular risk between RSG and PIO	68 of the 69 hazard ratios produced in this analysis showed an increased risk of RSG over PIO. "Comparisons of RSG with PIO consistently show a clinically meaningful increased risk of adverse cardiovascular outcomes, notably acute myocardial infarction, with RSG."
Update of meta-analysis of randomized control trials of RSG (10 new trials added to the 42 in the prior analysis)	For all outcomes except stroke, RSG-containing regimens compared with regimens not containing RSG are associated with odds ratios greater than 1.0; the increase was statistically significant for myocardial infarction (↑80%), serious myocardial ischemia (↑46%), total myocardial ischemia (↑34%), and congestive heart failure (↑93%).
Initial meta-analysis of randomized control trials of PIO (29 small and 2 large trials)	Hazard ratios were less than 1.0 for all outcomes except cardiovascular death (1.01) and congestive heart failure (1.41). "PIO tended to have lower or similar estimated risks as controls across the safety endpoints, except for congestive heart failure."
Epidemiologic study, using Medicare databases, of cardiovascular risk associated with RSG or PIO	All hazard ratios for individual cardiovascular events showed an increased risk of RSG over PIO: RSG was associated with increased risk for stroke (↑27%), heart failure (↑25%), death (↑14%), and myocardial infarction, stroke, heart failure, or death combined (↑18%).

PIO, pioglitazone; RSG, rosiglitazone.

FDA in August 2009, Gerald Dal Pan, the director of FDA/CDER's Office of Surveillance and Epidemiology, recommended to his bosses that they grant the Citizen Petition. In March 2010, Janet Woodcock, the director of FDA/CDER, ordered a new RSG safety review and set the advisory committee meeting to discuss the findings for July 13–14, 2010.

The Joint Meeting of the Endocrinologic and Metabolic Drugs Advisory Committee and the Drug Safety and Risk Management Advisory Committee, July 13–14, 2010

Two bombs were dropped in the morning press on July 13, 2010, the day the meeting was scheduled to begin. In a piece in the *New York Times*,[19] Gardiner Harris reported that the *Times* had recently obtained documents showing that SmithKline Beecham, GSK's predecessor, had conducted a head-to-head trial of RSG to PIO in 1999 which showed that, not only was RSG no better than PIO in glycemic control, RSG was riskier to the heart. The company never published the trial results or reported them to the FDA. Rather, internal company e-mails showed that the company "spent the next 11 years trying to cover them up," according to Harris. Harris also reported some damning news for the FDA— that John Jenkins, then the director of FDA/CDER's Office of New Drugs (the office that had maintained that RSG should stay on the market)—had routinely briefed GSK executives on the debate raging inside the agency.

That same day, Catherine Larkin of *Bloomberg* reported that sources had told her that GSK had agreed to pay about $460 million to resolve lawsuits against the company that alleged Avandia caused heart attacks and strokes.[20] Larkin noted that GSK was making the settlement just as an advisory panel to the FDA was to meet to decide whether Avandia's benefits outweighed its risk. An article in *Daily Finance* the same day reported that, in its first round of settlements, GSK had paid about $60 million to settle over 700 suits, and that as of July 13, 2010, "at least 3,000 cases are pending."[21]

The meeting room where the Advisory Committee convened was packed with spectators. The first presentation was by Mary Parks, director of the Division of Metabolism and Endocrinology within FDA/CDER's Office of New Drugs. She gave an account of events related to RSG that took place before, during, and after the 2007 advisory committee meeting.

GSK executives then began their presentations. While at the 2007 meeting GSK had assailed the limitations of meta-analyses, and marshaled evidence from an observational study (a database analysis) that they had commissioned to show that RSG was safe, at this meeting they assailed the limitations of observational studies. The reason for this tactic is clear. By mid-July 2010 there were many more such studies, most unfavorable to RSG. Sixteen had compared RSG with anti-diabetes drugs from other classes, and the great majority found an increased hazard ratio associated with RSG. An additional 14 compared RSG to PIO, and 12 of these found a hazard ratio for myocardial infarction that showed PIO was better than RSG. GSK presenters then devoted their time to discussing the now-completed RECORD trial. Summarizing, the GSK presenter told the audience that RECORD demonstrated that treatment regimens containing

RSG are not inferior to other regimens regarding cardiovascular events, do not increase all-cause or cardiovascular mortality, and have a similar rate of acute coronary events, but do increase the risk for heart failure and distal fractures.

Steven Nissen, the lead author of the meta-analysis published in May 2007 in the *New England Journal of Medicine*, was the next speaker. Going back to the original approval of RSG in May 1999, he reviewed the evidence for RSG's effects on lipid profiles and cardiovascular outcomes, and questioned whether the FDA's premarket approval process of RSG had been sufficiently rigorous. He noted that the observational study that GSK had paid for and presented at the 2007 advisory committee meeting—the one that showed no increase in cardiovascular risk associated with RSG compared to other glucose-lowering agents—had "one major issue—the study included data on all major comparator drugs except for pioglitazone." He then told the audience that Takeda, the maker of PIO, had paid the same commercial research vendor to use the same database to compare RSG to PIO, and the study showed RSG was associated with a statistically significant increase in hospitalizations for myocardial infarction. He devoted the last part of his podium time to the RECORD trial, opening his discussion with a title slide that said: "RECORD—How Not to Perform a Safety Study."

Next on the agenda was a review of RECORD by FDA officials from two offices within CDER's Office of New Drugs: Thomas Marciniak and his boss Ellis Unger from the Division of Cardiovascular and Renal Products, Karen Mahoney from the Division of Metabolism and Endocrinology, and statistician David Hoberman from CDER's Division of Biometrics. Marciniak's presentation was damning of RECORD and must have surprised some members of the Office of New Drugs, but Ellis's comments distanced himself from Marciniak, and Mahoney and Hoberman soft-pedaled any criticisms they had of RECORD. For example, Mahoney described the 20% non-inferiority margin used in RECORD as "conservative for the time."

Committee members were allowed to ask questions after the FDA presenters were finished. The first to speak was Thomas Fleming, a professor of biostatistics at the University of Washington. He first condemned Mahoney's review for several inaccuracies in the presentation of data and in her interpretation of it. But Fleming saved his most vehement condemnation for Hoberman, a PhD statistician like himself. In discussing risk for myocardial infarction in the RECORD trial, Hoberman had said, "we could have a big discussion of [statistical] power...but I want to sidestep power." He then went on to argue that since the 95% confidence intervals around the point estimate of the hazard ratio were of the same length in the Nissen meta-analysis (0.73, 1.38) and in RECORD (0.71, 1.44), the two studies provided "similar information." Hoberman then concluded that the lower myocardial infarction rate in RECORD resulted from a "weaker signal" for RSG (i.e., a truly lower risk than Nissen found) and not from "less information" (i.e., low statistical power to detect the signal). In challenging Hoberman, Fleming pointed out that simple calculations showed that RECORD had a statistical power of about 50%—the same probability as a flip of a coin—to detect a hazard ratio of 1.43 or 1.44, the estimate that Nissen had found. Fleming accused Hoberman of diluting the concerns that had been raised about RECORD "with irregularities, toward seeing estimates that are less than truth." The Chair finally ended the heated interchange, but not before Hoberman agreed with Fleming that RECORD's statistical power to detect an increase in risk for myocardial infarction was only 50%.

That afternoon officials from the FDA's Office of Surveillance and Epidemiology presented the findings of the studies of RSG they had performed (summarized in Table 3.1). One of the presenters was David Graham, who devoted part of his podium time to a systematic criticism of GSK's TIDE trial. For example, after pointing out the problematic design features we noted in an earlier section, he told the audience that GSK had designed TIDE as a non-inferiority trial and powered it for a non-inferiority margin of 20%. This meant that thiazolidinediones could be associated with nearly 20% more cardiovascular complications but still be considered non-inferior to (no worse than) placebo. Graham also raised ethical concerns about the trial, alleging that information about the trial was not presented in a straightforward way to potential subjects, and calling into question whether their consent to participate was truly informed. He pointed out that, not only was the name of the trial misleading for potential participants, the consent document did not contain a clear statement that the purpose of the study was to establish whether one drug was associated with more harm than the other. Graham had set the stage for the next day's presentation by renowned ethicists Ruth Faden and Steven Goodman, co-chairs of an FDA-commissioned Institute of Medicine panel, the Committee on Ethical and Scientific Issues in Studying the Safety of New Drugs.[22]

Faden and Goodman both spoke the next day. Regarding the justification for initiating or continuing a safety trial, Faden said, "the key, a first key, to the ethics of a post-marketing safety trial is a determination that a safety signal, if it represents a true risk, would warrant a policy decision, and that new knowledge is needed to determine the existence of and magnitude of that safety signal, that risk, in relation to benefits... If, for example, the existing information about a safety risk is judged to be sufficient to warrant the removal of the drug from the market, then it would be unethical to conduct a trial. The same reasoning applies to judgments about whether a current trial should be stopped." Faden and Goodman both spoke on the inextricable nature of methods and ethics in clinical trials. Goodman said, "A precondition for the ethical acceptability of any clinical trial is that it provide some degree of social good, and it can't provide that social good if it's improperly designed or conducted."

Regulatory decisions about drugs do count as a social good. Goodman went on, "The RCT [randomized control trial] should be designed in such a way as to directly inform the policy decision that FDA faces. The FDA should not be requiring a trial that does not fill the evidence gap needed to inform that decision."

Faden then addressed the issue of informed consent, saying that it is "key that the trial involve the highest possible standards of respect for participants. And these include standards that ensure that participants understand what the risks are and what makes them generally acceptable, so that participants can then make a personal self-referential decision that they want to accept those risks." But she cautioned, "as important as the meaningfulness of the informed consent process is to the ethics of research with human participants, these questions about informed consent only come into play if the trials are independently judged to be acceptable....The determination must be made first that the trial is ethically justified, or its continuation is ethically justified; and then and only then must you be very carefully attentive to assuring that the consents obtained or the refusals obtained are meaningful and valid." Faden and Goodman did not discuss the RECORD trial: they discussed the ethical principles that govern trials involving human subjects.

Faden and Goodman concluded speaking just before lunch on the second day of the meeting. After lunch, the Committee took up its deliberations and voting. A majority of the committee believed that the data for RSG were sufficient to raise safety concerns for ischemic cardiovascular events relative to non-thiazolidinedione anti-diabetes drugs (18 yes, 15 no or other) and relative to PIO (21 yes, 12 no or other), and that the TIDE trial should be continued if RSG were allowed to remain on the market (19 yes, 14 no or other). Regarding regulatory actions recommended for the FDA to pursue regarding RSG, one member abstained; three members voted to allow continued marketing and make no changes to the label; seven voted to allow continued marketing and revise the label to add additional warnings; 10 voted to allow continued marketing, revising the label to add additional warnings as well as adding additional restrictions on use (e.g., prescribing restrictions); and 12 voted for withdrawal from the U.S. market.

The Committee meeting had opened to media reports critical of the behaviors of some FDA officials. In the days after the meeting ended there was more bad press for the FDA. The *Wall Street Journal* published an article raising questions about whether the members of the Advisory Committee were free from conflict of interest regarding regulatory decisions on RSG and about FDA's diligence in assessing panel members for such conflicts.[23] One member had received over $14,000 in speaker's fees in recent years from GSK, but for promoting another drug, not Avandia. He was one of only three Committee members who had voted to keep Avandia on the market without further restrictions. When interviewed, he said that he had not reported the fees because "the FDA doesn't consider a different product for the same company to be a conflict of interest," and that he had not been asked about them by the FDA. Another member reported having received speaker fees from Takeda, the maker of PIO. He told the *Wall Street Journal* that he had reported this conflict to the FDA, but they had allowed him to serve. He was one of the 12 who voted to have Avandia removed from the market.

The FDA Decides

In early September 2010, John Jenkins, director of the Office of New Drugs (OND), submitted his office's recommendations to Janet Woodcock, the director of the FDA's Center for Drug Evaluation and Research. OND recommended that Avandia be kept on the market but with a revision of the product label to reflect current information on cardiac risk. (Only 7 of the 32 Advisory Committee members had supported this option.) OND also recommended the TIDE trial be continued using its current design, but with improvements in the consent form.

In mid-September Gerald Dal Pan, director of the Office of Surveillance and Epidemiology (OSE), submitted his office's recommendations to Woodcock. He said OSE continued to support the withdrawal of RSG from the market as an appropriate regulatory action. But, consistent with the Advisory Committee's recommendations, an acceptable alternative would be to allow RSG to be available through a restricted distribution program to patients for whom RSG was the only treatment option for glycemic control.

On September 22, 2010, Woodcock issued her decision, which was published in the online version of the *New England Journal of Medicine* the following day.[24] She endorsed OSE's recommendation to make RSG available only through a restricted access program. She also instructed GSK to "commission an independent re-adjudication of the RECORD study" and to put the TIDE trial on "full clinical hold" pending that re-adjudication. The day Woodcock's decision appeared in the *Journal*, Avandia suffered another breach. The European Medicines Evaluation Agency recommended suspending sales of all RSG-containing medicines, noting that "these medicines will stop being available in Europe within the next few months."

In May 2011 the components of the restricted access program, called a "risk evaluation and mitigation strategy" or REMS program, were announced. Prescribers of RSG-containing medicines would have to be specifically certified by and enrolled in the RSG REMS program; certification would involve reading the REMS Prescriber Overview and Medication Guide, completing and signing the Prescriber Enrollment Form, agreeing to complete and sign an Enrollment

Form for each patient who was prescribed RSG, and agreeing to review the Medication Guide with each patient. Furthermore, RSG-containing medicines would only be dispensed by specially certified pharmacies. GSK was to ensure that RSG-containing drugs would be dispensed only if there was documentation in the RSG REMS database that the dispensing pharmacy, the prescriber, and patient were all enrolled in the program. To notify the medical community about the restrictions, GSK was required to send "Dear Pharmacist" and "Dear Doctor" letters to all pharmacists and physicians in the United States within 60 days.

On November 4, 2011, the FDA announced that the RSG REMS would become fully operational on November 18, 2011, and that from then on RSG-containing medicines would not be available through retail pharmacies, but rather only by mail order from specially certified pharmacies participating in the program. Reviewing the history of Avandia,[25] the *New York Times* noted that sales of RSG in 2006 were $3.2 billion. Sales dropped after the 2007 Advisory Committee meeting but as late as 2010 were still a very substantial $1.19 billion, though they fell off in 2011 and 2012. The *Times* predicted that the FDA's RSG-REMS and the European actions will cause RSG sales to plunge to "almost nothing."

Conclusions

We know how to generate high-quality evidence about the benefits and harms of clinical interventions. But evidence can make winners and losers of parties that have a stake in the decisions that will flow from that evidence. Consequently, though this flies in the face of scientific objectivity, medical ethics, and the high ideals of methods and ethics of human subjects research, parties will try to manipulate the design and conduct of research so that the process yields answers favorable to their interests. Moreover, findings from even well designed and carefully executed studies can be equivocal, ambiguous, or subject to competing explanations, even by the most disinterested of interpreters. The tendency of human interpreters of data to see what they want or need to see is exacerbated when their economic interests or prestige depends on what the evidence is interpreted to mean.

The rosiglitazone story is a story about regulatory science. But even though the results of comparative effectiveness research mandated in laws passed in the 2000s will not be used to regulate medical products, the lessons the rosiglitazone story teaches are perfectly applicable. The results of federally mandated comparative effectiveness research will be used to make decisions that have economic implications—decisions by payers who use the findings in developing coverage and reimbursement policies rather than by federal regulators of medical products. Should we expect intimidation of scientists, manipulation of scientific methods and the execution of research studies, and conflicts of interest in the interpretation of findings?

Notes

1. Wilson D. Glaxo settles cases with U.S. for $3 billion. New York Times 2011 Nov 3.
2. U.S. Senate Committee on Finance. Staff report on GlaxoSmithKline and the diabetes drug Avandia. 111th Congress, 2d Session. Committee Print (S-PRT 111–41). January, 2010. [Public release February 20, 2010]. (Accessed September 19, 2012, at http://www.finance.senate.gov/newsroom/chairman/release/?id=bc56b552-efc5–4706–968d-f7032d5cd2e4.) Committee investigators conducted numerous interviews and reviewed over 250,000 documents provided by GSK, the FDA, the University of North Carolina, and others.
3. Information from the National Institute of Diabetes and Digestive and Kidney Diseases. Fast facts on diabetes. Available from http://diabetes.niddk.nih.gov/dm/pubs/statistics/#fast.
4. All elements of FDA's drug approval package for RSG, including the medical and statistical reviews, are available from http://www.accessdata.fda.gov/drugsatfda_docs/nda/99/21071_Avandia.cfm.
5. Investigational drugs designated for priority review by the FDA go through the same evaluative processes as drugs designated as standard review, but the agency completes the evaluation within a 6-month time frame rather than the standard 10-month time frame.
6. Cholesterol Treatment Trialists (CTT) Collaborators, Kearney PM, Blackwell L, Collins R, et al. Efficacy of cholesterol-lowering therapy in 18,686 people with diabetes in 14 randomised trials of statins: a meta-analysis. Lancet 2008;371:117–25.
7. Dormandy JA, Charbonnel B, Eckland DJA, et al. Secondary prevention of macrovascular events in patients with Type 2 diabetes in the PROactive Study (PROspective pioglitAzone Clinical Trial In macroVascular Events): a randomised trial. Lancet 2005;366:1279–89.
8. The results of this study were published in 2007: Dargie HJ, Hildebrandt PR, Riegger GAJ, et al. A randomized, placebo-controlled trial assessing the effects of rosiglitazone on echocardiographic function and cardiac status in Type 2 diabetic patients with New York Heart Association functional class I or II heart failure. J Am Coll Cardiol 2007;49:1696–704.
9. Kahn SE, Haffner SM, Heise MA, et al. Glycemic durability of rosiglitazone, metformin, or glyburide monotherapy. N Engl J Med 2006;355:2427–43.
10. The flaws in the ADOPT study were discussed in a briefing document dated July 9, 2007 prepared by Karen M. Mahoney and Mary H. Parks of FDA's Division of Metabolism and Endocrinology Products/Office of New Drugs II. Mahoney and David J. Graham (FDA/Office of Surveillance and Epidemiology) reviewed ADOPT's flaws at the July 30, 2007 Advisory Committee meeting. Their testimony before the Committee is available from http://www.fda.gov/ohrms/dockets/ac/07/transcripts/2007–4308t1-Part2.pdf and http://www.fda.gov/ohrms/dockets/ac/07/transcripts/2007–4308t1-Part3.pdf.
11. Nissen S, Wolski K. Effect of rosiglitazone on the risk of myocardial infarction and death from cardiovascular causes. N Engl J Med 2007;356:2457–71.
12. Transcripts are available from http://www.fda.gov/downloads/NewsEvents/Newsroom/MediaTranscripts/ucm123590.pdf.
13. FDA advisory committees are composed of independent experts who advise the agency on scientific, technical, and policy issues. The committees provide recommendations to the agency, but they are not binding: the agency makes the final decisions.
14. The DREAM Trial investigators. Effect of ramipril on the incidence of diabetes. N Engl J Med 2006;355:1551–6.

15. Here are views of the FDA's Office of Surveillance and Epidemiology (OSE) regarding GSK's RECORD: "RECORD does not now, nor will it at completion, provide meaningful evidence...The biased design of RECORD renders it useless as an objective measure of RSG's cardiovascular safety. Its results cannot be trusted because they are too subject to bias...it is probably unethical to continue the study because it cannot produce scientifically reliable or valid results...The preliminary and final results of RECORD should not be considered reliable or valid and should not be used by FDA in any consideration of risk or benefit associated with RSG use." Quotation from a July 6, 2007 letter from David J. Graham (FDA/OSE) through Gerald Dal Pan (director, FDA/OSE) to Mary Parks (director, Division of Metabolic and Endocrine Drug Products) included as part of the briefing materials (under Tab 4) for the July 2007 Advisory Committee meeting. (Accessed October 16, 2012, at http://www.fda.gov/ohrms/dockets/ac/07/briefing/2007-4308b1-02-fda-backgrounder.pdf.)

16. Home PD, Pocock SJ, Beck-Nielsen H, et al. Rosiglitazone evaluated for cardiovascular outcomes—an interim analysis. N Engl J Med 2007;357:28-38. Psaty BM, Furberg CD. The record on rosiglitazone and the risk of myocardial infarction [editorial]. N Engl J Med 2007;357:67-9.

17. The results of this analysis were published in 2010: Graham DJ, Ouellet-Hellstrom R, MaCurdy TE, et al. Risk of acute myocardial infarction, stroke, heart failure, and death in elderly Medicare patients treated with rosiglitazone or pioglitazone. JAMA 2010;304:411-8.

18. Nathan DM, Buse JB, Davidson MB, et al. Medical management of hyperglycemia in Type 2 diabetes: a consensus algorithm for the initiation and adjustment of therapy. Diabetes Care 2009;32:193-203. Note that John Buse, the physician-investigator that GSK called the "Avandia Renegade," is the second author of this paper.

19. Harris, G. Diabetes drug maker hid test data, files indicate. New York Times 2010 Jul 13.

20. Available from http://www.bloomberg.com/video/61464058/.

21. Alazraki M. GlaxoSmithKline settles majority of Avandia lawsuits ahead of FDA panel vote. Daily Finance, July 13, 2012. (Accessed October 16, 2012, at http://www.dailyfinance.com/2010/07/13/glaxosmithkline-settles-avandia-lawsuits-fda/.)

22. This IOM panel had been commissioned by the FDA in response to a letter from Congress to the FDA demanding a justification for the TIDE trial. See Mello MM, Goodman SN, Faden RR. Ethical considerations in studying drug safety—the Institute of Medicine report. N Engl J Med 2012;367:959-12.

23. Mundy A. Panelist who backed Avandia gets fees from Glaxo. Wall Street Journal 2010 Jul 20. Accessed at http://online.wsj.com/article/SB10001424052748704723604575379292803755042.html]

24. Woodcock J, Sharfstein JM, Hamburg M. Regulatory action on rosiglitazone by the U.S. Food and Drug Administration. N Engl J Med 2010;363:1489-91.

25. No author given. Avandia (drug). Last updated July 2, 2011. Available from http://topics.nytimes.com/top/news/health/diseasesconditionsandhealthtopics/avandiadrug/index.html.

4

Operate First, Evidence Later

The Special Case of Surgery

If evidence of effectiveness and safety in humans is a prerequisite for allowing all prescription drugs and some medical devices to enter routine clinical use, the situation differs with surgery, an unregulated medical technology. It is amazing to realize that the great majority of surgical interventions are put to fair tests of effectiveness in clinical trials only after they become widely used, if at all. Federal mandates for comparative effectiveness research offer much-needed opportunities for improving the evidence base for surgery. However, changing the existing paradigm for the diffusion of surgical innovations and addressing the unique challenges of trials of surgical procedures are obstacles that will need to be overcome. As we will see in this chapter, the forces inside and outside American surgery seem aligned to maintain the status quo.

First, let's provide some definitions. We define invasive therapeutic procedures to be treatments requiring the introduction of hands, instruments, or devices into the body via incisions or punctures of the skin or mucous membranes and that may or may involve the use of ionizing, electromagnetic, or acoustic energy. Invasive therapeutic procedures are performed not for diagnosis but rather with the intention of changing the natural history of a human disorder for the better. Some are performed by classically trained surgeons; others can be performed by proceduralists from other specialties such as cardiology, gastroenterology, or interventional radiology. Throughout the chapter we use the term "surgical" to denote all surgical, minimally invasive, endovascular, and endoluminal invasive procedures, and "surgeon" to denote surgeons as well as proceduralists from other specialties like cardiology.

Surgery: It's Where the Money Is

During the first two waves of interviews for this book, before comparative effectiveness research became law as part of the 2010 Affordable Care Act, we asked all of our informants to tell us their views on whether and how surgical procedures should be included in federal policy on comparative effectiveness research. Most had given it little thought. Contemplating clinical acumen and the motivations that drive clinical decision making, one person told us, "It's one thing to think that somebody might give you a drug that you don't need or do an X-ray that you don't need, but to actually cut somebody open and do something really invasive, would people really do that if you didn't need it?"

Others thought invasive therapeutic procedures were in fact in need of comparative effectiveness research, but to include them would ensure the failure of any new federal policy. To many of our informants, the mention of the word "surgery" in the context of federal policy on comparative effectiveness research immediately evoked memories of the near-death experience of the U.S. Agency for Health Care Research and Policy (AHCPR) in the mid-1990s. This small federal agency was almost eliminated by Congress, in part as a result of lobbying by spine surgeons who objected to the clinical practice guidelines issued by the AHCPR for the treatment of acute low back pain. (We will tell more of this story in Chapter 10.) A congressional staffer told us, "When you bring that up, probably the one thing that everyone thinks about is what happened 10 years ago with AHCPR and spinal surgery and what happened with the docs. They [*the policy makers*] worry about it from that perspective. If we start to say that we are not going to do some surgeries or we are not going to pay as much for a surgery over something else, then all the docs are going to freak out and drop out of Medicare or something like that."

A few of our respondents went straight to the heart of the matter: "surgery must be included in federal policy on comparative effectiveness research: it's where the money is."

It is the rare American who finishes out his or her life without "going under the knife" for some reason or other. The average American can look forward to nine invasive therapeutic procedures over an 85-year life span.[1] Americans undergo more surgery than citizens of other countries. In 2004, the rate of major operations per 100,000 population was 21,397 in the United States, 13,635 in the United Kingdom, and 12,242 in Canada—a 1.75-fold difference.[2] Some of the international variation in rates is attributable to the different incentives inherent in the way in which health care systems are organized and financed. Some may be attributable to national cultures. Compared with people from some other countries, Americans place a high value on technical innovation and quick fixes, and Americans prefer aggressive surgical intervention.[3]

Invasive therapeutic procedures account for a large proportion of U.S. national health expenditures. Over a quarter (26.4%) of the 44 million U.S. hospital stays in 2007 involved one or more major invasive therapeutic procedures, and the volume continues to increase.[4] Hospital stays involving a major surgical procedure cost nearly two and a half times as much, on average, than stays that do not. In 2007, the average cost of an operative hospital stay was $15,400; the average for a nonoperative stay was $6,300.[5] (These are hospital costs only and do not include the professional charges billed separately by surgeons, anesthesiologists, and so on.)

The most frequently performed major invasive therapeutic procedures are listed in Table 4.1 along with their prices.

Because of the way national statistics are kept, it is not possible to derive a firm estimate of the proportion of national health expenditures accounted for by major invasive therapeutic procedures. Making some calculations based on 2007 data,[6] we give a very conservative estimate that it is at least 23%.[7] In other words, expenditures for major invasive therapeutic

Table 4.1 **Selected High-Volume Operations Performed in U.S. Acute Care Hospitals in 2007**

Procedure	Frequency Rank, 2007	Prices by Fee Category, 2011, in US dollars			
		Physician	Hospital	Anesthesia	Total
Cesarean delivery	1	2,014	5,728	816	8,558
Percutaneous transluminal coronary angioplasty	2	1,132[a]	20,888	0	22,020
Arthroplasty of knee	3	2,795	18,305	522	21,622
Hysterectomy, vaginal, no cancer	4	1,495	6,136	942	8,573
Laminectomy, excision of intervertebral disk	5	2,451	9,600	1,159	13,210
Cholecystectomy, laparoscopic	6	1,229	4,750	956	6,934
Hip replacement	7	2,597	18,305	1,077	21,978
Oophorectomy	8	731	1,074[b]	885	2,690
Appendectomy	9	1,087	9,232	537	10,856
Spinal fusion	10	2,840	40,222	1,159	44,220[c]

[a] Angioplasty of a single vessel.

[b] Price is for ambulatory surgical center, where this procedure is now generally performed, except when performed as part of a total abdominal hysterectomy, an inpatient procedure.

[c] Price figures are for lumbar spinal fusion.

Source: Frequency data adapted from Elixhauser A, Andrews RM. Profile of inpatient operating room procedures in US hospitals in 2007. Ann Surg 2010;145:1201–8; price data from http://www.healthcarebluebook.com, a publicly available Web site for consumers, accessed May 4, 2011 for zip code 00000.

interventions account for at least 23 cents of every dollar spent on health care in the United States. This is more than two times what we spend on prescription drugs, which, in 2007, was 10% of national health expenditures or 10 cents of the health care dollar. A prominent Republican who believed it was critical to include surgery in the scope of comparative effectiveness research and whose strong backing of federal support for comparative effectiveness research put them at odds with some in the GOP said to us, "Tom Allen, being from Maine and on the drug industry's tail for years, looked at comparative effectiveness research initially as a strategy to try to limit the reimbursement of new, expensive pharmaceuticals . . . That is mostly what it's used for in the United Kingdom and other places, devices as well as drugs. For me, it's like, ten cents on the dollar *[referring to the fact that prescription drugs account for about 10% of U.S. health spending]*—I am not wasting my political capital for 10 cents on the dollar." (Representative Tom Allen (D-ME) was the first to propose comparative effectiveness research legislation, in 2002.)

A Look at the "Operate First, Evidence Later" Paradigm

The process by which a surgical innovation is developed and disseminated is overseen by internal professional and organizational norms rather than by an external regulatory body, and the evidential bar a surgical innovation must meet before it is used in routine clinical practice is much lower than pre-market requirements for prescription drugs and biologics. The contrasts can be seen in Table 4.2. Surgeon-innovators may or may not develop and test their innovation in animal or cadaveric experiments before they apply it to human patients; preclinical evaluation of a surgical innovation is not standardized or required as it is in drug development. The human studies that constitute the evidential bar are often case series or other weak study designs from which firm conclusions about clinical effects—benefits and harms—should not be drawn. When a surgical innovation is put forward in the literature or at a professional gathering, its use may be supported because "it makes clinical sense" given the prevailing notions of disease pathophysiology and because case reports and case series suggest it works. Rather than insisting that the surgical innovation be subjected to additional, more rigorous proofs of effectiveness and safety, many surgeons take up the new procedure and dissemination begins. As a consequence of this development and diffusion pathway, from a scientific standpoint, substantial uncertainty surrounds the typical surgical innovation at the time it is introduced and disseminated.

Table 4.2 **Contrasts between the Developmental Pathways of New Prescription Drugs and New Invasive Therapeutic Procedures**

Phase or Stage	Prescription Drug	Invasive Procedure
0	Preclinical experiments (animal, bench)	*Proof of principle*: "usually a report of case or small case series [in patients]...describing the technique"
1	Single-group trial conducted in 20–80 human volunteers	*Refinement and definition*: "modification of technique in light of early experience...this phase is often unreported, as surgeons hesitate to publish results of incompletely developed techniques"
2	Controlled trials in several hundred people with the target disease or condition	*Dissemination*: technique is "adopted rapidly by other surgeons...who report their personal case series"
3	Controlled and single-group trials including several hundred to several thousand people, for purpose of establishing overall benefit: risk of the drug	*Comparison with current standard treatment*: "Once a technique has achieved stability and popularity, it becomes important to determine whether it is better than current treatment, preferable by performing a randomized trial...but investigation often stops short of an RCT"
4	(Post-FDA approval) Post-marketing studies	*Surveillance and quality control*: Monitoring of complication rates

Note: Invasive procedure definitions from McCulloch P. Developing appropriate methodology for the study of surgical techniques. J Royal Soc Med 2009;102:51–5.

The Carotid Artery Surgery Stories

To illustrate the process of surgical innovation, we will tell the story of invasive procedures directed at atherosclerotic blockages in the carotid artery. Such blockages increase the risk of stroke (death of brain tissue) in the brain territory supplied by that artery. Carotid artery disease is responsible for about a quarter of ischemic strokes.[8] The story illustrates how procedures that look promising because they attack the presumed culprit in the prevailing model of disease[9] quickly disseminate into wide use, only later to be found, on the basis of randomized controlled trials, to be less effective or more harmful than originally believed.

The carotid arteries carry oxygenated blood from the arch of the aorta to large portions of the brain. Imaging tests can estimate the amount of atherosclerotic blockage (stenosis) in a carotid artery. The risk for a stroke in a region of the brain supplied by the diseased artery appears to be related to the amount of blockage and the presence or absence of signs and symptoms, such as a prior stroke in that circulatory distribution, or a stroke "warning" called a transient ischemic attack (TIA). Epidemiologic studies performed in the 1980s indicated that the risk of ipsilateral stroke in people with severe (>75%) stenosis was about 2.5% per year; in asymptomatic people with <75% stenosis it was about 1.3% per year.[10] The risk of stroke related to carotid stenosis has declined significantly over the subsequent decades, largely because of the control of risk factors such as hypertension.

Interventional procedures (surgery or stenting) on the blockages in a carotid artery can only reduce the risk of stroke due to the blockages that are the focus of the procedure. Blockages elsewhere in the cerebral circulation that may not be amenable to surgical intervention continue to present an unmitigated stroke risk, as does the risk of stroke due to other mechanisms such as hemorrhage and cardioembolism.

The goal of an interventional procedure on a diseased carotid artery is to reduce a person's risk of stroke below that which can be achieved by doing nothing or by medical treatment such as control of high blood pressure. The other side of the equation that must be factored in is the risk of serious or fatal complications from the interventional procedure itself. The procedures themselves carry a certain risk of causing a fatal or disabling stroke—the very thing they are intended to avert—or other serious perioperative complications.

Carotid endarterectomy involves making an incision in the neck to expose the carotid artery, and then incising the artery and removing the plaque from the inside. Sometimes a vascular patch or graft is involved. The first case reports of patients treated with carotid endarterectomy appeared in the early 1950s. On the basis of the case reports and case series, the procedure was picked up very quickly, and by the mid-1980s nearly a million Americans had undergone it. But many in the medical community questioned whether the procedure conferred net benefit over harm, and to which patients. An observational study of Medicare beneficiaries who had had the operation in 1981 showed only a third of patients had undergone the operation for indications considered by experts to be clinically appropriate. In the others, the operations were undertaken for reasons the experts considered equivocal or inappropriate. Moreover, 1 out of every 10 patients suffered a disabling stroke during or after the operation before they were discharged from the hospital or died within 30 days of the operation.[11]

Then, a series of randomized trials, most of which were reported in the 1990s, established that the procedure benefited some subgroups of patients but in others caused more harm than benefit. Carotid endarterectomy was highly effective in reducing the risk of ipsilateral stroke over a 5-year period in persons with symptoms and stenosis of 70%-99%, marginally effective in symptomatic persons with stenosis of 50%–69%, had no significant effect in symptomatic persons with stenosis of 30%–49%, and harmful—that is, it increased the risk of stroke instead of decreasing it—in symptomatic persons with less than 30% stenosis.[12] In persons with no symptoms (i.e., no prior mild stroke or TIAs on the side of the stenosis), carotid endarterectomy was less effective than when performed on persons with symptoms. It reduced the risk of ipsilateral stroke by only about 3% per year[13]; in other words, there was only a three percentage-point spread between the incidence of stroke in the operative group and the incidence of stroke in the control group. These multi-center trials also clarified the operative complication rates that could be expected with carotid endarterectomy, when performed by surgeons in the centers considered proficient enough to participate in the trial. The operation-related rate of stroke or death was nearly 3% in trials of the surgery on persons with no symptoms (prior stroke or TIA) and was 7% in trials of the surgery on persons with symptomatic carotid stenosis.

Before the answers were in on carotid endarterectomy, tens of thousands of Americans had undergone the operation. Substantial proportions were not benefited or suffered harm. After the results of the randomized trials of carotid endarterectomy were reported, the proportion of patients undergoing the procedure for inappropriate indications—no chance of benefit, or net harm over benefit—fell from 32% to under 9%.[14]

Another operation for stroke prevention, extracranial-intracranial arterial bypass, was launched on the basis of a case report in 1969 and performed widely for 15 years before the first randomized trial to test it showed that the operation increased rather than decreased the incidence of fatal and nonfatal strokes.[15] Few of these procedures are now performed in the United States.[16]

Percutaneous carotid artery angioplasty and stenting for stroke prevention were first described in the 1980s and diffused rapidly, in part because of the belief that a percutaneous procedure involving a small tube was less invasive and therefore had to be safer for patients than an incision-requiring endarterectomy. The first stent to be approved by the Food and Drug Administration (FDA) for deployment in the carotid artery was Guidant Corporation's Acculink™ carotid stent system. Guidant's pre-market approval application for this "first of its kind" class III device was approved in August 2004. The Acculink™ carotid stent system consists of the stent (a metal mesh tube that props open the blocked artery and remains there permanently) and a delivery catheter plus an embolic protection device (a micromesh filter basket which opens up like an umbrella in the carotid artery downstream from where the blockage is) and its delivery/retrieval catheter. The embolic protection device serves the purpose of trapping any particles of the plaque that break free during the deployment of the stent; such particles travel into the brain as emboli and cause strokes. It is removed once the stent is deployed. The FDA categorizes intravascular stents and their associated delivery systems as class III devices; such devices are evaluated by the FDA under the pre-market approval application pathway, and human studies are required.

We pointed out that carotid stenting for stroke risk reduction came into clinical use in the 1980s. The fact that the first carotid stenting system was not approved until 2004 means that the thousands of patients who underwent this procedure before then had stents implanted in their carotid arteries that had been developed and cleared by the FDA for use in other bodily locations, an example of off-label use. In fact, stents cleared by the FDA for use to prop open strictures of the biliary tree (ducts carrying bile in the liver and gall bladder) caused by malignancies—biliary stents—were the products most commonly used in the carotid arteries before 2004. As the clinical use of carotid stenting and stenting of other arteries expanded between the mid-1990s and the early 2000s, the FDA experienced a virtual flurry of pre-market notifications [501(k)] for metallic expandable stents indicated for the palliation of malignant neoplasms in the biliary tree from companies wanting a share of the market. Between 1999 and 2004, the FDA received over 125 [510(k)] submissions for such devices.[17] (Approval via the pre-market notification 510(k) pathway requires no clinical data.) One group estimates that between 2003 and 2006, a million biliary stents were implanted off label into carotid and other peripheral arteries.[18]

Early experience with carotid stenting showed that insertion of the device often inadvertently dislodged some of the plaque inside the artery, so that the debris traveled as an embolism into the brain and caused a stroke—the very condition the procedure was intended to avert. By the mid 1990s the need for "cerebral protection" against emboli during carotid angioplasty and stenting was recognized at least by some groups, and various protective techniques were developed and employed by groups performing the procedure.[19]

The FDA approved the Acculink™ carotid stenting system for marketing based on bench tests, animal studies, and three clinical trials conducted by the manufacturer. The trials involved 581 patients from 50 centers who got the device; their outcomes were compared with those of historical controls, subjects who had undergone carotid endarterectomy in two of the large randomized trials.[20] The goals of the trials were to show the non-inferiority of carotid stenting to carotid endarterectomy, and they were met. Patients in the stenting trials had about an 8% chance of death, stroke, or heart attack within 30 days of the stenting procedure, and an 8%–10% probability of having one of the 30-day endpoints plus an ipsilateral stroke within 365 days of the procedure.[21] The FDA approved the device system for use in patients judged to be high risk for adverse events during carotid endarterectomy and who had either symptomatic carotid stenosis of >50% or no symptoms but a carotid stenosis of >80%. Of course, it was, and still is, being used in much broader populations than that.

So how does carotid stenting compare, in terms of effectiveness and safety, with carotid endarterectomy? The results of the first randomized trial of stenting versus endarterectomy appeared in 2001,[22] 20 years after carotid stents began to be used in patients. A 2007 meta-analysis of 12 randomized trials of carotid stenting versus endarterectomy found that five had been stopped early, three because of safety concerns in the subjects allocated to stenting.[23] This meta-analysis found that the results of the seven completed trials indicated that endarterectomy was better than stenting in preventing death or any stroke within 30 days of the intervention, and that over the longer term (1 year), no significant differences in stroke prevention existed between the interventions. An analysis of the 2005 Nationwide Inpatient Sample, including 135,701 Americans undergoing carotid revascularization, found that the risk of in-hospital postoperative stroke and death was significantly higher in patients undergoing stenting compared with endarterectomy.[24] Moreover, the median total hospital charges for stenting were substantially higher: $30,396 per patient compared with $17,658 for endarterectomy.

We used carotid artery procedures to illustrate how surgical innovations are developed and disseminate rapidly into wide clinical use, in advance of valid evidence of their safety, efficacy, and comparative effectiveness, but we could have used many others. Arthroscopic lavage with or without debridement for relief of knee pain due to osteoarthritis, a story recounted in Chapter 1, is another example, as are the ten or so different procedures performed with curative intent on men with localized prostate cancer, most of the different endoscopic procedures directed at ablating or removing abnormal mucosa from the lower esophagus in persons with Barrett's esophagus, thought to be associated with a small risk of esophageal cancer, and so forth.

These procedures are performed by well-intentioned surgeons and proceduralists who are highly motivated to cure disease and improve health. The patients who choose to undergo these procedures believe doing so is in their own best interest. But the context in which these doctors and patients are interacting, at least in the U.S. health care system, is one in which doctors generally receive financial remuneration for each such procedure they perform, on patients who are generally unaware of the large gaps in evidence of effectiveness and safety of some of the procedures they give "informed" consent to undergo, in settings characterized by the lack of systematic observation of clinical outcomes and lost opportunities to learn. One of the challenges to be overcome is devising ways to maximize our learning from patients who agree to undergo promising but as-yet-unvalidated surgical procedures or to be treated with new medical devices outside the setting of randomized controlled trials. Such learning is not antithetical to innovation.

Roots of the Double Standard

As the methodological, ethical, and regulatory standards for the evaluation of new drugs and biologics became increasingly formalized over the past 60 years, a curious double standard—one for medicines, and the other for surgery—came into being. We may set down the double standard as follows: our contemporary society requires that only prescription drugs of demonstrated clinical effectiveness and safety can be used in routine clinical care, but it allows promising but unvalidated invasive procedures, often risky and costly, and causing anatomical changes that cannot be reversed, to be used in routine clinical care. Why do we have one level of effectiveness and safety expectations for prescription drugs and a much lower level of expectations for invasive procedures? Why is it that invasive therapeutic procedures are allowed to come into wide clinical use before their benefits and harms have been validated in fair tests? We will discuss four reasons: factors within the surgical profession itself, the U.S. regulatory framework for surgery, the regulatory framework for medical devices used in surgery, and the special challenges presented by designing and conducting fair tests of the effects of a surgical procedure.

Factors within the Profession of Surgery

For a substantial part of the last 60 years, from roughly 1950 to 1975, many surgeons and leaders of the profession believed that surgical procedures could not, should not, or need not be tested in randomized trials. Part of this belief can be traced to concerns about the ethical treatment of human subjects. It was a time before research protections were codified, and a variety of ethical violations were being noted.[25]

Some of the prejudice against randomized trials of surgical procedures may be attributable to the backlash to two very early controlled clinical trials, both sponsored by the National Heart Institute, of a surgical procedure undertaken to relieve chest pain attributed to coronary heart disease (angina pectoris).[26] The operation, ligation of the internal mammary arteries, was hypothesized to reduce angina by increasing the amount of arterial blood flowing to the myocardium. This simple procedure is performed under local anesthesia and entails incising the skin next to the sternum in the space between the second and third ribs, isolating the artery in the subcutaneous tissue, tying a ligature around it, and then closing the incision. The thoracic cavity is not entered. The results of early uncontrolled studies of the procedure were mixed.

In 1959, Leonard A. Cobb and coinvestigators reported a randomized trial in 17 subjects in which the subjects as well as the physicians conducting the postoperative follow-up examinations were blinded to group assignment. Local, not general, anesthesia was used in both the intervention and control groups in the trial. The placebo procedure consisted of parasternal skin incisions and exposure of the internal mammary artery but no placement of ligatures around the artery. In the operating room, after making the skin incision, the surgeon was handed a randomly selected envelop telling him whether to ligate the internal mammary arteries. During the first six postoperative months, five of eight ligated subjects and five of nine non-ligated subjects reported significant improvement in their angina. The investigators concluded that the operation had no effect on the pathophysiology of coronary artery disease and attributed the findings to the placebo effect associated with surgery. Using the same design as the Cobb trial, E. Grey Dimond et al. performed another trial and found the same results, also noting that, though the subjects reported much improvement in their angina, the abnormalities on the exercise electrocardiograms remained the same.

A key issue about these trials is the subsequent and enduring backlash against placebo-controlled surgery trials they caused. What was disclosed in the consent process met the time's prevailing ethical standards, but afterward it was deemed inadequate. Trial subjects were told that they were participating in an evaluation of internal mammary artery ligation for angina relief, but they were not told that there was a possibility they would receive a sham procedure.

The views of the surgical profession about the value of randomized trials of surgical procedures have since changed, though anti-trial sentiments have not disappeared entirely. In some subspecialties, the randomized clinical trial design is becoming the standard expectation in the evaluation of surgical innovations, and of untested but long-used procedures as well.[27]

The U.S. Regulatory Framework for Surgery

Some have said that another reason for the double standard is that no federal regulatory body oversees surgery: "There is no FDA for surgery."[28] Surgical innovation and the behavior of surgeon-innovators are regulated instead by the internal norms of the surgical profession and by the organizational expectations of the hospitals and academic departments in which surgeon-innovators work. Professional societies have attempted to set forth guidelines for surgical innovation. For example, the American College of Surgeons issued a "Statement on Issues to Be Considered before New Surgical Technology Is Applied to the Care of Patients"[29] in September 1995, which has not been rescinded. The Society for University Surgeons proposed, among other things, that the internal oversight of surgical innovation would be more effectively accomplished by local "surgical innovation committees" rather than institutional review boards,[30] the thorny problem being that not all surgical innovation seems to be "research" in the prevailing understanding of either term. However, neither the recommendations for posting innovative techniques nor those for local surgical innovation committees seem to have gained any purchase.

The primary mission of medical product manufacturers is to make a profit. The FDA was born and has evolved because of society's need for protection against product makers whose profit motive predisposes them to take undue risks with public health and well-being. U.S. statutes protect the makers of newly approved regulated medical products from material competition for a period of years. This affords the manufacturers and company shareholders some likelihood of recouping their outlays on research and development and of making substantial profits.[31]

A similar ability for a surgeon or a group of surgeons to recoup large outlays for research and development of a surgical innovation does not exist. Unlike medical product makers, a surgeon-innovator cannot patent a surgical innovation and has no statutory period of exclusivity on it. The innovator can patent a new device he or she developed for use in surgical procedures, but not the procedure itself.[32] (The issue of patents for "medical activities" and remedies for their infringements got a great deal of discussion in the mid 1990s, which culminated in 1996 with the passage of legislation. If such patents can be awarded, most infringements against them are nevertheless unenforceable.[33]) While it is true that a well-publicized surgical innovation may bring in a higher volume of cases for the innovator, it is not possible to commodify the surgical innovation to the extent or scale that a manufacturer of a drug or device can.

While we are not advocating for a change in the law, the inability to patent or to have a period of exclusivity for an innovative surgical procedure has one downside. Because a surgical innovation has such limited commercial potential, there is no justification for an industry devoted to the research and development of new invasive therapeutic procedures and to bringing them to market—a very great contrast to prescription drugs, biologics, and medical devices. This means that there is no commercial source of investment available for the support of research and development of surgical innovations. Research and development of surgical innovations must be, and is, underwritten by governmental and private sources, and such funding is in short supply.

The Regulatory Framework for Medical Devices Used in Surgery

Although "there is no FDA for surgery," the regulatory purview of the FDA does extend to medical devices used in surgery. As we saw in Chapter 2 from the example of the LARIAT device, the FDA's pre-market notification [510(k)] pathway has the unintended and perverse effect of encouraging the rapid and wide uptake of invasive procedures that have not been put to fair tests of clinical effectiveness and safety. That surgeons can legally use FDA-cleared devices for purposes not on the label has the same effect.

Challenges of Randomized Trials of Invasive Therapeutic Procedures

Factors within the profession of surgery and aspects of the U.S. regulatory system explain at least part of the status quo for how surgical innovations develop and disseminate. But there is an additional factor. More so than trials of pharmaceutical agents, trials of surgical procedures are challenging to design and even more challenging to perform well. The same design issues face all trialists: deciding whether a trial is justifiable, choosing the goal of the trial and the most appropriate comparator, laying plans to minimize selection bias and expectancy bias, calculating how large the trial needs to be in view of the expected effect size of the intervention and other factors, developing criteria for the kinds of subjects who should be recruited to participate, and strategizing on how to retain subjects, once enrolled, in the trial. Another set of issues that the drug trialist escapes lies in store for the surgical trialist. An experimental drug does not have an ego, bad days and good days in the operating room, or a learning curve. Once the pill containing the experimental drug is ready to be tested in a clinical trial, it has been "standardized"—it is not an intervention that must be standardized across multiple surgeons or proceduralists who vary in the way they do things in the operating room, or across complex multi-disciplinary teams involving surgeons, anesthesiologists, nurses, technicians, idiosyncratic hospital procedures, and institutional cultures and mixes of patients, payers, and socioeconomic status. Progress has been made in advancing the methods of trials of surgical procedures, but, as recent reviews of the quality of such trials indicate, much more work needs to be done.[34]

Another difference exists between investigational drugs and promising but unvalidated surgical procedures: a patient's ability to access the treatment outside the research setting. Such access is virtually nil for investigational drugs; even the humanitarian exemptions require data collection. This is not the case for innovative surgical procedures. As long as surgeons and hospitals can get reimbursed for performing a promising but unvalidated invasive therapeutic procedure and patients can get access to it outside a trial, then wide dissemination of the procedure in advance of any trial results will happen. Though it is a rare occurrence, groups of specialists have used their power and influence and taken a public stance that a surgical innovation must be put to the test in a randomized trial before the innovation is allowed to disseminate. Two examples are a trial of laparoscopically assisted colectomy for colon cancer and a trial of prenatal versus postnatal surgical repair of a type of spina bifida.[35]

More commonly, dissemination outruns the evidence. Surgeons and patients believe they know what is best and are unwilling to entertain the thought of random allocation in a trial, even though ethical safeguards in the design of clinical trials preclude testing an innovation against an intervention known to be less efficacious than what is considered "standard of care" at the time.

Think about the LARIAT story in the *Houston Chronicle* that we mentioned in Chapter 2. Suppose you are a patient with atrial fibrillation and are asked to enroll in a trial testing the LARIAT's effectiveness and safety in which you had a 50% chance of being randomized to the LARIAT and a 50% chance of being randomized to standard treatment with anticoagulants. What decision would you make? After all, trials are voluntary. If you do not enter the trial, you can make sure you will be treated with the LARIAT. Or make sure you are not.

Conclusions

Given the financial impact of major invasive therapeutic procedures on national health expenditures, and the serious deficiencies in the evidence base for most surgical procedures, it would have made no sense to leave them out of the 2010 federal mandate for comparative effectiveness research. But the challenges of evaluating the comparativeness effectiveness of surgical procedures loom very large. The federal mandates for comparative effectiveness research of the 2000s could improve the quantity and quality of surgical trials in several ways: by the infusion of additional funds for trials, by advancing the methodology of clinical trials, by providing support for the training of surgical trialists, and by increasing the demand for high-quality evidence from all the stakeholders in medical care.

Notes

1 Lee PH, Gawande AA. The number of surgical procedures in an American lifetime in 3 states. J Am Coll Surg 2008;207:S75.
2. Weiser TG, Regenbogen SE, Thompson KD, et al. An estimation of the global volume of surgery: a modelling strategy based on available data. Lancet 2008;372:139–44.
3. Payer L. Medicine and culture. New York: Penguin Books, 1988.
4. Data from analyses of the U.S. Hospital Care and Utilization Profile Nationwide Inpatient Sample, performed by the Agency for Healthcare Research and Quality (AHRQ). AHRQ's clinical classification system groups ICD-9-CM procedure codes into four types. "Major therapeutic" procedures are those performed in an operating room and that are for therapeutic reasons. See Merrill C, Elixhauser A. Procedures in U.S. Hospitals, 2003: Agency for Healthcare Research and Quality; 2006 May 2006. Report No.: HCUP Fact Book #7, and Elixhauser A, Andrews RM. Profile of inpatient operating room procedures in U.S. hospitals in 2007. Arch Surg 2010;145:1201–8. The 2007 data are based on the same databases and analytic strategies as the 2003 data.
5. Ibid.
6. Ibid.
7. In 2007, the 29.1 million hospital stays involving at least one major invasive therapeutic procedure accounted for 47% of total aggregate hospital costs in non-federal U.S. hospitals. For ease we round this up to 50%. In 2007, U.S. expenditures for hospital care were $686.8 billion; 50% of $686.8 billion is $343.4 billion. Because about half of operating room procedures are now performed in an outpatient setting, we assume

an additional 29.1 million major invasive therapeutic procedures for 2007. Since no overnight stay was required for those outpatient procedures, we use a single day cost of $2,900 per procedure. Therefore, outpatient procedures add $84.4 billion to the tab, giving a combined subtotal for hospital and outpatient expenditures of $427.8 billion. To that we must add expenditures for the professional services of surgeons, anesthesiologists, and other physicians, which in 2007 accounted for 20% of national health expenditures. We will assume that expenditures for physician services will boost our subtotal of $427.8 billion by 20% ($85.6 billion), giving us a grand total of $513.4 billion expended on major invasive therapeutic procedures in 2007. In 2007, U.S. national health expenditures totaled $2,283.5 billion; $513.4 billion divided by $2,283.5 billion equals 22.5%. We used 2007 data as the starting point for our estimates based on the analyses reported in the 2010 paper by Elixhauser et al. cited in note 4. More recent statistics are unavailable.

8. "Stroke" is defined as the abrupt onset of focal or lateralizing neurological deficits that last longer than 24 hours and are caused by irreversible death of brain tissue due to lack of oxygen (ischemia/infarction) or brain hemorrhage. Strokes due to ischemia/infarction are due to arterial thrombosis (locally formed clots) and/or emboli (elements such as clots formed elsewhere or broken-off particles of atherosclerotic plaques that travel and eventually obstruct the artery as its lumen narrows). About 85% of strokes are due to ischemia/infarction and 15% to hemorrhage. Of strokes attributable to ischemia/infarction, about one-fourth are due to thrombosis and about three-fourths to embolism. A transient ischemic attack (TIA), a harbinger of a future stroke, is the abrupt onset of focal or lateralizing neurologic deficits that disappear within 24 hours.

9. When imaging studies such as radiographs or angiographs can be used to document the etiology or consequences of a disease, physicians and surgeons are prone to develop disease and treatment models in which local or regional therapy directed against the seeable lesion, such as excision, amputation, bypass, or stenting, takes the central place. Such models may turn out to be wrong or suboptimal when tested in randomized control trials, as in the case of radical mastectomy for breast cancer. For a provocative and insightful discussion of "the tensions between visual and statistical evidence," see Jones DS.Visions of a cure. Visualization, clinical trials, and controversies in cardiac therapeutics, 1968–1998. Isis 2000;91:504–41.

10. See Norris JW, Zhu CZ, Bornstein NM, Chambers BR. Vascular risks of asymptomatic carotid stenosis. Stroke 1991;22:1485–90; and Klijn CJM, Kappelle LJ, Tulleken CAF, van Gijn J. Symptomatic carotid artery occlusion. A reappraisal of hemodynamic factors. Stroke 1997;28:2084–93.

11. Winslow CM, Solomon DH, Chassin MR, Kosecoff J, Merrick NJ, Brook RH. The appropriateness of carotid endarterectomy. N Engl J Med 1988;318:721–7.

12. Rerkasem K, Rothwell PM. Carotid endarterectomy for symptomatic carotid stenosis. Cochrane Database Syst Rev. 2011 Apr 13;(4): CD001081.

13. Chambers BR, Donnan G. Carotid endarterectomy for asymptomatic carotid stenosis. Cochrane Database Syst Rev. 2005 Oct 19;(4): CD001923.

14. Halm EA, Tuhrim S, Wang JJ, Rojas M, Hannan EL, Chassisn MR. Has evidence changed practice? Appropriateness of carotid endarterectomy after the clinical trials. Neurology 2007;68:187–94.

15. The EC/IC Bypass Study Group. Failure of extracranial-intracranial arterial bypass to reduce the risk of ischemic stroke. Results of an international randomized trial. N Engl J Med 1985; 313:1191–200.

16. Amin-Hanjani S, Butler WE, Ogilvy CS, Carter BS, Barker FG 2nd. Extracranial-intracranial bypass in the treatment of occlusive cerebrovascular disease and intracranial aneurysms in the United States between 1992 and 2001: a population-based study. J Neurosurg 2005;103:794–804.

17. Gonzalez G, Nipper JC, Yustein AS, et al. The use of a biliary stent clearance database in the review of metallic biliary stents for malignant neoplasms. [Abstract from the 2004

FDA Science Forum.] (Accessed September 25, 2012, at http://www.accessdata.fda.gov/
ScienceForums/forum04/J-01.htm.)

18. Bridges J, Maisel WH. Malfunctions and adverse events associated with off-label use of
biliary stents in the peripheral vasculature. Am J Ther 2008;15:12–8.

19. Theron JG, Payelle GG, Coskun O, Huet HF, Guimaraens L. Carotid artery stenosis: treatment with protected balloon angioplasty and stent placement. Radiology
1996;201:627–36.

20. See North American Symptomatic Carotid Endarterectomy Trial Collaborators.
Beneficial effect of carotid endarterectomy in symptomatic patients with high-grade
carotid stenosis. N Engl J Med 1991;325:445–53, and Executive Committee for the
Asymptomatic Carotid Atherosclerosis Study. Endarterectomy for asymptomatic carotid
stenosis. JAMA 1995;273:1421–8.

21. This information is from the summary of safety and effectiveness data on the Acculink™
carotid stenting system, available on the FDA Web site. (Accessed September 24, 2012,
at http://www.accessdata.fda.gov/cdrh_docs/pdf4/P040012b.pdf.)

22. Endovascular versus surgical treatment in patients with carotid stenosis in the Carotid
and Vertebral Artery Transluminal Angioplasty Study (CAVATAS): a randomised trial.
Lancet 2001;357:1729–37.

23. Ederle J, Featherstone R, Brown MM. Percutaneous transluminal angioplasty and stenting for carotid artery stenosis. Cochrane Database Syst Rev. 2007 Oct 17;(4):CD000515.

24. McPhee JT, Scanzer A, Messina LM, Eslami MH. Carotid artery stenting has increased
rates of post-procedure stroke, death, and resource utilization than does carotid endarterectomy in the United States, 2005. J Vasc Surg 2008;48:1442–50.

25. See, for example, the landmark paper by Henry K. Beecher: Ethics and clinical research.
N Engl J Med 1966;274:367–72.

26. The two trials are: Cobb LA, Thomas GI, Dillard DH, Merendino KA, Bruce RA. An
evaluation of internal-mammary-artery ligation by a double-blind technic. N Engl J
Med 1959;260:1115–8, and Dimond EG, Kittle CF, Crockett JE. Comparison of internal mammary artery ligation and sham operation for angina pectoris. Am J Cardiol
1960;5:483–6.

27. One example is the NIH-supported Urinary Incontinence Treatment Network, a group
of urogynecologists that conducts state-of-the-art multi-center trials of surgical procedures for the relief of urinary incontinence in women. Information is available from
http://www.uitn.net/index.asp.

28. Spodick DH. Numerators without denominators: there is no FDA for the surgeon. JAMA
1975;232:33–6.

29. American College of Surgeons: [ST-23] Statement on issues to be considered before new
surgical technology is applied to the care of patients. (Accessed September 24, 2012, at
http://www.facs.org/fellows_info/statements/st-23.html.)

30. Biffl WL, Spain DA, Reitsma AM, et al. Responsible development and application of surgical innovations: a position statement from the Society of University Surgeons. J Am
Coll Surg 2008;206:1204–9.

31. The U.S. Patent and Trademark Office defines a patent as "an intellectual property right
granted by the Government of the United States to an inventor to exclude others from
making, using, offering for sale, or selling the invention throughout the United States or
importing the invention into the United States for a limited time in exchange for public
disclosure of the invention when the patent is granted."

32. For example, LASIK surgery is intended to reduce a person's dependency on glasses
or contact lenses by using a laser to change the shape of the cornea; the abbreviation
stands for laser-assisted in situ keratomileusis. The first laser to be approved for use
in the LASIK procedure was one tested and put forth by Frederic B. Kremer, MD, of
Photomed, Inc. (The pre-market approval application for the Kremer Excimer Laser
System was approved by the FDA in July 1998.) Like many individuals, Dr. Kremer
holds patents for several kinds of apparatus used in LASIK surgery, including one that
measures corneal thickness. But no one can hold a patent for the operation itself.

33. The Omnibus Consolidated Appropriations Act signed into law by President Bill Clinton on September 30, 1996 amended Section 237 of the USC with a new subsection (c), the medical procedures reform provision. See Bennet VC. Limitations on patents claiming medical or surgical procedures. (Accessed on September 24, 2012, at http://www.myersbigel.com/library/articles/MedicalorSurgical.pdf.)

34. Wenner DM, Brody BA, Jarman AF, Kolman JM, Wray NP, Ashton CM. Do surgical trials meet the scientific standards for clinical trials? J Am Coll Surg 2012;215:722–30.

35. See The American Society of Colon and Rectal Surgeons. Approved statement on laparoscopic colectomy. Dis Colon Rectum 1994;37:8–12, and Adzick NS, Thom EA, Spong CY, et al. A randomized trial of prenatal versus postnatal repair of myelomeningocele. N Engl J Med 2011;364:993–1004.

5

Doctors and Evidence

Evidence-Based Medicine

The preceding chapters cover how clinical evidence is generated in the research process, how evidence is applied as part of the regulation of drugs and devices, and the role evidence plays in the uptake of surgical innovations. In this chapter we turn to the individual who stands at the intersection of scientific evidence in the abstract and its application to the care of the actual patient: the physician. All decisions about the use of prescription drugs, devices, hospitals, and operations are made in interactions between individual doctors and patients. How do doctors know what seems best for the patients in front of them? How do they use evidence?

The ideal for contemporary medical practice is what is called "evidence-based medicine," defined by David Sackett as "the conscientious, explicit, and judicious use of current best evidence in making decision about the care of individual patients...The practice of evidence-based medicine means integrating individual clinical expertise with the best available external clinical evidence from systematic research. By individual clinical expertise we mean the proficiency and judgment that individual clinicians acquire through clinical experience and clinical practice."[1] The tenets and approaches of evidence-based medicine have developed over the past six decades, but the term itself is just over 20 years old. Gordon Guyatt describes how, as the new director of the internal medicine residency program at McMaster University in Hamilton, Ontario in 1990, he presented to the assembled departmental faculty his plans for changing the program, calling his new approach "scientific medicine." Not surprisingly, some of the faculty bristled at the implication for what they were currently practicing. Trying again, Guyatt came up with the more acceptable "evidence-based medicine."[2]

Evidence is defined as "an outward sign" or "that which furnishes or tends to furnish proof." The physician deals with two kinds of evidence: the evidence he or she collects directly from the individual patient, and the evidence he or she obtains from research sources that guides clinical decision making. Sackett's definition and the definitive history of the evidence-based medicine effort[3] confirm that evidence-based medicine rests on information from the patient as well as information from the literature. But much more attention has been focused on appraising and synthesizing the literature than on collecting and interpreting hands-on data from the patient.[4] Advances in clinical research methods and the explosion of published research pose serious challenges for doctors. A whole field has grown up to help doctors use scientific literature to inform their clinical practice. This field includes the techniques of critical appraisal of medical literature as well as various approaches to finding and synthesizing the literature.

While it is safe to say that federal mandates for comparative effectiveness research were never on the mind of the originators of the evidence-based medicine approach, such mandates have made their work even more important. The historical overview we give here shows the evolving nature and relative recency of this thing called evidence-based medicine, and it provides insights on why it is difficult to achieve.

The Doctor as Clinical Epidemiologist: Alvan Feinstein and David Sackett

Evidence-based medicine grew out of the efforts of two giants in medicine, Alvan Feinstein, MD (1925–2001), who is called the father of the American branch of clinical epidemiology, and David Sackett, MD (1934–), the father of the Canadian branch.

Feinstein was born and raised in Philadelphia, Pennsylvania. He initially chose to study mathematics and received bachelor of science (1947) and master of science (1948) degrees in mathematics from the University of Chicago. Feinstein's education in mathematics established the basis for his analytic approach to the everyday things clinicians do. Believing he would be nothing more than a mediocre mathematician, Feinstein changed his career plans to medicine. He received his medical degree from the University of Chicago in 1952 and completed his training in internal medicine at Yale, Columbia, and the Rockefeller Institute. At the time he intended to pursue academic medicine, and academic medicine was entrenched in the laboratory. But at the Rockefeller Institute, Feinstein found biological specimens to be much less intriguing than patients, and he shifted his sights to clinical practice. He completed an additional year of formal training and then became clinical director of Irving House, a chronic care facility affiliated with New York University for patients suffering from rheumatic fever.[5]

It was at Irving House that Feinstein first began to develop his concepts about improving the accuracy, reliability, and validity of the data collected from patients by the history or physical exam. He was hired at Irving House to care for a set of patients with rheumatic fever who were enrolled in a trial of anti-streptococcal therapy. The goal of the trial was to determine whether drug therapy would prevent recurrent episodes of acute rheumatic fever. To be eligible to enter the trial, a subject had to have had a prior attack. Subjects were followed to determine whether they had subsequent attacks of rheumatic fever, which was the primary endpoint of the trial.

Feinstein noted that, while great care had been taken in designing the statistics for the trial and in standardizing the laboratory measurements, no comparable effort had been made to ensure the accuracy of diagnoses. The simple event of correcting an error in a resident physician's diagnosis of a cardiac murmur in a patient at Irving House made Feinstein realize the magnitude of the bias that inaccurate diagnosis could inject into the trial's findings. If individuals who had not in fact had a prior episode of rheumatic fever were entered into the trial—such persons are much less likely to have an attack of rheumatic fever than those who already had one—drug therapy would appear more effective in preventing recurrent attacks than it really was. The same would be true if physical findings indicative of recurrent rheumatic fever were missed or misinterpreted at follow-up examinations. Feinstein realized that these diagnostic errors would lead to spurious overestimates of the efficacy of anti-streptococcal therapy in the trial.[6]

Feinstein first presented his thoughts on the need to improve the accuracy of the history and physical exam in four articles entitled "Scientific Methodology in Clinical Medicine" published in 1964.[7] In these papers he noted that physicians practicing clinical medicine lagged far behind physician-scientists working in the laboratory. The latter were trained in the latest techniques to ensure accuracy and reliability of measurement. They applied strict scientific methods in their work, including selection of appropriate controls, standardization to ensure the reproducibility of reagents and procedures, and so forth—all efforts to optimize the accuracy and reliability of the data on which their conclusions would be based. In contrast, the clinician practiced the "art" of medicine informed by clinical acumen. Feinstein argued that, to understand disease and the effect it had on patients, clinicians had to measure the disease state as it occurred in patients with high levels of accuracy and reliability before therapy and again after therapy. In Feinstein's words, "The data obtained exclusively at the bedside must be acquired and interpreted by procedures specifically designed for the various human beings who are the observed and the observers. Using clinical skill, clinical settings and the sick people who constitute clinical material, clinicians must develop a scientific methodology of their own."

In his 1964 articles and his 1967 book *Clinical Judgment*,[8] Feinstein proposed how the practice of clinical medicine should change to adopt more rigorous scientific methods. Two things were essential. The first was to improve the accuracy of diagnoses made in the context of patient–physician interactions. This would require improvements in the validity of diagnoses (that the patient was in fact suffering from the disease that the doctor believed was present) as well as their reliability or reproducibility (that two doctors examining the same patient would arrive at the same diagnostic conclusions). The second was to be able to use data obtained during patient–physician interactions to identify important prognostic subclasses of patients within a diagnostic category, subclasses with differences in expected outcomes, for example, different survival times or different probabilities of developing complications. The effectiveness of any therapy in altering expected outcomes is highly dependent on their predicted rates in the untreated patient. Without classifying patients accurately, and sub-classifying them based on their prognostic outlook, it is impossible to assess accurately the effectiveness of a targeted treatment.

Feinstein was not the first to put the word "clinical" in front of the word "epidemiology" (both he and David Sackett give this credit to J. R. Paul[9]), but he infused the term with new meaning in a set of three articles published in 1968.[10] Though the initial work of the epidemiologist was in infectious diseases, defining population and patient-level characteristics, exposures, geographic distribution, and so on, to try to elucidate causative exposures or agents, Feinstein noted that epidemiology had evolved to include the study of chronic diseases. He saw clinical epidemiology as the way to improve diagnostic accuracy, the prognostic classification of patients, and the monitoring of changes in outcomes attributable to treatment.

It was about the time of Feinstein's 1968 papers that David Sackett became aware of his work. Born in 1934, Sackett received his medical degree in 1960 from the University of Illinois. Planning a career in academic internal medicine, he devoted the years from 1960 to 1966 to an internal medicine residency, chief residency, and subspecialty training in hypertension and nephrology. During this period he also did a 2-year stint in the U.S. Public Health Service. Sackett has said that the branch of clinical epidemiology he founded should be attributed to Alvan Feinstein and Nikita Khrushchev: Khrushchev because the Cuban Missile Crisis and the prospect of war with the U.S.S.R. led to the drafting of thousands of young physicians into the U.S. Public Health Service, Sackett among them.

Sackett's 2 years in the Public Health Service were devoted to performing surveys of cardiovascular disease. It was during this time that he was introduced to the principles of epidemiologic investigation. It dawned on him, he notes, that epidemiology and biostatistics could be made as relevant to improving clinical medicine as well as any research he might do in nephrology. Feinstein's paper on Boolean algebra and clinical taxonomy that appeared in the *New England Journal of Medicine*[11] solidified Sackett's thinking. He wrote a fan letter to Feinstein. Thus began the close, but never easy, relationship of the two men.[12]

After further graduate work, Sackett was awarded the degree of Master of Science in Epidemiology from Harvard in 1967. Shortly thereafter he was recruited to McMaster University in Hamilton, Ontario, for its new medical school, which had been launched in 1965. It was at this time that he wrote his paper defining a new field that he called clinical epidemiology.[13]

Sackett taught McMaster's physicians-in-training to improve the rigor with which they collected data from their patients. In the late 1980s he decided to expand his sphere of influence. Believing that an accessible series of articles summarizing the state of the literature on the validity of the history and physical exam would not only encourage physicians to improve their performance but also encourage academics to perform much-needed studies in this area, he approached the editors of the *Journal of the American Medical Association* about publishing such a series. In 1992, *JAMA's* Rational Clinical Examination Series was born.[14]

In the editorial introducing the series, Sackett noted that the initial history and physical examination are the tools that all physicians use to direct the development of the initial differential diagnoses and the subsequent diagnostic testing to be done to confirm or exclude diagnoses under consideration. For that reason, the initial history and physical exam is the dominant determinant of the subsequent evaluation of the patient, the cost of that evaluation, and its potential for leading to an accurate attribution for the problem that prompted the patient to seek care. The latter, of course, is the sine qua non for formulating a treatment plan likely to be effective. He noted that an accurate clinical history and proper physical exam "are the best series of diagnostic 'tests' we ever have." Sackett pointed out that we require the validity and reliability of laboratory tests to be predefined by rigorous testing against a gold standard; in contrast, we have few requirements for rigorous tests of the components of the history and physical exam and very little idea of their validity and precision.

Feinstein and Sackett came independently to defining this new area and calling it clinical epidemiology. In pursuing clinical epidemiology, both were devoted to improving clinicians' everyday practice of medicine. But the paths they took to achieve the improvement in practice were very different. Feinstein, through his program at Yale University and his generations of trainees, focused on improving the observation and measurement of clinical phenomena and on developing methods for more accurately identifying prognostic subclasses of patients.[15] Sackett, through his program at McMaster University and his trainees and protégés, focused on helping physicians interact intelligently and critically with published clinical research.

Visions Unrealized

Feinstein's principles of clinical epidemiology—the valid and reliable characterization of patients' clinical findings, diagnoses, and prognostic subclasses—have been widely applied in clinical research and have resulted in major improvements in the quality of such research. But his vision has not been realized that those same principles would be vigorously applied in the care of individual patients and lead to significant improvements in the everyday practice of medicine. And while the papers published in the Rational Clinical Examination Series increased attention to the challenges of physical diagnosis, Sackett's concerns about the poor state of the literature on physical diagnosis go unmitigated. For example, a 2010 article in this series investigated the utility of the history and physical exam in evaluating whether a patient's lower extremity pain was due to lumbar spinal stenosis, the most common indication for spinal surgery in patients older than 65 years of age.[16] A comprehensive search of electronic databases for published papers on physical diagnosis of this disorder uncovered only four articles of high enough quality to meet the authors' inclusion criteria—this for a condition that leads to 174,000 back operations per year among elderly Medicare beneficiaries, at a cost of over $44,000 per operation.[17]

Why has so little progress been made in improving the validity and reliability of the history and physical exam performed in routine clinical practice? The most likely explanation is that the explosive advances in diagnostic imaging seen over the past 40 years, and the ease of access and lucrative returns of using such imaging, have made the humble maneuvers of the physical exam seem quaint if not outmoded. Many physicians take the cynical but expedient view, a view that is technologically intensive and costly, that simply proceeding to testing is easier than trying to improve the accuracy of their history-taking and physical diagnosis skills.

There are several reasons why we should care about this. The first answer has to do with delayed, missed, and erroneous diagnoses. Accurate or not, the history and physical exam are the dominant determinants of the subsequent evaluation of the patient. If the physician's evaluation fails to detect the clues that a certain disease is present, the physician will fail to send that patient for the relevant confirmatory testing. Likewise, if the physician over- or misinterprets findings on the initial history and physical exam (or fails to perform key elements of the exam), the patient will be sent for unnecessary tests, increasing the costs of care as well as the potential for complications related to the testing itself. In both cases, the delay in making the right diagnosis means a delay in devising an appropriate treatment plan.

The second reason we should care is that diagnostic misclassification is a formidable limitation to the use of medical records data for comparative effectiveness research, as is the failure to capture accurate data on other factors that influence clinical outcomes. When data are swept from hardcopy or electronic medical records for use in research, there is no recourse but to assume they are accurate, even though we know they are not. If the large volume of data collected in the settings of everyday practice is ever to inform what works best in medical care, nothing is more critical than standardizing the collection of data from individual patients.

A resurrection of interest in Feinstein's principles of clinical epidemiology and their actual implementation are mandatory if the promise held out by the electronic medical record for comparative effectiveness research is to be fulfilled. Writing about the use of such data shortly after Americans were transfixed by the 112-day voyage of a New York City garbage barge sailing from port to port seeking one willing to accept its cargo, Feinstein cautioned, "Like the garbage barges of modern technological society, data barges do not contain garbage alone. In a garbage barge, some of the material may be unused and often quite valuable if retrieved in its original status; other material can readily be converted into useful forms of landfill or fertilizer; but much of it is garbage that cannot be otherwise redeemed. In the era of computerized data barges, the main challenge... is to distinguish between a valuable scientific retrieval or transformation, and an elaborate statistical processing of garbage."[18]

The Doctor as User of Scientific Literature: The Other Half of Clinical Epidemiology

Early in his career Sackett realized, as many physicians do, that the explosion of the volume of medical literature means that the average clinician, year over year, falls further and further behind in keeping current. To help practicing clinicians keep up with the literature, Sackett developed what is now called critical appraisal of the literature, launching it in 1981 with a series of five articles called "Clinical Epidemiology Rounds" in the *Canadian Medical Association Journal*. This series brought immediate recognition to Sackett and his Department of Clinical Epidemiology and Biostatistics at McMaster University.

Critical appraisal is based upon the principles of applicability and validity. In Sackett's method, the reader applies two filters. First, using a set of four screening questions,[19] the reader can quickly scan and discard a sizable majority of journal articles because they are not applicable to the reader's clinical practice. To the papers that remain the reader applies the second filter. This second step requires a more in-depth reading and the systematic application of the rules of evidence to assess the degree to which the findings are valid and free of bias. Because study designs vary based on the nature of the research questions they address, criteria for validity differ as well. The 1981 series covered research papers addressing four types of clinical questions: those to find out whether to use a new diagnostic test on patients, those to learn the clinical course or prognosis of a disorder, those to determine etiology or causation, and those to distinguish useful from useless or even harmful therapy. The questions the reader applies to assess internal validity differ by the type of article. To illustrate, Table 5.1 gives the internal validity questions for distinguishing useful from useless or harmful therapies.

In the early 1990s the McMaster Clinical Epidemiology group realized that the purpose of critical appraisal needed fundamental redirection. That redirection was apparent in the series of Users' Guides to the Medical Literature launched in 1993 in the *Journal of the American Medical Association*. The Readers' Guides provided a way to stay abreast with the medical literature to avoid falling short in clinical practice, but the Users' Guides provided a way to bring valid evidence to bear on a current clinical problem of a specific patient. Critical appraisal had matured into evidence-based medicine. This new paradigm for medical practice was described by the McMaster group as one that "de-emphasizes intuition, unsystematic clinical experience, and pathophysiologic rationale as sufficient grounds for clinical decision making and stresses the examination of evidence from clinical research."[20]

Within 7 years of its 1993 launch in the *Journal of the American Medical Association*, the Users' Guides series had examined 25 topical areas of clinical research with 33 separate articles. These 33 Users' Guides became the basis for a book written in a lively, accessible style, *Users' Guides to the Medical Literature*, first published in 2002.[21]

The McMasters group and others have developed strategies that practicing physicians need to critically appraise the medical literature and apply it to their patients. But many physicians, if not most, find the learning and application of these competencies to be a formidable prospect. A review of the formal steps of evidence-based practice shows why.

The first step is to identify the problem of the patient that needs to be addressed and develop a precise, structured, and answerable question that will be used to guide the literature search. The second is to conduct an efficient literature search and identify the most relevant articles to address the question.

Table 5.1 **Guiding Questions a Reader Can Apply to a Research Report to Distinguish Useful from Useless or Harmful Therapy**

1. Was the assignment of patients to treatments really randomized?
2. Were all clinically relevant outcomes reported?
3. Were the study patients recognizably similar to your own?
4. Were both statistical and clinical significance considered?
5. Is the therapeutic maneuver feasible in your practice?
6. Were all patients who entered the study accounted for at its conclusion?

Source: From Sackett DL. How to read clinical journals: V: to distinguish useful from useless or even harmful therapy. CMAJ *1981*;124:1156–62.

The third is to read and critically appraise this literature and assess its validity (closeness to the truth), impact (size of benefit or harm or other effect), and applicability (similarity of the patient at hand to those who were studied in the reports). The final step is to evaluate whether the findings from the literature review should be applied to the patient at hand given their unique biological state and their values and preferences.

Some of these steps are more difficult to learn than others, but each one requires practitioners to acquire new competencies, and each one is time consuming. How is it possible that a busy practitioner, who sees anywhere from 15 to over 40 patients in a typical day at the office, could adhere to the ideal of evidence-based clinical practice? Luckily, for many clinical questions, current clinical literature has already been searched for, found, appraised, and synthesized. Most proponents of evidence-based clinical practice advise the searcher not to start with primary articles, but rather to search for syntheses that have already been done. The development of approaches to performing what are called "systematic reviews" of the literature has been a major advance in helping clinical practice become more evidence based.

Synthesizing Evidence from Clinical Research: Archie Cochrane and Iain Chalmers

Archibald L. Cochrane (1909–1988) was the major proponent of the idea—an idea which seems self-evident now—that therapeutic interventions should be rigorously tested and known to be effective before they become part of the clinical armamentarium. A deeply held skepticism of medical practices based on belief rather than evidence was bred in him by his experiences in medical school and as a prisoner of war.

Cochrane, born in Scotland, started his medical studies at University College London in 1934 and qualified as a doctor in March 1938. Cochrane served from 1940 to 1945 as Captain in the Royal Army Medical Corps. He was taken prisoner in Crete on June 1, 1941, and spent 4 years in captivity. As he recounted in his landmark 1972 book, *Effectiveness and Efficiency: Random Reflections on Health Services*,[22] many of his thoughts about the value of medical interventions, or the lack thereof, were born during experiences he had as a prisoner of war. For example, he recalls, "The first experience was in the Dulag at Salonika where I spent six months. I was usually the senior medical officer and for a considerable time...the only doctor...There were about 20,000 POWs in the camp...The diet was about 600 calories a day and we all had diarrhea. In addition we had severe epidemics of typhoid, diphtheria, infections, jaundice, and sand-fly fever, with more than 300 cases of 'pitting oedema above the knee.' To cope with this we had a ramshackle hospital, some aspirin, some antacids, and some skin antiseptic...I expected hundreds to die of diphtheria alone in the absence of specific therapy. In point of fact there were only four deaths, of which three were due to gunshot wounds inflicted by the Germans. This excellent result had, of course, nothing to do with the therapy they received or my clinical skill. It demonstrated, on the other hand, very clearly the relative unimportance of therapy in comparison with the recuperative power of the human body."

After his release from the Royal Army Medical Corps, Cochrane returned to London and began his career as an epidemiologist, studying environmental lung diseases and tuberculosis. During a Rockefeller fellowship in preventive medicine at the London School of Hygiene and Tropical Medicine, Cochrane learned statistics from Austin Bradford Hill, the statistician credited with establishing the randomized clinical trial as the definitive test of the efficacy of an intervention. Bradford Hill was a major influence on Cochrane's arguments for the rigorous testing of medical interventions using the randomized trial design.

With his growing reputation as an epidemiologist, his advocacy for scientific rigor in medicine, and his intensifying concerns about the ever-increasing expenditures in the U.K.'s National Health Service (NHS), in 1971 Cochrane was awarded a Rock Carling Fellowship by the Nuffield Provincial Hospitals Trust to write a monograph evaluating the NHS. The book, the previously mentioned *Effectiveness and Efficiency* book, won him international renown. It focused on three issues in evaluating health care or a health care system: effectiveness, efficiency, and equity. Cochrane's legacy derives largely from his strong arguments that clinical therapeutics should have a basis in evidence. He argued that a treatment should not be considered effective until it is proven to cause more good than harm, preferably by way of a randomized trial to ensure that bias was limited as much as possible.

Seven years after his book appeared, Cochrane opened a new front when he noted, "It is surely a great criticism of our profession that we have not organized a critical summary, by specialty or subspecialty, adapted periodically, of all relevant randomized trials."[23] In the same essay he criticized the specialty of obstetrics as having done the least of all in basing its care on good scientific evidence. A young obstetrician, Iain Chalmers (1943-) would later take up Cochrane's challenge and bring into being what are now called systematic reviews.

Iain Chalmers[24] received his medical training at the Middlesex Hospital Medical School, qualifying for medicine in the mid-1960s. Upon graduation he went to Gaza and practiced in poorly funded settings, less extreme than those experienced by Cochrane in internment camps, but very resource poor in the way of antibiotics and other critical supplies. Chalmers's experiences during this time made him realize the limits of his knowledge and the devastating effects errors in clinical judgment could have.

In the early 1970s Chalmers returned to the United Kingdom and undertook training in obstetrics, during which he saw firsthand the degree to which practices could vary among the experts in his field. This prompted him to undertake a study comparing the outcomes of two groups of pregnant women, one cared for by an obstetrician who was more of an interventionist, and the other cared for by a more conservative obstetrician. Chalmers was unable to demonstrate any differences in the outcomes between the two sets of women and their babies. However, recognizing that the two groups of women varied on factors other than just the type of care they received that could have influenced outcomes, he did a second study on a subset of patients from each practice who were similar to each other. Again, he found no difference in outcomes.

Conducting these studies taught Chalmers the importance of bias and the difficulty in limiting it. Shortly afterward he became aware of Cochrane's *Effectiveness and Efficiency* book. Chalmers describes his experience in reading the book as "being given a compass in the jungle." In reflecting on his medical education, Chalmers notes: "I had managed to be let loose on the public as a medical graduate without having any conscious recognition of these terms [epidemiology, randomized trial] and what they implied. That is a pretty damning comment on me and on the education system to which I was exposed."

Unfortunately, even today, most U.S. medical schools fall far behind in educating doctors-in-training in the principles of epidemiology and study design, and the need for skepticism about therapeutic interventions not put to rigorous tests in randomized trials.

In the early 1970s Chalmers met Archie Cochrane and, inspired by the man and his book, took up his challenge. Chalmers's initial work that more intense and thus more expensive obstetric care did not lead to different outcomes compared with less intense and less costly care had drawn the attention of physician organizations. At the same time, patient advocacy groups were appealing for improved perinatal care. Thus, in 1978 the National Perinatal Epidemiology Unit was established at the University of Oxford, and Chalmers was appointed its first director. The Unit's first effort was to build a register of randomized trials of perinatal care. In 1979 Chalmers published his first systematic review, a review of randomized trials of fetal monitoring.

In building the trial registry, Chalmers saw immediately that the methods used to identify trials, if incomplete, could potentially lead to bias in the estimation of the effect of an intervention. For that reason, to identify relevant trials he and his colleagues not only searched the major electronic reference databases but also hand-searched the references listed in each article to identify any additional trials. The product of this enormous effort was the publication in 1985 of *A Classified Bibliography of Controlled Trials in Perinatal Medicine 1940–1984.*[25]

Chalmers knew that, despite his attempts to identify all published trials, this bibliography was incomplete because it did not include the results of trials that were never reported. Trialists and editors are more likely to report and publish the results of trials with positive results rather than those with equivocal or negative findings; this publication bias therefore leads to inflated estimates of the effect of a treatment. In subsequent updates of The Oxford Database of Perinatal Trials (the electronic version is regularly updated), Chalmers attempted to correct the publication bias by doing an international survey of pediatricians to uncover unpublished trials.

Another problem with the database was that it was a catalogue of the trials. It did not summarize their findings. The task of going from the identified articles to summaries of the findings was left to the individual physician. Chalmers knew that if the database was to alter practice, the information contained in the trials had to be readily accessible to the practicing physician. He and colleagues set out to create what are called systematic reviews.

The review article, summarizing information on a medical topic, is a time-honored type of publication, but because authors could choose what research to include and what to ignore, is variably, and to an unknown extent, influenced by bias. Chalmers thought that the review should be systematic. He thought that a review ought to be held to the same standards as other kinds of research: "As in any scientific endeavor, people are required to describe what it is they set out to do, what methods and materials they used to do it, how they made sense of the data they collected in terms of their analysis, and then what they concluded: what did it all mean?"

In 1985 Chalmers began to assemble an international group to assist with the production of the systematic reviews of relevant topics. In 1989 the massive *Effective Care in Pregnancy and Childbirth* was published by Oxford University Press. *Effective Care of the Newborn* was published 2 years later. These publications were the first texts to recommend what care should be provided based on systematic reviews of randomized trials.

Writing in 1987 about the anticipated *Effective Care in Pregnancy and Childbirth* book, Archie Cochrane called it "a real milestone in the history of randomized trials and in the evaluation of care" and suggested that other specialties should follow suit. He also said, "I now have no hesitation whatsoever in withdrawing the slur of the wooden spoon from obstetrics and I feel honored by being associated, even in an indirect way, with such an important publication."

Cochrane did not live to see it—he died in 1988—but his hope that other specialties would take up the practice of summarizing randomized trials was soon realized.

The Cochrane Center and the Cochrane Collaboration

Effective Care in Pregnancy and Childbirth was widely acclaimed by women, international health policy organizations, and health policy makers in the

United Kingdom and provided impetus for the establishment of an entity to realize Cochrane's dream of "critical summary, by specialty or subspecialty, adapted periodically, of all relevant randomized controlled trials." In 1992 the National Health Service awarded funds, and the Cochrane Centre opened at the University of Oxford in October under the direction of Iain Chalmers.

One of the Cochrane Centre's first efforts was to foster the development of similar centers in other countries for international collaboration. Within the first five years, Cochrane Centers opened in Canada, the United States (Baltimore, San Francisco, San Antonio, and New England), Denmark, Australia, Italy, the Netherlands, France, Brazil, South Africa, Germany, and Spain.

Cochrane Centers[26] function primarily as coordinating centers to support and facilitate the activities of specific Collaborative Review Groups, which are the entities that actually conduct and update the systematic reviews. The Centers maintain registries of individuals interested in specific health areas and facilitate the organization of Collaborative Review Groups, and they provide workshops to train reviewers. They also assist with the ongoing work of building and maintaining the databases that are the major products of the international effort, namely the Cochrane Database of Systematic Reviews and the Cochrane Central Register of Controlled Trials, which together are known as the Cochrane Library. The Cochrane Central Register of Controlled Trials is a catalogue of controlled trials that is built from comprehensive searches of other electronic databases and supplemented by hand searches of over 1,000 journals worldwide. This Register serves as the source of trials that are reviewed by the Collaborative Review Groups when they conduct systematic reviews.

The work of the Collaborative Review Groups is done predominantly by scientists who volunteer their time. Individuals interested in a topic, under the guidance of a Center, form a Review Group. Over the first few years, a diverse set of disease-based Review Groups were formed, including Review Groups in stroke, musculoskeletal diseases, infectious disease, schizophrenia, and so on. Other registered Review Groups focus on areas of heath care such as primary health care, complementary health care, health promotion, and health care of older people. Still other Review Groups focus on research methods, such as the statistics and quality of randomized controlled trials, individual patient data meta-analysis, and informatics methods.

The Cochrane review process is highly structured. Before a Review Group undertakes a systematic review of a specific condition or topic, the authors must submit a detailed plan outlining the questions they wish to address and the plan for analysis. This plan undergoes initial review by experts both in the disease area of focus and methodologists as well as ongoing review as the work proceeds, in order to ensure that the systematic review meets the high standards set for Cochrane Reviews. Contingent upon successful peer review, the final product is published in the Cochrane Database of Systematic Reviews.

Reviews are added to the Cochrane Database of Systematic Reviews at the rate of about 300 per year.[27] As of March 2011, the Database contained 4,574 Cochrane Systematic Reviews, and the Cochrane Library indicated that 2,006 review protocols were in progress.[28] Considering the enormous effect that the availability of accurate summary information from clinical trials could have on improving patient care, Naylor, writing in the *Lancet* in 1995, noted: "The Cochrane Collaboration is an enterprise that rivals the Human Genome Project in its potential implications for modern medicine."[29] More recently, during the debates before the passage of health care reform in general and federal mandates for comparative effectiveness research in particular, the Cochrane Collaboration received attention from the highest political levels in the United States. In the *New York Times* in October 2008, Billy Beane (of Moneyball fame), Newt Gingrich, and John Kerry said, "A health care system that is driven by robust comparative clinical evidence will save lives and money. One success story is [the] Cochrane Collaboration."[30]

Challenges Facing the Cochrane Collaboration

The greatest thing about the Cochrane Collaboration is the ideal for which it strives, that all clinical specialties should have easy access to accurate summaries of the findings of randomized clinical trials to guide their everyday practice. The effort is well on its way, but challenges continue to arise. The most serious is funding. Since its beginning, the Cochrane Collaboration has been able to obtain only limited funding, approximately half of which comes from UK governmental entities. Some funds are provided to the Centers and the Collaborative Review Groups, but many are struggling to survive and some have disbanded. The French Centre closed in 2002, though it did reopen in 2010, and two of the U.S. Centers, San Antonio and New England, have closed. The worsening financial situation for U.S. academic institutions over the last several years is adding increasing hardship, making it more difficult for scientists to volunteer their time for reviews.

Another challenge is gaps in the coverage of topics by systematic reviews. The volunteer structure of the Cochrane Collaboration means that the enthusiasm of individuals greatly influences the choice of topics to be reviewed. This has led to duplication, overlap, and wasted effort. Unfortunately, the gaps are not of arcane or rare health conditions. Some very important areas of health care have few if any reviews. Take, for example, heart conditions of high impact and/or high prevalence. In the March 2011 catalogue of the Cochrane Library, 365 systematic reviews are listed under the topic "heart and circulation."[31] However, when this is explored, only two reviews are listed under the topic "valvular heart disease," one on the use of anti-platelet drugs and anticoagulation for patients with prosthetic heart valves, and the other on the closely related topic "self-monitoring and self-management of oral anticoagulation," leaving numerous and complex therapeutic issues in the care of these patients unaddressed. A similar picture holds for the number of reviews that guide therapeutic interventions in people with congestive heart failure. Because of its high prevalence and high morbidity and mortality (heart failure is the number-one cause of hospitalization in U.S. Medicare beneficiaries over age 65), one would expect a full slate of reviews addressing all the important therapeutic decisions that physicians need to make to maximize cardiac function in these patients, thus limiting symptoms, maximizing quality of life, and reducing hospitalizations. However, only 18 of the 365 heart and circulation reviews address any issue in heart failure.

Beyond Cochrane Reviews of Randomized Trials: Other Evidence Syntheses

An increasing number of efforts have been undertaken to make clinical evidence more accessible to physicians. For example, searches of PubMed, an electronic reference database, can be restricted to retrieve only systematic reviews. Readers not qualified to judge the adequacy of systematic reviews on their own can access the free Database of Abstracts of Reviews of Effects (DARE), a database of abstracts of systematic reviews whose quality has been assessed.[32]

Other sources of systematic reviews exist besides the Cochrane Collaboration. A U.S. source of high-quality systematic reviews is the Effective Health Care Program of the Agency for Healthcare Research and Quality of the U.S. Department of Health and Human Services. As of August 2011, the Effective Health Care Program had listed on its Web site[33] 32 final research reviews on such diverse topics as "Comparative effectiveness of non-operative and operative treatments for rotator cuff tears," and "Comparative effectiveness of therapies for children with autism spectrum disorders." In addition, the professional medical press has launched print and/or online journals (e.g., the bimonthly *ACP Journal Club*) or books (e.g., BMJ Publishing Group's Clinical Evidence) that identify high-quality systematic reviews as well as high-quality individual articles and present short reviews or synopses of them for the busy reader. Because only about 1 in 150 articles in the peer-reviewed literature is deemed of high enough relevance and quality to be included, the summary journals are real timesavers for physicians. "Clinical Evidence" does not make specific recommendations about clinical care, leaving that up to physicians' judgment. The regularly updated *Physicians' Information and Education Resources* (PIER) textbook,[34] a product of the American College of Physicians, evaluates and summarizes available evidence and does make clinical practice recommendations.

From Systematic Reviews of Evidence
to Clinical Practice Guidelines

In the preceding sentence we used the term "recommendations for clinical practice." These practice guidelines are the last plank of some syntheses of best medical evidence. When based on high-quality evidence, such guidelines embody what might be called the standard of care, that is, the expectations for how the judicious and well-informed physician would approach a specific patient-care question. David Eddy was one of the leaders who moved guidelines from being based on the opinions of experts to being based on best evidence.[35]

The American Cancer Society assumed a leadership role in guideline development in 1980 when it set forth to develop guidelines for the care of people with cancer. Now many professional bodies produce evidence-based guidelines for physicians and patients. To make clinical practice guidelines more accessible, the Agency for Healthcare Research and Quality, the American Medical Association, and the American Association of Health Plans (now America's Health Insurance Plans) collaborated to create the National Guidelines Clearinghouse.[36]

The methodological standards for producing clinical practice guidelines are similar to those for producing a rigorous systematic review. First, a systematic strategy for searching the medical literature is developed and applied, with the intent of uncovering all the relevant evidence. Then, each piece of the evidence is critically appraised as to its quality and probable validity. Finally, all the evidence is summarized and synthesized. But here is where the paths diverge. The authors of a systematic review, if they determine that the existing evidence is of poor quality, can say so and stop at that point. With a systematic review, there is no obligation to guide practice with the "best" evidence if in fact the evidence is irredeemable. This is not true for clinical practice guidelines, which, if they are to fulfill their intended purpose of guiding clinical practice, must make recommendations for best practice regardless of how bad the best evidence is. In addition, practitioners attempting to apply the recommendations must be able to distinguish those based on high-quality evidence from those based on low-quality or no evidence.

Many groups have developed systems to grade the evidential strength of recommendations. One widely used and internationally endorsed grading system is GRADE, which stands for the Grading of Recommendations, Assessment, Development and Evaluation.[37] In 2011, the *Journal of Clinical Epidemiology* launched a 20-part series on how to apply the GRADE methodology in systematic reviews, technology assessments, and the creation of practice guidelines.[38] The lead author of the first paper in the series is Gordon Guyatt, the individual who coined the term "evidence-based medicine" in 1990.

Conflicts of Interest in Creation of Clinical Practice Guidelines

One threat to the validity of clinical practice guidelines is gaps in the coverage of clinical questions by randomized trials. Another threat is conflict of interest. Many physicians and most physician organizations—the parties who create and issue guidelines—have financial relationships of one sort or another to industry. Because guidelines drive the use (or non-use) of prescription drugs, devices, testing, and other medical technologies that are revenue generators for their makers and sellers, real or apparent conflicts of interest may lead individuals, consciously or unconsciously, to create guidelines that ignore or manipulate the evidence (when it exists) in order to favor a company's product.

The problem is pervasive. A study of the 17 most recent sets of guidelines issued by the American Heart Association and American College of Cardiology found that, of the 498 individuals who participated in the guideline development process, 56% disclosed one or more relationships with industry, such as serving on a company advisory board, receiving a research grant from industry, receiving speakers' honoraria, or owning stock.[39] Over 500 different companies were involved. This study adds to a mounting body of literature documenting a high level of real or potential compromise of practice guidelines resulting from conflicts of interest.[40]

But do the financial conflicts of interest of guideline developers and industry funding for guideline development lead to the production of guidelines that favor the use of an industry product over and above what the evidence indicates is justifiable? Two examples show that such conflicts of interest can indeed compromise the integrity of the guideline development process.

The first example is that of the biological agent recombinant human activated protein C, also known as drotrecogin alfa [activated], brand name Xigris™. This agent was developed by Eli Lilly, Inc., and was approved by the Food and Drug Administration (FDA) in 2001 for the reduction of mortality in adult patients with severe sepsis who have a high risk of death. (Sepsis is a highly fatal condition caused by bloodstream infection; severe sepsis is sepsis associated with organ dysfunction.) The approval, which was based on the results of one randomized trial that had methodological shortcomings, was contingent upon the manufacturer's agreement to perform further trials to confirm the efficacy and safety of the drug. A 2006 paper in the *New England Journal of Medicine* by Eichacker et al. revealed what Lilly did to increase sales of Xigris™.[41] Disappointed by the initially poor sales of the drug—one dose of which cost about $10,000, and there was scientific controversy about how the drug actually worked in the human body and how it had been tested[42]—the manufacturer engaged a marketing firm, which in turn developed a multi-pronged strategy to boost sales.

One strategy was to raise claims in the popular media that rationing was going on in intensive care units around the country. Another strategy was the "surviving sepsis campaign," an international effort to develop and implement a bundle of clinical practice guidelines for the treatment of patients with sepsis. The administration of Xigris™ was part of the bundle. Eli Lilly funded over 90% of the first two phases of the campaign and much of the third, and many of the experts involved in the campaign and in the development of the guidelines and performance measures had financial ties to Lilly. The "surviving sepsis" guidelines and performance measures that pertained to the use of Xigris™ ignored emerging safety concerns—use of the drug was associated with increases in the risks of serious hemorrhage—and led to overblown impressions of the drug's efficacy. There was also an indication of editorial suppression of information that a professional society had refused to endorse the guidelines because of how they were developed and who paid for them. Lilly voluntarily removed Xigris™ from the worldwide market in October 2011 after a placebo-controlled trial in patients with severe sepsis or septic shock showed the drug did not confer any survival benefit.

The second example is provided by clinical practice guidelines for the treatment of anemia with erythropoietin, a biologic agent, in people with chronic renal failure. Epoetin alfa was approved by the FDA in 1989 for the treatment of anemia associated with chronic kidney disease. The two companies that market an FDA-approved epoetin product in the United States are Amgen (Epogen®, epoetin alfa; Aranesp, darbepoetin alfa) and Ortho Biotech (Procrit®, epoetin alfa). The cost for a year of treatment with these agents ranges from about $4,000 to over $10,000. In 2006, the National Kidney Foundation's Kidney Disease Outcomes Quality Initiative (KDOQI) changed its clinical practice guidelines to say that the hemoglobin level of an individual with chronic kidney disease should be maintained between 11 and 13 g/dL instead of between the target of 11 and 12 g/dL it set in 2000. A higher hemoglobin target translates into a higher use of epoetin products. The guidelines were changed without the benefit of randomized trial evidence indicating the higher target was beneficial and safe.[43] In a commentary published in Lancet,[44] Robert Steinbrook pointed out that in 2005, the National Kidney Foundation received 57% of its total funding from corporate and organizational support; $4.1 million came from Amgen and $3.6 million from Ortho Biotech. Amgen supported the development of the anemia guidelines, and of the 18 panelists who developed the guidelines, two-thirds had financial ties to Amgen or other epoetin makers or sellers. After several randomized trials were reported showing that higher hemoglobin levels harmed rather than helped people with chronic kidney disease, the KDOQI revised its hemoglobin targets downward. The anemia guidelines story is further complicated by the way in which physicians and dialysis centers were reimbursed at the time by the Centers for Medicare and Medicaid Services for administering epoetin products to Medicare and Medicaid beneficiaries—the more epo, the more dollars.

Conclusions

The mandates of the 2000s for comparative effectiveness research will increase the amount of evidence available on the interventions that lead to desirable health outcomes. In this chapter, among other things, we described how massive amounts of published clinical research are transformed into vehicles that, it is hoped, can and will inform the routine care of patients. This begs the question, "To what extent does contemporary clinical practice conform with evidence-based clinical practice guidelines?" The short answer is, we have a long way to go. As we will see in Chapters 11 and 12, this will be true until the pressures and incentives in American medicine are aligned for the provision of care that is in line with evidence-based clinical guidelines.

Notes

1. Sackett DL, Rosenberg WMC, Gray JAM, Haynes RB, Richardson WS. Evidence based medicine: what it is and what it isn't. BMJ 1996;312:71.
2. Guyatt G, Rennie D, Meade MO, Cook DJ. Users' guides to the medical literature: a manual for evidence-based clinical practice. 2nd ed. New York: McGraw Hill, 2008.
3. Daly J. Evidence-based medicine and the search for a science of clinical care. Berkeley, CA: University of California Press, 2005. We acknowledge this book as a source of the much of the information we present in this chapter.
4. Straus SE, McAlister FA. Evidence-based medicine: a commentary on common criticisms. CMAJ 2000;163:837–41. Rosenberg W, Donald A. Evidence based medicine: an approach to clinical problem-solving. BMJ 1995;310:1122–7. Wyer PC, Silva SA. Where is the wisdom? I- a conceptual history of evidence-based medicine. J Eval Clin Pract 2009;15:891–8.
5. Acute rheumatic fever is a serious illness associated with group A streptococcal infections. It is far less common now in industrialized nations than in the mid-20th century, but it is still a major problem in poorer countries. It attacks mostly children aged 5–15 years as well as young adults. It attacks the joints, the heart, the nervous system, and the skin and subcutaneous tissues and can cause irreversible damage to heart valves, especially the mitral valve. There is no specific laboratory test that confirms the diagnosis. The diagnosis is a clinical one that rests on evidence of a recent streptococcal infection and the presence of major criteria (signs and symptoms of carditis, migratory polyarthritis, Sydenham's chorea, subcutaneous nodules, and erythema marginatum) and several nonspecific minor criteria.
6. The story is recounted by Feinstein in the preface to his 1967 book. Feinstein AR. Clinical judgment. Baltimore: Williams and Wilkins Co, 1967.
7. Feinstein AR. Scientific methodology in clinical medicine. I. Introduction, principles, and concepts. Ann Intern Med 1964;61:564–79. Feinstein AR. Scientific methodology in clinical medicine. II Classification of human disease by clinical behavior. Ann Intern Med 1964;61:757–81. Feinstein AR. Scientific methodology in clinical medicine. III. The evaluation of therapeutic response. Ann Intern Med 1964;61:944–65. Feinstein AR. Scientific methodology in clinical medicine. IV. Acquisition of clinical data. Ann Intern Med 1964;61;1162–93.

8. Feinstein AR. Clinical judgment. Baltimore: Williams and Wilkins Co, 1967.

9. Paul JR. President's Address: Clinical epidemiology. J Clin Invest 1938;17:539–41.

10. Feinstein AR. Clinical epidemiology. I. The populational experiments of nature and of man in human illness. Ann Intern Med 1968;69:807–20. Feinstein AR. Clinical epidemiology II. The identification rates of disease. Ann Intern Med 1968;69:1037–61. Feinstein AR. Clinical epidemiology. III. The clinical design of statistics in therapy. Ann Intern Med 1968;69:1287–312.

11. Feinstein AR. Boolean algebra and clinical taxonomy. I. Analytic synthesis of the general spectrum of human disease. N Engl J Med 1963;269:929–38.

12. Feinstein and Sackett had very different personalities. About a discussion he had with Feinstein, Sackett wrote, "And we got into a big fight, as everyone does who works with Alvan." Sackett also described letters and conversations with Feinstein as "often by no means cordial." In her book on the history of evidence-based medicine, Jeanne Daly says (see page 35 of reference in note 3), "Feinstein's contribution to clinical epidemiology cannot be doubted. It took a person with his caustic turn of phrase to attack the citadels of clinical research. Perhaps this same critical capacity meant that he did not go into team research to the extent that the researchers at McMaster University did—and which they see as crucial to their success. Instead he became the critical overseer of the discipline, its respected but feared gadfly. His criticisms could be devastating." But not everyone had this same experience of Feinstein. In an obituary of Feinstein, one of his oldest and best friends described him thus: "brilliant, articulate, erudite, incisive, original, witty, entertaining, engaging, charming, flamboyant, irreverent, iconoclastic. When called for outrageous. Others traits may have been less obvious, but were apparent to those who knew him well: warm, caring, concerned, empathic, generous, loyal, devoted, loving." As for Sackett, Brian Haynes, a student of Sackett who then became a close colleague, said that Sackett never ceased trying to surprise people: "He would wear jeans to an important meeting or a tuxedo to an informal meeting. He likes to shake up people's perception of the way the world is run. He really never lost the kid inside." Of himself, Sackett says, "My accomplishments are people. I don't care what I've given to medicine as a profession. If you look at what happens to people who focus only on their contributions, for example, identifying the issue or showing how this mechanism works or illustrating this principle, such an identity is good for three to five years. So many great people, especially towards the end of their careers, have destroyed themselves trying to make their one discovery their immortality. The way I try to achieve immortality is through the young people who have come to work with me. Those people are now teaching other people who will teach other people who will teach other people. That is immortality."

13. Sackett DL. Clinical epidemiology. Am J Epidem 1969;89:125–8.

14. The paper that introduced the series was: Sackett DL, Rennie D. The science of the art of the clinical examination. JAMA 1992;267:2650–2. JAMA's Rational Clinical Examination Series continues in 2012.

15. The evolution of Feinstein's thinking can be traced by reading his three books, now classics: Feinstein AR. Clinical judgment. Baltimore: Williams and Wilkins Co, 1967. Feinstein AR. Clinical epidemiology: the architecture of clinical research. Philadelphia, PA: WB Saunders Co., 1985. Feinstein AR. Clinimetrics. New Haven, CT: Yale University Press, 1987.

16. Suri P, Rainville J, Kalichman L, Katz JN. Does this older adult with lower extremity pain have the clinical syndrome of lumbar spinal stenosis? JAMA 2010;304:2628–36.

17. Data for 2007. In 2007, roughly 37 million people over age 65 were enrolled in Part A Medicare. Dartmouth Atlas data indicate that in 2007, the rate of back surgeries was 4.7 per 1,000 Medicare beneficiaries over age 65. According to http://www.health-carebluebook.com, accessed September 27, 2012, the average price for a lumbar spinal fusion operation (an operation commonly performed for spinal stenosis, the other being lumbar decompression) was $44,220.

18. Feinstein AR. Para-analysis, *Faute de mieux*, and the perils of riding on a data barge. J Clin Epidem 1989;42:929–35.
19. Sackett DL. How to read clinical journals: I. Why to read them and how to start reading them critically. CMAJ 1981;124:555–8.
20. Evidence-Based Medicine Working Group. Evidence-based medicine: a new approach to teaching the practice of medicine. JAMA 1992;268:2420–5.
21. Guyatt G, Rennie D, Evidence-Based Medicine Working Group. Users' guides to the medical literature: essentials of evidence-based clinical practice. Chicago, IL: AMA Press, 2002.
22. The book was originally published in 1972. It has been reissued. Cochrane AL. Effectiveness and efficiency: random reflections on health services. London: Royal Society Press Ltd., 1999.
23. Cochrane AL. 1931–1971: A critical review, with particular reference to the medical profession. In: Medicines for the year 2000. London: Office of Health Economics;1979:1–11.
24. Much of the information about Cochrane and Chalmers, and many of their quotations, are from: Daly J. Evidence-based medicine and the search for a science of clinical care. Berkeley, CA: University of California Press, 2005.
25. This book was published by Oxford University Press.
26. See http://www.cochrane.org.
27. Information from http://www.cochrane-net.org/openlearning/html/mod2–2.htm.
28. Accessed September 27, 2012, at http://www.thecochranelibrary.com/view/0/AboutTheCochraneLibrary.html#ABOUT.
29. Naylor CD. Grey zones of clinical practice: some limits to evidence-based medicine. Lancet 1995;345:840–2.
30. Beane B, Gringich N, Kerry J. How to take American health care from worst to first. New York Times 2008 Oct 24. (Accessed November 9, 2012, at www.nytimes.com/2008/10/24/opinion/24beane.html?_r+0.)
31. The contents of the Cochrane Library can be found at http://www.thecochranelibrary.com/view/0/index.html.
32. DARE is a free product of the U.K. National Health Service Centre for Reviews and Dissemination at the University of York. Information is available from http://www.crd.york.ac.uk/CRDWeb/AboutDare.asp.
33. See http://www.effectivehealthcare.ahrq.gov/index.cfm, accessed September 27, 2012.
34. PIER's disease-based modules are the primary sources for guidance for clinical practice; each provides relevant guidance statements and practice recommendations, all of which are all rated for the strength of the underlying evidence that supports them.
35. Eddy DM. Clinical policies and the quality of clinical practice. N Engl J Med 1982;307:343–7.
36. Information about the National Guideline Clearinghouse is available from http://www.guideline.gov.
37. Information about the GRADE Working Group is available from http://www.gradeworkinggroup.org/index.htm.
38. Guyatt GH, Oxman AD, Schunemann HJ, Tugwell P, Knotterus A. GRADE guidelines: a new series of articles in the Journal of Clinical Epidemiology. J Clin Epidem 2010;64:380–2.
39. Mendelson TB, Meltzer M, Campbell EG, Caplan AL, Kirkpatrick JN. Conflicts of interest in cardiovascular clinical practice guidelines. Arch Intern Med 2011;171:577–84.
40. See, e.g., Choudry NK, Stelfox HT, Detsky AS. Relationships between authors of clinical practice guidelines and the pharmaceutical industry. JAMA 2002; 28:612–7, Campbell EG, Weissman JS, Erlinghaus S, et al. Institutional academic-industry relationships. JAMA 2007;298:1779–86, and Holloway RG, Mooney CJ, Getchuis TS, Edlund WS, Miyasaki JO. Conflicts of interest for authors of American Academy of Neurology clinical practice guidelines [invited article]. Neurology 2008;71:57–63.
41. Eichacker PQ, Natanson C, Danner RL. Surviving sepsis—practice guidelines, marketing campaigns, and Eli Lilly. N Engl J Med 2006;355:1640–2.

42. Warren HS, Suffredini AF, Eichacker PQ, Munford RS. Risks and benefits of activated protein C treatment for severe sepsis. N Engl J Med 2002;347:1027–30.

43. Ingelfinger JR. Through the looking glass: anemia guidelines, vested interests, and distortions. Clin J Am Soc Nephrol 2007;2:415–7.

44. Steinbrook R. Haemoglobin concentrations in chronic kidney disease. Lancet 2006;368:2191–3.

PART TWO

POLITICS AND POLICY

Part I of this book, "Evidence," describes how clinical evidence is generated and how it is used in regulation and medical practice. In Part II, "Politics and Policy," we take a closer look at what comparative effectiveness research is (Chapter 6) and examine the legislative odyssey of federal policy governing comparative effectiveness research and the evidence it yields (Chapters 7–9). In Chapter 10, we take a step back to consider the scope, structure, and financing of federally mandated comparative effectiveness research and why they matter.

The story of federal policy on comparative effectiveness research begins in 2002 with a very short bill introduced in the House of Representatives that went largely unnoticed and never got out of committee. A year later the first game-changing event occurred: a law was passed that includes a provision for comparative effectiveness research, the Medicare Prescription Drug and Modernization Act of 2003. Five subsequent inflection points followed over the next 7 years, indicators that comparative effectiveness research as a policy alternative was gaining traction. The last was the enactment of the Affordable Care Act of 2010, which established and funded the Patient-Centered Outcomes Research Institute.

Each of the inflection points has its main players. Some, particularly the aides of legislators and of congressional committees, played critical roles in the crafting and molding of the policy but stay mostly unnamed and in the background. Organizations such as AcademyHealth, the Institute of Medicine, and trade groups such as the Pharmaceutical Research and Manufacturers of America (PhRMA) exerted strong influence on the course of events, as did the political, legislative, and economic contexts of the decade of the 2000s. Each inflection point left a legacy, a set of realities, that influenced how things happened next.

6

Comparative Effectiveness Research

A New "Silver Bullet" for U.S. Health Care Costs

Comparative effectiveness research is actually two things. It is a type of clinical research, which, in the abstract, is relatively free of political trappings. It is also a federal health care policy, having become so in the decade of the 2000s. As the policy evolved between 2002 and 2010, the term "comparative effectiveness research" took on specific meanings for many stakeholder groups and also came to denote a specific set of research approaches. In this chapter we explore the various meanings of comparative effectiveness research, the problem that policy makers hoped would be solved by an investment in it, and the justifications that emerged and gave sticking power to this policy alternative.

Comparative Effectiveness Research: What Is It?

Where did the term "comparative effectiveness research" come from? We were very interested in its origin, having ourselves been engaged in clinical or health services research since the early 1980s and never hearing the term until the early 2000s. During our first wave of interviews, conducted in the fall of 2008, we questioned our informants about it but were unable to discover who first used it in a policy context. The earliest use of the term in print that we have been able to find is in a guideline called "General Considerations for Clinical Trials (E8)" issued in July 1997 by the International Conference on Harmonisation.

Regardless of its new name, comparative effectiveness research is an eons-old type of research involving human subjects or data derived from human subjects. It involves comparing the effectiveness—the ability to produce net benefit over harm—of one preventive, diagnostic, therapeutic, or service delivery modality with that of some other. All therapeutics research in humans is inherently comparative. The comparator may be the historical experience of patients observed at an earlier period than those being observed in the current study, or the experience of a concurrent comparison group receiving a placebo, an active alternative treatment (a different drug, device, invasive procedure, or treatment modality), or an alternative comprehensive treatment protocol. Viewed from this perspective, the great preponderance of the clinical research portfolio would be classified as comparative effectiveness research.

But during the 2000s, "comparative effectiveness research" took on a restricted definition as the term became a buzz word among policy makers and those attempting to influence policy. The placebo-controlled trial was removed from the purview of comparative effectiveness research. During the policy evolution of comparative effectiveness research, the term came to denote research comparing two or more active interventions.

Table 6.1 provides the different definitions for comparative effectiveness research put forth during the 2000s by several federal entities,[1] Academy-Health (a Washington, DC-based organization representing the interests of

Table 6.1 **Definitions of Comparative Effectiveness Research Used during the 2000s**

Developer of Definition	Date	Definition
Academy Health[a]	Sep 2005	Comparative effectiveness research is defined as a rigorous assessment of the relative safety, effectiveness, and cost of treatment therapies or approaches for managing the same condition.
Congressional Research Service	Oct 2007	Comparative effectiveness research is a term that has been defined by people in many different ways. All agree that comparative effectiveness research compares the effectiveness of two or more health care services or treatments, and is one form of health technology assessment. It compares outcomes resulting from different treatments or services, and provides information about the relative effectiveness of treatments. Additional specifics about the research and its definition are sources of contention. In particular: Effectiveness—How should effectiveness be measured? Should the research compare only the effectiveness (the effect in routine clinical practice) or also the efficacy (the effect under optimal conditions) of treatments or services? Costs—Should costs be included in the research? Should the costs be reported separately from the effectiveness results? Or should a cost-effectiveness ratio be the ultimate goal?

(continued)

Table 6.1 **Continued**

Developer of Definition	Date	Definition
Congressional Budget Office	Dec 2007	As applied in the health care sector, an analysis of comparative effectiveness is simply a rigorous evaluation of the impact of different options that are available for treating a given medical condition for a particular set of patients. Such a study may compare similar treatments such as competing drugs, or it may analyze very different approaches, such as surgery and drug therapy. The analysis may focus only on the relative medical benefits and risks of each option, or it may also weigh both the costs and the benefits of those options.
Federal Coordinating Council[b]	Jun 2009	Comparative effectiveness research is the conduct and synthesis of research comparing the benefits and harms of different interventions and strategies to prevent, diagnose, treat, and monitor health conditions in "real-world" settings.
Institute of Medicine	Jun 2009	Comparative effectiveness research is a strategy that focuses on the practical comparison of two or more health interventions to discern what works best for which patients and populations.
Academy Health	Jun 2009	[Comparative effectiveness research is] a comparison of the effectiveness of the risks and benefits of two or more health care services or treatments used to treat a specific disease or condition (e.g., pharmaceuticals, medical devices, medical procedures and other treatment modalities) in approximate real-world settings.
Section 6301 of The Patient Protection and Affordable Care Act (P.L.-111–148)	Mar 2010	"Comparative clinical effectiveness research" and "research" mean research evaluating and comparing health outcomes and the clinical effectiveness, risks, and benefits of two or more medical treatments, services, and items...The medical treatments, services, and items...are health care interventions, protocols for treatment, care management, and delivery, procedures, medical devices, diagnostic tools, pharmaceuticals (including drugs and biologicals), integrative health practices, and any other strategies or items being used in the treatment, management, and diagnosis of, or prevention of illness or injury in, individuals.

[a] A Washington, DC–based organization representing the interests of health services researchers.

[b] The Council was established by the American Recovery and Reinvestment Act of 2009; the Department of Health and Human Services used the definition developed by the Council to allocate the $1.1 billion appropriated by the Recovery Act for comparative effectiveness research.

health services researchers),[2] and the Institute of Medicine,[3] and the definition provided in Section 6301 of the 2010 Affordable Care Act.

Comparative Effectiveness Research: Not a New Kind of Research

Many of the young congressional staffers whom we interviewed in 2008 seemed to think that comparative effectiveness research was a new idea and a new kind of research. But it is neither. In 2007, to inform the debate about the need for and shape of a federal mandate for comparative effectiveness research, AcademyHealth, an organization representing health services researchers, launched an analysis of how much comparative effectiveness research was going on at the time. Searching the clinicaltrials.gov database for the 14-month period January 2007 through February 2008 and the HSRProj database (Health Services Research Projects in Progress), the analysts identified 689 comparative effectiveness studies ranging across observational designs, research syntheses, and head-to-head trials.[4] (The denominator was not reported; therefore, the proportion of all studies listed in those databases that could be classified as comparative effectiveness studies is not known.)

Section 6309 of the 2010 Affordable Care Act specifies that, under the statute, acceptable methods of comparative effectiveness research are head-to-head trials, registry-based observational studies, and research syntheses of the results of multiple studies. Even if we restrict ourselves to randomized head-to-head trials of one treatment alternative compared with another, the portfolio was large even before federal mandates were in place.

First, let us take a look at research intended to gain regulatory approval for a new prescription drug or device. The ethical justification for the use of a placebo comparator in a clinical trial is that no efficacious treatment is known to exist for the condition in question, or if one does exist, that withdrawal or deferral of such treatment during the time of the trial would not cause serious or irreparable harm to the subjects. Because treatments of known efficacy do exist for many human conditions, placebo-controlled trials would be unethical for many of the new prescription drugs, biologics, and devices regulated by the Food and Drug Administration (FDA). Active comparators must be used, bringing such trials under the definition of comparative effectiveness research. It is true that a sizable number of the comparative effectiveness trials performed for regulatory purposes are non-inferiority trials, which are less informative than superiority trials, and that trials conducted with regulatory intent pose narrow questions, include very homogenous study populations, may use outcome measures that doctors and patients consider not very informative, and are often never fully reported in the medical literature. Nevertheless, even before the federal mandates of the 2000s, comparative effectiveness trials were already playing a very important role in how new drugs are brought to market.

Comparative effectiveness trials supported by taxpayer funds and performed for other than regulatory purposes were also under way before any new federal mandates. One example is the Antihypertensive and Lipid-Lowering Treatment to Prevent Heart Attack Trial (ALLHAT). ALLHAT was an 8-year, $102 million study funded by the U.S. National Heart, Lung, and Blood Institute (NHLBI),[5] one of the 26 institutes and centers that make up the National Institutes of Health. ALLHAT is the largest randomized trial ever conducted to examine the effects of antihypertensive drugs on clinical outcomes, and its results have been incorporated into national treatment guidelines. The trial was motivated not by a marketing motive but rather by clinical uncertainty as to which antihypertensive regimen was best for people over age 55 with heart disease or at high risk for it. ALLHAT included 33,357 participants older than age 55 (47% women, 36% diabetic, 35% black) from 623 North American centers. The trial evaluated the comparative effectiveness of three different antihypertensive medications, chlorthalidone (a thiazide diuretic), amlodipine (a calcium antagonist), and lisinopril (an angiotensin converting enzyme inhibitor), all of which had been FDA approved for marketing for some period, and all of which had an FDA label for the treatment of hypertension. The National Institutes of Health has always supported comparative effectiveness trials and continues to do so. Looking at just the NHLBI, for instance, a search of clinicaltrials.gov that we conducted in July 2011 uncovered 77 such trials that were actively recruiting subjects.

The well-regarded Cooperative Studies Program of the Veterans Health Administration, now over 60 years old, provides planning, infrastructure, and financial support for multi-center studies of therapeutic or diagnostic interventions. Most VA cooperative trials meet the definition of comparative effectiveness research.

Finally, we turn to trials testing invasive therapeutic procedures. The use of placebo or sham-procedure controls is extremely low in such trials for reasons touched on in Chapters 1 and 4. Almost all trials evaluating surgical procedures are comparative effectiveness trials.[6]

Comparative Effectiveness Research as Federal Policy

Before the definition of the term hardened, which our analyses suggest happened around mid-2009, "CER" became the buzzword for a policy option. According to three of our informants, comparative effectiveness research is "impossible to disagree with," "makes a lot of sense to a lot of people," and is "a good bumper-sticker slogan." One congressional staffer told us, "There is always a trendy silver bullet in health care policy. It was health information technology for awhile. I think comparative effectiveness is the next version of that."

Many of those we interviewed were conscious that the wide use of the term covered a lack of specificity about what the term meant. Perhaps this allowed comparative effectiveness research to gain traction as a policy option. A former Medicare official told us, "Everybody I've talked to says this [*comparative effectiveness research*] is one of the few ideas where there is bipartisan agreement that something needs to happen. The details matter, but it seems to me there is a lot of bipartisan support for CER. Some see it as a way to reduce costs, some see it as a way to improve evidence, and most people see it as a better use of dollars, if you know what works better with what kinds of patients." A former health plan executive saw things differently: "Whenever you have unanimous agreement about a policy concept in Washington it means nobody's sure what it is."

By the last half of the 2000s the concept of comparative effectiveness research as part of federal health policy to help control health care costs and improve the quality of care enjoyed broad support, except from the medical products industry and a few other groups such as the U.S. Chamber of Commerce. The areas of controversy were the policy specifics, which we will explore in the remaining chapters of Part II. Here we will examine the problem that policy makers hoped comparative effectiveness research would solve.

"Thirty Percent of Health Care Is Wasted:"
The Problem That Federal Policy on Comparative Effectiveness Research Was Intended to Solve

Wide geographic variations have existed for decades across the United States in levels of use of hospital care, ambulatory care, disease-specific health services, care at the end of life, and in per capita rates of preference-sensitive operations in Medicare beneficiaries aged 65 and older. For example, after adjusting for population differences in age, gender, and race, the rate of back surgery among Medicare beneficiaries in Houston, Texas, is more than twice that of Chicago, Illinois, and the rate of knee replacement is 40% higher.[7] These variations are not only observed in private-sector medicine in the United States. They have also been documented in the Veterans Affairs medical care system, a publicly funded system in which access to health services does not depend on ability to pay or commercial health insurance coverage, and in which physicians are salaried rather than paid on a fee-for-service basis.[8] The variations in care are unexplained by geographic differences in age, gender, or health status distribution in the population. Moreover, levels of use of various services do not appear to be correlated with health outcomes. High levels of use are not associated with better outcomes, nor are low levels of use with poorer outcomes.

Physician John E. Wennberg is credited with bringing the problem of unexplained geographic variation in American health care use to national consciousness and keeping it there. He and coauthor Alan Gittelsohn first documented the extent of variation in a paper they had difficulty getting published in the medical literature. Frustrated, Wennberg submitted it on a lark to the premier journal *Science*, which published it in 1973.[9] Over the next decades Wennberg and the group he put together at Dartmouth College in New Hampshire conducted numerous empirical studies of variation. Wennberg also founded and served as the first editor of the widely used and oft-quoted Dartmouth Atlas of Health Care.[10]

Early on, Wennberg and his colleagues posited that one explanation for the marked geographic differences in rates of certain kinds of clinical interventions was the lack of solid scientific evidence for or against their value.[11] For example, one of the conditions that Wennberg and his coauthors studied is prostatism, a collection of symptoms that older men suffer in trying to empty their bladder. Prostatism results from a benign aging-related increase in the size of the prostate gland. The condition can be treated by various invasive procedures to reduce the size of the prostate, including transurethral resection of the prostate (TURP). Across the State of Maine in the 1970s, Wennberg found a threefold variation in the probability of undergoing a TURP by age 75, and also discovered that the decision to intervene or wait was not based on high-quality evidence for net benefit over harm from randomized controlled trials. In addition, he discovered that TURP was associated with a much higher rate of long-term postoperative complications such as urinary dribbling and impotence than previously thought. Wennberg proposed that physicians' and patients' uncertainty about the benefits and harms of the procedure was a major contributor to the geographic variation in TURP rates. He made the case that, with operations aimed at improving function, like TURP, data on postoperative "quality-of-life" outcomes had to be obtained directly from patients in order to estimate the benefits and harms of surgery, and that patient participation in the decision to operate was critical. For this "preference-sensitive" operation, Wennberg credited the geographic variation in rates to doctors' lack of valid data on the outcomes of the condition, whether treated or observed, and on the exclusion of patient preferences in the decision-making process.

Wennberg's thinking was somewhat different about the roots of geographic variations in the volume of per capita utilization rates of ambulatory care services and hospital care. He calls these types of health services "supply-sensitive care" and attributes their variation to geographic differences in the supply of physicians and hospital beds. What permits these geographic variations in utilization rates to go unchecked is the lack of scientific evidence on which rates of use appear to lead to the best outcomes for patients.

In Wennberg's view, geographic variation in the rates of preference-sensitive interventions as well as in supply-sensitive care can be traced back to the "uncertainty principle." If Wennberg et al. are right, the antidote to unwarranted geographic variations in care would be more evidence on what interventions work best, including evidence from head-to-head trials comparing one treatment or health care strategy with another.

Elliott Fisher, a protégé and long-time collaborator of Wennberg's, took the variations work further with research examining how usage levels of health care services correlate with patients' outcomes.[12] In areas where Medicare expenditures were higher, neither access to care nor quality of care was better than in lower spending areas. Moreover, Medicare beneficiaries in higher spending areas did not have better outcomes in terms of mortality and functional status, and neither were they more satisfied with their care than beneficiaries in lower spending areas.

This line of research led to a serious and still unanswered question. If it is not better access, quality, outcomes, or satisfaction, exactly what is it that we are buying with the extra 30%–60% of Medicare expenditures going toward the higher spending Medicare regions? At meetings in 2008–2009 during which data were presented showing that per capita Medicare spending was twice as high in one hospital compared to one in a different city, despite the fact that both hospitals had received the same "best" quality ratings, speakers would ask the audience, "How can the best care in the United States cost twice as much as the best care in the United States?"[13]

Geographic variations in U.S. health care, the work of Wennberg's group, and an analysis supported by the Commonwealth Fund showing that the United States was paying 30%–40% more for health care than other developed countries[14] figured very prominently in the debates leading up to the inclusion of federal mandates for comparative effectiveness research as part of the 2010 Affordable Care Act.[15] Together with the imperative of finding a solution to inexorably rising health care costs, these factors exerted powerful influence on policy makers' beliefs and discussions during the debates about comparative effectiveness research that began in earnest in the mid-2000s. "Thirty percent of health care is wasted" became a mantra on Capitol Hill.

The problem was that no one knew how to distinguish the 30% waste from the 70% non-waste. A member of a Washington, DC think tank told us, "[CER] has risen to the top of the policy makers' discussions because they've run out of other bright ideas of how to get sustainable resource use in health care. Building on the work of Jack Wennberg and others who claim—they might argue with the number—but if you have the claim that 30% of everything we do is wasted, there is the general belief that if we could just identify the 30%, couldn't we do better? That is begging the question, because that is the tricky bit. But increasingly there is a sense that, maybe we can't identify all of the 30%, but we certainly know a number of areas."

Accordingly, as the debates progressed, comparative effectiveness research became the answer or at least part of the answer in the minds of policy makers. The thinking went like this: (1) Lack of good evidence makes physicians uncertain about what care works best. (2) Absent best evidence, physicians do what they think is best, but since opinions vary, this leads to geographic variations in use and costs. (3) Despite geographic variations in health expenditures exceeding 30%, the health status of Americans in high-use areas is not manifestly better than it is in low-use areas. (4) Therefore, 30% of health care expenditures are wasted. (5) Comparative effectiveness research will identify those services that are ineffective or less effective, positioning us to eliminate them, and increase value-for-money in the health care system.

This shaping of federally mandated comparative effectiveness research as the search for and elimination of waste was vitally important in the 2010 health care reform debates. The elimination of waste—health services that do not help and may in fact hurt patients—was a prospect much more palatable than the alternatives of rationing or across-the-board cuts of health services regardless of their effectiveness. Comparative effectiveness research became the antidote for rationing. Rationing claims had helped sink the 1993–1994 health care reform efforts of the Clinton administration. Talking to us about the stance of large employers in the recent health care reform debates, a staffer for a Senate Democrat said, "The value question and the efficiency question and the transparency question and the quality question are very much at the heart of why big business is willing to have these conversations about health reform again. Where they got skittish before [*in 1993–1994*], and were unwilling to stand with the Democrats, was with the rationing conversations. They are much more comfortable in that skin now. They are helping to drive a more aggressive approach to improving quality and reducing waste and inefficiency. It is all driven by their cost pressures."

We agree with Wennberg and others that the lack of evidence for or against some medical interventions drives variations in the volume and intensity of their use. But the situation has improved little over the past decades despite significant expansions in the evidence base for many health care interventions. A case in point is the use of percutaneous coronary stents for the treatment of stable coronary artery disease. Numerous randomized trials of stenting versus medical (drug) therapy have shown that stenting for stable angina confers no incremental benefits for longevity, preventing heart attack, reducing the frequency of effort-induced chest pain, and avoidance of subsequent procedures to revascularize the heart muscle. Yet each year there are nearly 650,000 U.S. hospital stays for coronary stent implantation,[16] with an estimated 40% being implanted for stable coronary artery disease. The explanation for this can be found in market forces and the way in which American physicians and hospitals are paid for delivering medical services. On its own, more and better evidence cannot and will not drive waste and ineffective or marginally effective health services out of the U.S. health care system.

Comparative Effectiveness Research: Producing a Public Good

Many of the people we interviewed for this book believed that a federal investment in clinical comparative effectiveness research was justifiable because such research produces a "public good." A public good is a good characterized by being non-rivalrous and non-excludable. "Non-rivalrous" means that consumption of the good by one party does not preclude its consumption by other parties. (As one person told us, "It's not like a Snickers bar.") "Non-excludable" means that it is not possible to exclude a party from using the good. Individuals and private entities have no incentive to produce or maintain such goods because there is no means of making a profit from them: they have no business case for producing them. Therefore, it generally falls to public entities—governments—to produce and maintain them.

A closer inspection of the business case for comparative effectiveness research is in order. The business case for a decision involving the outlay of funds rests on the projected effects on cash flow, revenue, and internal rate of return over a specific payback period.

The Medical Products Industry: A Business Case for Comparative Effectiveness Research?

We saw in Chapter 2 that, under current regulations, to gain FDA approval, a product need not be shown to be superior or even "non-inferior" to an alternative product already cleared for marketing. Drug or device makers only have a business case for evaluating the comparative effectiveness of a product when it will help them gain FDA approval for marketing their product or help expand its market share afterward.

Aggressive marketing is generally a better investment for the product maker than risky comparative effectiveness studies, especially for big-ticket devices. A health facility's decision to purchase high-dollar diagnostic and therapeutic medical devices such as a positron emission tomography (PET) scanner (a machine costs up to $2.5 million) and particle accelerators for proton therapy (construction of a proton therapy facility costs over $100 million) is based on the beliefs that insurers will cover and reimburse for procedures performed with the devices and that having such equipment will bring in doctors, patients, and revenue. Investments in such devices are based not on evidence that, compared to alternatives, they lead to superior patient outcomes (such evidence does not exist at the time purchasing decisions are made), but rather on the belief that they should be better "in principle." That is, the PET scan's ability to find areas of abnormal metabolic activity indicative of malignancy *should* more accurately stage the extent of disease, enable optimal treatment planning, and enhance the accuracy of prognostication; more focused delivery of a form of radiotherapy (proton beam therapy) to a cancerous lesion *should* lead to less collateral damage of surrounding normal tissue. Once a facility invests in such a device, doctors begin using it, and payers agree to cover its use, there is no incentive and many disincentives to actually putting the device to rigorous tests of comparative effectiveness.

Private Health Insurers: A Business Case for Comparative Effectiveness Studies?

In 2009, 32% of the dollars the United States spent on health care came from the private health insurance industry, which gets its funds from the individuals it insures and the companies that employ them. The private health insurance industry has an interest in making sure their health care payouts come in low enough to preserve the profit margin (or revenue, in the case of nonprofit insurers) desired by this industry and its shareholders.

The primary interests of a commercial firm are to make a profit and satisfy its investors. Health insurers make their profits on the difference between the total insurance premiums they collect and the total claims they pay out. (Some profits also come from interest income made during the lag between the collection of premium dollars and the payment of claims.) Out of the premiums collected the firm must pay providers for covered medical services (a price multiplied by volume element, minus the costs borne by beneficiaries in the form of deductibles, coinsurance, and co-payments); cover administrative costs for employee salaries, business overhead, marketing, and so on; and cover the firm's profits. The portion of the premium that covers administrative costs plus profits is called the "loading cost."

Obviously, to boost its profits, a commercial health insurer can target any one of the variables in this equation; scientific evidence on what works best in medicine is almost an irrelevancy. There are several variables in this equation where a health insurer might be interested in *using* the findings from comparative effectiveness research, such as in a value-based insurance design, and we will discuss those issues in Chapter 11. The question here, however, pertains to the business case for *sponsoring* such research. The funds to support such an effort would have to come out of loading costs, which could threaten the profit margin. Despite the perceptions of consumers, employers, and others that commercial health insurers have a profit margin of 19%–30%, credible analyses suggest the industry's mean margin is less than 5%.[17] A firm would have to think twice about making an investment in the sponsorship of research. Moreover, the sponsoring company would have an edge over its competitors only as long as they could be prevented from accessing and using the results of the comparative effectiveness research it had sponsored. The business case does not look good.

But the fact is that many private health insurers do make financial out-lays in order to determine whether and under what clinical circumstances coverage might or will be provided for specific clinical services and inter-ventions. They tend to make their investments in technology assessment groups, which conduct secondary comparative effectiveness research. For example, Aetna publishes on its Web site Clinical Policy Bulletins that com-municate the results of "Aetna's determination of whether certain services or supplies are medically necessary, experimental and investigational, or cosmetic." The company bases those conclusions "upon a review of currently available clinical information (including clinical outcome studies in the peer-reviewed published medical literature, regulatory status of the technol-ogy, evidence-based guidelines of public health and health research agencies, evidence-based guidelines and positions of leading national health profes-sional organizations, views of physicians practicing in relevant clinical areas, and other relevant factors)." Another example is the BlueCross BlueShield Association's Technology Evaluation Center, established in 1985, which pro-duces evidence-based technology assessments that are of very high quality and are publicly accessible. To the extent that the results of the technology assessments conducted by private insurers are publicly accessible, these com-panies are producing a public good.

A fair conclusion to be drawn is that private insurers contribute substantially to comparative effectiveness research. However, the studies are motivated or at least influenced by concerns about profit margins, often of uncertain qual-ity, sometimes difficult or impossible to access, and duplicative. Several of our informants pointed out that a reason they favored a national entity that would oversee and conduct comparative effectiveness research is that it would elimi-nate the duplication of effort occurring across insurance companies and health plans. A former official of Kaiser Permanente told us, "We advocate more col-lective activity here. There is a huge amount of waste because there are tens, hundreds, maybe even thousands of entities that are looking at these same questions, pulling the same evidence base around what is there...Our point of view evolved to say, why could this work of comparative effectiveness research not be done in a public space so that everyone could have access to it? It could be done once really well, updated as necessary, and then organizations could make individual decisions based on what they saw as the evidence and the val-ues they brought to it."

Conclusions

Many of the staffers and members of Congress who were leading the charge for federally mandated comparative effectiveness research during the 2000s would have been surprised that so much comparative effectiveness research was already taking place. This is not to say that it is enough—we saw in preceding chapters the great gulfs that exist in evidence—but it does indicate that a mandate for more research will not solve problems that are stemming from the failure to apply the evidence we already have.

Notes

1. These include the Congressional Research Service (CRS), the Congressional Budget Office (CBO), and the Federal Coordinating Council for Comparative Effectiveness Research in the Department of Health and Human Services. The CRS is a nonpartisan legislative branch agency that is part of the Library of Congress. It provides policy and legal analysis to committees and members of the House and Senate. It provided its definition in: Jacobson GA. Comparative clinical effectiveness research and cost-effectiveness research: background, history, and overview. CRS report for Congress, RL34208, October 15, 2007. The CBO is also a nonpartisan agency that works exclusively for Congress; it provides objective analyses of budgetary and economic issues. Its definition was given in: A CBO paper: research on the comparative effectiveness of medical treatments. Pub. no. 2975, December 2007. (Accessed October 29, 2012, at http://www.cbo.gov/sites/default/files/cbofiles/ftpdocs/88xx/doc8891/12-18-comparativeeffectiveness.pdf.) The Federal Coordinating Council gave its definition in: U.S. Department of Health and Human Services. Federal Coordinating Council for Comparative Effectiveness Research. Report to the President and the Congress, June 30, 2009. (Accessed September 27, 2012, at http://www.hhs.gov/recovery/programs/cer/cerannualrpt.pdf.) The Federal Coordinating Council was established by the 2009 American Recovery and Reinvestment Act and abolished by a provision in the 2010 Affordable Care Act. Agencies within the Department of Health and Human Services continue to use the Council's definition.
2. AcademyHealth. Placement, coordination, and funding of health services research within the federal government. September 2005. (Accessed September 27, 2012, at http://www.academyhealth.org/files/publications/placementreport.pdf.) Holve E, Pittman P. A first look at the volume and cost of comparative effectiveness research in the United States. AcademyHealth. June 2009. (Accessed September 27, 2012, at http://www.academyhealth.org/files/FileDownloads/AH_Monograph_09FINAL7.pdf.)
3. Institute of Medicine Committee on Comparative Effectiveness Research Prioritization. Initial national priorities for comparative effectiveness research. Washington, DC: National Academies Press, 2009: xiii.
4. Holve E, Pittman P. A first look at the volume and cost of comparative effectiveness research in the United States. AcademyHealth. June 2009. (Accessed September 27, 2012, at http://www.academyhealth.org/files/FileDownloads/AH_Monograph_09FINAL7.pdf.)
5. The ALLHAT officers and coordinators for the ALLHAT Collaborative Research Group. Major outcomes in high-risk hypertensive patients randomized to angiotensin-converting enzyme inhibitor or calcium channel blocker vs. diuretic. JAMA 2002; 288:2981–97.
6. Wenner DM, Brody BA, Jarman AF, Kolman JM, Wray NP, Ashton CM. Do surgical trials meet the scientific standards for clinical trials? J Am Coll Surg 2012;215:722–30. Of 290

influential trials of invasive therapeutic procedures whose findings were reported in the peer-reviewed literature between 2000 and 2008, 96% were comparative effectiveness trials.

7. Our calculations, based on data from the Dartmouth Atlas, accessed September 27, 2011, at http://www.dartmouthatlas.org.

8. See, for example, Ashton CM, Petersen NJ, Souchek J, Menke TJ, Yu HJ, Pietz K, Eigenbrodt ML, Barbour G, Kizer KW, Wray NP. Geographic variations in utilization rates in Veterans Affairs hospitals and clinics. N Engl J Med 1999;340:32–9.

9. Wennberg J, Gittelsohn A. Small area variations in health care delivery: a population-based health information system can guide planning and regulatory decision-making. Science 1973;182:1102–8.

10. The Dartmouth Atlas is available from http://www.dartmouthatlas.org/. According to its homepage, "For more than 20 years, the Dartmouth Atlas Project has documented glaring variations in how medical resources are distributed and used in the United States. The project uses Medicare data to provide information and analysis about national, regional, and local markets, as well as hospitals and their affiliated physicians."

11. Wennberg reviews this work and his thinking in Chapter 6 of his book, Tracking medicine: a researcher's quest to understand health care. New York: Oxford University Press, 2010.

12. Fisher ES, Wennberg DE, Stukel TA, Gottlieb DJ, Lucas FL, Pinder EL. The implications of regional variations in Medicare spending. Part 1: the content, quality, and accessibility of care. Ann Intern Med 2003;138:273–87. Part 2: health outcomes and satisfaction with care. Ann Intern Med 2003;138:288–98.

13. This query has been attributed to Elliott Fisher, Uwe Reinhardt, and Peter Orszag.

14. Reinhardt U, Hussey PS, Anderson GF. U.S. health care spending in an international context. Health Aff 2004;23:10–25.

15. Wennberg's variations work was also a strong influence in the debates leading up to the unsuccessful health care reform efforts in 1994 during the Clinton administration. His work also helped shape the program of the Agency for Health Care Policy and Research and its successor agency, the Agency for Healthcare Research and Quality.

16. Auerbach DI, Maeda JL, Steiner C. Hospital stays with cardiac stents, 2009. HCUP Statistical Brief #128, April 2012. (Accessed September 28, 2012, at http://www.hcup-us.ahrq.gov/reports/statbriefs/sb128.pdf.)

17. Austin DA, Hungerford TL. The market structure of the health insurance industry. Congressional Research Service 7–5700 R40834, November 17, 2009.

7

The Legislative Odyssey of Comparative Effectiveness Research

Birth in 2002 to the First Federal Mandate in 2003

Our analyses indicate that the legislative odyssey of federal policy on comparative effectiveness research started in earnest in 2002. However, several bills before then included provisions for comparative effectiveness research. Most notably, the Food and Drug Modernization Act of 1997 (P.L. 105–115) directed the Secretary of Health and Human Services to establish a demonstration program on centers for education and research on therapeutics (CERTs). One of the three statutorily required activities of these centers is "the conduct of research on the comparative effectiveness and safety of drugs, biological products, and devices."[1] This language notwithstanding, the CERTs program never became known as a nidus of comparative effectiveness research, and the CERTs program was not mentioned in any of the 117 interviews we conducted for this book. Comparative effectiveness research as a promising solution to the problem of unsustainable rises in national health expenditures did not emerge with any stickiness until after the first stand-alone bill was introduced in 2002.

Representative Tom Allen and the First Stand-Alone Comparative Effectiveness Research Bill

The story starts on May 23, 2002, during the second session of the 107th Congress, when Representative Tom Allen (D-ME) introduced in the House a very short bill, H.R. 4832, the "Prescription Drug Comparative Effectiveness Act of 2002." This bill, the full text of which is given in Box 7.1, would have required the Director of the Agency for Healthcare Research and Quality "to conduct studies on the comparative effectiveness and cost-effectiveness of prescription drugs that account for high levels of expenditures or use by individuals eligible Medicare or Medicaid" and would have authorized[2] the appropriation of $25 million to the Agency for Healthcare Research and Quality in 2003 and thereafter for these purposes.

Box 7.1 First Comparative Effectiveness Research Bill, Introduced by Representative Tom Allen (D-ME)

H.R. 4832—Prescription Drug Comparative Effectiveness Act of 2002 (Introduced in House—IH)

107th CONGRESS

2d Session

H.R. 4832

To require the Director of the Agency for Healthcare Research and Quality to conduct studies on the comparative effectiveness and cost-effectiveness of prescription drugs that account for high levels of expenditures or use by individuals eligible for Medicare or Medicaid, and for other purposes.

IN THE HOUSE OF REPRESENTATIVES
MAY 23, 2002

Mr. ALLEN (for himself, Mr. BERRY, Mr. LANGEVIN, Mr. BROWN of Ohio, Mr. STARK, Mr. RANGEL, Ms. KAPTUR, Mr. BALDACCI, Ms. DELAURO, and Mr. WAXMAN) introduced the following bill; which was referred to the Committee on Energy and Commerce

A BILL

To require the Director of the Agency for Healthcare Research and Quality to conduct studies on the comparative effectiveness and cost-effectiveness of prescription drugs that account for high levels of expenditures or use by individuals eligible for Medicare or Medicaid, and for other purposes.

Be it enacted by the Senate and House of Representatives of the United States of America in Congress assembled.

SECTION 1. SHORT TITLE

This Act may be cited as the "Prescription Drug Comparative Effectiveness Act of 2002."

SEC. 2. STUDY ON EFFECTIVENESS OF CERTAIN DRUGS USED BY INDIVIDUALS ELIGIBLE FOR MEDICARE OR MEDICAID

(a) STUDY—The Director of the Agency for Healthcare Research and Quality shall conduct studies or other analyses, which may include clinical research, to develop or analyze valid scientific evidence regarding the comparative effectiveness and cost-effectiveness of covered prescription drugs relative to other drugs and treatments.

(b) COVERED PRESCRIPTION DRUGS—For purposes of this section, the term "covered prescription drugs" means prescription drugs that account for high levels of expenditures or use by individuals entitled to benefits under the medicare or medicaid programs under titles XVIII or XIX of the Social Security Act (42 U.S.C. 1395 et seq.; 1396 et seq.), respectively.

(c) REPORT—Each year the Director of the Agency for Healthcare Research and Quality shall—

(1) submit to the Congress a report on the results of the studies or analyses conducted under subsection (a); and

(2) make such report publicly available, including by posting the report on the Internet.

(d) AUTHORIZATION OF APPROPRIATIONS—There are authorized to be appropriated to carry out this section $25,000,000 for fiscal year 2003, and such sums as may be necessary for fiscal years thereafter.

As Mr. Allen explained to us (Box 7.2), his idea of comparative effectiveness research grew out of his concerns about high prescription drug prices. At the time he introduced his 2002 bill, Republicans held a majority. (During the 107th Congress, 2001–2002, the House had 221 Republicans, 211 Democrats, and 2 Independents, and the Senate was evenly divided.) H.R. 4832 was referred to the Subcommittee on Health of the House Energy and Commerce Committee, from which it never emerged, and it died on November 22, 2002 along with the second legislative session of the 107th Congress.

Box 7.2 Representative Tom Allen's Account of the Birth of His Ideas on Federally Mandated Comparative Effectiveness Research and His 2002 Bill

The bill in 2002 grew out of our continuing interest in prescription drug prices. That started [*in*] spring of 1998 when I wound up talking to a group of seniors in Sanford, Maine. A retired firefighter brushed off what I was saying about Medicare and Social Security by saying, "Well, that's all well and good but I just got another prescription from my doctor. It costs $100.00 a month and I'm not going to fill it because my wife and I can't afford the cost of our prescription drugs." Through the Democratic staff of the House Government Reform Committee we did two studies of prescription drug pricing. Then in September of 1998 we introduced legislation to provide a discount for all Medicare beneficiaries on the price of their prescription drugs. There were studies showing that the market for pharmaceuticals was driven by marketing more than by the inherent additional value of a new drug in treating a particular illness or condition. So that 2002 legislation grew out of reading about the way the pharmaceutical market worked.

Before we introduced that bill, we'd been following a little bit what Governor Kitzhaber had done in Oregon. We met with him and with Mark Gibson here in Washington to discuss what they were doing and how they were doing it. We also looked [at other countries]. Australia and New Zealand had national systems for evaluating the comparative effectiveness of different prescription drugs and their national health care policy board. It was a long time ago, but I remember the Australian system. The companies would come in and make a pitch for a certain price for a new drug and then there'd be some evaluation of how much better that drug was than other drugs in the same class, drugs treating the same illness or condition. And then the board would decide how much of an increase was justified.

Well, obviously prescription drugs were a lot cheaper in Australia and New Zealand and everywhere else in the world than they are in the U.S. where the ability to establish price is pretty much the domain of the manufacturer. And if you don't have a truly competitive market then you wind up paying a lot for prescription drugs. So we introduced that bill H.R. 4832 [2002] the Prescription Drug Comparative Effectiveness Act. That was the first federal bill to provide funding, $25 million, to the Agency for Healthcare Research and Quality. That was the beginning, the core beginning.

The next year, on June 5, 2003, during the first legislative session of the 108th Congress, Mr. Allen and a Republican co-sponsor, Jo Ann Emerson (R-MO), introduced another version of the bill, H.R. 2356, called the "Prescription Drug Comparative Effectiveness Act of 2003." The scope of the 2003 bill was broader: the comparative effectiveness of prescription drugs was to be established relative not only to other drugs used for the same purpose, but to other treatments for the same condition. The 2003 bill stipulated that "The Director of the National Institutes of Health, in coordination with the Director of the Agency for Healthcare Research and Quality, shall conduct research, which may include clinical research, to develop valid scientific evidence regarding the comparative effectiveness, cost-effectiveness, and, where appropriate, comparative safety of covered prescription drugs relative to other drugs and treatments for the same disease or condition." The bill authorized the appropriation of $50 million to the National Institutes of Health (NIH) and $25 million to the Agency for Healthcare Research and Quality (AHRQ) for this purpose in 2004 and thereafter.

During this period Mr. Allen met several times with a group called the Alliance for Better Health Care that consisted of large employers, health insurers, trade organizations, professional organizations, consumer organizations, and others.[3] He observed a phenomenon that would figure significantly in the traction that comparative effectiveness research eventually developed as a policy option: "It [*the Alliance for Better Health Care*] was truly a broad-based group. To me that was very important: it meant at least some employers were starting to think of their interests as being separate from the pharmaceutical and health insurance industries."

Mr. Allen told us that the 2003 bill, which he had co-sponsored with a Republican, had bipartisan support. (During the 108th Congress, the House of Representatives had 227 Republicans, 210 Democrats, and 1 Independent aligned with the Democrats. The Senate had 51 Republicans, 48 Democrats, and 1 Independent aligned with the Democrats.) He related that he had participated for several years in the bipartisan health policy retreat for congressional members held by the Commonwealth Fund each January in Florida—a bipartisan, closed meeting with no press, characterized by frank, open, and collegial discussions—and recalled that comparative effectiveness research was a topic at some of them. He said, "This concept [*comparative effectiveness research*] grew because it made sense no matter which side of the aisle you were on, because the notion of having a market with good, independent information that will drive decisions of consumers and providers is a free market concept."

The Allen-Emerson bill H.R. 2356 was referred to the House Committee on Energy and Commerce. The bill received little attention, and no further action was taken on it during the 108th Congress. A government official of the Agency for Healthcare Research and Policy explained the politics (recall that this was during the George W. Bush administration): "When the [*2003*] Allen Bill was [*introduced*], in my world, this is about as important as Patrick Kennedy introducing this really glorious IT [*information technology*] bill—fun to think about but it ain't going anywhere because they [*Democrats*] are in the minority, it ain't going to get a hearing, we are not gonna talk about it."

But even though the 108th Congress took no action on H.R. 2356 in 2003, as we will see later, much of what was in that bill actually did become law that year, as part of the massive Medicare Prescription Drug, Improvement, and Modernization Act of 2003 that created a prescription drug benefit for Medicare beneficiaries.

The First Federal Mandate for Comparative Effectiveness Research: Section 1013 of the Medicare Prescription Drug, Improvement, and Modernization Act of 2003

On June 11, 2003, only days after Representatives Allen and Emerson introduced their comparative effectiveness bill, Senate Majority Leader Bill Frist (R-TN) introduced in the Senate S. 1. "Prescription Drug and Medicare Improvement Act of 2003." A few weeks later, on June 25, 2003, Representative Dennis Hastert (R-IL), the Speaker of the House, introduced the companion bill in the House, H.R. 1, the "Medicare Prescription Drug, Improvement, and Modernization Act of 2003." After much acrimony, a version of this bill was signed into law (P.L. 108–173) by President George W. Bush on December 8, 2003. Among other things, this law amended title XVIII (Medicare) of the Social Security Act to add a new Part D to the Medicare program, a prescription drug benefit for beneficiaries as of January 1, 2006.[4]

As first introduced, neither the House or Senate version (H.R. 1; S. 1) included provisions relating to comparative effectiveness research. In fact, neither included as much as the words. Yet the final bill that came out of the conference committee, was passed by both houses, and was signed into law includes Section 1013, "Research on Outcomes of Health Care Items and Services." Section 1013 requires the Secretary of Health and Human Services to conduct and support research on "the outcomes, comparative clinical effectiveness, and appropriateness of health care items and services."[5] How did this come about, and who was responsible?

The Medicare Modernization Act of 2003 was a bill proposed by Republicans, favored by most Republicans (though opposed by conservative Republicans who were against a major expansion of Medicare, a huge federal entitlement program), and opposed by most Democrats. The bill became law at a time when Republicans were in the majority in both houses of Congress and a Republican, George W. Bush, was president. That a federal mandate should exist for comparative effectiveness research was a proposal that originated with Democrats, as we saw in the preceding section. Though it had some bipartisan support, a mandate for comparative effectiveness research was opposed by the medical products industry.

On June 24, 2003, 2 weeks after Senator Frist introduced S. 1 into the Senate, Senator Hillary Clinton (D-NY) proposed that S. 1 be amended to include provisions for comparative effectiveness research of prescription drugs. The amendment, No. 1000, was titled "Study on Effectiveness of Certain Prescription Drugs." The texts of Amendment 1000 and the Allen-Emerson bill of 2003 are virtually identical in structure and content, with four exceptions: they have different titles, the Allen-Emerson bill includes cost-effectiveness studies in its scope while the Clinton amendment does not, the Clinton amendment includes the FDA along with the NIH and AHRQ as responsible agencies but the Allen-Emerson bill does not, and the Clinton amendment authorizes $75 million for 2004 while the Allen-Emerson bill specifies that $50 million is to go to NIH and $25 million to AHRQ.

The Clinton Amendment 1000 was debated on the floor of the Senate on June 25, 2003. Senators Mike Enzi (R-WY) and Charles Grassley (R-IA) opposed it. Senator Grassley's arguments against passage of the amendment were largely procedural in nature, but Senator Enzi's centered on themes heard from the opposition to comparative effectiveness research throughout the remainder of the 2000s. Those themes are that a federal mandate for comparative effectiveness research would "get the federal government even further into the business of making medical decisions," "promote one-size-fits-all medicine," "fail to recognize the value of incremental advances in drug developments," "fail to recognize the differences in the way individuals and sub-populations respond to different drugs," and so forth. Clinton's Amendment 1000 to S. 1 was rejected by the Senate (52 nays and 43 yeas). Interestingly, among the Senators voting against Amendment 1000 were Senate Majority Leader Bill Frist,[6] who, as we will see later, cited the final bill's comparative effectiveness provisions as a reason the Senate should pass it, and Senator Max Baucus (D-MT), who would in 2008 propose his own legislation for comparative effectiveness research[7] and figure heavily in how the federal mandate for comparative effectiveness was styled in the 2010 Affordable Care Act.

On June 27, 2003, H.R. 1 was agreed to in the House. On July 7, 2003, H.R. 1 was received in the Senate, and it was passed in the Senate in lieu of S. 1. (Recall that neither version had any comparative effectiveness research provisions.) Because of disagreements about amendments, the two chambers agreed to send the bill to conference and appointed their conferees.[8] Between September 9, 2003 and November 18, 2003, actions taken on the bill were basically procedural in nature. An examination of the Congressional Record shows that no amendments were proposed while the bill was in conference, and there is no mention of comparative effectiveness research related to the bill.

The conference report on H.R. 1 (H. Rept. 108–391) was filed on November 21, 2003. The excerpt pertaining to comparative effectiveness research is given in Box 7.3.

During the subsequent considerations of the conference report in the House, Representative Doug Bereuter (R-NE) advocated for the comparative effectiveness research provision when he spoke on the importance of the authorization of "$50 million for fiscal year 2004 for the Agency for Healthcare Research and Quality to conduct research on health care outcomes, comparative clinical effectiveness and appropriateness of health care items and services, including

Box 7.3 **Excerpt Pertaining to Provisions on Comparative Effectiveness Research from the Conference Report Accompanying H.R. 1, Medicare Prescription Drug, Improvement, and Modernization Act of 2003, Filed on November 21, 2003**

Research on Outcomes of Health Care Items and Services. (Section 1014 of the Conference Agreement)

PRESENT LAW

The Agency for Healthcare Research and Quality (AHRQ) is an agency within the Department of Health and Human Services. AHRQ's mission is to support, conduct, and disseminate research that improves access to care and the outcomes, quality, cost, and utilization of health care services. The research agenda is designed to be responsive to the needs of its customers, including patients, clinicians, institutions, plans, purchasers, and federal, state, and local governments. The research conducted by AHRQ is used to inform medical practice, educate consumer understanding of health care, and expand policy makers' ability to monitor and evaluate the impact of system changes on outcomes, quality, access, cost, and use of health care, and to devise policies to improve system performance.

HOUSE BILL

No provision.

SENATE BILL

No provision.

CONFERENCE AGREEMENT

The conference agreement authorizes $50 million for fiscal year 2004 for the Secretary through the Agency for Healthcare Research and Quality to conduct research to address the scientific information needs and priorities identified by the Medicare, Medicaid, and State Children's Health Insurance Programs. The information needs and priorities will relate to the clinical effectiveness and appropriateness of specified health services and treatments, and the health outcomes associated with such services and treatments. The needs and priorities also will address strategies for improving the efficiency and effectiveness of those health care programs. The Secretary is required to establish a process for developing research priorities. Not later than 6 months after the date of enactment, the Secretary must establish an initial list of priorities. The

Secretary must complete the evaluation and synthesis of the scientific evidence related to that initial list within 18 months after development of such a list and disseminate the research findings to the public, prescription drug plans, and other plans. Not later than 18 months after the date of enactment, the Secretary is required to identify voluntary options that could be undertaken by public and private entities to improve information sharing regarding outcomes and quality of care, adopt innovative quality improvement strategies, develop management tools to improve oversight by state officials, support federal and state initiatives to improve the quality, safety, and efficiency of services, and provide a basis for estimating the fiscal and coverage impact of federal or state policy changes of the Medicare, Medicaid, and State Children's Health Insurance Programs. The Administrator for the Center for Medicare and Medicaid Services may not use data from the research conducted to withhold coverage of a prescription drug, to mandate a national standard, or require a specific approach to quality measurement and reporting.

prescription drugs. This Member has been a strong advocate for such research, as evidenced by his amendment to the Labor, Health and Human Services, and Education appropriations bill (H.R. 2660).[9] ... This Member is pleased that the conference report language authorizes the AHRQ to conduct such research and that comparative clinical effectiveness is referenced but is concerned that cost-effectiveness is also not mentioned."

When the conference report was considered in the Senate, Senate Majority Leader Bill Frist, who a few months earlier voted against Amendment 1000 proposed by Senator Clinton, put forth the report's provisions for comparative effectiveness research as a strength of H.R. 1. He said, among other things, "Not only will the Medicare agreement help lower prices, it will help give consumers more information about their medical options. This bill expands federal research into the comparative effects of different drugs and treatments. With this new information, seniors will be able to comparison-shop in the medical marketplace, just like they would for any other product or service. Patients and their doctors will be able to compare treatment options and choose the course of action that best addresses their medical needs. And Medicare and health consumers will get better value for their money." During the debate Senator Hillary Clinton spoke of her opposition to passage of the bill but noted her support for its comparative effectiveness research provisions: "This is a sad day for seniors and a sad day for America. I have long fought for a prescription drug benefit, and I am truly disappointed that this bill fails to adequately address this need. Seniors deserve a comprehensive, reliable prescription drug plan. This is no such bill. It is a weak benefit meant to cover the true intentions of its authors—privatizing Medicare. In short, the bill Republicans are passing today is a wolf in sheep's clothing. Fortunately, there are some provisions included that I support [*she went on to mention five*]...And finally, this bill contains a proposal that I offered as an amendment on the Senate floor—the comparative effectiveness research provision. This will assure that we spend money on drugs that are most effective, not just the ones that are most advertised. These positive provisions, however, should have been attached to a good bill. They are not enough to justify undermining the promise of Medicare."

The final vote for the Medicare Prescription Drug, Improvement, and Modernization Act of 2003 was very close in the House. Final consideration of the conference report on the bill in the House began just before midnight on November 21, 2003. The way in which Mr. Hastert worked to secure the votes of enough recalcitrant conservative Republicans so the bill would pass put some in mind of Lyndon Johnson's heavy-handed management of the Senate.[10] Hastert made the unusual move of extending the period of debate allowed on the measure from 1 hour to 3 hours so he had time to secure enough votes. The roll call vote at 5:53 AM on November 22, 2003 in the House was 220 yeas (204 Republicans and 16 Democrats) and 215 nays (25 Republicans, 189 Democrats, and 1 Independent). The Senate voted a few days later, November 25, and at a more reasonable hour, 9:23 AM. In the Senate there were 54 yeas (42 Republicans, 11 Democrats, and 1 Independent) and 44 nays (35 Democrats and 9 Republicans), and 2 senators not voting, both Democrats. Mr. Hastert and Senator Majority Leader Bill Frist worked closely together to assure passage of the legislation. In fact, there was so much conflict that, reportedly, it was only the intervention of the two leaders that produced an acceptable compromise. With the passage of H.R. 1 and its Section 1013, the first federal mandate to conduct comparative effectiveness research was established.[11]

Section 1013 appears to have originated as a stand-alone piece of legislation making its way around Democrats in Congress whose advocates were trying to find a "must-move" bill to which to attach it.[12] Supporting this contention is the fact that Section 1013, which became law as part of the Medicare Modernization Act of 2003, is identical in every respect to Section 613 of S. 1926 "Support Our Health Providers Act of 2003," which was introduced by Senator Debbie Stabenow (D-MI) on November 21, 2003. This bill, one of the co-sponsors of which was Senator Tom Daschle (D-SD), was referred to the Senate Finance Committee and no further action was taken on it. Senator Daschle, a conferee on the Medicare bill, was a vocal proponent of federally mandated comparative effectiveness research, and he will come back into our story later.

Despite interviewing many of the individuals who were in some way involved in the negotiations on the Medicare Modernization Act of 2003, we were unable to determine with certainty who drafted Section 1013, how it got into the conference report, and how it was able to survive as part of the final bill.

It was almost certainly not Senator Hillary Clinton, though a few of our interviewees speculated that it was. Clinton was not a member of the conference committee that crafted the final bill, although she could have had some conversations with Senator Frist. Clinton does deserve the credit for raising the issue of comparative effectiveness research with the Amendment No. 1000 she proposed during the initial Senate floor debates on the bill. But an examination of Amendment S. 1000 and Section 1013 (the comparative effectiveness provisions) from the Medicare Modernization Act of 2003 shows that the two differ in structure and content. Finally, she must have thought Section 1013 of the Medicare Modernization Act of 2003 was insufficient. The day after it became law, on December 9, 2003, Senator Clinton introduced S. 2003 "Health Information for Quality Act." Section 203 of this bill, "Study on Effectiveness of Certain Prescription Drugs" was nearly identical to her Senate Amendment No. 1000.[13]

Several of our informants indicated that Senate Majority Leader Bill Frist was the one responsible for getting provisions for comparative effectiveness research into the final bill. For example, a legislative aide who was working for one of the involved federal agencies in 2003 told us that "The MMA's [*Section*] 1013 was a product primarily of Senator Frist, who by that time was Majority Leader and was in a position to have it inserted into the MMA. It built on other things and broader consensus developed by others. There had been a number of bills regarding CE [*comparative effectiveness*] either introduced or floating or developed, so I think there was a fairly broad bipartisan consensus. But Senator Frist was the primary actor in this case and negotiated the deal to put it in the bill outside of the regular channels. To the best of my knowledge the HELP [*Senate Committee on Health, Education, Labor and Pensions*] Committee was not consulted,[14] and the negotiators on the House side in Energy and Commerce and Ways and Means, they made the agreement with the Majority Leader. As a result it was not necessarily controversial. It was certainly something the Majority Leader wanted to do and he didn't want to have to negotiate with a million people so he arranged it so he did not have to do so."

Though we do not know Senator Frist's motivations, perhaps he wanted the comparative effectiveness research provisions in the bill in order to secure some additional votes for passage of the legislation. A former Congressional Budget Office (CBO) official who had been at CBO during the congressional debates and actions on the Medicare Modernization Act of 2003 put it this way: "History will judge the process for the MMA itself, but there is no question that the Bush Administration wanted a signature accomplishment. Republicans wanted an inroad with the AARP, a political objective. Then there was the research community's observation that, 'Jeez, drugs are part of modern medicine and it doesn't make much sense they aren't covered.' And Ted Kennedy signed on, which was an enormous help in getting the coalition. At that point it just became raw politics, the best and the worst. Every lobbyist that you can name came to town and waited on that bill. [*Regarding Section 1013*] There are constituencies out there who believe in CER [*comparative effectiveness research*]. Either they want more market-based approaches and the information is not there, or they believe the government should do this and be able to make these decisions. Regardless, they're all trying to get something in. And the ultimate political aspect of the process is that, once something becomes a must-move piece of legislation, you want to get your language in there because then you're going to get it into law. And that's what happened here with CER. It was not central to the bill, but there were a lot of things in the bill that were not central."

Or perhaps Senator Frist was trying to get something accomplished—a change in its authorities? New or more money?—for the Agency for Healthcare Research and Quality, and did it by attaching the language to a much larger piece of legislation he knew was going to pass. Frist was a long-time supporter of the agency, and that agency had a major stake in a federal mandate for comparative effectiveness research. Under Section 1013, AHRQ would be responsible for comparative effectiveness research and would receive any funds appropriated for the purpose. (Section 1013 authorized the appropriation of up to S50 million to AHRQ for fiscal year 2004 and "such sums as may be necessary" for subsequent years.) Officials at the agency itself, for one thing, hoped that Section 1013 would increase its funding for health services research and the predictability of that funding, as well as fix some of the perceived limitations in its existing statutory authority. These included the need to get rid of what one of our informants from the agency called "that old guideline language" in Section 1142 of the Social Security Act. The agency's issuance of clinical practice guidelines in the mid-1990s—an activity clearly within its statutory authority—drew the ire of some physician groups and members of Congress and contributed to what has been called "the near-death experience" of the agency. We will examine the later more closely in Chapter 10. Another limitation was that the existing statutory authorities did not require the agency to involve Medicare and the other federal health programs in setting agency research priorities. Consequently, much of the research the agency funded was of little interest to those programs, and the agency did not enjoy the support of those program officials or their advocacy during the annual appropriations process. Another limitation, according to our informants, was that the existing authorities of the agency did not include the crucial step of learning and teaching how to use in actual practice the information gained by the research.

In fact, as one of our informants pointed out, Section 1013 of the Medicare Modernization Act of 2003 did not confer new statutory authority on the Agency for Healthcare Research and Quality. The agency, as well as its predecessor agency, the Agency for Health Care Research and Policy, already had the authority to conduct and support comparative effectiveness research. That statutory authority was granted to it under Title IX of the Omnibus Budget Reconciliation Act of 1989[15] as amended by the Healthcare Research and Quality Act of 1999 (PL 106–129), a bill introduced by Senator Frist. Though the words "comparative" and "effectiveness" are not found together in the pre-2003 statutes, research on "effectiveness" and "cost-effectiveness" as found in the statutes obviously can be interpreted as including comparisons between alternative health technologies for the same condition. In effect, Section 1013 increased research funding for comparative effectiveness research. It allocated additional dollars to the agency, over and above its usual appropriation,[16] and earmarked the funds for comparative effectiveness research.

Section 1013 made two other changes to the agency. First, it directed it to have a public and transparent process for setting research priorities, and that the Secretary of Health and Human Services would set research priorities based on the needs of the Medicare, Medicaid, and State Children's Health Insurance programs. In other words, researchers would no longer be the ones to establish the research priorities. Second, it directed the agency to disseminate the results of its research and evidence syntheses in a way that made them accessible to multiple audiences.

The Legacies of Section 1013 and the Fight over the Medicare Modernization Act of 2003

The three most important legacies relating to the legislative odyssey of federally mandated comparative effectiveness research of Section 1013 and the fight over the Medicare Modernization Act of 2003 were a new program at the Agency for Healthcare Research and Quality, a nascent but substantial bipartisan attachment to the concept of comparative effectiveness research as a way to address unsustainable rises in national health expenditures, and a developing animosity between the proponents of federally mandated comparative effectiveness research and the medical products industry, which strongly opposed it.

After the passage of the Medicare Modernization Act of 2003 and its Section 1013, AHRQ established the Effective Health Care Program in order to carry out the authorities conferred to it by the statute. According to the agency, its

Effective Healthcare Program reviews and synthesizes published and unpublished scientific evidence, generates new scientific evidence and analytic tools, and compiles the evidence and translates it into useful formats for various audiences. Because the 2003 law was enacted outside of the congressional appropriations cycle, no funds were appropriated the first year (fiscal 2004). The agency got its first appropriation for Section 1013 in fiscal 2005, the sum of $15 million (the statute authorizes up to $50 million).[17] Proponents of federally mandated comparative effectiveness research thought this a paltry sum given the crisis in national health expenditures, and we will see marked increases as the decade of the 2000s progresses.

The negotiations pertaining to including comparative effectiveness research provisions in the Medicare Modernization Act of 2003 raised awareness of this policy alternative and its potential value for addressing health care costs, and nurtured the development of some bipartisan support. As a former Medicare official told us, "Part of what I think happened, more in the Democratic side but not exclusively on the Democratic side, were areas of common interest, looking at this [comparative effectiveness research] as a broader strategy to try to slow down spending, and I think the potential for having this reach across the aisle." The bipartisan support for comparative effectiveness research gave this policy option staying power as well as momentum over the next years of the 2000s.

Opposition to a federal mandate for comparative effectiveness research crystallized within the medical products industry, particularly in the pharmaceutical industry, during the discussions about including such provisions in the Medicare Modernization Act of 2003. (Even though the scope of Section 1013 clearly included devices, the lobbying group for the medical device industry seems to have been largely inattentive to federal policy on comparative effectiveness research at the time, a situation that changed later in the 2000s.) The shape of the arguments against, which as we saw were first heard on the floor of the Senate from the lips of Senator Mike Enzi in June 2003, changed little over the ensuing years, although oppositional tactics changed. Industry could not keep Section 1013 out of the legislation, but industry was able to get language into the bill that limited how the findings from such research could be used: "The Administrator of the Centers for Medicare and Medicaid Services may not use data obtained in accordance with this section [Section 1013] to withhold coverage of a prescription drug."

But the stance of the medical products industry against the inclusion of comparative effectiveness research in the bill had serious consequences. Using the term "pharma," which can refer to the pharmaceutical industry in general, any of its companies, or the industry's advocacy organization called the Pharmaceutical Research and Manufacturers of America, one House staffer told us, "Pharma, for a lot of Democrats, is still a four-letter word. Democrats don't trust them, and their opinion is informed by our experience during the

MMA [*Medicare Modernization Act of 2003*] . . . It was Democrats versus Pharma and Republicans. Pharma shot themselves in the foot by associating so closely with Republicans." Not only did the medical products industry lose regard in the eyes of the Democrats, their opposition to comparative effectiveness research actually fostered Democratic interest in this policy option. A Senate Committee staffer told us, "Pharma started to lobby against CE [*comparative effectiveness research*] so Democrats started to think that CE was a good idea."

Notes

1. The Centers for Education and Research on Therapeutics (CERTs) program is a national initiative to increase awareness through education and research of the benefits and risks of new, existing, or combined uses of therapeutics. The Agency for Healthcare Research and Quality, in consultation with the FDA, administers the CERTs program and its six centers.

2. Authorization laws establish, continue, or modify federal programs, and they are a prerequisite under the House and Senate rules for the Congress to appropriate budget authority for the programs. Some authorization laws provide spending directly (i.e., the authorizing legislation itself creates budget authority); the authorization laws providing for this "mandatory" or "direct" spending may be permanent or may require periodic renewal. The other kind of spending is called "discretionary." For this kind of spending, the role of the authorizing congressional committees is to enact legislation that serves as a basis for operating a program, and to guide the Appropriations Committees as to the appropriate level of funding for the program. Such authorizations may be provided as specific dollar amounts (definite authorizations) or "such sums as necessary" (indefinite authorizations). In addition, authorizations may be permanent and remain in effect until changed by the Congress, or they may cover only specific fiscal years. When a time-limited authorization expires, Congress may reauthorize it or simply extend a program by providing new appropriations. Information is available from http://appropriations.senate.gov/about-budget-process.cfm.

3. The Alliance was supported by the advocacy arm of AcademyHealth, the Coalition for Health Services Research, which was active in the 2000s. Coalition functions were absorbed into AcademyHealth in the early 2010s.

4. For an account of how the MMA legislation passed, see Iglehart J. The new Medicare prescription-drug benefit—a pure power play. N Engl J Med 2004; 350:826–33.

5. The authenticated text of the Medicare Modernization Act of 2003 is available from http://www.gpo.gov/fdsys/pkg/BILLS-108hr1enr/pdf/BILLS-108hr1enr.pdf. Section 1013 starts on page 373.

6. Senator Bill Frist, a physician and surgeon, served two terms as a Republican United States Senator representing Tennessee. He was the Republican Majority Leader from 2003 to 2007.

7. The Baucus-Conrad bill, S. 3408, Comparative Effectiveness Research Act of 2008.

8. The Senate conferees were Grassley (R-IA), Hatch (R-UT), Nickles (R-OK), Frist (R-TN), Kyl (R-AZ), Baucus (D-MT), Rockefeller (D-WV), Daschle (D-SD), and Breaux (D-LA). The House conferees were Tauzin (R-LA), Thomas (R-CA), Bilirakis (R-FL), Johnson (R-CT), DeLay (R-TX), Dingell (D-MI), Rangel (D-NY), and Berry (D-AR). The conference committee was chaired by Representative Bill Thomas (R-CA).

9. On July 10, 2003, Representative Bereuter (R-NE) offered Amendment No. 5 to the Departments of Labor, Health and Human Services, and Education, and Related Agencies Appropriations Act, 2004. His amendment, which was passed, "requires the Agency for Healthcare Research and Quality to spend $12 million for the conduct of research on the comparative effectiveness, cost-effectiveness, and safety of drugs, biological products and devices under their existing authorization." Representative

Bereuter's amendment did not increase AHRQ's appropriation by $12 million; rather it required AHRQ to allocate $12 million of its existing appropriation to comparative effectiveness research. The text of his arguments for the amendment can be found in the Congressional Record for the 108th Congress on July 10, 2003, pages H6560-1. Representative Nancy Johnson (R-CT) spoke in support of Mr. Bereuter's amendment. (It should be noted that Representative Johnson was a member of the conference committee on the Medicare Modernization Act of 2003.) Representative Nethercutt (R-WA) spoke against it, saying it "may set AHRQ in the wrong direction," "encourages the federal government to direct medical care," and "promotes a 'one-size-fits-all' approach to medicine which is bad for patients."

10. See Hulse C. Fight to pass Medicare measure raised House Speaker's profile. New York Times 2003 Dec 6. (Accessed August 12, 2012, at http://www.nytimes. com/2003/12/06/us/fight-to-pass-medicare-measure-raised-house-speaker-s-profile. html?scp=1&sq=hulse%20december%206%202003&st=cse.)

11. This is an overstatement, given the 1997 bill (P.L. 105–115) that authorized the CERTs demonstration program. But the conduct of comparative effectiveness research by the CERTs never reached much, if any, public notice or notice within the research community.

12. As a civil servant at the Agency for Healthcare Research and Quality told us, "This legislation that became Section 1013 of the MMA [*Medicare Modernization Act of 2003*] had been traveling around Congress for a while as stand-alone legislation that was bipartisan in terms of its support in both the House and the Senate. In previous years, variations, different forms...the scope changed a little bit, and then there was acceleration as the MMA was being shaped...a train, so to speak, to roll this legislation into the MMA. This is a common thing to do on the Hill when you have legislation that can be attached to other larger legislation because it is either not controversial or is insignificant in size to the other legislation."

13. The bill was referred to the Senate Committee on Finance; no further action on it was taken.

14. In fact, jurisdictional concerns between Senate Committees were raised by Section 1013. As a former Senate committee staffer told us, "Majority Leader Senator Frist wanted that comparative effectiveness research provision in the MMA [*Medicare Modernization Act of 2003*], and so it was in the MMA (chuckles). I was working for the HELP [*Senate Health, Education, Labor and Pensions*] Committee at the time, and the MMA was a bill that was written out to the Finance Committee. We at the HELP Committee were very concerned that the legislation impinged on our jurisdiction, and we urged that that provision be considered in our Committee rather than be included in the MMA bill. We lost. The bill provided AHRQ with funding to do these [*comparative effectiveness research*] studies. We were interested in having that debate in a full setting rather than having something that was not a focal point and was an attachment to a much larger bill. We wanted to have that debate in our Committee."

15. Reconciliation acts are not assigned a public law number.

16. AHRQ received a total appropriation of $318,695,000 in fiscal year 2005.

17. In each fiscal year 2005, 2006, and 2007, Congress appropriated AHRQ $15 million to carry out the authorities in Section 1013. The appropriation was increased to $30 million for fiscal 2008 and to $50 million in 2009. In fiscal 2010, the appropriation was $21 million but the 2009/10 Recovery Act provided an additional $300 million. For fiscal 2011, $21 million was appropriated under a Continuing Resolution, and an addition $8 million was transferred to AHRQ from the Patient Centered Outcomes Research Trust Fund. Information is available from http://www.ahrq.gov/about/cj2012/cj2012.pdf.

8

2005 to 2007

*The Health Services Research Community Stirs,
the "B" Word Awakens Policy Makers,
and the House CHAMP Act Creates Divisions*

Storms of controversy and partisan acrimony—about the size of the new entitlement program, its provisions for increasing payments to Medicare managed care plans, the Bush administration's suppression of actuarial evidence about the estimated cost of the new program, and many other aspects of the legislation—surrounded the passage of the 2003 Medicare Modernization Act and continued afterward. Along with the sheer size of the bill, that meant that many of its provisions, including Section 1013 and its authorization of "up to $50 million" to the Agency for Healthcare Research and Quality (AHRQ) for comparative effectiveness research in fiscal year 2004, got little notice. Those in the health services research community who *had* noted the passage of Section 1013 had to wait until 2005 for the first appropriation of funds, which was only $15 million for that year. In fact, Congress kept the appropriation for Section 1013 to $15 million for 2005, 2006, and 2007.

AHRQ created its Effective Health Care Program with Section 1013 funds, but the years 2003 to 2005 (and even 2006) were quiet ones as far as legislation on comparative effectiveness research was concerned. However, because of initiatives taken by its main organization, AcademyHealth, the health services research community began to see the potential for federal policy on comparative effectiveness research. This awareness, and a belief that comparative effectiveness research might help control rising health care costs, spread rapidly in the community of health policy makers, especially after a prominent Republican health policy expert announced in November 2006 that the federal government should create a center for comparative effectiveness research and support it with billions of dollars. In 2007, the House passed the CHAMP Act, which contained provisions for the establishment of a Center for Comparative Effectiveness Research within AHRQ. The act never became law, but the House passage indicated that a significant consensus had been reached, and the debates revealed where the fault lines were for future legislation. In this chapter, we tell the story of how these events and processes built the momentum for eventual enactment of additional comparative effectiveness research legislation and began to shape what form it would take.

The Health Services Research Community Stirs: AcademyHealth's "Placement Report"

The health services research and health policy communities in the United States include many individuals who rotate regularly among governmental, academic, and "think tank" positions. AcademyHealth is the nation's largest organization representing the interests of health services researchers. Through its advocacy arm, AcademyHealth interacts with members of Congress and congressional staff to secure increased funding for health services research via the annual appropriations process to AHRQ, a major sponsor of extramural health services research, and other federal entities that fund such research.

AHRQ, like the National Institutes of Health (NIH), is an agency of the Department of Health and Human Services. AHRQ's operating funds are appropriated each year by the Congress to the Department from the general receipts of the U.S. Treasury. The amount of the annual appropriation is a matter of negotiation among the White House and both houses of Congress. NIH's annual appropriations are much larger than AHRQ's; for example, in 2005 the NIH appropriation was $28.5 billion while AHRQ's was $319 million. Federal funding for investigator-initiated health services research is chronically perceived by the field as being in short supply. Moreover, while the NIH's sacrosanct place in the American psyche seems to protect it from congressional attacks on its existence or its budget, the continued existence of AHRQ has seemed chronically imperiled, a matter to be covered in Chapter 10.[1]

In the first half of the 2000s AcademyHealth and its advocacy arm, the Coalition for Health Services Research (hereafter, the Coalition), were finding the annual AHRQ appropriations process to be tough sledding. Part of the difficulty seemed to be the prosaic nature of health services research ("It's harder to understand; it's not the glamorous 'search for the cure'"), and part was how some congressional staffers perceived AHRQ: "We struggled with John Eisenberg [a late AHRQ director[2]] telling us that we needed to get a billion dollars for AHRQ. I'm up on the Hill, and congressional staff would say, 'For what? And to do what? What has AHRQ done with what it's been given already?'"

To be fair, the Coalition had been advocating for increased funding for health services research during a period when Republicans controlled the Congress[3] and the White House. At the same time, though, AHRQ was having image problems with some health services researchers in the field. As a former

Board member of AcademyHealth told us, "There has been disappointment by many in the health services research field, particularly among researchers themselves, that AHRQ has moved away from a traditional role of having a significant amount of its money directed at investigator-initiated research. Today, when you look at its portfolio, it is driven by a set of congressional mandates, at least that's how AHRQ has described them."

The law that established AHRQ in 1999 authorized appropriations to it only for fiscal years 2000 through 2005, meaning that Congress would have to decide to reauthorize the agency in 2005.[4] The prospect of AHRQ's congressional reauthorization, along with the image and funding problems AHRQ was having, stimulated AcademyHealth to take the opportunity to evaluate its vision for the federal role in health services research.

In late 2003 AcademyHealth launched an analysis of the funding, the placement, and the coordination of health services research at the federal level, to be ready in time to inform the congressional reauthorization process for AHRQ. It established what came to be called the "Placement Committee," which was chaired by Sheila Burke, the former chief of staff for Senate Majority Leader Bob Dole, and co-chaired by Jeanne Lambrew,[5] a leading health policy expert who had held important positions in earlier Democratic administrations. Burke had strong Republican credentials, which, as one of our AcademyHealth's informants told us, "could get us access to Senator Frist," the Senate Majority Leader. Gail Wilensky,[6] a former administrator of the Health Care Financing Administration (now called the Centers for Medicare and Medicaid Services) in the administration of George H.W. Bush, also with sterling Republican credentials, was a member of the Placement Committee.[7]

Although not a prime motivator for establishing the Placement Committee, the passage of comparative effectiveness research provisions in the Medicare Modernization Act of 2003 had not gone unnoticed by the organization or by the Committee members. They quickly grasped its potential significance for the field and soon made it the primary focus of the Committee. A Committee member told us, "The upcoming AHRQ reauthorization is what kick-started the Placement Committee, and then CER [*comparative effectiveness research*] came up and then it became an issue of where to place CER, and then for the Placement Committee and for the staff, it became a question of which is the dog and which is the tail. The thinking was that CER spending, if you want to do it right, would have to be huge. There were some examples that came out about that time; the National Institute of Mental Health had done a comparison of schizophrenia drugs that came out about that time[8] and that study alone cost $15 million—and that was all Congress was willing to authorize for the AHRQ CER in the MMA. [*In fact, $50 million was authorized but only $15 million was appropriated to AHRQ the first year for CER.*] So [CER] was seen as potentially a huge opportunity, and that the field of health services research, if Congress was willing to go along this way and could be convinced, could be looking at maybe $100 million a year, which is a third the size of AHRQ alone ... CER became a potential driver that could really push either health services research and/or AHRQ into a bigger sphere."

Over 12 months, the Placement Committee interviewed roughly 40 individuals who were distinguished health services researchers, congressional staff, or opinion leaders.

Though an array of issues pertaining to the field of health services research was considered by the Committee, a central issue that emerged was where federally mandated comparative effectiveness research should be "placed," that is, the different agencies, forms of public entities, or types of public-private entities that could oversee funding for comparative effectiveness research. In fact, the placement of federal comparative effectiveness research, which basically came down to inside AHRQ or in some other entity, turned out to be the most enduring controversy of the entire legislative odyssey. A Committee member crystallized the main points for us: "It was really a question of how best to set up a system. Who was best able to gather people around those questions? Were there agencies in the federal government capable of doing it [comparative effectiveness research]? Did it require a third party external to the government to do it? Who would participate? What was the environment in which one would have to play, and how did you increase the support for this entity, whatever it was? What would the Congress support? What would the agencies support? We talked to people on the Hill. We talked to people in the agencies. Some of what you see is the traditional internecine warfare of one agency against another. They tend to think in stovepipes. 'If they get money, I don't get money. If they get decision authority, I don't.' Will the third parties come to the table? Are there trust issues? The goal was to decide who was best able to do this. Did you need to create something new or could you use AHRQ or some other organization within the government and empower them? Everybody remembered the back surgery brouhaha and how they were savaged."

After several iterations, the Committee identified four placement options, some they knew were not likely to be politically viable but were nonetheless important to view within the spectrum of choices. The Committee deliberately resisted endorsing one option over the others. Instead, they developed and put forth a set of five principles designed to guide policy makers' decisions. Offering principles to guide decision making rather than an actual recommendation for placement seems to have been wise. It sent the message that the most important thing at this juncture was a commitment to a federal mandate for comparative effectiveness research; placement should be a secondary concern. Box 8.1 gives the placement options and principles.

Box 8.1 Options for Placing Responsibility for Comparative Effectiveness Research, and Principles to Guide Decisions about Placement

Option 1: The Agency for Healthcare Research and Quality (AHRQ) sponsors and conducts comparative effectiveness studies with oversight and guidance from an external board and panel of experts.

Option 2: ARHQ sponsors and conducts comparative effectiveness studies with oversight and guidance from an external board and panel of experts, and establishes a Federally Funded Research and Development Center (FFRDC).[a]

Option 3: AHRQ remains as currently structured and a new separate quasi-government entity is established to fund and conduct comparative effectiveness research.

Option 4: AHRQ is reconstituted as a quasi-governmental agency retaining most existing functions and adding comparative effectiveness research.

Principle 1: Overall funding for the field of health services research should continue to support a broad and comprehensive range of topics

Principle 2: Assessments should be based on scientific evidence and kept separate from funding and coverage decisions.

Principle 3: Entity commissioning or conducting comparative effectiveness research should maintain close linkage to the lead agency for health services research.

Principle 4: Entity commissioning or conducting comparative effectiveness research should be subject to congressional oversight.

Principle 5: Entity commissioning or conducting comparative effectiveness research should involve key stakeholders to assure transparency of the methods and process, promote public acceptance of research findings, and support for the entity's mission.

[a] According to the AcademyHealth Report, "FFRDCs receive their funding primarily from federal government agencies but operate as private, not-for-profit organizations. They are usually located at a university or an autonomous nonprofit organization. FFRDCs are not subject to federal personnel rules but are prohibited from competing for government contracts to ensure their independence, objectivity, and freedom from organizational conflicts of interest. They do not have a prescribed organizational structure but must be sponsored by an executive branch agency that monitors, funds, and is responsible for the overall use of the FFRDC. FFRDCs fall into categories such as research laboratory or study and analysis center. In some instances, an FFRDC may be a unit of a larger organization, such as the National Defense Research Institute, which is part of the RAND Corporation."

Source: AcademyHealth. Placement, coordination, and funding of health services research within the federal government. September 2005.

AcademyHealth released its "Placement Report" in September 2005,[9] as a staffer told us, "to little fanfare." While the Report might have gone unnoticed by many in the field, it was not allowed to go unnoticed on Capitol Hill. Members of the Placement Committee engaged in a series of post-Placement Report rounds on the Hill, intended to present the Committee's findings and so influence policy. Though sometimes they visited members of Congress or their staffs jointly, generally the Committee members with Republican credentials went to the Republicans, and those with Democratic credentials went to the Democrats. Among others, they met with those who supported Section 1013 in the Medicare Modernization Act of 2003, the staff of Senator Hillary Clinton, and with Representative Tom Allen (D-ME) and his staff. After the face-to-face visits, Committee members followed up with congressional staff.

Perhaps influenced by the Placement Report or post-Report meetings, Representative Tom Allen and seven co-sponsors on July 28, 2006, during the 109th Congress, introduced H.R. 5975, the Prescription Drug Comparative Effectiveness Act of 2006. The bill required the Director of AHRQ to conduct or support reviews of existing evidence and research to develop evidence on comparative effectiveness, outcomes, and appropriateness of prescription drugs, medical devices, and procedures, and authorized the appropriation of $100 million to AHRQ and NIH for this purpose for fiscal year 2007 and thereafter. It was referred to the Subcommittee on Health of the House Committee on Energy and Commerce, where it died.

The Congressional Record for 2006 includes two other references to comparative effectiveness research in relation to bills.[10] One of these links comparative effectiveness to potential reductions in health care costs, a linkage that would become controversial in later stages of the legislative journey. On March 14, 2006, Senator Max Baucus (D-MT), ranking minority member of the Senate Finance Committee, offered an amendment (S.A. 3060) to a budget resolution stating that it is "the sense of the Senate" that the budget should include funding for "innovative initiatives to reduce the rate of growth in health care costs...such as...investing in comparative clinical effectiveness."

The Legacies of AcademyHealth's "Placement" Activities

The activities of AcademyHealth and the advocacy of the Coalition did not succeed in getting Congress to reauthorize AHRQ. AHRQ continues to operate today under authority that expired in 2005, receiving de facto authorization in the way of the annual appropriation of funds. The annual appropriation to AHRQ grew moderately, from $204 million in FY00 to $372 million in FY10,[11] but this was a lower growth rate than occurred in the overall federal budget during that period.

But if the Coalition and AcademyHealth's Placement Committee were unsuccessful in the matter of AHRQ's reauthorization, the same cannot be said with regard to effects on policy for comparative effectiveness research. The activities leading up to the formation of the Placement Committee, its interviews and deliberations, and the post-Placement Report rounds on the Hill created a fairly large network of policy makers and policy influentials who were knowledgeable and held strong opinions about federally mandated comparative effectiveness research and what it might have to offer if expanded and structured in alternative ways. This network of primary actors can be credited with the substantial diffusion of interest in comparative effectiveness research as federal policy that occurred in the subsequent years. After the Placement Committee's activities, there was an exponential increase in the number of meetings and lay and professional press reports about federally mandated comparative effectiveness research. Though Washington was the epicenter, meetings and press coverage extended throughout the United States and involved more and more groups with a stake in the issue.

The activities of the Institute of Medicine[12] (IOM) merit special note in this regard. The IOM's interest in "effectiveness research" can be traced to its Clinical Research Roundtable,[13] active between 2000 and 2004. Issues about research into the effectiveness of health services, and their comparative effectiveness, had surfaced during the Roundtable's work. In the fall of 2004, the Roundtable devoted some time to a consideration of a proposal for the creation of a new structure for research on health care effectiveness developed by Joel Kupersmith, a former medical school dean who was at that time a scholar-in-residence at the Institute of Medicine and the American Association of Medical Colleges. These considerations were subsequently reported in a paper published in March 2005.[14] The paper focuses on effectiveness research—the qualifier "comparative" is not used. The authors propose the creation of a public-private consortium for effectiveness research and give some examples of existing successful consortia. One is the Transportation Research Board, which is one of the six major divisions of the National Research Council, the operating agency of the National Academies of Science, which includes the IOM. By invoking the Transportation Research Board model, the Kupersmith paper had raised the possibility of an operational role for the IOM in the performance of effectiveness studies of one sort or another, a role both resource intensive and politically sensitive.

In view of external forces and the proposals of Kupersmith and his coauthors, in January 2005 the IOM recruited J. Michael McGinnis[15] and commissioned him to head the exploration of the potential leadership role that the National Academy of Sciences and the IOM might play in fostering progress on comparative effectiveness research. Recognizing that nothing could happen without stakeholder and constituent involvement, McGinnis suggested that the

IOM establish a roundtable to explore the issues of comparative effectiveness research, including current and future capacity for such research. In January 2006, the IOM established and convened the Roundtable on Evidence-Based Medicine, later renamed the Roundtable on Value and Science-Driven Health Care. The Roundtable was sponsored by many stakeholders of all types,[16] and, like all IOM Roundtables, held open workshops and symposia. It eventually expanded its activities to include five "stakeholder collaboratives,"[17] extending its reach even further. Four months later, in April 2006, the IOM launched another activity related to comparative effectiveness research, a consensus study, requested and funded by the Robert Wood Johnson Foundation, titled "Reviewing Evidence to Identify Highly Effective Clinical Services." The consensus committee was appointed in June 2006 and was chaired by Barbara MacNeil, professor and head of the Department of Health Care Policy at Harvard Medical School, and Hal Sox, editor of the *Annals of Internal Medicine*. The activities of the IOM greatly expanded further the network of persons interested in federal policy on comparative effectiveness research.

The other legacy of AcademyHealth's Placement Committee is that their deliberations about the structure and placement of the entity responsible for comparative effectiveness research laid the groundwork for congressional negotiators later in the decade. It might be said that the structure and placement selected for comparative effectiveness research in the 2010 Affordable Care Act falls under "Option 3" proposed by the Placement Committee.

Work on the Placement Committee crystallized the opinions and resolve of two of its members in particular, Jeanne Lambrew and Gail Wilensky. Both of these individuals had developed substantial political capital in the course of their prior work in government, and both enjoyed access to many members of Congress and the Administration. They subsequently played important roles in raising the profile of comparative effectiveness research and in framing it as a solution to a national problem of gigantic proportions: runaway health care costs. In 2009, Lambrew, together with former Senate Majority Leader Tom Daschle (D-SD), President-elect Obama's original choice for Secretary of Health and Human Services, published a book on health care reform.[18] In it they proposed a quasi-governmental body called the Federal Health Board that would operate for the health care industry the way the Federal Reserve works for the banking industry. As they envisioned it, the "Fed Health" could use information on the comparative clinical and cost effectiveness of various treatment options to set standards for federal programs. During the years remaining in the decade of the 2000s, Wilensky testified on behalf of comparative effectiveness research at several congressional hearings. And in 2006 she published a widely noted paper in *Health Affairs* on the need for a federal center for comparative effectiveness research, a paper that changed the game.

A Prominent Republican Puts the "B" Word on Comparative Effectiveness Research: Gail Wilensky's November 2006 Paper in *Health Affairs*

Two important things happened on November 7, 2006. For one thing, it was Election Day, and as on all federal election days, all 435 seats in the House of Representatives and a third of those in the Senate were in play. For the 110th Congress, the House "turned" and Democrats regained control by a 31-seat margin over the Republicans (233 Democrats, 202 Republicans), and Democrats gained five seats in the Senate, which, counting the two Independents that caucused with them, gave them a 51–49 margin. A Republican, President George W. Bush, still held the White House but was in the last 2 years of his second term. That same day, *Health Affairs*, a journal that has been called "the Bible of health policy" and is widely read by health policy makers and their staffs, published a paper by Gail R. Wilensky.[19] Working from the premise that comparative effectiveness research was a "mechanism that will help the United States make better spending and coverage decisions," the focus of Wilensky's paper was "to assess the various options regarding the structure, placement, financing, and functions of an agency devoted to comparative (clinical) effectiveness assessment."

But what got the paper broad notice was that Wilensky, a health economist and Republican with an impeccable record of supporting small government, said in the article that this new agency needed to be financed annually at the "multibillion-dollar" level. (As a referent, in 2006, AHRQ's appropriated budget did not reach $319 million, and the additional appropriation earmarked for comparative effectiveness research was $15 million.) As one of our informants said, "Gail Wilensky put the 'b' word on it. She's the one who put the b word on it, nobody else." Though Wilensky said "multi-billion" in her paper, somewhere in the aftermath the $5 billion figure got attached. As a federal political appointee told us, "The $5 billion number really, really got people excited."

The *Health Affairs* paper was a product of Wilensky's prior work and analyses, her experience with the deliberations of AcademyHealth's Placement Committee, and a series of interviews she conducted with stakeholders after the Placement Committee completed its work. Democratic as well as Republican policy makers took note of the paper. One congressman told us, "Gail's article in *Health Affairs* saying we need a big, bold, billion dollar program [*in comparative effectiveness research*] changed the dynamics."

Some Republican policy makers and some members of the business community were interested in an investment in comparative effectiveness research because it would support market-based reforms of the health care system and consumer-directed health care. As one congressional staffer told us, "If consumers are going to have more skin in the game and have some responsibility for their [*health care*] decisions, they need to have a whole lot better and more reliable information than they presently do to make those decisions."

The Legacies of Wilensky's *Health Affairs* Paper

Had anyone else in the United States authored that paper, chances are that it would have gone largely unnoticed. The paper had the far-reaching effects it did because of its author's credentials and her political capital. Wilensky's analyses and propositions brought attention to, and bipartisan support for, a policy alternative, and the specifics in the paper about options for structuring it and financing it served as a starting point for crafting legislation. The timing of the paper was fortuitous as well. With the Democrats gaining a majority in Congress, and the resultant changes in the chairpersons and membership of congressional committees having jurisdiction over health care, events that Election Day started Democrats thinking that reform of the health care system might be a real prospect, depending on the results of the presidential election 2 years away.

Shortly after Wilensky's paper appeared, another staunch advocate for federal policy on comparative effectiveness research stepped into her wake. On January 18, 2007, Peter Orszag left his post at the Brookings Institution to become the Director of the Congressional Budget Office.[20] Orszag's energetic speaking schedule on federally mandated comparative effectiveness research earned him the label "ubiquitous."

Wilensky's *Health Affairs* paper of November 2006 sparked increased activity with regard to federal policy on comparative effectiveness research. During the first half of 2007, four bills were introduced in Congress that contained comparative effectiveness research provisions, indicating that an increasing number of legislators were willing to take up serious debate on the issue. On January 4, 2007, Senator Harry Reid (D-NV) introduced S.3, the Medicare Prescription Drug Price Negotiation Act of 2007, which was basically a 10-line "sense of the Senate" bill. S.3 was referred to the Senate Finance Committee, chaired by Senator Max Baucus (D-MT). By the time (April 13, 2007) Senator Baucus reported S.3 to the Senate (S.3 RS), the bill had expanded to 21 pages and included two sections on comparative effectiveness, one directing the Secretary of Health and Human Services to "develop a comprehensive prioritized list of comparative clinical effectiveness studies that are most critical to building the evidence needed to advance value-based purchasing of covered Part D drugs," and the other authorizing that comparative effectiveness studies could be considered in making formulary decisions about such drugs. The Senate never debated S.3 RS. Motions that the full Senate consider the bill failed.

On January 18, 2007, Senator Ron Wyden (D-OR) introduced S. 334, the Healthy Americans Act. Sections 701 and 702 offer various incentives and pressures on drug and device manufacturers to encourage them to conduct comparative effectiveness studies on their products. The bill was referred to the Senate Finance Committee and was never reported out.

On May 7, Representative Tom Allen (D-ME) introduced H.R. 2184, a bill "to amend the Medicare Prescription Drug, Improvement, and Modernization Act of 2003 to expand comparative effectiveness research and to increase funding for such research to improve the value of health care." We have more to say about this bill in the next section.

On July 24, 2007, Representative Brian Baird (D-WA) introduced H.R.3163, the Healthy Americans Act. This bill was referred to four House Committees and was never reported out by any of them. H.R. 3163 includes the same sort of incentives for the medical products industry to conduct comparative effectiveness studies as the related Wyden bill, but in addition, the Baird bill includes a Title VIII, "Enhanced Health Care Value," which pertains to research on the comparative effectiveness of health care items and services. (Title VIII of this Baird bill is word for word the same as Allen's H.R. 2184, except for one provision.[21])

The "Mystery Tax at Midnight": Comparative Effectiveness Research Provisions in the House Children's Health and Medicare Protection (CHAMP) Act of 2007

At the start of calendar year 2007, Democrats controlled both houses of Congress and had begun mobilizing for a presidential election in November of 2008 they hoped would put a Democrat in the White House. On January 20, 2007, Senator Hillary Clinton (D-NY) announced her candidacy for the Democratic nomination for the presidency; 3 weeks later, Senator Barack Obama (D-IL) announced his.[22] Senator John McCain (R-AZ) entered the race for the Republican presidential nomination on April 25, 2007.[23] Prospects for reforming the health care system to extend coverage to the roughly 47 million uninsured Americans were looking up. At the same time, it was widely recognized that the annual increases in national health expenditures were unsustainable and had to be reined in. The proportion of the U.S. Gross Domestic Product expended on health care had reached 16.4%, and per capita spending on health care had been increasing about two and a half percentage points faster than other spending for decades. When the base amount was small, the annual increases could be ignored, but no longer.

It was the legislative staff of the Health Subcommittee of the House Ways and Means Committee who were destined to weave together several threads of comparative effectiveness research in 2007.

In the fall of 2006, the staff of the Health Subcommittee had learned from Gail Wilensky of the increasing bipartisan interest in comparative effectiveness research as a policy alternative, and of the options described in her upcoming paper on the topic. Subsequent meetings with representatives of the business community substantiated Wilensky's claim of broadening support for a major investment in comparative effectiveness research. Health Subcommittee Chairman Pete Stark's support for AHRQ and his deeply held opinion that much more information is needed on what works in health care provided the framework for committee staff to begin to work on drafting legislation.

Early in 2007 the Health Subcommittee staff contacted Mike McGinnis, executive director of the IOM's Roundtable on Evidence-Based Medicine, for information on the IOM's activities in this area. Later McGinnis invited legislative aides from the Health Subcommittee to come to the February Roundtable Workshop to share where the Hill was on legislation for comparative effectiveness research. The staff director of the Health Subcommittee, Cybele Bjorklund, was on leave, and Deb Mizeur, who was acting in that capacity in Bjorklund's absence, gave the talk. Mizeur's message was that some members of Congress did not know what comparative effectiveness research is, that others were nervous about it to the extent it sounded like rationing, and that others, including Mr. Stark, were very interested, but a lot of distance had to be covered between interest and the passage of policy.

After the IOM Workshop, the Health Subcommittee staff made contact with Susan Lexer, legislative assistant to Representative Tom Allen, because of that office's long-standing interest in comparative effectiveness research. Lexer had been working in Mr. Allen's office for about 7 years by this time, and she had worked on all prior versions of comparative effectiveness research bills that Mr. Allen had introduced in the House (2002, 2003, and 2006). They were in fact working on another version, to be introduced in 2007, and Lexer shared it with the Health Subcommittee staff. Lexer also connected staff with Jeanne Lambrew, co-chair of AcademyHealth's Placement Committee, and Lambrew alerted Emily Rowe Holubowich, the lead for AcademyHealth's advocacy arm, the Coalition, and the coordinator of the Alliance for Better Health Care, a broad-based group of health insurers, large employers, consumer groups, and other stakeholders. Between January and June 2007 Health Subcommittee staff participated in a bipartisan Ways and Means and Energy Commerce working group focusing on physician payment reform, along with individuals from the Congressional Research Service, the Congressional Budget Office (two agencies that would issue reports on comparative effectiveness research later in 2007[24]), and the Medicare Payment Advisory Commission. Threads were coming together.

On May 7, 2007, Representative Tom Allen and co-sponsor Jo Ann Emerson (R-MO) introduced H.R. 2184, a bill "to amend the Medicare Prescription

Drug, Improvement, and Modernization Act of 2003 to expand comparative effectiveness research and to increase funding for such research to improve the value of health care."[25] Among other things, the bill would establish a Comparative Effectiveness Research Advisory Board composed of the Director of AHRQ and up to 14 additional members representing broad stakeholder groups; this Board was to report to Congress within 2 years "regarding the establishment of one or more federally funded research and development centers." The bill also would establish the Health Care Comparative Effectiveness Trust Fund, which would consist of appropriated funds, transfers from the Medicare Trust Fund, and fees levied on health insurance and self-insured plans. That same day, May 7, 2007, the BlueCross BlueShield Association held a press conference "strongly recommending that Congress pass legislation creating a new Institute that would support research comparing the effectiveness of new and existing procedures, drugs, devices and biologics." In a statement later that day Democratic presidential front-runner Senator Hillary Clinton praised BlueCross BlueShield's call for comparative effectiveness research legislation and announced her intention to introduce such legislation.[26]

Eight days later Representative Allen held a press conference outside on the steps of the Capitol to announce the bill he had introduced. May 15, 2007 was a bright, sunny day. Standing with him to endorse the bill were Helen Darling, president and chief executive officer of the National Business Group on Health; Jeanne Lambrew, the co-chair of AcademyHealth's Placement Committee; and W. David Helms, president and chief executive officer of AcademyHealth, among others.

Over the subsequent weeks the Health Subcommittee staffers worked with Mr. Stark through the issues relating to a major new federal initiative in comparative effectiveness research. On June 12, 2007, Mr. Stark held a hearing on strategies to increase research and information on comparative clinical effectiveness. The hearing lasted nearly 3 hours. The goals of comparative effectiveness were discussed as were potential structures and financing mechanisms for it. Leading off the nine witnesses was Representative Tom Allen; the next four were Carolyn Clancy (director, AHRQ), Peter Orszag (director, CBO), Mark Miller (director, Medicare Payment Advisory Committee), and Gail Wilensky (senior fellow, Project Hope).[27]

But in 2007 the attention of Congress was not focused on comparative effectiveness research. Congress was preoccupied by two issues of gigantic proportions, both pertaining to health care entitlement programs. One was the need to reauthorize, by September 30, 2007, the 10-year-old State Children's Health Insurance Program (SCHIP), which had greatly expanded publicly funded health care for children of low-income families not poor enough to qualify for Medicaid.[28] The other was the "doc fix"—addressing the prospect that, under current law, the sustainable growth rate formula in the Medicare physician fee schedule would lead to a 10% cut in Medicare reimbursements to physicians in 2008 and deeper cuts thereafter.

States, advocacy groups, religious organizations, and Democrats (and some Republicans) in Congress strongly favored SCHIP reauthorization, but in mid-summer 2007, the Bush Administration began to attack congressional efforts to reauthorize SCHIP, using a combination of speeches, letter campaigns to newspapers, threats of veto, and the release of highly controversial data that minimized the problem of uninsured children. This galvanized Democrats in the 110th Congress, and SCHIP reauthorization began to appear as "must pass" legislation. Then provisions pertaining to the Medicare program (including the "doc fix" and other elements of physician payment reform) were brought into the SCHIP reauthorization bill, as well as provisions for comparative effectiveness research. Staffers to the Subcommittee on Health of Ways and Means were committed to trying to get provisions for comparative effectiveness research in the bill (one staffer reportedly believed that, in the bill "the Children's Health Insurance Program stuff and the doc fixes [are] interim fixes—but getting something up and running on comparative effectiveness research would be an enduring contribution"), but other less closely involved members of the House also shared the interest. A staffer for a Democratic legislator not on any of the involved committees told us, "I wasn't part of the conversation at that point...our involvement came later, after all of that [comparative effectiveness research and information technology] was included in the CHAMP Act. With the CHAMP Act, we finally had a chance to do all the things that Democrats wanted to do to improve health care and the Medicare program for the first time in 10 years, more than 10 years actually, so we were looking at all the ways to lay the groundwork for 2009 [after the inauguration of the next president], to get the ball rolling on comparative effectiveness research and put some money in place. Then we can build on that when there is an administration that is willing to dump in more resources."

Accordingly, staffers on the Health Subcommittee of Ways and Means explored various ways that the comparative effectiveness research function could be structured, governed, and financed, considering which options had the best political viability. The 2007 Allen bill served as an important resource. Parts of it even served as a template, but there are several differences. For example, while the Allen bill would have housed comparative effectiveness research within a federally funded research and development center (outside government), the CHAMP bill housed it within AHRQ (inside government).

A Health Subcommittee staffer told us, "We talked through the different options and governance options [for comparative effectiveness research]. Pete Stark obviously did not like the idea of having a private entity doing all this and didn't like the idea of giving government money in a mandatory appropriation to a private entity to do with as it saw fit. Of the various federal agencies, they are very sympathetic with AHRQ and thought that funding a center at AHRQ to do this made sense and then having a public-private oversight body to sort of manage the politically difficult stuff would be a solution. We spent a lot of time looking into the federally funded research and development center model, but decided that, if you looked at all the issues that people were trying to deal with by creating a public-private activity rather than just doing it in government, it didn't seem like that in the end an FFRDC did enough to fix that. [*In writing the legislation*] the idea of an all payer tax was in, was out, was in again . . . For obvious reasons, it was viewed as a lightning rod . . . We all knew we had to come up with money for [*the comparative effectiveness research provisions*] from somewhere. At the time we had not figured out that we could do a mandatory appropriation from general revenue which is the dodge that the Senate Finance Committee tried in the fall [*of 2007*] and now is part of Baucus-Conrad [*referring to S. 3408, the Comparative Effectiveness Act of 2008, sponsored by Senators Max Baucus and Kent Conrad*], and some didn't like the idea of funding it in all from the Medicare program. [*NAME*] made the analogy to graduate medical education financing: if you have Medicare fund it initially, waiting for other people to come on board, then that just means that only Medicare will pay for it. That was actually the alternative that stakeholders were proposing at that time, because nobody thought that doing it through annual appropriations was a good idea—that was sort of off the table. So in the end we did bill it 'all-payer financing.'"[29]

A staffer explained to us that the CHAMP Act was a bill jointly developed by Energy and Commerce and Ways and Means. Some provisions had single jurisdiction, a lot of provisions had joint jurisdiction, and though it was unclear where the comparative effectiveness research provisions would fall, everybody agreed that it was going to be part of the final package. In 2007, the staffs of the two committees worked together effectively and there was give-and-take on the controversial elements. "The people are different, the personalities are different, and the strengths and weaknesses are different, but people worked hard and pulled together a 500-page bill that addressed children's health insurance and a bunch of good government stuff."

On July 24, 2007, John Dingell (D-MI), chairman of the House Energy and Commerce Committee, introduced H.R. 3162, the Children's Health and Medicare Protection Act of 2007 (CHAMP Act), a 465-page bill. Section 904 of Title IX "Miscellaneous" contained the comparative effectiveness provisions. Acknowledging the impact one individual can make, several people we interviewed credited the efforts of Eugene C. Rich, a Robert Wood Johnson Health Policy fellow working on the Health Subcommittee. A legislative aide to a congressman told us, "This wouldn't have happened, Allen [*Representative Tom Allen*] wouldn't have had a hearing in Ways and Means, we wouldn't have had the package in the CHAMP bill, without Gene Rich. We had to have a staff member on the committee who spent his time, a good portion of his time, working with us and taking an interest in this... Having Gene here made all the difference."

The day the CHAMP Act was introduced in the House, July 24, 2007, the bill was referred to the Committees on Energy and Commerce and Ways and Means. Energy and Commerce referred the bill that same day to its Subcommittee on Health, and on July 26 and 27 the Subcommittee considered the bill and held its markup session.[30] The House Ways and Means Committee did not refer the bill to their Health Subcommittee.[31] Rather the full committee took up consideration of the bill on July 26 and held its markup that day; working into the night, shortly before 2 AM on Friday July 26, the Ways and Means Committee finally ordered the amended bill to be reported (24 yeas, all Democrats, and 17 nays, all Republicans).[32]

The events of July 26–27 were much more dramatic than the aforementioned account suggests, as indicated by a description given to us by an observer (Box 8.2). On July 27, 2007 the Republicans on the Ways and Means Committee issued through its press office a release titled "Ways and Means Democrats' Mystery Midnight Tax Provision: Taxes Health Insurance, Raids Medicare Trust Fund." The release describes a "stealth tax increase that will drain money from the Medicare trust fund and increase taxes on every American with a health insurance plan. Worse, this tax hike was hidden in a non-tax portion of the bill and Democrats were utterly unable to explain it."

On July 30, 2007, Peter Orszag, CBO director, wrote a letter to Charles Rangel (D-NY), chairman of the House Committee on Ways and Means, explaining the impact of the CHAMP Act, as ordered reported by the Committee on Ways and Means on July 27, 2007, on federal spending, revenues, and deficits.[33] By law, the Congressional Budget Office is required to develop a cost estimate for virtually every bill reported by congressional committees to show how it would affect spending or revenues over the next 5 or more years. A bit of buoyancy was given to the CHAMP Act's comparative effectiveness provisions when the CBO "scored" them favorably, though the Health Subcommittee staffers did not know the results of the CBO's scoring until the day of the markup. As a staffer said, CBO "scored them as at least paying for themselves in the last two of the first ten years." Actually, Orszag's letter of July 30 does not mention the bill's comparative effectiveness research provisions specifically, and the scoring of Section 904 is difficult to grasp from the spreadsheets attached to the letter. (Orszag clarified how CBO scored Section 904 in a letter to Pete Stark dated September 5, 2007.)

On August 1, 2007, the day the House debate and vote was scheduled on the CHAMP Act, Ranking Member Jim McCrery (R-LA) sent around a "Dear Colleague" letter (Box 8.3). Dear Colleague letters are short member-to-member

Box 8.2 Narrative Told by an Observer of the House Ways and Means Committee Markup of the CHAMP Act in July 2007

Then [*Ways and Means*] had the markup. The Republicans were pissed off about some other things that were happening, so they required a reading of the bill for several hours [*recall that the bill was over 450 pages*]. They never stopped that on the Energy and Commerce side—if you recall, the Energy and Commerce markup never occurred on the CHAMP Act. They were going through the reading of the bill for the second or third time, and they just gave up.[a] Time had run out on the calendar and leadership decided to move on. But Charlie Rangel (D-NY) [*chairman, House Ways and Means*] and Jim McCrery (R-LA) [*ranking minority member*] worked out in the afternoon that they were done with the reading of the bill, and the markup could go on.

So the markup resumed at 6 o'clock in the evening. Peter Orszag was there. He did answer a question about the fact that CER [*comparative effectiveness research*] saved money. But the Republicans didn't say anything about the CER section until after midnight, thereby setting up the news press release the next day of the "mystery at midnight tax." So [*staffer's name*] is the person being interviewed at that point, Peter Orszag long since having gone home, and they brought up a procedural question about how that component of the full bill was dealt with in the tax section of the bill. [*Staffer's name*] did find it but they were obviously fatigued and it took a moment. This was not a great time of the day for Pete Stark [*chairman of the Health Subcommittee of Ways and Means*] either, although he didn't say anything that was really incorrect. Then there was a press announcement that this bill had had a mystery midnight tax on health insurance that no one even understood and that not even the members—not even the Democrats—understood what it was.

---

[a] According to an article published on July 27, 2007 in *CQ Today* written by Drew Armstrong, Alex Wayne, and Richard Rubin, "The Energy and Commerce Committee—which shares jurisdiction over the package—gave up for the night around 10:30 PM Thursday. It resumed its markup Friday morning, but again, Republicans stalled progress on the legislation, forcing the committee clerk to read aloud every one of the bill's hundreds of pages. At about 4:30 PM Friday, nearly 30 hours after the committee convened and 160-some pages into the 495-page bill, Chairman John D. Dingell (D-MI) used his last remaining option to end the deadlock. He said he would discharge the bill to the full House, without any amendments. Lawmakers and staff stood to applaud Sharon Davis, the clerk who undertook the marathon reading chore. Dingell adjourned the committee, ending the markup and any chance of altering the bill there."

Box 8.3 **August 1, 2007 "Dear Colleague" Letter Sent by Ranking Member Representative Jim McCrery before the House Vote on the CHAMP Act (H.R. 3162)**

August 1, 2007
Democrat's "CHAMP" Act Contains Mystery Tax on Health Insurance
Even the Democrats Can't Explain the Hidden Provision

Dear Colleague:

Hidden near the back of their massive bill that will cut Medicare by $200 billion is a tax increase on health insurance. That's right, the tax and spend Democrats are at it again proposing yet another new tax, this time on health insurance.

Section 904 of the so-called "CHAMP" Act establishes, through the tax code, a "Health Care Comparative Effectiveness Research Trust Fund." The stated goal is to support research that will give information to health care providers and insurers that will allow them to identify the most cost effective treatment options. This could include research on the comparative effectiveness of drugs, devices, and therapies.

I'll get to the funding in a minute, but this program is worth a critical review because it could easily pave the way in the future for a government bureaucrat, intent on holding down health care costs, to make it difficult for physicians to use "disfavored" drugs or therapies when treating a Medicare beneficiary.

As for financing, from 2008 through 2010, $300 million would be raided from the Medicare Trust Funds to fund this research. Beginning in 2011, those transfers will be supplemented with a new, mandatory tax on health insurance. Total receipts for the research fund will reach $375 million per year, with at least $285 million coming from the new tax on health insurers. Although a formal revenue estimate for the proposal is not yet available, the Joint Tax Committee did expect the Trust Fund to generate gross revenues of more than $2.9 billion during the 10-year budget window.

The amounts involved in the tax increase—at this point—may sound relatively modest. But this is dangerous territory. Once a tax on health insurance is created, it will be impossible to get rid of, and very easy to increase.

I urge all of you to protect your constituents and vote against H.R. 3162. If you have any questions, please contact Jon Traub with the Ways and Means Committee at x54021.

With kindest regards, I am
Sincerely yours,
/S
JIM McCRERY
Ranking Member

letters sent electronically and in hard copy before a House vote urging recipients to vote a certain way on the measure at hand. This heading of this letter is "Democrat's [sic] 'CHAMP' Act Contains Mystery Tax on Health Insurance; Even the Democrats Can't Explain the Hidden Provision." The letter urged recipients to "protect your constituents and vote against H.R. 3162." A House staffer on the Democratic side explained the motivation: "The Republicans were looking for anything to sink that bill [*the CHAMP Act*] and to get people to vote no for it. They were looking for anything to sink the whole package, and this—the so-called midnight tax on health insurers—was a really easy shot. Once they did that, it made it difficult to get Republicans [*on board*]."

The House of Representatives debated the CHAMP Act on August 1, 2007. The measure passed on a roll call vote at 7:37 PM, with 225 yeas (220 Democrats) and 204 nays (194 Republicans). A Ways and Means staffer had this impression of the floor debate: "Every third Republican specifically mentioned the vile tax on health insurance...their primary concern was the tax on health insurance, but there were some people who were worried about government funding research. Mostly it was the tax on health insurance."

Over the subsequent 2 months, the Senate passed its version of the House CHAMP Act—the comparative effectiveness research provisions were removed, as were the provisions relating to the Medicare program—and the two houses resolved their differences and crafted a bill that passed both chambers. On October 2, the Children's Health Insurance Program Reauthorization Act of 2007 was presented to President George W. Bush, who vetoed it the next day. The House was not able to muster enough votes to over-ride the President's veto. On December 12, 2007 the President vetoed another version of the bill, and again the House did not have the votes to over-ride the veto. In the end, Congress passed stop-gap legislation that authorized the extension of the State Children's Health Insurance Program until March 2009. President Bush signed the extension into law on December 29, 2007.

What was going on in the Senate with regard to comparative effectiveness research while the House was laboring over and debating Section 904 in the CHAMP Act?[34] Senate Budget Committee staffers had taken note of the November 2006 *Health Affairs* paper by Gail Wilensky, and the Senate Budget Committee advanced the agenda for comparative effectiveness research by including a reserve fund for it in the budget resolution that Chairman Kent Conrad introduced in mid-March of 2007. The Concurrent Resolution on the Budget for Fiscal Year 2008, agreed to in the House and Senate on May 17, 2007, included Section 305, "Deficit-neutral reserve funds for health care quality, effectiveness, efficiency, and transparency." Subsection (b) stated, "The Chairman of the Senate Committee on the Budget may revise the aggregates, allocations, and other appropriate levels

in this resolution for a bill, joint resolution, amendment, motion, or conference report that establishes a new Federal or public-private initiative
for comparative effectiveness research, by the amounts provided in such
legislation for that purpose."

For a number of reasons, the House Ways and Means Committee got out in
front of the Senate in 2007 with regard to comparative effectiveness research
with the inclusion of Section 904 in H.R. 3162, the CHAMP Act. The staffers
of the Senate Finance and Budget Committees had been working on comparative effectiveness legislation in 2007. When the Allen-Emerson bill was
introduced in the House in early May 2007, Senate Budget Committee staffers initiated conversations about federal policy on comparative effectiveness
research with the staff of the Senate Finance Committee. As one of the staffers told us, "I thought this would be a perfect meeting of the minds. It's an
issue we all probably could get interested and engaged in. Our bosses are both
very much aligned in terms of wanting to get more value out of the health
care dollars that we are spending, since their perspectives are Chairman
of the Finance Committee and Chairman of the Budget Committee. So we
started talking about working together on a bill, and we independently got
the go-aheads from each of our bosses in early 2007 to start working on a
bill, so we did. We started spec-ing things out and trying to figure out what
exactly we wanted this entity to look like. As we were thinking through the
issues, we sent a joint letter over to the Congressional Budget Office asking
for their advice, assistance on structure issues, scope issues, funding issues,
what's the best way to disseminate the information and the evidence that is
generated by this entity so that patients and providers actually use it . . . They
[CBO] later in the year came out with their report [*The December 2007 CBO
report on "Research on the Comparative Effectiveness of Medical Treatments"*].
A lot of what they [CBO] ended up coming out with in that report they also
testified before the House Ways and Means Committee in June 2007. So a lot
of what they were going to say in the report they put out in a teaser, I guess
you could say, in testimony before the Ways and Means Committee . . . Even
before that happened [*Section 904 of the House CHAMP Act*], we had come to
the conclusion that we wanted to create an entity that was outside of the federal government. So their [*The House*] vision, while a great vision and a great
place marker out there, was different than what we wanted to put forward.
So we [*Budget and Finance*] continued to work on our effort and were actually
hoping to include it in the Medicare package that was moving in December
[*2007*], but we got into a situation with the Medicare package where the
scope was getting narrowed down. We were in the situation where we had
to pass something by Christmas or it wasn't going to get enacted into law.
Anything that wasn't narrowly focused on the doc fix and some of the other
Medicare extenders wasn't going to get included."

The Legacy of Comparative Effectiveness Research in the CHAMP Act of 2007

The inclusion of Section 904 in the CHAMP Act, along with the increasing scrutiny comparative effectiveness research was garnering from legislative and other sectors, made the political viability of this policy alternative, if not its inevitable passage, obvious to anyone paying attention. Proponents for federal policy on comparative effectiveness research intensified their advocacy, opponents mobilized and intensified their objections, and stakeholders still undecided realized it was time to study the issues and take a position.

The results of the CBO's scoring of the comparative effectiveness provisions in the bill increased the political viability of this policy alternative. In his September 5, 2007 letter to Pete Stark, chairman of the Subcommittee on Health of Ways and Means, Orszag explained how CBO had evaluated the comparative effectiveness research provisions in the bill. In the letter Orszag stated, "CBO estimates that the information produced by enacting Section 904 would reduce total spending for health care services. Specifically, total spending—by public and private purchasers—would be reduced by about $0.5 billion over the 2008–2012 period and by about $6 billion over the 2008–2017 period." Orszag's support for comparative effectiveness research comes through in this letter, though he acknowledges that its effects on health care spending over the next 10 years would be "modest." That the CBO scored Section 904 the way it did gave the prospect of comparative effectiveness research as federal policy a boost, and it also injected a dose of reality into the debates. As one of our informants told us, "The CBO score of the CHAMP Act was good and bad, depending on what side of the aisle you sit on. For those who support CER, it was great: 'Oh my God, we get a score—it actually saves money.' On the downside, 'Oh, it will take a long time and doesn't save much money—it's barely making a dent.' But there is starting to be more talk. This is not a panacea. The same is true for health IT [*information technology*]. If you say it's going to solve everything, you're setting yourself up for failure. Now it's starting to be seen as part of a broader strategy to drive costs down. This is one thing we can do as part of a larger health reform. It certainly can't hurt. We think it can help."

By specifying one version of how a federal mandate for comparative effectiveness research would be structured, placed, and financed, Section 904 induced the proponents of a federal mandate for such research to begin to seriously analyze the pros and cons of each option. The one thing they seemed to agree upon at this point was that trying to use the congressional appropriations process to launch and sustain a major effort in comparative effectiveness research was not going to work. And opponents, while not resigned to the inevitability of eventual passage, did the same, to be ready to influence the policy elements so that any new entity or initiative on comparative effectiveness research would be configured in ways that would least conflict with their interests. One of the Health Subcommittee staffers who had observed the August 1st House floor debate on the CHAMP Act told us, "It was an interesting experience, being on the floor and hearing the [*comparative effectiveness research*] provision regularly attacked. After that, from the middle of August through the beginning of December [*2007*] we heard from all the stakeholders all the reasons why what we did wasn't really what they had had in mind."

Section 904 of the CHAMP bill and the debates surrounding it made the various stakeholders realize that they did not necessarily share the same interests in comparative effectiveness research policy, at least as far as how it was structured and financed. For example, on July 31, 2007, the U.S. Chamber of Commerce, in a letter to the members of the U.S. House of Representatives, stated, "Chamber opposes a proposed tax on health plan premiums to fund a Center for Comparative Effectiveness Research . . . The Chamber opposes a new tax levied on individual insurers and group health insurance premiums that would establish a trust fund to conduct comparative effectiveness research. While many employers are very interested in further analysis of outcomes and effectiveness of health care services, this tax increase on health insurance policies will negatively impact the ability of employers who are struggling to continue to provide affordable insurance for their employees." On the other hand, in its August 17, 2007 Washington-Business Health Update, the National Business Group on Health stated that "The Business Group is working with Congressional staff to assure that employers have a meaningful say in determining research priorities and that information produced be credible and independent. The Business Group believes that our capacity for comparative effectiveness studies should be significantly expanded and produce reliable, independent information through a transparent and accountable process." Divisions became apparent in the Alliance for Better Health Care as well, the coalition of all types of stakeholders that had so impressed Representative Tom Allen (D-ME) when he began working on comparative effectiveness research legislation back in 2002 and 2003. A member of the Alliance described for us one of the fall 2007 meetings: "As the debate evolved, we as a coalition struggled to hold it all together. BlueCross and AHIP [*America's Health Insurance Plans*] took strong positions about the financing and where it [*comparative effectiveness research*] should be. After the CHAMP Act, probably September, the fall of 2007, you have the employers saying, 'We're against all-payer financing,' which was a bomb being dropped. All through that process, just to see those dynamics . . . [*NAME*] called a meeting of the Alliance to order, and we were trying to push the discussion, but it was literally 'cricket, cricket' all around the table. No one wanted to speak . . . Bizarre dynamics."

The scene of the action now shifts to the Senate.

Notes

1. This point is illustrated by the following anecdote told to us by one of our informants: "When they formed AHCPR [*Agency for Health Care Research and Policy, the predecessor agency of AHRQ*] they made it in the org chart equivalent to these mega-agencies [*in DHHS*] in terms of structure. Here sits little AHCPR and then AHRQ and it is on a parallel structurally with FDA, CMS, HRSA, etc. We are reminded of this agency's vulnerability when George Bush gets elected and there is a new Secretary of DHHS, Tommy Thompson. Tommy Thompson is looking around at the structure of this big enterprise, and he is a management-oriented kind of guy, and he looks at this and says, 'This doesn't make any sense, this little thing [*AHRQ*] sitting out here.' He was quoted in the press as saying, 'Well, I've looked at what they are doing and there is nothing useful.' What he meant—and he did backtrack when pressed—was that there was nothing that would inform the Medicare prescription drug bill. Well, that was a tough indictment of the agency [*AHRQ*]. It was decided that it would be rude to eliminate it or cut it when John Eisenberg [*then the director of AHRQ*] was dying from brain cancer. Shortly after his death Carolyn Clancy [*deputy director of AHRQ under Eisenberg, and then acting director after his death*] has Secretary Thompson out to meet with her and he gets kind of enthused about the agency."

2. John M. Eisenberg served as the director of the Agency for Healthcare Research and Quality from 1997 to 2002. He died of a brain tumor in 2002.

3. Republicans controlled both houses of Congress from 1995 to 2007 except for 2001–2002, when the Senate was evenly divided.

4. If an agency's statutory authority expires and Congress continues to appropriate funds for it nonetheless, the agency's reauthorization is, de facto, the appropriations process.

5. Lambrew earned her doctoral degree from the Department of Health Policy at the University of North Carolina at Chapel Hill. Part of the Department of Health and Human Services, she worked on the unsuccessful Clinton health care reform effort in the mid-1990s, and then served as a health policy aide to President Clinton at the White House. From 1997 through 2000, she was the program associate director for health at the Office of Management and Budget and from 1997 to 2001 the senior health analyst at the National Economic Council. In these positions, she worked on the creation and implementation of the Children's Health Insurance Program, development of the president's Medicare reform plan and long-term care initiative, and implementation and oversight of Medicaid and disability policies. Lambrew headed the Office of Health Reform at the Department of Health and Human Services during the Obama administration's health care reform process, and in March 2011, she became President Obama's Deputy Assistant for Health Policy.

6. Wilensky, who earned a PhD in economics at the University of Michigan, is an elected member of the Institute of Medicine. She served as Administrator of the Health Care Financing Administration, overseeing the Medicare and Medicaid programs, from 1990 to 1992. As Deputy Assistant for Policy Development to President George H.W. Bush from 1992 to 1993, she advised the President on health and welfare issues. She chaired the Physician Payment Review Commission from 1995 to 1997, and from 1997 to 2001 she chaired the Medicare Payment Advisory Commission, which advises Congress on payment and other issues related to Medicare. She is a prolific writer, testifies frequently before congressional committees, speaks on health affairs to many national and international groups, and serves on many councils and boards. She serves as the John M. Olin Senior Fellow at Project HOPE, an international health foundation.

7. The other members of the Placement Committee, and their positions at the time, were David Abernethy, senior vice president, Operations, HIP Health Plans; Michael Chernew, PhD, professor, Department of Health Management and Policy, School of Public Health, University of Michigan; Jordan Cohen, MD, president, Association of American Medical Colleges; Judith Feder, PhD, dean of Public Policy, Georgetown University; Harold S. Luft, PhD, Caldwell B. Esselstyn professor and director, Institute

for Health Policy Studies, University of California, San Francisco; Nicole Lurie, MD, senior natural scientist and Alcoa chair, RAND Corporation; and Donald M. Steinwachs, PhD, professor and chair, Department of Health Policy and Management, Bloomberg School of Public Health, Johns Hopkins University.

8. The trial referred to was the first phase of the Clinical Antipsychotic Trials of Intervention Effectiveness (CATIE): Lieberman JA, Stroup TS, McEvoy JP, et al. Effectiveness of antipsychotic drugs in patients with chronic schizophrenia. N Engl J Med 2005;353:1209–23.

9. AcademyHealth's Placement Report of 2005 is available from http://www.academy-health.org/files/publications/placementreport.pdf.

10. The other mention is in a bill on which no congressional action was taken. On September 14, 2006, Senators Max Baucus and Chuck Grassley introduced S. 3897, the Medicare Data Access and Research Act. In giving the rationale for the bill, Finance Committee Chairman Grassley stated that the data-access provisions of the bill would "help [Federal agencies] to fulfill their missions to... conduct research on the comparative effectiveness of prescription drugs."

11. For fiscal year 2000, Congress appropriated $17.8 billion to the NIH; the amount increased every year over the decade, and for 2010, the appropriation was $31 billion. During the same period, appropriations to AHRQ were $204 million for 2000, increasing to $372 million for 2010. In 2010, AHRQ also received a one-time appropriation of $300 million in 2-year dollars via the American Reinvestment and Recovery Act of 2009. Sources: National Institutes of Health: History of Congressional Appropriations, Fiscal Years 2000–2010, and Office of the Director, Agency for Healthcare Research and Quality.

12. The Institute of Medicine (IOM) was established in 1970 and is the health arm of the National Academy of Sciences. It is an independent, nonprofit organization that works outside of government to provide unbiased and authoritative advice to decision makers and the public. The IOM serves as adviser to the nation to improve health. The IOM undertakes several different kinds of activities, with the various kinds of bodies operating under specific rules and processes; only some of these bodies may issue recommendations. A description of these is available from http://www.iom.edu/About-IOM/Study-Process/Activities.aspx.

13. The IOM Clinical Research Roundtable was chaired by William Gerberding and co-chaired by Tom Beauchamp. It was charged to discuss the challenges facing clinical research and ways to create a supportive environment for conducting a broad agenda of high-quality clinical research.

14. Kupersmith J, Sung N, Genel M, et al. Creating a new structure for research on health care effectiveness. J Invest Med 2005;53:67–72.

15. J. Michael McGinnis is a physician, epidemiologist, and long-time contributor to national and international health programs and policy. Before joining the Institute of Medicine as senior scholar in 2005, McGinnis served as founding director, respectively, of the Robert Wood Johnson Foundation's Health Group, the World Health Organization's Office for Health Reconstruction in Bosnia, the federal Office of Research Integrity, and the federal Office of Disease Prevention and Health Promotion. He held continuous appointment through the Carter, Reagan, Bush, and Clinton administrations at the Department of Health and Human Services, with policy responsibilities for disease prevention and health promotion (1977–1995), including the Healthy People process and the U.S. Preventive Services Task Force.

16. The IOM Roundtable on Value and Science-Driven Health Care was chaired from 2006 to 2011 by Denis A. Cortese, MD, of the Mayo Clinic; the executive director is J. Michael McGinnis. The Roundtable, which continues its activities as of this writing (March 2012), has convened 15 public workshops, with 7 or 8 of them occurring between 2006 and 2008.

17. These collaboratives include (1) Best Practices: health professional societies and organizations; (2) Clinical Effectiveness Research: research scientists and public, private, and

academic institutions; (3) Digital Learning: care delivery and information technology organizations; (4) Evidence Communication: marketing experts and decision scientists; and (5) Value Incentives: health financing and health care organizations.

18. Daschle T, Lambrew JM, Greenberger SS. Critical: What we can do about the health-care crisis. New York: Macmillan, 2009. In this book the authors propose the creation of a quasi-governmental Federal Health Board, structured like the Federal Reserve, that would be insulated from political influence and would be charged with establishing the health care system's framework. The Board, among other things, "would have a staff of analysts charged with assessing and producing the research required to make sound decisions," which would presumably include comparative effectiveness research.

19. Wilensky GR. Developing a center for comparative effectiveness information. Health Affairs 2006;26:w572–8. Published online on November 7, 2006. The paper was supported by a grant from the Commonwealth Fund. Two supportive commentaries accompanied the paper, one from the IOM: Rowe JW, Cortese DA, McGinnis JM. The emerging context for advances in comparative effectiveness assessment; and the other, from AHRQ: Clancy CM. Getting to "smart" health care.

20. Orzag headed CBO from January 2007 to November 2008 when he resigned his CBO post to become Director of the White House Office and Management and Budget.

21. Both bills include provisions for levying fees on health insurers to generate revenue for the Comparative Effectiveness Research Trust Fund. The bill (H.R. 284) introduced by Representatives Allen and Emerson in May 2007 includes a provision for levying that fee on self-insured health plans (as well as other types of private and public plans), while the Baird bill of July 2007 does not.

22. Contenders for the 2008 Democratic presidential nomination included Senator Hillary Clinton (D-NY), Senator Barack Obama (D-IL), Senator Joseph Biden (D-DE), Senator Christopher Dodd (D-CT), former North Carolina senator John Edwards, former Alaska senator Mike Gravel, Representative Dennis Kucinich (D-OH), and New Mexico Governor Bill Richardson.

23. Contenders for the 2008 Republican presidential nomination included Senator John McCain (R-AZ), former Massachusetts governor Mitt Romney, former Arkansas governor Mike Huckabee, former mayor of New York City Rudolph Giuliani, Senator Sam Brownback (R-KS), Representative Tom Tancredo (R-CO), former Virginia governor Jim Gilmore, Representative Duncan Hunter (R0CA), Representative Ron Paul (R-TX), and former Wisconsin governor Tommy G. Thompson.

24. The Congressional Research Service issued a Report for Congress (Order Code RL34208) on October 15, 2007, titled "Comparative clinical effectiveness and cost-effectiveness research: background, history, and overview." The report was written by Gretchen A. Jacobsen. The Congressional Budget Office issued a CBO paper (Pub. No. 2975) in December 2007 titled "Research on the comparative effectiveness of medical treatments: issues and options for an expanded federal role." No author was listed.

25. The "Enhanced Health Care Value for All Act of 2007" was referred to the Subcommittees on Health of the House Ways and Means and Energy and Commerce Committees. No further congressional action was taken on H.R. 2184.

26. Senator Clinton never introduced the legislation. Her staff indicated that her campaign for the Democratic presidential nomination precluded her from working on the bill.

27. The other witnesses were David Dale (president, American College of Physicians), Gail Shearer (director, Health Policy Analysis, Consumers Union), Susan Hearn (Dow Chemical Co.), and Steve Teusch (Merck & Co.). The full transcript of the hearing is available from http://www.gpo.gov/fdsys/pkg/CHRG-110hhrg45994/html/CHRG-110hhrg45994.htm.

28. See Kenney G, Yee J. SCHIP at a crossroads: experiences to date and challenges ahead. Health Affairs 2007;26:356–69.

29. Section 904 of the CHAMP Act would have funded the comparative effectiveness research institute trust fund by a combination of appropriated dollars and fees levied on public and private insurers. To set the fee amount, the Secretary of Health and Human

Services was required to calculate an amount "equivalent to the fair share per capita" that would yield a target total figure for the fiscal year. The annual total obligation of an insurer (Medicare, private or self-insured employer) was the "fair share per capita" multiplied by the number of covered lives. The default amount was set at $2 per covered life.

30. "Marking up a bill" refers to the process by which a congressional committee or subcommittee goes through a piece of legislation to consider its provisions, propose and debate revisions, and to insert new sections and new wording. During these markup sessions the views of both sides are studied in detail. At the end of the markup session a vote is taken to determine the action of the subcommittee: it may decide to report the bill favorably to the full committee, with or without amendment, or unfavorably, or without recommendation. The subcommittee may also suggest that the committee "table" it or postpone action indefinitely. Information from http://thomas.loc.gov/home/lawsmade.bysec/considbycomm.html#, accessed October 2, 2012.

31. Though many committees adopt rules requiring referral of measures to the appropriate subcommittee, the full committee can vote to retain the measure at the full committee.

32. The Ways and Means Committee Report on H.R. 3162 was filed on August 1, 2007.In the Dissenting Views section of the Report, dissenters expressed disappointment that the Committee rejected an amendment by Representative Jim McCrery (R-LA) "to strike a second tax increase in the bill, which is to be used to fund research on the comparative effects of various treatments. While a laudable goal, the funding mechanism, a tax on health insurance policies along with transfers from the Medicare Trust Funds, seems to be at cross-purposes with the Majority's stated goal of getting more people health insurance coverage."

33. As of March 20, 2012, this letter could no longer be retrieved from the CBO Web site, although the Web site indicates it exists, and we have a hard copy.

34. A bill introduced by Senate Majority Leader Harry Reid (D-NV) on January 4, 2007, S.3, "Medicare Prescription Drug Negotiation Act of 2007" included provisions that would have prioritized studies of comparative clinical effectiveness of covered Part D drugs and authorized the use of such studies in developing formularies under the Medicare Prescription Drug Program. Reported out to the Senate by the Finance Committee (Chairman, Max Baucus), it never came to a floor vote because of a Republican filibuster and an unsuccessful cloture vote.

9

2008 to 2010

*The Baucus-Conrad Bills, the American Recovery
and Reinvestment Act, and the Patient Protection
and Affordable Care Act*

The back and forth in 2007 about the CHAMP Act between the Congress and the White House took place against a backdrop of campaigns of people seeking their party's nomination as its candidate for president of the United States. In the fall of 2007 campaigns were in full swing. Presidential and congressional elections were coming up in November 2008 and the caucuses and primaries were slated to begin in January 2008. With no sitting president or vice-president running, the field of Democratic and Republican presidential hopefuls was large. It was clear that health care reform would be a major campaign issue. In the fall of 2007 Senator Hillary Clinton was leading Senator Barack Obama by 20 points in the polls for who would win the Democratic nomination. Clinton, who had headed the task force on health reform during the first term of her husband President Bill Clinton, was unarguably the politician most informed about the U.S. health care system and its ills and about what the politics of health care reform would be.

Representative Tom Allen (D-ME), who had represented the State of Maine since 1997 and was the original "running back" for federal policy on comparative effectiveness research, was campaigning for the U.S. Senate seat held by Republican Susan Collins. Term limits enacted by the State of Maine precluded him from any more time as a U.S. Representative.

During the last months of 2007, the energies of the Congress remained focused on the reauthorization of the Children's Health Insurance Program and on the 12 appropriations bills necessary to fund the federal government in fiscal year 2008. Between October 1 and December 22, 2007, the 110th Congress passed four continuing resolutions to keep the government running. Only the Defense Appropriations bill was signed into law before Christmas.

In the fall of 2007 signs of economic trouble could no longer be ignored. Home prices had been falling, mortgage delinquency rates and foreclosures rising. The profits of mortgage lenders were threatened, and investment banks holding mortgage-backed securities were sustaining serious losses. Some banks failed. After peaking in early October 2007, the U.S. stock market began to decline. The unemployment rate held steady at 4.7% in September, October, and November 2007, but the job creation rate slowed. Predictions of an economic recession began to be heard, and by December 2007 a recession seemed inevitable.

Senators Baucus and Conrad Introduce a Comparative Effectiveness Research Bill in 2008

With the failure of the House CHAMP Act of 2007, House members and their staffs seemed to lose interest, at least temporarily, in proposing new legislation containing a federal mandate for comparative effectiveness research. Not so in the Senate. Staffers of the Senate Committees on Budget and Finance continued work on their version of a comparative effectiveness research bill. They started by reviewing the comparative effectiveness research provisions in the Medicare Modernization Act of 2003. The issue of committee jurisdiction arose: the 2003 provisions center on the Agency for Healthcare Research and Quality (AHRQ), and AHRQ falls under the jurisdiction of the Senate Committee on Health, Education, Labor, and Pensions (HELP), not Senate Finance or Senate Budget. The Finance and Budget staffers had to decide whether to write a draft bill that would not fall under either Committee's jurisdiction. They told us, "We said, 'Let's start with a blank slate. We don't care if it's in our jurisdiction or not. It doesn't matter. What do we think is the right thing to do?' First we said, 'what are all the functions that need to happen? Let's list out all the functions.' We met with CRS [*Congressional Research Service*]; they're the people who help develop policy. We said, 'What are all the options? Should it be at AHRQ or not?' We looked at all the models, from AHRQ to a Federal Reserve model to an FFRDC [*federally funded research and development center*] to just funding it in the private sector."

By early March 2008, Senate Budget and Finance staffers thought they had a bill ready for their chairmen to introduce, and by that time committee jurisdiction had come to matter to the staffers. A problem with jurisdiction led to a 5-month delay in the dropping of the bill. As the staffers told us, they "had to go back to the drawing board because we were told by the parliamentarians that it was going to get referred to the [*Senate*] HELP Committee. In the Senate when you introduce a bill there is no such thing as joint referral. In the House if you introduce a bill it can get referred to multiple committees at the same time. And we wanted to retain ownership by the Finance Committee...so we pulled back and ended up adding in the all-payer tax which got it squarely in the jurisdiction of the Finance Committee."

After a bill or resolution is introduced, it is the parliamentarian's office that refers bills to the Senate committee with jurisdiction over the subject of the bill, based on the rules of the Senate. The parliamentarian decided that the bill fell under the jurisdiction of the Senate HELP Committee, not the Senate Finance Committee, in part because of the content pertaining to AHRQ and the Secretary of Health and Human Services, which are in the jurisdiction of the Senate HELP Committee, and the fact that the comparative effectiveness research entity would be funded by means of congressional appropriations. Changing the financing by adding the tax on health plans would put the bill in the jurisdiction of the Senate Finance Committee.

The U.S. economic situation grew into a full-blown crisis in early 2008, distracting Congress and the nation from much focus on health policy. In January 2008, in an unusual display of bipartisanship, both houses of Congress approved and President Bush signed a $168 billion economic stimulus bill. Gasoline prices soared in February. That same month a Gallup poll indicated that Republicans as well as Democrats believed that Barack Obama, not Hillary Clinton, would win the Democratic presidential nomination. In March, the Bush administration forced a sale of the investment house of Bear Stearns in order to avert a bankruptcy filing. The economy was losing tens of thousands of jobs each month, and in May 2008, the unemployment rate, which was at 5.5%, started what seemed to be an inexorable monthly increase. (It increased each month until October 2009, when it peaked at 10.1%.) During the 3-month period ending September 2008, 966,000 Americans lost their jobs; this nearly doubled for the subsequent 3-month period, to 1,814,000. The number of failures of mortgage lenders, investment banks, commercial banks, and savings institutions skyrocketed. Fannie Mae (Federal National Mortgage Association) and Freddie Mac (Federal Home Mortgage Corporation), after steep losses in their value, were placed under the conservatorship of the federal government in September 2008, the same month that Merrill Lynch sold itself "at a fire-sale price," the investment bank of Lehman Brothers collapsed and was forced to file for bankruptcy, and the U.S Treasury Department rescued American International Group, an insurer with a global reach, with $85 billion of taxpayer dollars. The failures of Fannie Mae and Freddie Mac, two types of nongovernmental but government-sponsored enterprises, dampened any enthusiasm for the placement of federally mandated comparative effectiveness research in a non- or quasi-governmental entity.

On July 31, 2008, Senator Max Baucus (D-MT), the chairman of the Senate Finance Committee, and Senator Kent Conrad (D-ND), the chairman of the Senate Budget Committee, finally introduced their comparative effectiveness

research bill, S. 3408, the Comparative Effectiveness Research Act of 2008
(the "Baucus-Conrad bill"). Highlights are given in Box 9.1. Filed the day before
the August recess started, and with just a few weeks remaining in the legislative calendar of the second session of the 110th Congress, it was intended
only to be a marker bill, that is, a bill that stakes out a certain topical territory

---

Box 9.1 **Key Elements of S. 3408 (Introduced in Senate-IS), the
Baucus-Conrad Comparative Effectiveness Research Act of 2008**

- Amends the Social Security Act to provide for the conduct of comparative effectiveness research and amends the Internal Revenue Service
  code to establish a Comparative Effectiveness Research Trust Fund
- Defines comparative clinical effectiveness research as research evaluating and comparing the clinical effectiveness, risks, and benefits of two
  or more medical treatments, services, and items, that is, interventions,
  protocols for treatment, procedures, medical devices, diagnostic tools,
  pharmaceuticals (including drugs and biologicals), and any other processes or items being used in the treatment and diagnosis of, or prevention of illness or injury in, patients
- Establishes the Health Care Comparative Effectiveness Research
  Institute which is neither an agency nor establishment of the U.S.
  government
- Charges the Institute to improve health care delivered to individuals
  in the United States by advancing the quality and thoroughness of evidence concerning the manner in which diseases, disorders, and other
  health conditions can effectively and appropriately be prevented, diagnosed, treated, and managed clinically through research and evidence
  synthesis, and the dissemination of research findings with respect to
  the relative outcomes, effectiveness, and appropriateness of medical
  treatments, services, and items
- Sets the Institute's scope of methods to include systematic reviews and
  assessments of existing research and evidence; clinical research, such
  as randomized controlled trials and observational studies; any other
  methodologies recommended by the methodology committee
- Authorizes the Institute to enter into contracts with federal agencies,
  appropriate private sector or study-conducting entities for the conduct
  of research
- Charges the Institute to establish a Methodology Committee and sets
  out its purpose, scope, and other elements
- Authorizes the Institute to coordinate comparative effectiveness
  research conducted by public and private agencies and organizations

in order to ensure the most efficient use of the Institute's resources, and to build capacity for comparative clinical effectiveness research through appropriate activities, including making payments of up to 5% of funds credited to the Trust Fund in a given fiscal year to the Cochrane Collaboration (or its successor)

- Directs that the Institute shall have a Board of Governors (18 members to be appointed by the Comptroller General) and sets out its membership, terms, and processes; medical products industry to be represented on the Board
- Invests the responsibility for oversight of the Institute in the U.S Comptroller General
- Sets out requirements for public comment periods, public availability, and transparency
- Warns that nothing in the bill shall be construed as permitting the Institute to mandate coverage, reimbursement, or other policies for any public or private payer
- Creates a Comparative Effectiveness Research Trust Fund in the U.S. Treasury, and appropriates funds to the Trust Fund for FY 2009–18, adding, for 2012 and beyond, amounts received from fees on health insurance (private as well as some public programs, namely the Federal Hospital Insurance Trust Fund and Federal Supplementary Medical Insurance Trust Fund) and self-insured plans
- Describes the fees, the nature of the entities required to pay the fees, the amounts of the fees (for fiscal year 2012, $0.50 per covered life and $1.00 in subsequent years), and adjustment in fees for increases in U.S. National Health Expenditures.

as belonging to a specific legislator, and a conversation piece filed in order to foster serious discussion about its provisions among stakeholders. Just after the bill was introduced a staffer told us, "So we have our bill out there and people are commenting…Even though we talked to a lot of people while we were developing it, it's not the same as working on legislation. We didn't give people the language. Now we want to get feedback on the actual language…We will take the feedback into consideration and rewrite the bill as we think it needed and reintroduce it beginning of next year. And so there it's out there again and potentially ready—what I'm saying is—as a ready product to put into any health care reform or Medicare reform package. The bill really has more potential for next year [2009]."

In August 2008, polls showed that Democratic presidential nominee Barack Obama led presumptive Republican nominee John McCain for the first several weeks, but then a tie developed and McCain briefly edged ahead. In mid-September, however, Obama's numbers in the polls began to rise and McCain never caught up. By the end of October, 2008, Obama led McCain in the polls 53% to 40%. More and more people in Congress and out began to believe there would be a Democratic president and a Democratic majority in both houses of Congress. With that came the possibility of major legislation reforming the nation's health care system, and the chance to enact comparative effectiveness research provisions as part of health reform.

From August through December 2008, Senate Finance and Budget staff solicited comments and feedback from stakeholders interested in comparative effectiveness research, meeting, as they said, "with everybody under the sun," including the health insurance industry, the medical products industry, patient groups, consumer groups, business leaders, and health services researchers. "We want to make sure we have a bill that is politically viable [*for the next Congress*]." No further action was taken on S. 3408 and it died with the 110th Congress.

The Legacies of the Baucus-Conrad Bill of 2008

With the introduction of the Baucus-Conrad bill on July 31, 2008, eventual passage of some form of a federal mandate for comparative effectiveness research took on the air of inevitability. By 2008, this policy alternative for helping to control health care costs and increase value for money had been discussed around Capitol Hill for 6 years by ever-widening circles of legislators and congressional staffers and by stakeholder groups outside Washington. The concept of federally mandated comparative effectiveness research had shown itself to be a survivor. Moreover, several versions of actual legislation on comparative effectiveness research were floating around Capitol Hill, ready to be pulled "off the shelf" and quickly attached to larger bills that looked like they had a chance of passage. The prospect of there being "a larger bill" was coming closer to reality. In August of 2008 a staffer to a House Committee told us, "Things are heating up behind the scenes right now. The Democratic caucus has been meeting with Obama and his folks pretty regularly. The rumor is that if Obama is elected he wants major health reform and he wants it in 100 days. The Democrats want to get their ducks in a row so they can support Obama's plan."

What had to happen next with regard to comparative effectiveness research was a more thorough consideration of the alternative forms the elements of the policy might take and their intended and unintended consequences. The 2007 CHAMP Act debates initiated that process, and the 2008 Baucus Conrad bill provided it with great momentum. The meetings that the Senate Finance and Budget Committee legislators and staffers held with various stakeholder groups before and after the bill was introduced forced them to consider alternative specifications and advocate explicitly for those most favorable to their interests. But by the time the Baucus-Conrad bill was introduced in summer 2008, enough parties had done enough thinking that some battle lines were beginning to develop, battle lines about whether the comparative effectiveness research entity should be inside government or outside of it, how it should be financed, and whether the medical products industry should be part of its governance.

Battle Lines Are Drawn

Strongly held differences of opinion about the specifics of legislation on comparative effectiveness research were emerging between different Senate committees, between House and Senate, and among various stakeholder groups outside government. In the Senate, while the Finance and Budget Committees believed the entity should be "a nonprofit corporation...which is neither an agency nor an establishment of the United States Government,"[1] the Senate Health, Education, Labor, and Pensions (HELP) Committee disagreed. The Senate HELP Committee, which was chaired by Senator Edward Kennedy (D-MA), the "Lion of the Senate," had jurisdiction over AHRQ. Some believed that any new funds for comparative effectiveness research should simply be placed at AHRQ, where they would be handled by a well-established federal agency and stay under congressional authority and oversight. As a HELP staffer told us, "I don't make it a secret...Everybody on Senate Finance knows that I don't like their version of the bill [*Baucus-Conrad 2008*]. I don't think it's the right thing. It's great to have it [*the bill*] out there, but creating additional infrastructure that, from everything I've read, does nothing but dole out money without setting priorities, makes no sense to me. It seems like a $100 million boondoggle."

The Senate HELP Committee's 2008 activities and influence on the comparative effectiveness research front (and others) had been undermined by Senator Kennedy's diagnosis, in May 2008, of an incurable malignant brain tumor, a high-grade glioblastoma, and his subsequent treatment. Though HELP Committee staffers had been working on a version of a comparative effectiveness research bill, they did not get the legislation introduced in 2008. Also sapping the HELP Committee's energies was the fact that two of its members, Senator Hillary Clinton and Senator Barack Obama, were fully engaged in a run for the Democratic nomination for President. Even after Barack Obama won the Democratic nomination on June 3, 2008, Senator Clinton's eventual role in his administration took most of her attention.

The Senate HELP Committee had other considerations in 2008. Ted Kennedy, now terminally ill, had labored his entire tenure in Congress for health care reform. Now that comprehensive health care reform was likely under the

Obama administration, many people thought that it would be given to him to lead as the capstone of his career. A committee staffer told us in mid-August 2008, "Whether HELP introduces a bill this year depends on what happens in November... There's no desire to put out something that binds Senator Obama's hands. People would assume that Obama would be in favor of anything with Kennedy's name on it, and that's too controversial right now. If he wins in November, I could easily see us dropping a bill after that. I am getting everything ready for Senator Kennedy so we can have something."

Battle lines were drawn also between the Senate and the House. Although the outlines were known of the Senate HELP Committee's version of comparative effectiveness research policy, the position of the Senate Finance and Budget Committees dominated in the Senate—that the federal mandate for comparative effectiveness research would be realized in an extra-governmental nonprofit corporation. The House had declared its stance with the provisions in the CHAMP Act: a Center for Comparative Effectiveness Research to be established inside government, within AHRQ.

The Medical Products Industry

In weekly publications covering key developments affecting the medical products industry (e.g., "The Pink Sheet" for pharmaceuticals and "The Gray Sheet" for devices), articles about proposed federal policy on comparative effectiveness research and its implications had begun appearing in the second half of 2007. The industry was closely following comparative effectiveness research proposals and was mobilizing to affect the outcome of legislation.

A member of a pharmaceutical industry trade group told us, "From our perspective the Senate bills are much better than Stark's bill [the 2007 CHAMP Act] because they do say that the pharmaceutical industry will have some role and be at the table. The main difference between the Baucus and Kennedy bills from my perspective is where CER [comparative effectiveness research] is located. Baucus wants this independent facility and Kennedy wanted to house it at AHRQ. I think it could be done at either place as long as you have the right governance and transparency. So we've been supportive of both Kennedy and Baucus."

The "right governance"—meaning that the medical products industry would have a seat on the governing board—would position the industry to influence what the Institute did and did not study, the research methods to be used, and so forth. It would also ensure that the industry would know from the outset what was in the comparative effectiveness research docket so they could mobilize their forces to be ready to undermine any research results unfavorable to their products. The claims heard against the comparative effectiveness provisions in the 2003 Medicare Modernization Act—"get the federal government even further into the business of making medical decisions," "promote one-size fits-all medicine," "failure to recognize the value of incremental innovation," and "failure to recognize differences in subpopulations"—were ready to go, and industry had begun funding to disease advocacy groups from which they could draw specific individuals to make the public believe that government policy on comparative effectiveness research was harming real people. This fear-mongering tactic was called the "human shield" defense by one of our informants.

In late August 2008, it was announced that the Pharmaceutical Research and Manufacturers of America (PhRMA), the Biotechnology Industry Organization (BIO), and the Advanced Medical Technology Association (AdvaMed), the major trade organizations representing the medical products industry, had formed a coalition "to promote an industry agenda on comparative clinical effectiveness research."[2] The news spread quickly. One of our informants told us, "The device industry seems to think they have the most to lose in CE [*comparative effectiveness*] in terms of revenue, so they are probably the loudest voice expressing significant concerns...The drug industry and the biologics industry are also vocal. They have formed an organization to weigh in on CE and they have hired a lobbyist to work separate and apart from their own individual efforts on these issues. PhRMA, BIO, and AdvaMed formed a new organization just on CE and they hired lobbyists."

The coalition's stated aim sounds innocuous enough, but the proponents of comparative effectiveness policy were not fooled. An informant from the health insurance industry told us, "We heard that they are spending $10 million—PhRMA, AdvaMed, and BIO—to attack this and dilute it or destroy the whole concept entirely."

Though we have been unable to confirm this,[3] it seems likely that this coalition of PhRMA, BIO, and AdvaMed morphed into the Partnership to Improve Patient Care (PIPC), which was established in November 2008. In any case, the PIPC[4] got down to business quickly. It set out its goals, established a set of principles to which any comparative effectiveness legislation should adhere (Box 9.2), and, together with an influential Washington public relations firm it had engaged,[5] developed a multi-faceted strategy for shaping the legislative proposals for comparative effectiveness research that were circulating around the Congress. The situation was urgent, given how close Section 904 of the House CHAMP Act of 2007 came, the fact that numerous proposals were floating around Congress, and the fact that comparative effectiveness research was a plank in the platforms of virtually all the presidential contenders, Republicans as well as Democrats.

Box 9.2 **Supporting Principles for Comparative Effectiveness Research as Put Forth by the Partnership to Improve Patient Care**

To put patients and providers first, any CER proposal must do the following:

- Define CER as a tool to improve patient care
- Enhance information about treatment options and about how to close the gap between care known to be effective and the care patients receive
- Focus on communicating research results to patients, providers, and other decision makers, not making centralized coverage and payment decisions or recommendations
- Provide information on clinical value and health outcomes, not cost-effectiveness assessments
- Design studies that reflect the diversity, including racial and ethnic diversity, of patient populations and communicate results in ways that reflect the differences in individual needs
- Assure that studies are technically excellent and appropriate
- Require open and transparent processes where all stakeholders have input into research priorities and design and have an equal voice in governance of a CER entity
- Examine all aspects of health care, including care management, medical interventions, benefit design, and processes of care for all patients
- Support continued medical advances, including personalized medicine and other advances that can help improve patient care and control health care costs
- Recognize the unique nature and value of targeted therapies that benefit specific groups of patients with rare and orphan diseases.

Source: Statement for the Record, PIPC, "Implementing Best Patient Care Practices," before the Senate Health, Education, Labor, and Pension Committee, February 5, 2009. See PIPC Web site for most current version of principles.

The American Recovery and Reinvestment Act of 2009, "A Giant Christmas Tree" with a $1.1 Billion Ornament for Comparative Effectiveness Research

On November 4, 2008, Democrat Barack Obama was elected President of the United States, and the Democratic Party held onto its majority in both houses. When the 111th Congress convened on January 6, 2009, the House of

Representatives had 257 Democrats—a gain of 24 seats—and 178 Republicans, and the Senate had 57 Democrats, 2 Independents who caucused with the Democrats, and 41 Republicans. Representative Tom Allen (D-ME), who in 2002 started the congressional ball rolling on comparative effectiveness, was unsuccessful in his 2008 run for a U.S. Senate seat, and term limits ended his tenure as a Maine Representative.

In the months after the November 2008 elections, political and economic events pushed federal policy for comparative effectiveness research further down on the agenda. The country's attention was taken by the excitement of a new president and administration, the shift in party control of the White House, the groundwork being done for health care reform, but most of all, by the economic downturn. It was the economic downturn, and the economic stimulus bill enacted to ameliorate it, that gave federal legislation for comparative effectiveness research its next toehold.

Barack Obama had made it clear throughout his campaign that health care reform would be a top priority for his first term in office. With Democrats now in control of the White House and both houses of Congress, health care reform looked to be within reach. But the inevitable threats to presidential agendas emerged. Three months before the election it had already become obvious to campaign staff that the economy could trump health reform. A top advisor to Republican Presidential candidate John McCain told us, "In 2007 when I was looking at the policies we needed to have ready—we were in a Republican primary—every candidate had to have a health care reform proposal. Unbelievable—unprecedented, in fact…Coming into this election, if you looked at the focus groups or polling, the number-one domestic issue is health reform. That's no longer true. Recently health reform is falling behind energy and the economy."

The 2 months preceding the election were marked by failures of some of the nation's financial giants. Credit markets constricted and job losses spiked. October 2008 ushered in a 6-month period in which monthly job losses averaged 712,000, the highest numbers since 1945.[6] A few days after Barack Obama was elected, the U.S. Labor Department released figures showing that one of every six workers, 17.5% of the labor force, were unemployed or underemployed, and the *New York Times* reported that personal bankruptcies had increased by 34% from the prior year.[7] The economy would have to be the Obama administration's first priority.

President-elect Obama's transition team worked quickly to get the new administration in place. On November 20, 2008, Barack Obama officially nominated former Senator Tom Daschle (D-SD) as his choice for Secretary of Health and Human Services, and named Daschle as the Director of a new White House Office on Health Care Reform, making Daschle the highest-ranking White House health policy advisor and the leader of the health care reform effort. In the same speech, Obama named Jeanne Lambrew, who had served as co-chair of AcademyHealth's Placement Committee, as deputy director of the

White House Office on Health Reform. Two days after he nominated Daschle for Health and Human Services, Obama nominated Senator Hillary Clinton (D-NY) for Secretary of State. The same week, Peter Orszag was nominated as director of the White House Office of Management and Budget. President-Elect Obama held press conferences on three successive days—November 24, 25, and 26—to explain to the nation plans for how his administration would address the financial crises. Rumors began to be heard of plans for a fiscal stimulus program in the range of $500 billion to $700 billion. Barack Obama encouraged Congress to work quickly so that the stimulus legislation would be ready for him to sign right after his inauguration in January 2009.

In early December 2008, an important shift in framing occurred. Health care reform went from being a problem to being a solution to the nation's fiscal problems.[8] On December 5, 2008, at a speech in Denver, Colorado, Tom Daschle said, "There is no question the economy is going to be directly related to our ability to reform the health care system in the years ahead." The same day, President-elect Obama said that the nation's financial outlook "will have a hard time improving as long as skyrocketing health care costs are holding us down."[9] It is doubtful that anyone believed then or now that the nation's 2008 banking, credit, and housing meltdowns were caused by the conditions in the U.S. health care system, though the resultant job losses caused sharp upswings in the number of Americans without health insurance and in medical-related personal bankruptcies. But forging a link in the minds of Americans between fiscal recovery and health care reform, even if more convenient than real, would certainly ease the path for reform.

Meanwhile in Congress, although Senator Kennedy might have been worried about tying President-elect Obama's hands, other members with a long-standing devotion to health care issues vied to be the first out of the gate and get their names associated with major reform legislation. "Without waiting for President-elect Barack Obama,"[10] on November 12, 2008 frontrunner Senator Max Baucus (D-MT), chairman of the Senate Finance Committee, released a white paper called "Call to Action: Health Care Reform 2009." A few days later, on November 18—the day after he returned to the Senate for the first time since July, having been undergoing treatments for his brain cancer— Senator Kennedy, chairman of the Senate HELP Committee, announced that he would put forth a health care reform plan in early 2009. Senator Ron Wyden, who had introduced a comprehensive health care reform bill (S.334, The Health Americans Act) in January 2007, had reworked his bill and, according to what an aide told us, planned to reintroduce it in January 2009, "barring a counter request from President-elect Obama." In the U.S. House of Representatives in November 2008, Pete Stark (D-CA), chairman of the Health Subcommittee of Ways and Means, intimated during a press conference that he would be offering a health care reform proposal, and two powerful Democrats were vying for the chairmanship of the Energy and Commerce Committee, a committee that would play a critical role in any health care reform legislation. Representative John Dingell (D-MI), who had been the senior Democrat on the Committee for over a quarter-century, was locked in a battle with Representative Henry Waxman (D-CA). On November 20, 2008, the Democratic caucus gave Waxman the chairmanship by a vote of 137–122. Waxman and Dingell later agreed that Dingell, not Waxman, would be the lead sponsor of any health care reform legislation coming out of the Committee.[11]

The November 2008 flurry of activity on health care reform in the Congress was summed up by a House staffer, who told us, "Right now everyone—all the various committees—all the players—are developing their own [*health care reform*] plans. Senator Baucus is releasing his blueprint, and we had Chairman Stark doing his press conference last week announcing his intentions to do a bill. Senator Kennedy is doing his thing as well. If John Dingell hangs on, or even if it's Henry Waxman on Energy and Commerce, they won't just sit by and let their jurisdiction be interfered with. It's going to depend on Obama and how hard he cracks the whip. We could be wrangling over this forever. More of the House and Senate dynamics will come into play and those are not good. At times I think we've got more unity with Republicans on the House side than with Democrats on the Senate side. If that gets bridged, it will be up to Obama."

As the 110th Congress came to a close, congressional leaders and the President-elect worked on prioritizing his legislative agenda and the economic recovery and jobs package that they hoped would be ready for the President to sign into law on his inauguration day, January 20, 2009. President-elect Obama and congressional advisors decided that the legislative vehicle would be a supplemental appropriations act with substantial mandatory spending and revenue components.[12] Any such act would have to have bipartisan support and be filibuster-proof in order to make it to the President's desk in such a short period of time. Though the 111th Congress would convene on January 6, 2009, there would be few days of work before Inauguration Day. The need for a massive economic stimulus was undeniable and intensifying by the day.

A few days before Christmas 2008 the *Washington Post* reported that Obama advisors were "working to convince lawmakers of the wisdom of limiting the [*economic stimulus*] package to projects that would create a large number of jobs quickly or make a down payment on Obama's broader economic goals, such as improving the health care system."[13] At this time both the House and Senate were operating under internal "pay-as-you-go" (PAYGO) rules, which prohibited the consideration of mandatory spending (basically, entitlement program spending) or revenue legislation that would cause or increase a budget deficit.[14] The economic stimulus package, because it would include mandatory spending, revenue, and discretionary spending provisions, would be subject in part to

PAYGO rules, but the chambers had special rules and actions that would enable them to consider a PAYGO waiver. A waiver of the PAYGO rules meant that provisions in the stimulus bill did not have to have budget offsets that made them budget neutral. The relaxation of normal budget discipline led to justifiable concerns about any eventual stimulus package being "larded up" with legislators' pet projects and initiatives. In addition, members of Congress and congressional committees who had "ready to go" measures now could hang them on a piece of must-move legislation—the stimulus bill—that could carry them into law when they might not have made it as stand-alone bills. And that is exactly what happened. One of our informants described the American Recovery and Reinvestment Act that President Obama signed into law into mid-February 2009 as "a giant Christmas tree of things that people have already thought about—it is a combination of different bills."

One of the ornaments on the tree was a $1.1 billion provision for federal funding of comparative effectiveness research. This was a product of much cooperation across committees and chambers. A Senate committee staffer told us that as early as mid- December 2008 plans were being laid to get federal funding for comparative effectiveness research into the stimulus bill: "We're still hammering out details but it looks like there's some desire to put it [*comparative effectiveness research funding*] in a stimulus package for January 20, 2009. The Senate HELP Committee is working across the Senate with the Senate Finance Committee and across the House, with Ways and Means and Energy and Commerce."

On January 15, 2009, the House Committee on Appropriations issued to the press a summary of the American Recovery and Reinvestment Act that Chairman David Obey (D-WI) planned to introduce in the House. Accompanying the press release was a 76-page discussion draft of the Committee on Appropriation's Report on the provisions of the legislation.[15] This $825 billion bill included a $1.1 billion supplemental appropriation for comparative effectiveness research. The Committee's press release explained, "Substantially increasing the federal investment in comparative effectiveness research has the potential to yield significant payoffs in reducing health care expenditures and improving quality."

On January 26, 2009 Chairman Obey introduced H.R. 1, the American Recovery and Reinvestment Act of 2009, into the House. The bill designated "each amount in the Act as an emergency requirement necessary to meet certain emergency needs in accordance with the FY2008–FY2009 congressional budget resolutions; and as an emergency for Pay-As-You-Go (PAYGO) principles." The House began consideration of the measure the next day and passed H.R. 1 on January 28, 2009, as amended, by a vote of 244–188. Title VIII of the bill included the previously mentioned supplemental appropriation to AHRQ for comparative effectiveness research, directed the Secretary to "enter into a contract with the Institute of Medicine, for which no more than $1,500,000 shall be made available from funds provided in this paragraph, to produce and submit a report to the Congress and the Secretary by not later than June 30, 2009, that includes recommendations on the national priorities for comparative effectiveness research to be conducted or supported with funds provided in this paragraph and that considers input from stakeholders" and directed the Secretary "to consider any recommendations of the Federal Coordinating Council for Comparative Effectiveness Research established by Section 804 of this Act and any recommendations included in the Institute of Medicine report." The duties of the Federal Coordinating Council included (1) assisting federal offices and agencies in coordinating the conduct or support of comparative effectiveness and related health services research; and (2) advising the President and Congress on strategies regarding the infrastructure needs of comparative effectiveness research within the federal government, and related matters.

The Senate took up consideration of H.R. 1 on February 2, 2009 and passed it, as amended, on February 10 by a vote of 61–37. Sixty votes are required in the Senate to end debate on a bill. Republicans Susan Collins (R-ME), Olympia Snowe (R-ME), and Arlan Specter (R-PA) joined with the 56 Democrats and 2 Independents to reach the mark of 61 votes. Democratic Senator Ted Kennedy, at home because of deteriorating health, had returned to the Senate to cast his aye vote. The same day both chambers agreed to a conference on the bill in order to resolve the significant differences between the two versions.

The conference report (H. Rept 111–16) was filed on February 12, 2009. The House agreed to the conference report the next day by a vote of 246–183 (7 Democrats and all 176 Republicans voted nay), as did the Senate that same day, by a vote of 60–38. Four days later President Obama, who had been sworn in as the nation's 44th President less than 3 weeks before, signed the $787 billion American Recovery and Reinvestment Act of 2009 into law as P.L. 111–5. His administration estimated it would save or create 3.5 million jobs. P.L. 111–5 provided a supplemental appropriation for FY2009 of $1.1 billion to AHRQ for comparative effectiveness research, making such funds available for obligation through FY2010. The law required AHRQ to transfer $400 million of this to the National Institutes of Health (NIH) for the conduct or support of comparative effectiveness research and to allow an additional $400 million to be allocated at the discretion of the Secretary of Health and Human Services. (Recall that Tom Daschle was President Obama's nominee for Secretary of Health and Human Services.) It also established the aforementioned Federal Coordinating Council for Comparative Effectiveness Research. Because the Recovery Act was an appropriations bill, the funding it included for comparative effectiveness research had to go to existing agencies with the statutory authority to expend it—hence, the funds went to AHRQ and to NIH.

How did comparative effectiveness research provisions get in to the original economic stimulus package introduced by House Appropriations Committee Chairman Obey on January 26, 2009? The congressional staffers and policy influentials we interviewed uniformly believed that "someone in the White House" wanted comparative effectiveness research in the economic stimulus package. In mid-January 2009 a legislative aide told us, "Someone in the White House wanted it [comparative effectiveness research] in the stimulus package. Just like health IT [information technology], it is being viewed as something that has to happen. We haven't been able to get over the hump in Congress, so we put something in there...We need to hash out the policy differences, and I think those questions might still be open after the stimulus."

White House staff included several strong proponents of federally mandated comparative effectiveness research. President-elect Obama had nominated Senator Tom Daschle (D-SD) for Secretary of Health and Human Services on November 20, 2008. Daschle was still only a nominee in December 2008 and January 2009 when the initial bill was being crafted, but he had also been named Director of the White House Office of Health Reform, a post that did not require Senate confirmation. Daschle and his deputy director Jeanne Lambrew could well have been pushing for its inclusion in the initial stimulus package. In fact, the provisions in the Recovery Act for a Federal Coordinating Council for Comparative Effectiveness Research hearken directly back to AcademyHealth's 2005 "Placement Report," which came out of the committee that Lambrew had co-chaired. However, the White House had even deeper bench strength in advocacy for comparative effectiveness research than just Daschle and Lambrew: Peter Orszag, the director of the Office of Management and Budget. Orszag had been a vocal and staunch advocate of federally mandated comparative effectiveness research since 2007, just after Gail Wilensky's "billionize" paper appeared and as he became Director of the Congressional Budget Office.

The inclusion of funds for comparative effectiveness research in the proposed stimulus bill delighted many health services and clinical researchers across the country, but many wondered whether those provisions would survive the legislative process. And indeed, within a week of the January 15, 2009 Appropriations Committee release of the summary of the planned legislation and the accompanying "Discussion Draft of the Joint Explanatory Statement to Accompany the Spending Provisions of the American Recovery and Reinvestment Act," a firestorm of opposition erupted. The flashpoint was the language used in one sentence in the Discussion Draft. The sentence reflects the policy goals behind comparative effectiveness research, avoidance of wasteful spending by identifying services that work best: "By knowing what works best and presenting this information more broadly to patients and healthcare professionals, those items, procedures, and interventions that are most effective to prevent, control, and treat health conditions will be utilized, while those that are found to be less effective and in some cases, more expensive, will no longer be prescribed." The fear mongers were ready, and the sentence was just enough. In an "Information Alert" published a week later (January 23, 2009), the Republican Study Committee[16] warned that this sentence, together with the provision for a Federal Coordinating Council for Comparative Effectiveness Research, was evidence that the stimulus bill under consideration "will grant Obama's nominee for Secretary of Health and Human Services, Tom Daschle, his wish of a permanent government rationing board prescribing care in place of doctors and patients."[17] (Recall that in the 2009 book that Daschle and Jeanne Lambrew co-authored, they proposed the creation of a Federal Health Board.)

The prospect that the proposed stimulus bill's comparative effectiveness provisions would give the federal government broad powers to dictate, monitor, and ration care spread with amazing rapidity throughout the country.[18] On his February 9, 2009 radio show, titled "The March to Socialized Medicine Starts in Obama's Porkulus Bill,"[19] Rush Limbaugh warned his listeners that "the national coordinator of health information technology will monitor treatments that your doctor gives you to make sure your doctor is doing what the federal government deems appropriate and cost-effective." He also said, "Let me translate this for you. You are a seasoned citizen. You come down with a disease that is not immediately life-threatening. You go into your doctor. The doctor consults the federal database to get your health care records. He then has to consult this new health council board. They then figure the cost of treating whatever's wrong with you, based on the statistics that tell 'em how long you're going to live—and if the cost vastly outweighs the number of years you're going to live, they will deny you treatment."

The informants we spoke to speculated that someone at PhRMA, one of the industry groups, or the Partnership to Improve Patient Care, the alliance formed in 2008 by PhRMA, BIO, and AdvaMed, got the Republican Study Committee "riled up" about the comparative effectiveness provisions in the proposed stimulus bill and that one or more of these groups was behind the million-dollar oppositional campaign. "The drug companies and the device companies have been very worried from the outset, and they've been trying to draw attention to the fact that this [*comparative effectiveness research*] could limit Americans' access to cures. They have been out there funding and stoking patient advocacy groups to say 'This is un-American,' that we're going to deny coverage to people for care they need to sustain their lives and so on...In a time when we are trying to move quickly and there's a lot of negative press that's not even factually correct, it's very easy for Senators to hide behind any excuse for not supporting this. I would agree with [*NAME*] that PIPC [*Partnership to Improve Patient Care*] is behind this. We have known since summer 2008 that they would be pouring millions and millions into a public relations blitz. We were waiting for it to rear its ugly head. And here we are. They are very mobilized and they have been able to infiltrate news figures like Rush Limbaugh, not credible but very popular in some states. And now we are starting to see the fear campaign take hold."

The furor over the Report language on comparative effectiveness research ostensibly centered on the possibility that the expense of treatments might be part of the calculus of comparisons between treatments. Understandably, the backlash caught the Appropriations Committee staffers off guard. Their goal was to increase the value of health care dollar by identifying wasteful services. One of the staffers told us, "Chairman Obey believes, 'If this isn't about decreasing costs, why are we doing it?' He's a very cut-and-dried sort of guy."

Whether the scope of federally mandated comparative effectiveness research included cost-effectiveness and not just "clinical" effectiveness had been a sticking point since 2003 and Section 1013 in the Medicare Modernization Act. The most vehement objections to including cost-effectiveness came from the medical products industry. Besides the fight about the language used in the House Appropriations Discussion Draft of January 15, 2009, there was a fight between the House and Senate over the use of the word "clinical" before "comparative effectiveness research" in the Senate version of the Appropriations Committee report on the stimulus bill, filed January 27, 2009. The belief was that, if the word "clinical" precedes "comparative effectiveness research" in the statute, than the statute would preclude any consideration of comparative costs. Ultimately, the word "clinical" was not included in the Conference Report (H. Report 111–16). However, months after the Recovery Act became law the scope of comparative effectiveness research—just "clinical" or "clinical and cost"—was still debated.

To lessen opposition and allay fears, the House-Senate Conference Committee Report (H. Report 111–16) on the stimulus bill filed on February 12, 2009 included language circumscribing what the data obtained by comparative effectiveness research could be used for (Box 9.3). Though some Republicans

---

Box 9.3 **Excerpt Signaling Congressional Intent for Comparative Effectiveness Research Funding from House-Senate Conference Committee Report (H. Rept 111–16) on the American Recovery and Reinvestment Act of 2009**

The conference agreement includes $1,100,000,000 for comparative effectiveness research, which is the same level as proposed by both the House and the Senate. The conference agreement uses the term "comparative effectiveness research," as proposed by the House and deletes without prejudice the term "clinical," which was included by the Senate. Within the total, $300,000,000 shall be administered by the Agency for Healthcare

Research and Quality (AHRQ), \$400,000,000 shall be transferred to the National Institutes of Health (NIH), and \$400,000,000 shall be allocated at the discretion of the Secretary of Health and Human Services.

The conferees do not intend for the comparative effectiveness research funding included in the conference agreement to be used to mandate coverage, reimbursement, or other policies for any public or private payer. The funding in the conference agreement shall be used to conduct or support research to evaluate and compare the clinical outcomes, effectiveness, risk, and benefits of two or more medical treatments and services that address a particular medical condition. Further, the conferees recognize that a "one-size-fits-all" approach to patient treatment is not the most medically appropriate solution to treating various conditions and include language to ensure that subpopulations are considered when research is conducted or supported with the funds provided in the conference agreement.

had comparative effectiveness research on the list of things they wanted to eliminate from the stimulus bill, the provisions survived the House-Senate Conference Committee. One of the conferees was Senator Max Baucus, who, the reader will recall, had introduced a stand-alone comparative effectiveness research bill in 2008 and who had promised to reintroduce it in 2009.

Legacies of the American Recovery and Reinvestment Act of 2009

The Recovery Act left four principal legacies for federal policy on comparative effectiveness research. First, while not a legacy of the law itself but rather of the anti-comparative effectiveness research campaigns that occurred during the crafting and passage of the legislation, "death panels," "rationing," "denial of care," and "government interference in medical care" became part of the lexicon for some Americans in considering federal policy on comparative effectiveness research, and on health care reform in general.

Second, the Recovery Act did provide a "down payment" on the infrastructure for comparative effectiveness research and paved the way for the subsequent evolution that would be impelled by the Patient Protection and Affordable Care Act of 2010. The Recovery Act of 2009 was a supplemental appropriation that provided a massive infusion of new funds—\$1.1 billion—for comparative effectiveness research into the NIH, AHRQ, and the Office of the Secretary of Health and Human Services. Until this point, the only federal funds earmarked for comparative effectiveness research came through the appropriation that AHRQ received under Section 1013 of the 2003 Medicare Modernization Act, which totaled only $30 million in FY2008. But the research dollars provided by the Recovery Act had only a 2-year life span. They had to be expended or obligated by the close of FY2010. The funds had to be gotten out of the door quickly. The initial NIH request for grant applications was posted on March 4, 2009, less than 3 weeks after President Obama signed the Recovery Act into law. Ultimately, with funds provided by the law, the Department of Health and Human Services funded 114 research projects and training grants focusing on comparative effectiveness research.[20] It is not unreasonable to assume that four to five times as many grant applications on comparative effectiveness research topics were submitted than were funded. Through its infusion of new funds for grants, the Recovery Act stimulated enormous interest in comparative effectiveness research among the nation's clinical and health services researchers and created a cadre of scientists versed in its research methods. It is still too early to know what effects their research might exert on the health of Americans.

Third, the Act's 2-year down-payment dollars for comparative effectiveness research made it clear to everyone on Capitol Hill that comparative effectiveness research would come up again as part of comprehensive health care reform. Despite the large amount of federal funds earmarked in the Recovery Act for comparative effectiveness research, sustained, predictable investments are needed if research programs are to achieve long-range outcomes.

Fourth, reports issued by two distinguished panels established by the law provided well-considered analyses of the current status of comparative effectiveness research in the United States as of 2009 and rational plans for how a new federal investment in it should be styled. The Institute of Medicine released its consensus report on 100 initial national priorities for comparative effectiveness research[21] on June 30, 2009, the deadline specified in the Recovery Act. The first seven topics of the highest priority group are given in Box 9.4. Also on June 30, 2009, the Federal Coordinating Council for Comparative Effectiveness Research submitted its report to the President and the Congress.[22] Among other things, the Council created an organizing framework for comparative effectiveness research that integrated types of activities (research, capacity-building, data infrastructure, and dissemination and translation) and themes for research (conditions and disease states, patient populations, and types of clinical interventions). The Council used this framework to analyze the existing landscape for comparative effectiveness research in federal agencies, inventory ongoing activities, and make priority recommendations for the funds that the Recovery Act allocated to the Office of the Secretary of Health and Human Services. The IOM's Consensus Committee and the Federal Coordinating Council did an enormous amount of work over a very short period in order to make their June 30, 2009 deadlines (recall that the Recovery Act was signed into law in mid-February 2009.) The information the reports contain—and the effects exerted on committee members and

---

Box 9.4 **The Institute of Medicine's Seven Highest Priority Topics for Comparative Effectiveness Research**

- Compare the effectiveness of treatment strategies for atrial fibrillation, including surgery, catheter ablation, and pharmacologic treatment.
- Compare the effectiveness of different treatments (e.g., assistive listening devices, cochlear implants, electric-acoustic devices, habilitation and rehabilitation methods [auditory/oral, sign language, and total communication]) for hearing loss in children and adults, especially individuals with diverse cultural, language, medical, and developmental backgrounds.
- Compare the effectiveness of primary prevention methods, such as exercise and balance training, versus clinical treatments in preventing falls in older adults at varying degrees of risk.
- Compare the effectiveness of upper endoscopy utilization and frequency for patients with gastroesophageal reflux disease on morbidity, quality of life, and diagnosis of esophageal adenocarcinoma.
- Compare the effectiveness of dissemination and translation techniques to facilitate the use of comparative effectiveness research by patients, clinicians, payers, and others.
- Compare the effectiveness of comprehensive care coordination programs, such as the medical home, and usual care in managing children and adults with severe chronic disease, especially in populations with known health disparities.
- Compare the effectiveness of different strategies of introducing biologics into the treatment algorithm for inflammatory diseases, including Crohn's disease, ulcerative colitis, rheumatoid arthritis, and psoriatic arthritis.

Source: Released on June 30, 2009. (The full list of 100 topics is given on the Institute of Medicine's Web site.)

---

others who provided input to their deliberations—are clearly among the legacies of this legislation.

Across the Finish Line: Comparative Effectiveness Research Becomes Law as Part of the Affordable Care Act of 2010

Like many new administrations since that of Franklin Delano Roosevelt, President-elect Obama's team was working feverishly to achieve great things before its 100-day mark and trying to get key cabinet and other posts in the executive branch filled expeditiously. The plummeting economy conferred a sense of immediacy. But some of the President's nominations for key posts of his administration went awry, and critics said haste had undermined due diligence. One of the most important of these fiascos occurred on February 3, 2009 during the critical final negotiations surrounding the passage of the American Recovery and Reinvestment Act. On that day, Senator Tom Daschle, because of scrutiny over unpaid taxes, withdrew as the nominee for Secretary of Health and Human Services and left his White House post as Director of Health Reform. A few weeks before another Cabinet nominee, Tim Geithner, slated for Treasury Secretary, also had come under scrutiny for unpaid taxes, but he managed to survive and was confirmed in January by the Senate Finance Committee.

The news of Daschle's withdrawal was a shocker. Serendipitously, hundreds of the nation's health policy researchers were meeting at AcademyHealth's annual National Health Policy Conference in Washington when the announcement came over their BlackBerrys and smart phones at midday. The energy and attendance at the 2009 conference was much higher than usual: health care reform was finally in reach, as was comparative effectiveness research legislation. Just the day before at the Conference, Jeanne Lambrew had given a keynote address about the health care overhaul.

Daschle's withdrawal and the consequent leadership void stalled health care reform efforts. On March 2, 2009 President Obama named Nancy-Ann DeParle[23] to head the White House Office of Health Reform, and he nominated Kansas Governor Kathleen Sebelius[24] for the post of Secretary of Health and Human Services. Sebelius received Senate confirmation as Secretary of Health and Human Services on April 28, 2009, the confirmation process hastened by a public health emergency: a swine flu epidemic. Lambrew left the White House Health Reform Office and on April 11, 2009 was appointed Director of the Office of Health Reform in the Department of Health and Human Services.

So many elements and proposals of the massive health care reform effort were contentious (e.g., the possibility of a "public option," a government-run health insurance plan) that federally mandated comparative effectiveness research seemed too small of an issue for many Americans and politicians to worry about. However, we will continue our focus on it, leaving others to tell the full story of health care reform as a whole. Several books have been published about how the Patient Protection and Affordable Care Act of 2010 that President Obama signed into law on March 23, 2010 came to be, and many more will be.

Both the House and Senate were working hard on various aspects of health reform. In the Senate, on June 9, 2009, Senator Baucus, chairman of the Finance Committee, and co-sponsor Senator Conrad, chairman of the Budget Committee, introduced a somewhat re-worked version of the comparative effectiveness bill they had introduced on July 31, 2008. According to Senate staffers, this bill had undergone some "tweaks and iterations" in the process of negotiations with people on the Senate HELP Committee; negotiations with the House did not progress.

Our comparison of the 2009 bill to the 2008 version indicates that 2009 bill contained changes that were somewhat more than "tweaks"[25] and that probably reflect the influence of industry rather than concessions to the HELP Committee. For example, the name changed. The name of 2008 Baucus-Conrad bill was the "Comparative Effectiveness Research Act" (S. 3408), but the 2009 version was called the "Patient-Centered Outcomes Research Act" (S. 1213).

How did the "Health Care Comparative Effectiveness Research Institute" become the "Patient-Centered Outcomes Research Institute"? It appears to have come about as a result of pressure by industry. This shift in language, little noted, had begun in mid-2007, just as the House Ways and Means Committee was preparing its version of comparative effectiveness research provisions that would be eventually folded into the CHAMP bill. Around that time the medical products industry began using the term "patient-centered care" in its statements about comparative effectiveness research. For example, in a statement submitted for the record of the June 12, 2007 Hearing on Strategies to Increase Information on Comparative Clinical Effectiveness before the Health Subcommittee of the House Ways and Means Committee, the Advanced Medical Technology Association offered four principles to ensure that comparative effectiveness research is carried out appropriately. The first was, "Patient-centered care and independent professional medical judgment:...its [CER's] objective should be to provide better evidence for physicians and patients to use in making individual clinical decision for each patient's unique condition."[26]

S. 1213 was referred to the Senate Finance Committee. No further action was taken on S. 1213. However, it was later taken largely unchanged into the Affordable Care Act of 2010 and became law. The name change persisted in the comparative effectiveness provisions of the Affordable Care Act of 2010 and eventually had significant implications for how the new Patient-Centered Outcomes Research Institute spent much of its first year: coming up with a definition of "patient-centered outcomes research."

Senator Ted Kennedy (D-MA) had been a decades-long advocate of comprehensive health care reform. He and many of his supporters hoped that that health care reform would be his legacy. His illness had sidelined him for much of the debate and undermined his ability to influence people and legislative processes. On June 9, 2009 (which happened to be the same day Senators Baucus and Conrad introduced their Patient-Centered Outcomes Research Act), Senator Kennedy unveiled the health reform bill that he and his Senate Health, Education, Labor, and Pensions (HELP) Committee had crafted. It was called the "Affordable Health Choices Act." On July

15, 2009, after a month-long markup, one of the longest in congressional history, according to the Senate HELP Committee press release,[27] the HELP Committee passed the bill. Section 937 of the bill would have established a Center for Health Outcomes Research and Evaluation within AHRQ and charged it to "collect, conduct, support, and synthesize research with respect to comparing health outcomes, effectiveness, and appropriateness of health care services and procedures in order to identify the manner in which diseases, disorders, and other health conditions can most effectively be prevented, diagnosed, treated, and managed clinically." The bill would have funded this Center through the congressional appropriations process. No dollar amount was stated; the bill "authorized to be appropriated such sums as may be necessary." Senator Kennedy succumbed to his brain cancer on August 25, 2009 at the age of 77. The Senate HELP Committee Affordable Health Choices Act (S. 1679) was introduced into the Senate on September 17, 2009 by Senator Tom Harkin (D-IA).

It is worth commenting on the differences of opinion about comparative effectiveness research that existed within the Senate between the Finance Committee and the HELP Committee. The most important centered on whether the function would be housed within and as part of government or without, as a non-governmental entity. Recall that the HELP Committee has jurisdiction over the NIH and AHRQ, among other things, and so has a particular interest in these agencies. The story told to us by a former staffer points out the contrasts between the Senate versions and describes how and why things evolved as they did (Box 9.5).

Box 9.5 **A Staffer's Description of the Differences Regarding Comparative Effectiveness Research between the Senate Finance Committee and Senate HELP Committee and How Events Unfolded as They Did in the Passage of the Affordable Care Act**

We all agreed that there needed to be an increased effort to focus on CE [*comparative effectiveness research*], but there was a debate, even among Democrats, about how that would best be done, given that we have AHRQ and NIH in existence, that they should be doing the CER. The HELP bill, because it clearly had jurisdictional boundaries, focused so much more so on AHRQ and NIH. The Senate Finance Committee had their bill. At the same time we knew the House, through Waxman and Stark, had their version as well.

So the food fight, so to speak, started in the stimulus bill. As the money went out the door to AHRQ and the NIH we wanted to make sure, we being the HELP Committee, that money continued to go to AHRQ and the NIH. Baucus and Conrad really had their eyes set on this entity that now exists by statute [*the Patient-Centered Outcomes Research Institute*]. The House also favored what Kennedy's staff and a lot of the HELP Committee felt was the right thing to do, which was to put that really into AHRQ and let AHRQ just be more muscular. AHRQ went through so many of its own morphs and iterations in its life. We felt like CER was just one more iteration and morphing of AHRQ. This would be a good thing because AHRQ had been so under-funded in the Bush administration.

But what ended up happening—I mean, Senator Kennedy was obviously sick, and priorities were set differently on the HELP committee when it was clear that he was not going to be there to champion a lot of these causes. What you saw was a compromise between Finance and HELP to merge these bills. In the Senate you really have to think about how much you want to fight for your issue. In the merging of the bill we didn't really mind having this institute or entity, even though it wasn't necessarily the way we would have gone. It wasn't such an awful idea . . . we thought, well, at the end of the day, if it's this or nothing, we'll take this. The House was in the same operation mode, you know, "If it's this or nothing, we'll take this." The House knew at that time it was the Senate bill that was probably going to be the ultimate bill.

Now some of those problem areas that we thought were really problematic, like the publications issue,[a] got dealt with in the manager's amendment that Harry Reid put out, which helped to fix some of those issues. But there are still issues with that bill that probably would've been worked out in conference had we not had kind of this unfortunate sequence of political events where Scott Brown won and we lost our super majority and then we basically had to pass the Senate bill as it was written and as it was passed in December of 2009.

---

[a] For information on this issue, see Selker HP, Wood AJJ. Industry influence on comparative effectiveness research funded through health care reform. N Engl J Med 2009;361:2595–7.

Ultimately, the Senate Finance Committee version prevailed.[28] As a staffer for that committee told us, "A lot of [*HELP's capitulation*] came from an understanding that our office has been working on this for a long time. Granted, we did go through our process without [*Senator*] Kennedy, but we did allocate a lot of funding to AHRQ that we had originally decided the Patient-Centered

Outcomes Research Institute would handle[29]... At the end of the day, the Finance Committee's structure did win out, but we made sure to accommodate certain issues the HELP Committee had. We didn't bully them out of anything. I think we convinced them on the importance of why we needed to have an outside entity as opposed to an AHRQ-based entity."

On June 8, 2009, the day before Kennedy had unveiled the draft of the Senate HELP Committee's Affordable Health Choices Act, the House released a discussion draft of what came to be called the "Tri-Committee House bill on health reform"—tri-committee because it was the product of a joint effort among the House Ways and Means Committee (Chairman Charles Rangel; Chairman of the Health Subcommittee Pete Stark), the Energy and Commerce Committee (Chairman Henry Waxman), and the Committee on Education and Labor (Chairman George Miller). Section 1401 of the Tri-Committee bill would have established a Center for Comparative Effectiveness Research within AHRQ and funded it with a combination of initial appropriated dollars ($90 million in FY2010, $100 million in FY2011, and $110 million in FY2012) and, beginning in FY2013, an all-payer tax on health insurers ($375 million for FY2013, increasing thereafter). This bill (America's Affordable Health Choices Act of 2009) was introduced into the House on July 14, 2009 by Representative John Dingell.

The Kennedy bill of the Senate, the health reform bill passed on October 13, 2009 by the Senate Finance Committee (America's Healthy Future Act, S.1796, unveiled by Chairman Max Baucus on September 16, 2009) and the tri-committee House bill were never debated or voted on by either chamber. Instead, a health care reform bill introduced into the House on September 17, 2009 by Representative Rangel, the Patient Protection and Affordable Care Act (H.R. 3590), was passed by the House on November 7, 2009 (220 ayes; 215 nays), and was passed, amended, by the Senate on December 24, 2009: 60 ayes (59 Democrats and 1 Independent), 39 nays (all Republicans), and 1 Republican not voting. The Congress recessed for the holidays.

The early 2009 negotiations and horse-trading among the lawmakers (Democrats vs. Democrats as well as Democrats vs. Republicans) and between the two chambers as they tried to resolve their differences with H.R. 3590 were intense, sometimes bitter and sometimes laughable, and seemed interminable. As if this were not enough, in early January it looked like the Massachusetts Senate seat that had been vacated by Senator Ted Kennedy's death might be won by a Republican. Kennedy, a Democrat, had held that seat since 1962. Democrat Martha Coakley, the Massachusetts' state attorney general, was running for the seat against Republican Scott Brown, a little known Massachusetts state senator. The election would be held in mid-January. Coakley had been leading the race comfortably and had been considered a sure win until the last few weeks before Election Day. A victory by Brown would mean that the Democrats no longer held a 60-vote majority in the Senate and would certainly be unable to control Republican senators' filibusters against the health reform bill.

On January 18, 2010, Republican Scott Brown decisively defeated Democrat Martha Coakley. The stakes were raised for the "informal" resolution of differences between the two Houses, instead of a conference committee. The outcomes seemed all the more uncertain.

To become law, identical versions of a bill must be passed by each house of Congress. Ordinarily with important or controversial legislation, when the House passes a bill and the Senate amends and agrees to that bill, a House-Senate conference committee is established to resolve differences. The conference committee issues a conference report, which must be agreed to by both chambers before it is cleared for consideration by the President.[30] But the loss of Ted Kennedy's seat to a Republican meant that a House-Senate conference report might not survive the Senate. In the Senate, 60 votes are required for cloture. Without 60 votes, the Republican opponents could kill the bill with a filibuster.

Accordingly, congressional Democrats began thinking of a way to avoid the potential failure of the health care reform bill in the Senate. The Senate had passed a health care reform bill in December, but it contained amendments that were not favored by many members of the House. How could these differences be resolved without going to conference committee and risking the bill's death by filibuster? Eventually, the Democrats decided to use another means of resolving differences between House and Senate versions. Party leaders would work to get the House to approve the Senate-passed amended bill, and then, once the President signed it into law, pass a budget reconciliation bill to modify it so that House-Senate compromises on some of the tax and spending provisions could be enacted.[31] Reconciliation bills need only 51 votes to pass in the Senate—not 60 like other legislation does—and the Democrats thought they could muster at least 51 votes. This pathway had two realities. First, the only changes that could be made in the bill passed by the Senate that could be changed to the satisfaction of the House were provisions related to tax and spending, because these are the only issues that can be corrected in a subsequent budget reconciliation bill. Second and more important, this pathway required House Democrats to trust Senate Democrats to keep their promise to pass a reconciliation bill containing the agreed-upon tax and spending changes, a tough proposition, given the long years of distrust between the two bodies.

But on March 21, 2010, Speaker Nancy Pelosi (D-CA) was able to deliver the House. The House voted 219 (all Democrats) to 212 (34 Democrats; 178 Republicans) on a motion to concur in Senate amendments. Two days later President Obama signed into law the Patient Protection and Affordable Care Act.[32] The law included a federal mandate for comparative effectiveness research, and the vision for its placement, governance, and funding was that of the Senate Finance Committee. The Patient-Centered Outcomes Research Institute would be "neither an agency nor establishment of the Federal Government" and, after initial support with appropriated dollars, would be funded primarily by fees on federal and private health insurers.

Scott Brown's election and the consequent loss of the Senate Democratic super majority had far-reaching consequences for the form federally mandated comparative effectiveness research eventually took. Our informants told us that many lawmakers and staffers believed that a House-Senate conference committee would be called to reconcile differences and come up with a bill that both houses could pass. As one person told us, "My understanding is, that prior to the election in Massachusetts, when it looked like there would be a conference, there was an agreement between the House and Senate staff responsible for the CER [*comparative effectiveness*] components that the final product would look more like the House version. CER might not have been established at AHRQ per se but in the Office of the Secretary [*of Health and Human Services*], with a direct line of funding from there to AHRQ, NIH, and other agencies with the Department or other departments, with a governing board. Once Scott Brown won Massachusetts, talks of a conference imploded. By virtue of the bigger political tidal wave, we ended up with the Senate version. Though I can't document it, my impression from folks in Senate Finance who were working on this intended all along to go with something closer to the House model, but they were humoring industry all the way to keep them at bay. They knew if they crossed them too early the whole thing had the potential to unravel a la Rush Limbaugh, euthanasia, rationing, killing Grandma, death panels, etc. There was a lot of that going on anyway. If it had gone to conference, they [*Finance Committee*] could have just said, 'Oh, well, it happened in conference and we lost and now it's too late. The train has left the station. The bill is going to pass.'"

Conclusions

In Chapters 7, 8, and 9 we have traced how comparative effectiveness research evolved from a "good idea" put forth by Representative Tom Allen (D-ME) in 2002 into a federally mandated activity envisioned as a support of the "value for money" needs in the 2010 U.S. health care reform law. In this 8-year story, relatively few individuals played key roles, and several of these individuals can be credited with more than one of the game-changing events in the evolution from good idea to policy. The opposition to federally mandated comparative effectiveness research, which came (and still comes) almost exclusively from the medical products industry and the disease-specific patient groups funded by the industry, became much more organized and much better funded over the 8 years, but the claims opponents made did not change at all: "cookbook medicine," "rationing of care," "the interference of the federal government between doctor and patients," and "stifling innovation." However, around 2008, when the eventual passage of some version of comparative effectiveness legislation appeared to be inevitable, the opposition changed its strategies. They continued trying to forestall the passage of *any* comparative effectiveness research legislation but also worked to ensure that proposed legislation was written in ways that protected their interests, and then, once the legislation was passed, to influence how it was implemented. The Partnership to Improve Patient Care, established in 2008 by PhRMA, BIO, and AdvaMED, has styled itself as the watchdog of the Patient-Centered Outcomes Research Institute.

Notes

1. Language from S. 3408, the Baucus-Conrad Comparative Effectiveness Research Act of 2008.
2. See Rawson K. PhRMA, BIO alliance promotes industry agenda on comparative effectiveness. The Pink Sheet 2008 Aug 25.
3. Our emailed inquiries to the PIPC about its origin have gone unanswered. We have found no publicly available information stating that the coalition became the PIPC, and no information to the contrary. The first three members of the PIPC were the three that formed the coalition: PhRMA, BIO, and AdvaMED.
4. On its Web site, the Partnership to Improve Patient Care states, "PIPC is dedicated to supporting comparative effectiveness research that strengthens physician and patient decision making, improves health care quality, and supports continued medical progress. To make that happen, we raise awareness . . . about the need to ensure that proposals to expand the government's role in CER are *centered on patient needs*" (PIPC's emphasis). (Accessed March 20, 2012 at http://www.improvepatientcare.org/about.)
5. See Mundy A. Drug makers fight stimulus provision. Wall Street Journal 2009 Feb 22.
6. Goodman CJ, Mance SM. Employment loss and the 2007–09 recession: an overview. Monthly Labor Review April 2011, pp. 3–12.
7. Bernard, TS, Anderson J. Bankruptcies by consumers climb sharply. New York Times 2008 Nov 16.
8. See, for example, Gruber J. Medicine for the job market. New York Times 2008 Dec 4.
9. See Carey MA. Health overhaul essential to economic recovery, Daschle says. CQ Healthbeat News 2008 Dec 5.
10. Pear R. Senator takes initiative on health care. New York Times 2008 Nov 12.
11. In mid-December 2008, a health legislative assistant to a representative told us, "The news I got today was that Dingell will basically take the lead on all health care stuff. I did not hear, however, that he would be Health Subcommittee Chair and bump Palone, though. That is an interesting dynamic there. I did hear that any health reform bill that comes out of Energy and Commerce, the lead co-sponsor will be Mr. Dingell, not Chairman Waxman. Chairman Waxman cares a lot about health care but it is not the priority for him that it is for Mr. Dingell."
12. Clinton TB, Vincent CH, Jackson PJ, Lake JE, Spar K, Keith K. American Recovery and Reinvestment Act of 2009 (P.L. 111–5): summary and legislative history. Congressional Research Service Report R40537, April 20, 2009.
13. Montgomery L. Obama expands stimulus goals. The Washington Post 2008 Dec 21. Available from http://www.washingtonpost.com/wp-dyn/content/article/2008/12/20/AR2008122001395_pf.html.

14. PAYGO procedures help to enforce budget policies with respect to congressional consideration of revenue legislation and direct spending (entitlement spending such as Social Security) legislation. PAYGO procedures do not apply to discretionary spending, which is provided in annual appropriations acts. Statutory PAYGO requirements expired in 2002, but the House and Senate put into place their own internal PAYGO rules and operate under them. See Keith R. Pay-as-you-go procedures for budget enforcement. Congressional Research Service Report RL34300, November 20, 2008.

15. The Joint Explanatory Statement to Accompany the Spending Provisions of the American Recovery and Reinvestment Act, submitted by the House Committee on Appropriations to the Committee of the Whole House on January 15, 2009. Accessed through Congressional Quarterly's Hot Docs on March 6, 2012. The Senate Committee on Appropriations issued its Committee Report to Accompany the American Recovery and Reinvestment Act of 2009, S. 336, on January 27, 2009.

16. According to its Web site, the Republican Study Committee is "a group House Republicans organized for the purpose of advancing a conservative social and economic agenda in the House of Representatives" (Accessed April 4, 2012 at http://rsc.jordan.house.gov/AboutRSC/.)

17. Conservative concerns on the comparative effectiveness research provision in the American Recovery and Reinvestment Act, January 23, 2009. Accessed November 12, 2012, at http://rsc.jordan.house.gov/uploadedfiles/advisoryhealthbd1_23_09.pdf.

18. See Avorn J. Debate about funding comparative effectiveness research. N Engl J Med 2009;360:1927–9.

19. The transcript of Rush Limbaugh's show of February 9, 2009 is available from http://www.rushlimbaugh.com/daily/2009/02/09/the_march_to_socialized_medicine_starts_in_obama_s_porkulus_bill. Limbaugh's commentary was based largely on a commentary on the stimulus bill written by Betsy McCaughey (a former lt. governor of New York), accessed April 9, 2012, at http://www.bloomberg.com/apps/news?pid=newsarchive&sid=aLzfDxfbwhzs.

20. Information obtained March, 8, 2012 from http://gold.ahrq.gov/projectsearch/cer_search_result.jsp?TEXT=comparative+effectiveness.

21. IOM (Institute of Medicine). 2009. Initial national priorities for comparative effectiveness research. Washington, DC: The National Academies Press.

22. Federal Coordinating Council for Comparative Effectiveness Research. Report to the President and the Congress, June 30, 2009. (Accessed April 01, 2012, at http://www.hhs.gov/recovery/programs/cer/cerannualrpt.pdf.)

23. DeParle served as the Director of the Health Care Financing Administration from 1997 to 2000.

24. Sebelius was first elected to the Kansas House of Representatives in 1986, and in 1994 left the House to run successfully for the office of State Health Insurance Commissioner. She was elected Governor of Kansas in 2002 and re-elected in 2006.

25. We offer a few more examples. Words like "genomics" and "molecularly informed" appeared, a nod to industry's drive to develop personalized drugs. Content was added that would assure that studies of medical devices would have to take into account where they were in the innovation cycle as well as the skill of the operator. Content was added instructing the Institute to support patient and consumer representatives. Requirements for advisory panels and comment periods for various stages of individual research projects were intensified. Examination of the methods of cost-effectiveness studies was removed from the responsibilities of the Institute's Methodology Committee. An entirely new section was added that was called "Limitations on use of comparative effectiveness research by the Secretary [of Health and Human Services]." Language was added in several areas to the effect that none of the reports of research findings disseminated by the Institute shall be construed as mandates, guidelines, or recommendations for payment, coverage, or treatment.

26. The full statement can be found in the transcript from the U.S. Government Printing Office.

27. See Coley A. In historic vote, HELP Committee approves the Affordable Care Act, July 15, 2009. HELP Committee Newsroom. (Accessed April 11, 2012, at http://www.help.senate.gov/newsroom/press/release/?id=e38929e7-8b99-4df9-9d41-bba123036c94&groups=Chair.)

28. For an insider's account, see Patel K. Health reform's tortuous route to the Patient-Centered Outcomes Research Institute. Health Aff 2010;29:1777–82.

29. Under the Affordable Care Act provisions for comparative effectiveness research, the trustee of the Patient-Centered Outcomes Research Trust Fund is directed each year to transfer 20% of the funds appropriated to or credited to the Trust Fund to the Secretary of Health and Human Services; of the amounts transferred, the Secretary retains 20% and must distribute 80% to the Agency for Healthcare Research and Quality's office of communication and knowledge transfer.

30. See Senate Legislative Process, Chapter 4: Resolving Differences with the House. (Accessed April 11, 2012, at http://www.senate.gov/legislative/common/briefing/Senate_legislative_process.htm#4.)

31. Van de Water PN, Horney JR. Using reconciliation process to enact health reform would be fully consistent with past practice. Center on Budget and Policy Priorities, March 3, 2010. (Accessed April 12, 2012, at http://www.cbpp.org/cms/index.cfm?fa=view&id=3059.)

32. The authenticated version of the Affordable Care Act is available from http://www.gpo.gov/fdsys/pkg/PLAW-111publ148/pdf/PLAW-111publ148.pdf, accessed October 30, 2012. Section 6301 begins on page 609. The Affordable Care Act was amended by the Health Care and Education Reconciliation Act of 2012, which was signed into law on March 30, 2010, 7 days after the Affordable Care Act became law.

10

The Structure, Financing, and Processes of Federally Mandated Comparative Effectiveness Research and Why They Matter

At the time of this writing, parts of two federal authorizing statutes specifically mandate the conduct of comparative effectiveness research, Section 1013 in the 2003 Medicare Modernization Act, and Section 6301 in the 2010 Affordable Care Act.[1] (Although it did earmark a sizable amount of funds for comparative effectiveness research, the American Reinvestment and Recovery Act of 2009 was an appropriations bill that is no longer relevant.) Each of the two laws confers specific attributes on federally mandated comparative effectiveness research, and those attributes differ. Lawmakers made choices among various forms and options to avoid some of the real or perceived pitfalls of prior incarnations or alternative versions of federal policy and to balance the influence of parties with competing interests. In this chapter, we will discuss the major elements of Section 6310 of the Affordable Care Act in view of earlier policies or the alternative forms that might have been chosen, and evaluate their implications.

The Patient-Centered Outcomes Research Institute (PCORI): "Neither an Agency Nor Establishment of the United States Government"

The 2010 Affordable Care Act established a new nonprofit corporation and specified that it was "neither an agency nor establishment of the United States Government." In contrast, the 2003 Medicare Modernization Act mandated that an existing federal agency, the Agency for Healthcare Research and Quality (AHRQ), conduct comparative effectiveness research, and it authorized the appropriation of additional federal dollars to the agency for that purpose. As we saw in the preceding chapters, a major point of debate about federal policy throughout the decade of the 2000s was whether to get the research done by expanding the mandate of an existing federal research agency—AHRQ and/or the National Institutes of Health (NIH)—or by creating a new entity. The 2007 CHAMP Act would have placed the function at AHRQ, as would have the House versions of the 2009 health care reform legislation. In fact, several congressional staffers we interviewed told us that, had the two chambers gone to conference on the Affordable Care Act, it is likely that the law that President Obama signed would have housed comparative effectiveness research at AHRQ.

Arguments *for* the AHRQ version included that, as an agency expending taxpayer dollars, its activities were subject to congressional oversight, that it already had the statutory authority to include comparative effectiveness research in its portfolio, that it had the infrastructure and well-worked-out, time-honored, peer-reviewed processes for awarding and monitoring federal research grants, and that creating a new organization when AHRQ could do the job was duplicative and wasteful. The most powerful argument *against* the AHRQ version was that its activities were subject to congressional oversight.

Staffers to the Senate Budget and Finance Committees described it to us like this: "We decided that we wanted this entity to be removed from political influence from the executive and the legislative branch as much as possible. How do you do that? You know, NIH does it pretty well. I mean, they get their appropriations. The people believe it's so important on so many different dimensions to fund basic science research, that its funding levels have never been [threatened] though sometimes they're flat. Nobody's ever talked about getting rid of the NIH. We felt that because these decisions that this entity would make—because of the experience that AHRQ had [*referring to the near-death of AHRQ's predecessor agency*]—because these decisions are going to directly affect certain industries, certain high-tech industries potentially, that it couldn't withstand the political pressure being within an agency or being a congressional support agency…So we looked for something that was more insulated. We settled on this congressionally chartered nonprofit, kind of like an Institute of Medicine. But it stops there—it's not funded the same, the board is totally different, and so forth."

Like all departments and agencies within the executive branch of the U.S. federal government, AHRQ, an agency within the U.S. Department of Health and Human Services, is subject to congressional oversight. (Congressional oversight has been likened to having a 535-member board of directors.) Congress exerts its control and oversight of federal agencies via the congressional committee system using the tools of authorization and the appropriation of funds. Housing the comparative effectiveness research function within an existing executive-branch agency meant that a future Congress could eliminate the function or the entire agency. Even if opponents in Congress cannot muster enough votes to eliminate an agency or change its authorities, they may still be able to sharply curtail its activities by holding up the appropriation of funds or keeping it at low levels. It is often said that the most powerful person in the House of Representatives, after the Speaker, is the Chairman of the House Appropriations Committee.

As does the executive branch, the legislative branch of the federal government also has research entities, for example, the Congressional Budget Office. These agencies are also subject to congressional will, as we will see later with the defunct Office of Technology Assessment.

In contrast to AHRQ, governmental oversight of PCORI is the responsibility of the Comptroller General of the United States, who heads the Government Accountability Office (GAO). The GAO, established in 1921, is an independent, nonpartisan agency that works for Congress and supports congressional oversight by audits, investigations, reports, policy analyses, and the issuing of legal opinions. While it is part of the legislative branch of the federal government, unlike congressional committees composed of elected lawmakers, the GAO serves in an advisory role to Congress, not a decision-making one. If, for example, the GAO were to advise Congress that PCORI was not fulfilling its statutory mandates, in order to eliminate or change PCORI a bill would have to be passed by both chambers (including achieving at least 60 votes in the Senate) and signed into law by the president. Obviously this would be much more difficult to achieve than convincing the members of the House Appropriations Committee to put a financial squeeze on a federal agency perceived to be underperforming or going in an undesirable direction. By using the GAO for oversight, Democratic lawmakers were trying to make the Institute less vulnerable to threats coming from a divided and increasingly partisan government.

There is another aspect of the decision to create a new organization to carry out a political mandate, regardless of whether it is a governmental, quasi-governmental, or extra-governmental organization. Organization-building from the ground up is messy, requires tremendous internal energy that distracts from the achievement of external mandates, and is not infrequently unsuccessful. Nevertheless, creating a new organization is a way of bypassing the ones that exist, which, like all organizations, have developed an internal life of their own and ways of resisting control by the authorities to whom they answer. While our research indicates that this sort of distrust of AHRQ swayed some lawmakers to take the PCORI route, the more powerful motivator seems to have been AHRQ's chronically imperiled existence and the so-called near-death experience of its predecessor agency.

The Near-Death Experience of the Agency for Health Care Research and Policy

The near-death experience of AHRQ's predecessor agency, the Agency for Health Care Research and Policy (AHCPR),[2] was fresh on the minds of many congressional staffers and policy influentials during the debates of the 2000s and came up repeatedly during our interviews. The AHCPR was established by Congress in 1989 during the administration of George H.W. Bush as a new agency within the U.S. Public Health Service, part of the Department of Health and Human Services. Its predecessor agency was the National Center for Health Services Research and Health Care Technology Assessment (NCHSR), which had been established in 1968 during the Lyndon B. Johnson administration as part of the Health Services and Mental Health Administration of the Department of Health, Education, and Welfare (later renamed the DHHS). The NCHSR had no explicit congressional authorization; its activities were authorized under Sections 301 and 304 of the Public Health Service Act. The NCHSR had grown out of the Health Services Research Study Section of the NIH. Both the NCHSR and the AHCPR emphasized medical treatment effectiveness research,[3] but the AHCPR also had a mandate from Congress to "arrange for the development and periodic review and updating of clinically relevant guidelines that may be used by physicians and health care practitioners to assist in determining how diseases, disorders, and other conditions can most effectively and appropriately by diagnosed and treated."

It was clinical practice guidelines that pushed AHCPR into harm's way. In December 1994 the agency released guidelines for the treatment of acute low back pain. Noting that nine out of ten sufferers will recover on their own in a month, and that "overall, surgery benefits only about one in 100 people with acute low back problems," the guidelines recommended treating most acute low back problems with over-the-counter analgesics and mild exercise. The 23-member guideline development panel was chaired by an eminent orthopedist and consisted of private sector clinician-experts and consumers. It reviewed over 3,900 studies, held public meetings, and subjected the guidelines to an extensive pre-release review by back care experts.

Nevertheless, the National Association of Spine Surgeons (NASS) found the guidelines objectionable. It responded by launching a letter-writing campaign to members of Congress, and one of the orthopedists on the NASS board founded a lobbying organization called the Center for Public Advocacy. At a Ways and Means subcommittee hearing in July 1995, Representative Sam Johnson (R-TX) attacked AHCPR for interfering with the practice of medicine and mocked it by calling it the "Agency for High Cost Publications and Research." He proposed an amendment to an appropriations bill that would have zeroed out the agency's funding. When the FY96 appropriations bill was finally passed in April 1996, it included a 21% budget cut for the agency. In 1999, the Congress passed and President Bill Clinton signed the Healthcare Research and Quality Act of 1999 (P.L. 106–129), which reauthorized the agency, renamed it the Agency for Healthcare Research and Quality, and modified its authorities. The agency had ended its guidelines program in 1996.

Many of the people we interviewed attributed the near-death of the AHCPR to the fact that the agency's guidelines program inflamed doctors who were at that time powerful enough to get some lawmakers to eliminate or at least choke the agency via the appropriations process. They viewed the AHCPR experience as "an object lesson" for the consequences of placing the comparative effectiveness research function within a federal agency, especially AHRQ.

But the AHCPR situation was considerably more nuanced. First, the Republicans assumed control of the House of Representatives in January 1995, the first time they and not the Democrats had controlled the House in 40 years. House Speaker Newt Gingrich and other Republicans in Congress drew up a list of discretionary federal programs to be eliminated. AHCPR was on that list. The issuance of guidelines that would have cut into the income of back surgeons was a convenient provocation. Another casualty of the "Republican Revolution" and the frenzy of government downsizing was the Office of Technology Assessment (OTA), which Congress eliminated in 1995.[4] The OTA, established in 1972 during the Nixon administration, was a highly respected agency within the legislative branch: it was called the "think tank" of Congress. It provided unbiased assessments not just of medical technologies but also of matters and technologies pertaining to space, energy, climate change, and so on. The elimination of the OTA led to accusations that some members of Congress were anti-intellectual and anti-science.

Second, AHCPR did have some other baggage that made it unusually vulnerable to its committed enemies. According to an in-depth analysis involving nearly 100 interviews,[5] the agency had too few friends in Congress, was thought to be wasteful and inefficient based on the findings of reviews by several congressional agencies, and was identified with partisan politics and the failed Clinton health care reform plan.

After it survived its close call of the mid-1990s, the agency was reinvented as a result of the internal redirection and culture change undertaken by its leaders and staff as well as the refocusing of authorities and processes in its 1999 reauthorization by Congress. Perhaps some features of the reinvention would have made any new federal mandate and funding for comparative effectiveness research placed there in the late 2000s too vulnerable to congressional action. The failure to pass reauthorization legislation for AHRQ in 2005 signified a dangerous kind of congressional ambivalence.[6] Or perhaps the policy makers and policy influentials who advocated for placing that function outside of AHRQ believed that AHRQ simply could not do the job as well as it needed to be done. After all, AHCPR and then AHRQ had had the authority to conduct comparative effectiveness research since AHCPR was established in 1989—a 20-plus year period—and yet such research seemed to be crowded out by other topics on the agency's agenda. Agency funding levels were always too low to support much primary and/or extramural research.

Interestingly, while it was the medical profession—orthopedists to be specific—who spearheaded the attack on AHCPR that almost led to its demise in the mid 1990s, opposition to the new federal mandate for comparative effectiveness research came not from doctors but rather from the medical products industry. When we asked congressional staffers about the input from doctors they were getting about proposed comparative effectiveness research legislation, they told us they were not getting any: doctors were too worried about the "doc fix" (reimbursement rates under Medicare/Medicaid) to pay attention to anything else.

Other Potential Organizations for Federally Mandated Comparative Effectiveness Research

As we saw in Chapter 8, when AcademyHealth's Placement Committee was at work in 2003–2004 evaluating possibilities at the federal level for the placement and coordination of health services and comparative effectiveness research, one model they entertained was that of a federally funded research and development center (FFRDC) to be established by AHRQ.

FFRDCs grew out of research centers established in the 1940s to bring the scientific and engineering expertise and capabilities of the private sector into the service of the government to help it meet national security challenges.[7] They are brought into existence and sponsored by an executive branch federal agency but operated and managed by a university, a university consortium, a nonprofit organization, or an industrial firm. (For example, the RAND Corporation operates three FFRDCs.) FFRDCs are not subject to federal hiring and employment regulations, which affords them greater flexibility in composing and managing their workforces.

An institutional unit must meet federally specified criteria before it can be designated an FFRDC. Among other things, the special research and development activity for which the FFRDC is established by a government agency must not be able to be met as effectively, at the time, by existing in-house or contractor resources. Also, the FFRDC must receive at least 70% of its financial support from the government, with a single agency predominating, and have an annual budget of at least $500,000. As of October 2011, 39 FFRDCs were in existence.[8] Most are funded by the Department of Energy (16) and the Department of Defense (9). Only one is health related: the National Cancer Institute at Frederick, MD, established in 1974, designated as an FFRDC in 1975, and funded by the Department of Health and Human Services.

The FFRDC model has many appealing features. However, it is doubtful that AHRQ or its parent agency, the Department of Health and Human Services, could have made a convincing case to government regulators that an FFRDC needed to be created in order to carry out the federal government's research and development needs in comparative effectiveness research. After all, the Department of Health and Human Services, with its agencies, the NIH, AHRQ, Centers for Disease Control, and others, have well-established intramural and extramural research programs that have existed for decades, and their research portfolios already contained studies classified as comparative effectiveness research. In addition, an FFRDC would still have been vulnerable to the vagaries of funding. As elements of executive-branch federal agencies, FFRDCs are still subject to congressional oversight and control via the appropriations process. Because an FFRDC must receive at least 70% of its financial support from its sponsoring agency, appointed officials at that agency can respond to budget constraints or changes in agency strategic initiatives by phasing out the FFRDC or downsizing it.

Another option that was entertained, albeit briefly, was placing the federal mandate for comparative effectiveness research at the Institute of Medicine (IOM). This option seems never to have developed wide appeal outside the IOM.

The Financing of Comparative Effectiveness Research and PCORI

If situating PCORI outside the federal government establishes (more than) arm's length between it and the Congress, the way the Institute and its operations are financed increases the distance. Whereas AHRQ's mandate for comparative effectiveness research contained in the Medicare Modernization Act of 2003 is funded solely through the congressional appropriation of funds from the U.S. Treasury, for PCORI the 2010 Affordable Care Act creates a trust fund that has a triple revenue stream: appropriations from the general fund of the Treasury, funds transferred from the Medicare Trust Funds[9] (Medicare Federal Hospital Insurance and Federal Supplementary Medical Insurance Trust Funds), and fees imposed on health insurance and self-insured plans. By the mid-2010s, Trust Fund transfers and fees will account for the lion's share of PCORI's operating funds.[10] While the individual taxpayer and the "covered life" are the ultimate sources of the dollars that go into the PCOR Trust Fund, a revenue stream that comes from a source outside government (even though Congress sets the fee amount) seems to be more reliable than one that must pass through congressional appropriations committees.

To the extent that health insurance and self-insured plans use in their benefit designs the information on comparative effectiveness generated by PCORI, an analogy can be drawn with the user fees that, under federal statute, the medical products industry must pay the Food and Drug Administration to fund a portion of the agency's drug and device review activities.

Governance

Because the 2003 Medicare Modernization Act places the mandate for comparative effectiveness research at AHRQ, governance is that of the agency itself: a director who is appointed by the Secretary of the Department of Health and Human Services who answers to that Secretary through the elements of the Department's organizational chart, and through that Secretary to congressional committees with jurisdiction over the Department. External input to the AHRQ director is provided by a 21-member National Advisory Council for Healthcare Research and Quality (the Council) made up of distinguished experts who are representatives of the public, other federal agencies, or federal officials. As openings on the Council occur, a call for nominations is issued via the Federal Register. Nominations are submitted to the AHRQ director, who then presents the slate of nominees to the Secretary of the Department of Health and Human Services for selection and appointment to the Council. By statute the Council advises the AHRQ director and the Secretary "on matters related to activities of the Agency to improve the quality, safety, efficiency, and effectiveness of health care for all Americans." The Council serves in an advisory rather than steering capacity and its recommendations to the director are non-binding. According to the May 3, 2012 call for nominations, the Council meets "three times a year to provide broad guidance on the direction of and programs undertaken by AHRQ."

In contrast, the Affordable Care Act of 2010 placed PCORI under the direction of a 19-member Board of Governors, which "shall carry out the duties of the Institute." The law specifies the types of members, qualifications, term lengths, and responsibilities. The Board is composed of representatives of key stakeholder groups; the numbers specified for each reflect an attempt to balance opposing interests. The Comptroller General of the United States (head of the Government Accountability Office) appoints the members of the Board and designates its Chairperson and Vice-Chair. The Board "may employ and fix the compensation of an Executive Director and such other personnel as may be necessary to carry out the duties of the Institute."

The key difference between the two governance structures lies in the amount of influence that can be exerted on the organization by stakeholders outside of the federal government versus those inside, who are appointed executive-branch officials and career federal employees.

The Topical Scope of Federally Mandated Comparative Effectiveness Research

Although the comparative effectiveness legislation introduced in 2002 by Representative Tom Allen (D-ME) pertained only to prescription drugs, his

2003 bill and all subsequent draft and enacted comparative effectiveness research legislation encompassed not just prescription drugs but all other medical treatments, items, and services with therapeutic modalities (devices, invasive procedures) as well as the manner in which those treatments, items, and services are organized, managed, and delivered in efforts to prevent, diagnose, treat, and manage illnesses and injuries. This broad topical scope ensures that federal mandates for comparative effectiveness research will pull in not just clinical researchers whose province is how well specific preventive, diagnostic, therapeutic, and restorative interventions work but also health services researchers who focus more broadly on how organizational and financing contexts in the health care system influence the outcomes of care.

We saw in earlier chapters that, by 2009, the issue of whether relative costs should be included as an important dimension of comparative effectiveness had become a matter of contention. Objections to including cost came for obvious reasons from the medical products industry, and also from individuals who believe that an economic cost can never be assigned to human life or health. A suite of measures is available for estimating the relative values of alternative clinical strategies. Some involve measures of cost per year of life saved, and, because (at least to some individuals) not all years of life are equally desirable, some analysts adjust the life-year for its desirability or utility to the individual. The 2009 Affordable Care Act specifically forbids PCORI from developing or employing "a dollars-per-quality adjusted life year (or similar measure that discounts the value of a life because of an individual's disability) as a threshold to establish what type of health care is cost-effective or recommended."

However, there is no language in the Act that specifically precludes PCORI from allowing considerations of health care costs to enter into the comparative effectiveness research it funds or oversees. Clearly, third-party payers and insurers who use the findings of comparative effectiveness research conducted with PCORI funding or otherwise will find it relatively easy to build cost considerations into the structure of their coverage and reimbursement policies.

PCORI's Statutory Research Structures and Processes

Regardless of the forms of specific legislative provisions, grant-making clinical research organizations must engage in five activities: establishing topical research priorities and selecting a means of allocating scarce resources among the priorities; generating the actual research—deciding what research questions will be answered, by what methods, and by which research groups; interpreting the evidence generated by the research, which includes challenges like dealing with ambiguity, handling conflicting results among studies of the same intervention, and understanding the implications of the research findings for the various stakeholders; disseminating the evidence generated by the research in the right form to the right people and at the right time; and finally, assisting in the implementation of the research findings into everyday clinical practice. Without this last activity the anticipated benefit to patients and the health care system from the investment in clinical research cannot be realized. The success of PCORI will be judged in large part on how well it accomplishes these five research activities. For two of these—priority-setting and implementation of research findings—we will examine what the 2009 Affordable Care Act has to say about how PCORI must address them.

Establishing Research Priorities

Priority setting is inescapable in a context of limited resources, and, whether done to establish the family budget or the federal budget of the most powerful nation on Earth, is a value-laden activity. The further it extends into the "applied" end of the spectrum, biomedical research is also a value-laden activity. Clearly, comparative effectiveness research is value laden throughout its entire cycle, from selecting a topic for research all the way to deciding how research results should be interpreted and implemented in routine clinical practice. Box 10.1 shows the approach to priority setting taken by the Institute of Medicine, one of the entities that established priorities for comparative effectiveness research, as we saw in Chapter 9.

Box 10.1 **The Institute of Medicine (IOM) Committee on Comparative Effectiveness Research Prioritization: Priority-Setting Approach**

The first step was to consult stakeholders. The committee made more than 20,000 solicitations and received input from direct mail, a public session, and a Web-based questionnaire. At the public session, 54 individuals representing consumers, patient advocacy groups, provider groups, insurers, manufacturers, and academia spoke directly to the committee and responded to follow-up questions. The Web-based questionnaire requested nominations, was open for 3 weeks, and received 1,758 submissions of more than 2,600 topics.

The committee developed criteria for assessing the importance of these recommended topics and a process for prioritization. Criteria included condition-level criteria (e.g., burden of disease, cost, and variability) and priority topic-level criteria (e.g., appropriateness for comparative effectiveness research, gaps in existing knowledge, and the likelihood that the results would improve health). Through three rounds of voting, the committee narrowed the list to 100 highest-priority research topics.

To evaluate a topic's importance, the committee formulated criteria that would identify not only those diseases and conditions with the greatest aggregate effect on the health of the U.S. population but also less common conditions that severely affect individuals in vulnerable subgroups of the population. Among the high-priority topics were interventions such as disease prevention, systems of care, drug therapies, devices, surgery, and monitoring of disease. The priority list includes 29 research areas, affecting a broad range of age and ethnicity.

Source: From Institute of Medicine Report Brief. Initial national priorities for comparative effectiveness research. June 2009.

Beginning with Section 1013 of the Medicare Modernization Act (MMA) 2003, all federal legislation on comparative effectiveness research has included directives on the priority-setting process as well as the attributes of topics that should be rated as of the highest priority for research. For example, Section 1013 of the MMA instructed the Secretary of of the Department of Health and Human Services to "establish a process to develop priorities" that includes "broad and ongoing consultation with relevant stakeholders" and encompasses health care items and services that impose a high cost on federal health programs and high direct or indirect costs on patients and society. To achieve the federal mandate for comparative effectiveness research contained in the 2003 MMA, AHRQ in 2005 launched its Effective Health Care Program, which conducts systematic reviews of existing research on the effectiveness of health care interventions, develops new evidence, advances research and dissemination methods, and translates research results into user-friendly forms for the various stakeholder groups. Making up the Program are Evidence-Based Practice Centers, which conduct systematic reviews; the Developing Evidence to Inform Decisions about Effectiveness (DEcIDE) Network; the Centers for Education and Research on Therapeutics (CERTs); and the Eisenberg Center for Clinical Decisions and Communications Science. AHRQ has developed a priority-setting process involving stakeholders and expects that stakeholders will be engaged at every step of the research process in its Effective Health Care Program.[11]

The 2010 Affordable Care Act also includes directives on priority setting for comparative effectiveness research. Subsection (d)(1)(A&B) of Section 6301 specifies that the duties of the Patient-Centered Outcomes Research Institute include "identifying research priorities and establishing the research project agenda." The Institute is charged to identify national priorities for research using a framework of multiple attributes, topical as well as pertaining to research design. The topical attributes include (1) disease incidence, prevalence, and burden; (2) the existence of gaps in evidence that are seen to exist by virtue of variations in clinical practice, disparities in the delivery of health services, and disparities in patients' outcomes; (3) the potential that new clinical evidence will improve patients' health and well-being and the quality of medical care; (4) the costs of a particular treatment plan or of the medical condition itself; (5) the needs, outcomes, and preferences of patients; (6) relevance for informed decision making by patients and their clinicians; and (7) consistency with the priorities in the national strategy for quality of care as laid out in Section 399H of the Public Health Service Act.

The statute specifies that once the Institute establishes the national priorities for research, it must establish and update a specific research project agenda for each of the priorities. The types and mix of individual studies comprising the research project agenda under each priority, that is, systematic reviews, observational studies, clinical trials, or studies using other methods approved by PCORI's Methodology Committee[12] must be chosen based on what they will cost compared to the amount of useful information each will produce.

The common denominators of these priority-setting processes are, first, establishing a working definition for comparative effectiveness research; second, engaging stakeholders to identify and then rank order the health care topics and questions that are in greatest need of research; third, deciding the kind of investments and activities that would be needed to achieve the goals of the federal mandate. Investments can be made in research projects of various methodologies, in building capacity for this type of research by training investigators, and in creating infrastructure to facilitate the conduct of comparative effectiveness research, for example, building databases for observational research, establishing research centers, and advancing the science and capacity to translate and disseminate research findings in optimally usable forms.

During the first 18 or so months of its existence, PCORI engaged in a range of priority-setting activities, and in May 2012 the PCORI Board of Governors adopted national priorities for research (Box 10.2) and PCORI's initial research agenda.[13]

Implementing Research Findings

Those who drafted Section 6310 of the Affordable Care Act were determined to ensure broad dissemination of the findings of research performed under the auspices of the Institute, to all audiences with an interest in such findings, and in a range of forms that would assure a wide reach. Implementing research

---

Box 10.2 **PCORI's National Priorities for Research, Adopted by the PCORI Board of Governors in May 2012**

The five priorities were developed in light of PCORI's statutory requirements, its working definition of patient-centered outcomes research, and previous research prioritization efforts. They are as follows:

1. Assessment of prevention, diagnosis, and treatment options—comparing the effectiveness and safety of alternative prevention, diagnosis, and treatment options to see which ones work best for different people with a particular health problem

2. Improving health care systems—comparing health system-level approaches to improving access, supporting patient self-care, innovative use of health information technology, coordinating care for complex conditions, and deploying workforce effectively

3. Communication and dissemination research—comparing approaches to providing comparative effectiveness research information, empowering people to ask for and use the information, and supporting shared decision making between patients and their providers

4. Addressing disparities—identifying potential differences in prevention, diagnosis or treatment effectiveness, or preferred clinical outcomes across patient populations and the health care required to achieve best outcomes in each population

5. Accelerating patient-centered outcomes research and methodological research—improving the nation's capacity to conduct patient-centered outcomes research, by building data infrastructure, improving analytic methods, and training researchers, patients, and other stakeholders to participate in this research

---

Source: Patient-Centered Outcomes Research Institute. National priorities for research and research agenda. May 21, 2012.

---

results, however, is a different endeavor than dissemination. The ultimate intent of comparative effectiveness research is to improve the health and well-being of patients by means of research and evidence synthesis that reveals which course of action, relative to other options, is most likely to lead to the desired outcomes. Health improvements cannot occur if front-line clinicians and system organizers do not adopt new ways of doing things based on valid evidence of superior effectiveness. Implementing research means changing behavior.

Pick up virtually any piece examining the impact of clinical research on clinical practice and you will read authors deploring the fact that it takes "an average of N years (often the figure quoted is 17)" for research findings to change clinical practice. For the sake of argument, let us presume that a certain set of research findings is indeed worth implementing (which is not always true); that is, the research used designs that minimized bias and was otherwise of high methodological quality, that the findings were interpreted fairly and appear to fit in understandably with prior research on the topic, and that the results are applicable to the clinical situation at hand. What are the reasons for the delays in implementation?

A substantial amount of work has been done in the past two decades on implementation. In fact, implementation science is now considered a bona fide field of inquiry.[14] One of the first realizations was that simply putting research results out there—reporting the results in the usual venues—is not enough. Nor is it enough to put the findings in more accessible formats and deliver them in other ways than just journal articles, though those things help. Much work has been done investigating interventions that cause physicians to change their behavior, for example, the promulgation of clinical practice guidelines embodying best evidence, and audit and feedback of compliance. Unfortunately, the behavioral effects of most interventions are modest at best—that is, all except changes in financial incentives, at least in the U.S. health care system.

When the Congressional Budget Office (CBO) favorably scored the comparative effectiveness provisions of the 2007 CHAMP Act, finding that they would reduce health care costs over a 10-year time horizon, the assumption CBO analysts made was that the effect of the law would make itself felt primarily through changes in physicians' practice patterns, especially if better information about the costs and benefits of different treatment options were combined with new incentive structures, and secondarily through changes in coverage rules.[15] In other words, the implementation lever would be payment policy: incentive, coverage, and reimbursement policies that would create change in how health services are delivered.

The Centers for Medicare and Medicaid Services in the U.S. Department of Health and Human Services (HHS) is responsible for administering the federal portions of the Medicare, Medicaid, and Childrens' Health Insurance Programs. Because of their impact on federal entitlement spending, the Secretary of Health and Human Services will be a major user or implementer of the findings of comparative effectiveness research conducted under the auspices of PCORI. Of course, states and private payers will also be avid users of the findings, implementing them through payment policy. Section 6301 of the Affordable Care Act prohibits PCORI from policy making: "Nothing in this section shall be construed to permit the Institute to mandate coverage, reimbursement, or other policies for any public or private payer." And further: "Materials, forums, and media used [by AHRQ's Office of Communication and Knowledge Transfer] used to disseminate the findings, informational tools, and resource databases shall...not be construed as mandates, guidelines, or recommendations for payment, coverage, or treatment."

However, nothing in the statute prohibits the Secretary of Health and Human Services from using the findings of comparative effectiveness research as a factor in configuring payment policies. The statute specifies under what conditions the Secretary *may* use the findings in administering the federal health care entitlement programs. As Box 10.3 shows, these fall roughly under the topics of making coverage decisions in general; payment policies that impact elderly, disabled, or terminally ill individuals; protections of individuals' preference for decisional tradeoffs for length of life versus risk of treatment-related disability; and a prohibition against using quality-adjusted life years or similar discounting metrics as thresholds in determining payment policy. Coverage and reimbursement decisions made in the Medicare program have "spillover" effects into the private health insurance and health plan market.

Box 10.3 **Statutory Conditions under Which the Secretary of Health and Human Services May Use PCORI Research Findings in Administering Federal Health Entitlement Programs**

Section 1182 (1)(a) The Secretary [of Health and Human Services] may only use evidence and findings from research conducted [under the auspices of the Patient-Centered Outcomes Research Institute] to make a determinations regarding coverage under title XVIII [Title XVIII-Health Insurance for the Aged and Disabled, of the Social Security Act] if such use is through an iterative and transparent process which includes public comment and considers the effect on subpopulations.

Section 1182(1) (b) Nothing in section 1181 [the section pertaining to the Patient-Centered Outcomes Research Institute] shall be construed as superseding or modifying the coverage of items or services under title XVIII [of the Social Security Act] that the Secretary determines are reasonable and necessary under Section 1182 (l)(1) [of the Social Security Act: Factors and Evidence Used in Making National Coverage Determinations], or authorizing the Secretary to deny coverage of items or services under such title solely on the basis of comparative clinical effectiveness research.

Section 1182(1) (c) Paragraph (1) The Secretary shall not use evidence or findings from comparative clinical effectiveness research conducted under section 1181 [the section pertaining to the Patient-Centered Outcomes Research Institute] in determining coverage, reimbursement, or incentive programs under title XVIII [of the Social Security Act] in a manner that treats extending the life of an elderly, disabled, or terminally ill individual as of lower value than extending the life of an individual who is younger, nondisabled, or not terminally ill. Paragraph (2): Paragraph (1) shall not be construed as preventing the Secretary from using evidence or findings from such comparative clinical effectiveness research in determining coverage, reimbursement, or incentive programs under title XVIII [of the Social Security Act] based upon a comparison of the difference in the effectiveness of alternative treatments in extending an individual's life due to the individual's age, disability, or terminal illness.

Section 1182(1) (d) Paragraph (1) The Secretary shall not use evidence or findings from comparative clinical effectiveness research conducted under section 1181 [the section pertaining to the Patient-Centered Outcomes Research Institute] in determining coverage, reimbursement, or incentive programs under title XVIII [of the Social Security Act] in a manner that precludes, or with the intent to discourage, an individual from choosing a health care treatment based on how the individual values the tradeoff between extending the length of their life and the risk of disability. Paragraph (2): Paragraph (1) shall not be construed to (i) limit the application of differential copayments under title XVIII [of the Social Security Act] based on factors such as cost or type of service; or (ii) prevent the Secretary from using evidence or findings from such comparative clinical effectiveness research in determining coverage, reimbursement, or incentive programs under such title based upon a comparison of the difference in the effectiveness of alternative health care treatments in extending an individual's life due to that individual's age, disability, or terminal illness. Paragraph (3): Nothing in the provisions of, or amendments made by the Patient Protection and Affordable Care Act, shall be construed to limit comparative clinical effectiveness research or any other research, evaluation, or dissemination of information concerning the likelihood that a health care treatment will result in disability.

Source: Patient Protection and Affordable Care Act (P.L. 111–148), Section 1182.

Balance of Power, Conflicts of Interest, and Transparency in PCORI

No matter how avidly scientists and individuals engaged in science policy, sponsorship, dissemination, and implementation believe that they are objective ("presenting facts uncolored by feelings, opinions, or personal bias; disinterested," according to the *Oxford English Dictionary*), they do not necessarily share the same values. This is particularly true for comparative clinical effectiveness research because it can create winners and losers. The challenge for democratic endeavors is designing and adhering to processes that balance interests.

Section 6301 embeds three strategies to manage the reality of different values among stakeholders in comparative effectiveness research: balancing power by having the key groups represented on the Board of Governors of PCORI, and in specific numbers, and by specifying groups to be represented on advisory panels; defining the term "conflict of interest" and specifying what must be done in case of it; and transactional processes that invite the public to see and participate in PCORI's activities and decisions. Moreover, the statute instructs PCORI as an organization not to compromise itself with real or perceived conflicts of interest: "The Institute, its Board or staff, shall be prohibited from accepting gifts, bequeaths, or donations of services or property. In addition, the Institute shall be prohibited from establishing a corporation or generating revenues from activities other than as provided under this section."

The level of transparency and public input statutorily required of PCORI is extraordinary; unprecedented, in fact. It is far above what is required of the NIH and AHRQ and researchers funded by those agencies, and quantum leaps ahead of what is required of industry and the research it conducts for regulatory purposes. The statute specifies that meetings of PCORI's Board of Governors, unless solely concerned with matters of personnel, shall be advertised at least 7 days in advance and open to the public. Public comment periods of not less than 45 days or more than 60 days are mandated for PCORI's national research priorities, the research agenda, the methodological standards developed and updated by the Methodology Committee, the peer-review process, and after the release of draft findings with respect to systematic reviews of existing research and evidence. Among other things, PCORI must make available and disclose through its official Web site (1) information contained in research findings; (2) the process and methods for the conduct of research, including the identities of the entities and individuals who conducted it, and any conflicts of interest they may have; (3) research protocols, including measures taken and methods of research and analysis; (4) the identities of peer reviewers; (5) comments received during each of the public comment periods; and (6) proceedings of the Institute, in accordance with applicable laws and processes and as the Institute deems appropriate. One may question the intentions behind these extraordinary requirements for transparency and disclosure, which found their way into the 2009 Baucus-Conrad bill because of concessions to the medical product industry. Have these requirements been taken too far? Will they retard the speed of research cycles and paralyze the research process? To what extent do they position parties who do not like the research being undertaken or the results being found to undermine the process at every step of the way?

Conclusions

The Affordable Care Act specifies funding for PCORI only through September 30, 2019, meaning that Congress will have to find some way of continuing PCORI if it is to exist and continue to operate after that. We are likely to hear the same sort of back-and-forth discussions about scope, placement, financing, and so forth, once the time arrives to begin planning for that reauthorization. So many factors can intervene between now (2012) and 2019 that it is impossible to predict the outcomes of whether PCORI's existence will be continued after 2019, and, if so, what form it will take. However, only a limited set of options exist, as we saw in this chapter.

Notes

1. The medical research authorizations included in statutes governing the NIH, AHRQ, VA, and other several other federal agencies, while not mentioning comparative effectiveness research specifically, have always been interpreted as including it.
2. Much has been written on the history of U.S. agencies devoted to health services research. See White KL Health care research: old wine in new bottles. Pharos Summer 1993:12–16. Salive ME, Mayfield JA, Weissman NW. Patient outcomes research teams and the Agency for Health Care Policy and Research. Health Serv Res 1990;25:697–708. Gray BH, Gusmano MK, Collins SR. AHCPR and the changing politics of health services research. Health Aff (Web exclusive) 2003, June W3–285. Deyo RA, Psaty BM, Simon G, Wagner EH, Omenn GS. The messenger under attack—intimidation of researchers by special-interest groups. N Engl J Med 1997;336:1176–80. Institute of Medicine. Health Services Research: Report of a Study. National Academy of Sciences, Washington, DC 1979.
3. Under Section 4111 of P.L. 101–239, the Omnibus Budget Reconciliation Act of 1989, the law which established AHCPR, the agency was also authorized to "conduct and support research with respect to the outcomes of health care services and procedures in order to identify the manner in which diseases, disorders, and other health conditions can most effectively and appropriately be diagnosed and treated." Though the word "comparative" is not used, this statement is a clear description of the focus of comparative effectiveness research.
4. An excellent account of the work of the Office of Technology Assessment and newspaper accounts of its demise are available from //www.princeton.edu/~ota/.
5. Gray BH, Gusmano MK, Collins SR. AHCPR and the changing politics of health services research. Health Aff (Web exclusive) 2003, June W3–285.
6. AHRQ is still imperiled. The July 15, 2012 working bill making FY 2013 appropriations for the Departments of Health and Human Services, and Education, and related agencies included the following provision (line 18, p. 90): "Effective October 19, 2012, the Agency for Healthcare Research and Quality is terminated." The bill was put aside by the passage of a continuing resolution to keep the government running until the new administration is in place after the November 2012 elections, but the issue will come up again. (Accessed November 1, 2012, at http://appropriations.house.gov/uploadedfiles/bills-112hr-sc-ap-fy13-laborhhsed.pdf.)

7. See Hruby JM, Manley DK, Stolz RE, Webb EK, Woodard JB. The evolution of federally funded research & development centers. Public Interest Report, Spring 2011 (Federation of American Scientists).

8. Data from the National Science Foundation (accessed June 4, 2012, at http://www.nsf.gov/statistics/ffrdclist.)

9. The Medicare Hospital Insurance Trust Fund is funded by means of payroll taxes paid by most employees, employers, and people who are self-employed and other sources such as income taxes paid on Social Security benefits, interest earned on the trust fund investments, and Part A premiums from people ineligible for premium-free Part A benefits. The Supplementary Medical Insurance Trust Fund is funded with funds authorized by Congress, premiums from people enrolled in Part B and Part D, and other sources such as interest earned on fund investments.

10. According to information provided to us in June 2012 by PCORI staff, federal projections on revenues that will credit to the PCOR Trust Fund are as follows (in millions): 2012: $150; 2013: $320; 2014: $543; 2015: $613; 2016: $645; 2017: $676; 2018: $710. Projections are revised periodically by the federal government.

11. The Agency for Healthcare Research and Quality. AHRQ Effective Health Care Program Stakeholder Guide. AHRQ Pub. No. 11-EHC069-EF, July 2011.

12. Subsection (d)(2)(A) of Section 6301 of the Affordable Care Act instructs that the Institute "shall carry out the research project agenda . . . using methods including the following: systematic reviews and assessments of existing and future research and evidence including original research conducted subsequent to the date of the enactment of this section (March 2010); primary research, such as randomized clinical trials, molecularly informed trials, and observational studies; and any other methodologies recommended by the methodology committee and adopted by the Board."

13. Patient-Centered Outcomes Research Institute. National priorities for research and research agenda. May 21, 2012. Available from http://www.pcori.org/assets/PCORI-National-Priorities-and-Research-Agenda-2012-05-21-FINAL.pdf.

14. Eccles MP, Armstrong D, Baker R, et al. An implementation research agenda. Implementation Sci 2009;4:18.

15. Information from a letter of September 5, 2007 from CBO Director Peter Orszag to the Honorable Pete Stark, chairman, Subcommittee on Health, House Ways and Means Committee.

PART THREE

INTERESTS

What gave comparative effectiveness research staying power as a policy alternative was the inexorable rise in U.S. health care costs coupled with concerns that about 30% of national health expenditures appear to be going for services that do not improve health or outcomes. In this third and final part of the book, "Interests," we examine the challenges to be overcome if we are to reap the returns on federal investments in comparative effectiveness research.

A good start has been made in research funding and workforce development. The establishment of PCORI in 2010 added a completely new stream of funding for comparative effectiveness research, and as its Trust Fund grows, the Institute will have more dollars every year to invest in comparative effectiveness research. Projections are that annual deposits to the PCOR Trust Fund will grow from $150 million in 2012 to $710 million by 2018.[1] In 2012, the total U.S. public outlay for comparative effectiveness research was $578 million. While this is admittedly a paltry investment in learning what works best for a nation whose national health expenditures for 2012 are projected to be nearly $2.84 trillion, the PCOR Trust Fund contributed $46 million of the $578 million, funds that would not have existed otherwise. The other public sponsors of comparative effectiveness research are the National Institutes of Health (NIH) and Agency for Healthcare Research and Quality (AHRQ). Of the $578 million that made up the 2012 outlays, the NIH contributed the lion's share, $511 million (which was <5% of the NIH's agency's total 2012 expenditure on clinical research),[2] and AHRQ contributed $21 million (just over 5% of AHRQ's total 2012 budget of $405.1 million). Provided that the NIH does not realign its funding priorities away from the support of comparative effectiveness research (AHRQ has

already signaled its intent to do so),[3] by the mid-2010s public sponsorship of such research will approach a billion dollars a year. The situation
is unclear after 2019, when the Patient-Centered Outcomes Research
Institute must be reauthorized or phase out its operations.

Not only is research funding growing; the research workforce for
comparative effectiveness research is being enhanced as well. The first
major infusion of new federal funds for workforce development in comparative effectiveness occurred with the passage of the Recovery Act in
February 2009. With these funds, AHRQ awarded individual (K12) and
institutional (T32) training grants, programs that will have produced
20–25 individuals with advanced credentials in comparative effectiveness research methods. Although the Recovery Act was a one-time infusion of funds, PCORI's investments in training are long term. By law, a
certain amount of funds must be transferred each year out of the PCOR
Trust Fund and provided to AHRQ for the purpose of training researchers to conduct comparative effectiveness research. Using funding allocated to it through that route, in 2012 AHRQ established two new career
development programs and an infrastructure program.[4] In addition, in
AHRQ's 2012 quinquennial national re-competition for institutional
training grants, comparative effectiveness research was one area of
interest. These AHRQ initiatives add to other federally funded options
for training in comparative effectiveness research.[5] As many as 100 individuals each year are receiving training in federally funded and other
comparative effectiveness research programs.

But as necessary as more research dollars and more researchers are,
they will not be sufficient to achieve the nation's goal of getting better
value for the health care dollars it spends. To achieve health care of better
value, the knowledge generated from comparative effectiveness research
must be put into practice. How can we bring medical practice into alignment with what scientific evidence there is of comparative effectiveness,
and what is the best course of action under conditions of clinical uncertainty, when evidence about what works best is unavailable? A link must
be forged between evidence—its use or its generation—and the practice
of health care, and that link is payment policy.

Notes

1. According to information provided to us in June 2012 by PCORI staff, federal projections on revenues that will credit to the PCOR Trust Fund are as follows (in millions):
   2012: $150; 2013: $320; 2014: $543; 2015: $613; 2016: $645; 2017: $676; 2018: $710.

2. As the NIH defines it, clinical research is research with human subjects, including patient-oriented research, that is, studies involving direct interaction between investigators and human subjects for the study of mechanisms of human disease, therapeutic interventions, clinical trials, and development of new technologies, epidemiological and behavioral studies, and outcomes research and health services research. Comparative effectiveness research is the segment of clinical research devoted to comparing one clinical strategy with alternatives in order to determine which one is best for patients. The NIH Research Portfolio Online Reporting Tools indicate that, in 2012, the NIH allocated about $10.5 billion to clinical research, or roughly a third of its $30.9 billion budget. The remainder goes to support basic research.

3. In its FY2012 budget estimate justification, AHRQ stated, "The FY 2012 Request level reflects a deliberate budget policy decision to fund only activities outside the scope of the funding anticipated from the Patient-Centered Outcomes Research Trust Fund."

4. RFA-HS-12–007: Patient-Centered Outcomes Research Pathway to Independence Award (K99/R00), PAR-12–115: Mentored Career Enhancement Award in Patient-Centered Outcomes Research for Mid-Career and Senior Investigators (K18), and PAR-12–114: Infrastructure Development Program in Patient-Centered Outcomes Research (R24).

5 Chilingerian J, Flieger SP, Hart A. Establishing an AHRQ learning collaborative (final report contract no. 290–10–000190), 2012. See Appendix 2 for training opportunities.

11

Aligning Clinical Practice with Best Evidence of Comparative Effectiveness

Payment Policy for Evidence-Based Medical Care

In 2003, in an article titled "The quality of health care delivered to adults in the United States" published in the *New England Journal of Medicine*, Elizabeth McGlynn and colleagues reported the extent to which adults in 12 metropolitan areas were provided medical care in line with the best medical evidence for preventive, acute, and chronic conditions representing the leading causes of illness, death, and use of health services. Their findings: "Participants received 54.9 percent of recommended care. We found little difference among the proportion of recommended preventive care provided (54.9%), the proportion of recommended acute care provided (53.5%), and the proportion of recommended care provided for chronic conditions (56.1%)." Further analyses showed only small differences in receipt of evidence-based care among sociodemographic subgroups defined by gender, age, and household income. In other words, regardless of their age, gender, and social status, Americans receive care in line with best medical evidence only about half the time.

The findings of the McGlynn study found their way into the halls of Congress, where they figured prominently in debates culminating in the 2010 Affordable Care Act. One way the findings were used was to ward off objections that federally mandated comparative effectiveness research would somehow get between the doctor and the patient. As one informant told us, "I have to bite my tongue every time I hear a politician say, 'We can't let anything get between the patient and the physician.' Excuse me? The same physician who is getting it right about 53% of the time? That is only slightly better than a crapshoot."

Medical Care in America: Following the Evidence or Following the Money?

Numerous examples exist of the under-use of health services of demonstrated benefit. One that affects large numbers of Americans is the under-treatment of hypertension. High blood pressure affects two-thirds of Americans over age 65 and three-fourths of those over 75. Uncontrolled high blood pressure is a major etiologic factor of the leading causes of morbidity and mortality in developed countries. Yet over half of Americans who have been told they have hypertension have uncontrolled blood pressure; their blood pressure exceeds best-evidence targets (systolic pressure >140 mm Hg and/or diastolic pressure >90 mm Hg).[1]

This is not for a dearth of effective therapies. Over 50 drugs in numerous drug classes have been approved by the Food and Drug Administration (FDA) for the treatment of high blood pressure. They vary in price more than they vary in effectiveness and side effects. The landmark Antihypertensive and Lipid-Lowering Treatment to Prevent Heart Attack Trial (ALLHAT), which we mentioned in Chapter 6, showed that thiazide-based antihypertensive regimens are more cost-effective than other regimens. This finding has been incorporated into current U.S. national hypertension treatment guidelines. But despite the high-quality evidence generated by this trial, national treatment guidelines incorporating its findings, extensive publicity, and a post-ALLHAT dissemination project based on academic detailing, implementation of the ALLHAT findings into routine clinical practice has been disappointing. By 2007, 5 years after the trial results were reported, the percentage of people receiving thiazides for hypertension had increased by only 7%. The overall prevalence of use of thiazide-based antihypertensive regimens has never exceeded 40%. This means that fewer than four of ten people with high blood pressure are using a thiazide-based regimen.[2] Thiazide diuretics are one of the oldest and cheapest classes of antihypertensive drugs. For example, in the Veterans Affairs medical care system, the drug acquisition price to treat one individual for 30 days with hydrochlorothiazide 12.5 to 50 mg once daily is $0.13 to $0.35.[3] Thirteen to thirty-five cents for a month's supply of the drug.

Opponents of federally mandated comparative effectiveness research showcased ALLHAT as an example of why such a mandate was not worth undertaking. If doctors fail to treat their patients in compliance with findings from medical research, even when the research comes from large, exemplary comparative effectiveness trials like the ALLHAT, what good will a federal mandate for more research do? Putting the research out there, and even incorporating the findings into national treatment guidelines, does not change practice.

The McGlynn study and the hypertension stories are examples of the under-use of treatments of established effectiveness compared with alternatives. Let's now look at an example of the other side of the coin: over-use.

Heart disease is the leading cause of death in the United States. Coronary heart disease—disease due to atherosclerotic blockages in the coronary arteries supplying the heart muscle—is responsible for one of five deaths in the United States. Implanting stents into coronary arteries is one of the most commonly performed invasive therapeutic procedures in the United States. In 2007 (the most recent data available), percutaneous transluminal angioplasty (PCTA), usually performed in conjunction with coronary stent implantation, was the second most commonly performed operating room procedure in the United States, accounting for 722,000 procedures.[4] (Cesarean delivery was the most common.) Of all operating room procedures, PCTA was the most costly. On average, it cost a hospital $16,200 to "produce" a PCTA in 2007.[5] The manufacturer's or distributor's list price for a drug-eluting coronary stent is about $3,000; for a bare metal stent, about $1,000. Most patients receive more than one stent during their interventional procedure. The Medicare program pays hospitals for a PCTA stay from about $10,000 to nearly $18,000 (2011 rates). PCTAs are also performed at outpatient surgical centers, which Medicare reimburses at lower rates, $5,700 to $7,300 (2011 rates). In addition, Medicare reimburses the physician who implants the intracoronary stents $873 for the first stent and $243 for each additional one in the same patient (2011 average rates).

Propping open the "culprit" coronary artery in people who are suffering an acute myocardial infarction, in conjunction with other measures, is of proven effectiveness in relieving ischemia, preserving viable heart muscle, and improving long-term outcomes. But the benefits of placing stents in the coronary arteries of people who have *stable* coronary artery disease, that is, partial blockages in coronary arteries but no acute threat to the part of the heart muscle nourished by that artery, have not been demonstrated. In fact, numerous randomized trials comparing coronary stenting in this population with medication therapy alone have shown that stents are no better than medications in lengthening life, preventing heart attacks, reducing the frequency of effort-induced chest pain, and avoiding further interventional procedures on the heart. Yet of the 722,000 procedures performed in 2007, about one-third were elective, meaning they were probably performed in a patient with stable coronary artery disease rather than an acute coronary syndrome. Clinical practice seems immune to the results of the randomized controlled trials and systematic reviews of multiple trials showing that stents, though much more costly—and much more lucrative for the physicians inserting them—are no better than medications. Many other examples exist of the over-use of health services.

The bottom line with under-use as well as over-use is that large proportions of patients are not receiving treatment that is in accordance with evidence showing what works best for their conditions. Our outlays for health insurance premiums, deductibles, and copayments are buying us suboptimal medical care. The situation is allowed to continue because of payment policies that reimburse physicians and hospitals for the services they deliver on the basis of volume rather than appropriateness, evidence of effectiveness, or value. But numerous natural experiments have shown that policies on how individual providers (e.g., doctors) and institutional providers (e.g., hospitals) are paid for the services they render are major influences on how they provide medical services. We give a few examples to show that providers act in predictable ways when financial incentives are changed.

Because prostate cancer cells are fueled by male hormones, androgen deprivation therapy is a cornerstone of palliative treatment in men with advanced prostate cancer. Estrogens were long used for this purpose, as was surgical removal of the testicles, but in the 1980s drugs were developed that specifically interfere with the production of testosterone in men. The FDA approved leuprolide acetate, a gonadotropin-releasing hormone agonist, for this indication in 1985. By the 1990s, those drugs, which are administered by injection in doctors' offices, had become the predominant method of androgen deprivation. The side effects of these drugs are numerous. Long-term use increases the risk of fractures, diabetes, heart attack, and stroke.

Research has demonstrated that androgen deprivation therapy confers a survival benefit only for certain subgroups of men with prostate cancer. Yet the drugs are used in significant numbers of men who will have no benefit from them. In a study reported in 2010[6] in the *New England Journal of Medicine*, a population of nearly 55,000 American men newly diagnosed with prostate cancer in 2003 to 2005 was divided into three groups according to whether their clinical characteristics indicated that the androgen deprivation therapy they were receiving, based on best scientific evidence, was appropriate, inappropriate, or discretionary (of uncertain benefit). In 2003, 38% of men, or nearly four of every ten, were receiving this therapy for inappropriate reasons and had no likelihood of benefit from it.[7] But by 2005, the proportion of men receiving this therapy inappropriately had fallen to 26%, just over one in four men. The proportion of men receiving androgen deprivation therapy *appropriately* did not fall.

What accounted for the decline in inappropriate use? A 2004 change in Medicare rates that halved the reimbursements to urologists for providing these injections.

Just like doctors, hospitals respond predictably to financial incentives. In the early 1980s, Medicare changed the way it reimbursed hospitals for stays of Medicare beneficiaries (Part A Medicare). It shifted from a per diem and per service basis to a stay-based payment calculated prospectively according to the diagnosis-related groups (DRGs) in which patients fall. As a form of "bundled payment," the inpatient prospective payment system (PPS) incentivizes hospitals to produce hospital stays that cost them less than what Medicare will pay for them. When Medicare phased in the inpatient PPS, hospitals responded predictably. As hoped, lengths of stay dropped. The unintended but not unexpected effect was that the number of stays per 1,000 beneficiaries increased. Now Medicare is exploring ways to use its payment policies to dis-incentivize readmissions.

The Centers for Medicare and Medicaid Services (CMS) has extended this prospective payment system approach to include not only short-term acute care hospitals (the inpatient PPS) but also other programs such as inpatient rehabilitation and home health care. Under the inpatient PPS, the hospital bears financial risk for each patient who stays longer than the pre-established expected length of stay for that DRG. By shifting some financial risk onto the provider, bundled payments incentivize them to deliver care in more efficient ways, which may or may not also include ways that are more evidence-based.

The Leveraging Power of Third-Party Payers

The American health care system is built upon a foundation of public and private health insurance, and the overwhelming majority of Americans use the medical care system within a context of the payment policies of third-party payers. Almost all Americans over age 65 are covered by Medicare, a publicly funded health insurance program. In 2010, 81.5% of Americans under age 65 had health insurance.[8] It is estimated that this will increase to 91% by 2016, when the Affordable Care Act and its individual mandate are fully implemented.[9] The coverage policies of health insurers exert enormous power on how patients use health services and the medical care system.

However, while patients initiate contact with doctors, it is doctors who drive the demand for medical care, as well as the volume and mix of health care items and services that are used in the health care system. A doctor's order is required for all health care items and services except for over-the-counter remedies, supplies, and equipment and complementary and alternative therapies. A doctor's order is required for a patient to be admitted to a hospital. Hospitals depend for their existence on doctors who will admit patients to their facility and refer patients for tests and treatments to be delivered at hospital-based outpatient clinics and surgery centers. The use of physician services and the health care items and services physicians prescribe account for over 61% of U.S. national health expenditures—over 61 cents of every dollar spent on health care.[10]

In turn, third-party payers can exert considerable leverage over how doctors and hospitals provide medical care. Through their reimbursement policies, federal and state governments and private health insurers pay for large proportions of health care items and services. Medicare, Medicaid, and other government funds constitute 27% of the revenue of physicians' offices and 40% of hospitals' revenue.[11] Private health insurers pay over 51% of physicians' revenue and 43% of hospital revenue.

Since the coverage and reimbursement policies of third-party payers exert so much influence on the types of health services that are used and their utilization levels, it is worthwhile examining how insurers decide what to include in their benefits packages.

How Do Health Insurers Decide What to Include in Benefits Packages?

According to the 2010 Affordable Care Act, essential health care benefits fall into 10 categories: (1) ambulatory patient services; (2) emergency services; (3) hospitalization; (4) maternity and newborn care; (5) mental health and substance use disorder services; (6) prescription drugs; (7) rehabilitative and habilitative services; (8) laboratory services; (9) preventive care, wellness services, and chronic disease management services; and (10) pediatric services. Each of these 10 categories covers an enormous range of possible clinical elements, a range that increases every year. How do insurance companies decide what health services they will cover in each category of benefits? The under-use and over-use examples given earlier in this chapter suggest that scientific evidence of effectiveness and comparative effectiveness seems to play a minor role in the determination of what benefits will be covered. However, the situation is changing. Evidence is playing an ever-increasing role, and federally mandated comparative effectiveness research will accelerate the trend.

At the watershed moment in American health care when the Medicare program was established by the Social Security Amendments of 1965, the randomized control trial as a way of evaluating therapeutic interventions was not yet two decades old. Very little of the prevailing medical practice at that time was based on what we would call today the "gold-standard evidence" of the randomized clinical trial. Most was based on clinical observations and pronouncements of medical luminaries. The legislation authorizing Medicare stipulated that payment could be made only for items and services that are "reasonable and necessary" for the diagnosis or treatment of illness or injury.

We saw in Part I how the accepted standards of care have changed over the past 50 years from authority to evidence. For example, Aetna, one of the nation's leading health insurers, says on its Web site that its coverage decisions are developed from "evidence from objective, credible sources: scientific literature, technology reviews, consensus statements, expert opinions, guidelines from national professional health care organizations, and public health agencies." Calls for insurance benefit design to be more "evidence based" began to appear in the literature as the 2000s began[12] but by that time, the industry had been investing in health technology assessments as a way of informing coverage decisions for over a decade. A case in point is the BlueCross BlueShield Technology Assessment Center, established in 1985.

While Medicare continues to try and define care that is "reasonable and necessary,"[13] it, like private insurers, uses scientific evidence in its coverage decisions to some extent. In the Medicare program, coverage for items and services is based on decisions made at the national level (national coverage determinations, NCD), or in the absence of an NCD, decisions made by a fiscal intermediary or carrier (local coverage determinations, LCD). These NCDs and LCDs are based on evidence that a particular item or service is reasonable and necessary for diagnosis or treatment of an illness or injury and falls within the scope of a Medicare benefit category. When making an NCD, the Centers for Medicare and Medicaid Services (CMS) conducts its own evaluation of the evidence supplemented in some cases by outside technology assessment and/or consultation with the Medicare Evidence Development and Coverage Advisory Committee (MEDCAC).[14] CMS's assessment of the evidence base for an item or service revolves around three points: first, the quality of the individual studies that make up the evidence base; second, the relevance of the findings from those studies to the Medicare population; and third, the conclusions that can be drawn from the evidence base regarding the direction and magnitude of the risks and benefits of the item or service. CMS does not use cost information in its determinations of coverage.

The Medicare national coverage process[15] may result in one of several decisions: (a) non-coverage: coverage not allowed for Medicare beneficiaries; (b) coverage without special conditions for all Medicare beneficiaries; (c) coverage with special conditions (coverage only for certain beneficiaries, or when provided by physicians or facilities meeting certain criteria, or when specific data are provided in addition to routine claims data); or (d) coverage only with study participation (in a randomized trial or an observational study that meets CMS expectations for safety, patient protections, monitoring, and clinical expertise). The intentions behind the last category are to generate data on which CMS can judge the appropriateness of use of the item or service in the Medicare population, consider the need for future changes in coverage, and improve the medical evidence base for the item or service.

Each of Medicare's national coverage determinations must be supported by a publicly available record of the decision-making process, the evidence that was considered and how it was assessed, and the rationale for the final determination. The record also includes public comments. For example, the Decision Summary posted by CMS in June 2012 for its coverage determination ("not reasonable and necessary for the treatment of chronic low back pain; coverage only with study participation") on transcutaneous electrical nerve stimulation for chronic low back pain (CAG-00429N) is 67 pages long, not counting appendices.

Coverage determinations made in the Medicare program exert massive influence. This is in part because of the large size of the Medicare beneficiary population (nearly 49.5 million in 2012) and the fact that this population tends to use a higher volume of health services than other segments. CMS coverage decisions extend far beyond the Medicare program. Given the thoroughness and quality of the evidence reviews conducted as part of Medicare coverage determinations, most private insurers use the Medicare determinations as the basis for their own policies instead of investing their own resources in duplicative evidence reviews and assessments. Where Medicare goes, the private health insurance industry follows.

Though we have more gold-standard evidence now, the pace of medical innovation continues to outstrip our ability to evaluate systematically benefits and harms before widespread adoption. Coverage with evidence development strategies may ameliorate that, as we will see in the next chapter. But uncertainty in medicine is a chronic, incurable condition: what works best today may not be the strategy or health service that works best tomorrow. As additional evidence emerges, items and services that are currently covered may no longer be the best way to approach a preventive, diagnostic, or therapeutic issue. As we will see later, when a public or private health insurer moves to restrict or discontinue coverage for an item or service it previously covered, these "take-backs" are often met with an extreme backlash from the public as well as from practitioners and medical product makers.

State-Mandated Health Insurance Benefits

During the pre-passage debates about the Affordable Care Act in general and its comparative effectiveness provisions in particular, opponents often raised the claim that health reform would "insert the government between you and your doctor." In fact, the government has been there for a long time. For decades state governments have mandated that health plans cover certain items and services. A 2010 analysis identified 2,156 such benefit mandates on the books of the 50 states and the District of Columbia.[16] The intent behind some of these is to ensure that citizens have access to services that private insurers may be unwilling to cover, for example, substance abuse treatment. The intent behind others seems to be to protect the incomes of certain types of providers. Without such mandates, citizens who choose to use these services may pay for them out of pocket. But coverage mandates shift out-of-pocket costs previously paid by individuals onto the pool of insured persons, leading to higher insurance premiums. There is also evidence that removal or lessening of out-of-pocket costs increases the use of services, which drives up costs.

It is fair to say that the decision-making process underlying many state-mandated health insurance benefits is not based on a thorough, systematic, and open assessment of the quality of the scientific evidence for the item or service, the relevance of the existing body of evidence for the state's population, and the magnitude and direction of the evidence for its benefits and harms. Many believe that state-mandated health insurance benefits drive up the cost of health care and health insurance without improving population health. Others see them as a way of ensuring equitable access. Others take issue only with certain mandates. For example, many states mandate that private insurers include in vitro fertilization in their benefits packages; opponents believe this is an expense the users of the service should bear. Trends toward making coverage decisions and benefits packages more evidence based are not likely to affect the number and type of state-mandated benefits or the decision-making process behind them. States run on politics, not on evidence, and respond to advocacy efforts by powerful constituents, including professional organizations, industry, and patient groups.

Health Insurance Industry Trends and the Influence of Comparative Effectiveness Research

The health insurance industry is intensifying its efforts to align payment policies with the delivery of evidence-based care. Federal mandates for comparative effectiveness research in the Affordable Care Act will provide more scientific evidence on which the insurance industry can base its benefit and purchasing designs. The fact that the 2010 Affordable Care Act requires public and private health insurers to fund the PCOR Trust Fund by means of fees per "covered life" will undoubtedly give those insurers a sense of entitlement in linking their payment policies to evidence of comparative effectiveness.

"Value-based" coverage and reimbursement strategies that are being developed by the health insurance industry began about 15 years ago. The intent behind them is to encourage the insured and their providers to move to the use of more effective services over less effective ones. They grew out of the tiered prescription drug benefits that came onto the scene in the mid-1990s. In the original tiered plans, the amount that enrollees paid in the way of co-payments was based on drug acquisition costs (the lowest co-pays for a generic drug in the class, the middle for a preferred brand name drug, and the highest for a non-preferred brand name drug), but people quickly realized the potential for linking the tiered co-payments to therapeutic value, not just drug acquisition costs. Assessments of therapeutic value are based on evaluations of scientific evidence of benefits, harms, and effectiveness relative to alternatives.

Value-Based Benefit Designs

Value-based benefit design (or value-based insurance design) is the use of incentives by insurance plans to encourage enrollees to adopt appropriate use of high-value services, adopt healthy lifestyles, and/or use high-performing providers who adhere to evidence-based treatment guidelines.[17] Incentives can include rewards, reduced premium share, adjustments to deductible and co-pay levels, and contributions to fund-based plans such as a health savings account. In 2005, a government official concluded that "consumer incentive strategies are in their infancy."[18] However, they have now been around long enough to offer some empirical evidence of how patients respond to changing levels of co-payments and of estimated returns on insurance company investments. For example, in a randomized trial conducted with Aetna beneficiaries recently discharged from the hospital after treatment for an acute myocardial infarction,[19] compliance with life-saving medications was higher in the group for whom the usual out-of-pocket medication co-payment was eliminated. This lowered the rates of first major vascular events and did not increase overall health care costs. Another study, a secondary analysis of Medicare managed-care utilization databases, found inverse associations between the amount of cost-sharing for screening mammography and the likelihood women would have the test.[20]

The health insurance industry is applying pressure to the medical products industry for better evidence of comparative effectiveness of their products. As a condition of market access to their beneficiaries, for example, in the way of having their pharmaceutical products listed on plan formularies, payers have begun to demand from drug and device makers evidence of relative value about specific products. In a trend that can be dated to the comparative effectiveness research provisions in the 2003 Medicare Modernization Act, medical product makers are responding in several ways to the increasing demand that their products perform better than or at least as well as those from competitors.[21] More and more companies are having health economics teams work with clinical development teams in the pre-approval phases of product testing—as early as Phase 2—so that study endpoints can be chosen that will provide information not only on efficacy but on patient-relevant outcomes and cost-effectiveness. Companies are using such data aggressively to pull products out of development if the results of early trials indicate their efficacy or price profiles relative to other products will not assure them a strong market post-approval. In addition, many companies are interacting with payers well before a product reaches the approval phase, to understand payers' concerns about price and their likely formulary, coverage, and reimbursement policies for the product. Companies are beginning to understand that an expensive product for which a payer institutes large co-payments or coinsurance has little chance of succeeding in the market, especially when that expensive product works no better than a cheaper product already on the market.[22]

The health insurance industry is likely to increasingly use evidence of the value of an item or service in its benefits and coverage policies. We can envision some of those changes. A health insurer might develop a new insurance "product"—a comprehensive evidence-based managed care plan in which the categories of covered benefits include only those items and services with credible, high-quality evidence that they lead to substantial benefits and few harms; which covers promising but not-yet validated services under an "only-in-research" arrangement; and in which deductibles and co-pays are tiered based on the strength of evidence that the finite set of diagnostic and therapeutic alternatives for a given condition can be ordered according to their benefit:harm (or benefit:cost) ratios. The benefits and coverage policies in such a plan could be complemented by reimbursement policies such as selective contracting that restrict the providers in the plan to only those whose performance data demonstrate adherence to evidence-based care of high quality. An insurer might market an evidence-based plan by making the annual premiums low relative to other plan types, or, in the case of employer-sponsored insurance, reducing the share of the premium paid by the employee. Based on empirical research, there are reasons to believe that enrollees in such a plan would have health outcomes as good as, if not better than, people enrolled in plans less based on best evidence.

In lieu of offering such a comprehensive plan, insurers might build certain components of it into their existing insurance products. The one most quickly in reach is tiered cost-sharing for covered items and services, with graduated payments and coinsurance based on evidence of benefit, risk, and/or costs.

Value-Based Purchasing

In the preceding section we discussed value-based benefits design, which is a contractual agreement about coverage between an insurer and the insured person. Here we discuss value-based purchasing, an arrangement that governs how an insurer will pay an individual or institutional provider. (Viewing these as bilateral arrangements is over-simplifying because all three parties interact in context.) Value-based purchasing agreements, because they may be configured to directly or indirectly induce providers to adhere to evidence-based care practices, rest on a foundation of clinical comparative effectiveness research.

Value-based purchasing agreements try to align provider payment with the "value" of the care they provide. Currently the value of care is denoted by its quality and the efficiency with which it is delivered. Through its many demonstration projects involving payment reform over the last decades, Medicare has been the leader in testing the effects of various value-based purchasing strategies. Such strategies have three characteristics in common: the provider bears some financial risk for the valued outcomes; they involve Medicare stepping back and allowing providers to decide how best to achieve the valued outcomes; and they require a reorganization of how care is delivered.

Some of the strategies that have been or are being explored include pay-for-reporting, pay-for-performance, bundled payments, accountable care

organizations, and medical homes.[23] Regarding pay-for-reporting, the 2003
Medicare Modernization Act mandated that, beginning in 2004, hospitals participating in Medicare Part A report data on certain clinical performance measures or take a reduction in their Annual Payment Update for inpatient hospital
services. Since 2005 hospital-level performance data have been posted on the
public Web site Hospital Compare. This Medicare hospital value-based purchasing plan, now called the Hospital Quality Alliance, is based on the assumption that the public reporting of data provides an incentive for hospitals to
improve. A similar program was put into place for physician reporting in 2007,
the Physician Quality Reporting Initiative. Physicians who report their data on
clinical quality measures receive a financial incentive of 1.5% to 2.0% of their
allowed Medicare charges for covered professional services. Because paying for
reporting is a weaker incentive for real change than paying for performance,
CMS has been testing several methods of providing bonuses to hospitals and
physicians for improving the quality of care in specific areas. Note that while
CMS targets the areas of care that need improvement, it leaves the "how" up
to doctors and hospitals. Presumably, improving care means bringing it into
line with best-evidence based practices, for which comparative effectiveness
research is the keystone.

Other initiatives focus on improving efficiency through better coordination between Part A (hospital) and Part B (professional fees) services. In the
1990s CMS supported a demonstration project that involved negotiated, single
payments for coronary artery surgery in which fees for hospitals and surgeons
were bundled together. Hospitals and surgeons had to figure out how to divide
the fees and how to configure the clinical care so that the quality of care could
be improved and revenue sustained. Several other bundled payment demonstrations are under way as part of the Medicare Acute Care Episode projects.
Large variations exist between providers in the cost of some inpatient surgeries, indicating that bundled payment programs may curb the utilization of services that do not improve patients' outcomes.[24]

Another value-based purchasing model being tested by CMS is the accountable care organization (ACO). In this model, CMS contracts with an organized group of physicians, hospitals, and other providers that is responsible
(accountable) for both the cost and the quality of care for a defined population
of a certain size. They are intended to create incentives to care for patients effi-
ciently across care settings. ACOs may take many forms. They may be made up
of multiple physician group practices, individual practice networks, partnerships between hospitals and providers, and so on. The payment structure also
varies, though most are built upon fee-for-service models. Though promising in
theory, accountable care organizations require massive investments in infrastructure, organization building, workforce, and workflow redesign, and may
take many years to become smoothly functioning.[25]

Private payers (employer-purchasers and health insurance companies) are very interested in these forms of value-based purchasing, but CMS has been much more successful than they have been in getting the programs and demonstrations up and running.

A relatively simple example of value-based purchasing that is increasingly common for procedures is the "center of excellence" model. Under this arrangement, the insurer covers the service only if the beneficiary has it at a center that has met the payer's criteria for "excellence." This arrangement enables the payer to ensure that services are being provided according to at least minimum standards of quality and expertise. In turn, the provider sees increases in patient volume and revenue. Certain national coverage decisions issued by CMS require that only providers working in facilities certified as Medicare approved for the procedure in question can be reimbursed for performing it on Medicare beneficiaries. In mid-2012, these procedures were carotid artery stenting, ventricular assist device destination therapy, bariatric surgery, certain oncologic positron emission tomography scans in Medicare-specified studies, and lung volume reduction surgery. Private insurers are also using center of excellence strategies to incentivize providers to improve quality and bring care into line with best evidence. An example is the Blue Distinction® Centers program of the BlueCross BlueShield Association.

A business case for bringing care into alignment with best evidence can be created not only with direct financial incentives as described earlier, but rather with reputational ones as well. We saw earlier that hospitals responded predictably to the financial incentives inherent in the Prospective Payment System that was phased in during the early 1980s. Hospitals also respond to rankings and report cards. For more than two decades, the *U.S. News and World Report* magazine has influenced how American hospitals behave by means of its annual ranking of "Best Hospitals." The focus is on hospitals that care for patients with complex conditions. The rankings are based on data for volume, mortality outcomes, reputation, and other factors. A high ranking helps to attract doctors, patients, and health plan contracts, especially in hospital-dense urban markets. Hospitals work hard to merit a "Best Hospital" ranking.

One of the rating factors for hospitals is called "technology." In the 2011–2012 rankings, hospitals were evaluated on how many of 15 "key technologies or advanced services" they offered.[26] Some are diagnostic technologies, others therapeutic, but all are costly. The scientific evidence of effectiveness and comparative effectiveness underlying several of them is iffy at best. One of them is robotic surgery, a technology that *U.S. News and World Report* claims is relevant in cancer, heart surgery, gynecology, nephrology, and urology. In essence, *U.S. News and World Report* is incentivizing hospitals, and doing so very effectively, to invest in high-cost health technologies of uncertain value as long as health insurers will cover the costs. And once a hospital invests in a piece of high-cost equipment, there are revenue incentives to ensure that doctors on staff use it, regardless of its value compared with other clinical approaches.

The point of this story is to show that hospitals respond predictably to incentives. They see the business case in being ranked as a "Best Hospital." If measures of adherence to evidence-based medicine were built into the "Best Hospitals" rankings, hospitals would move in that direction. And comparative effectiveness research is the foundation for evidence-based medicine.

Some Cautionary Tales: What Happens When Payment Policies Are Changed to Incorporate New Evidence of Comparative Effectiveness

Rational stakeholders respond to a policy or situation in a way they think will advance their own interests. Patients have a legitimate interest in having access to affordable medical care that is of high quality, with quality being defined by the Institute of Medicine as "the degree to which health services increase the likelihood of desired health outcomes and are consistent with current professional knowledge." Third-party payers for health care have legitimate interests in their financial solvency, in making a profit in the case of commercial entities, in satisfying expectations of investors (private or taxpayers) and government regulators, and in competing successfully in the marketplace by offering desirable, valuable, and affordable products.

If it were this simple, we could just conclude that more and better comparative effectiveness research is something that will unequivocally advance the interests of patients as well as third-party payers. After all, this kind of research shows which course of clinical action leads to the best value for money. But the situation is not so simple. Individuals and firms view their interests and respond to perceived threats through a lens colored by prevailing social, economic, and political conditions and the national "mood."

Most evidence-based recommendations and clinical practice guidelines pass quietly into being without causing much fuss in the public. Outside the ivory tower of academia, few people care about evidence in medicine until it is linked to payment policy. Like many politicians, many consumers and doctors do not care about evidence until it is linked to coverage decisions, which impact patients' out-of-pocket costs, providers' income, and medical product company revenue.

The two examples we give in the next section provide some insight into how the American public might respond to medical care payment policies that are increasingly and explicitly linked to scientific evidence of comparative effectiveness, evidence that, as it accumulates, requires changes in coverage and reimbursement policies.

The Mammography and PSA Wars

Two high-profile controversies have occurred recently that centered on changes in recommendations for preventive health measures. These recommendations were drawn up by experts and were based on systematic and comprehensive analyses of evidence generated by clinical research. Though the words "comparative effectiveness" are not used, the recommendations make it clear that, based on current best evidence, one course of action appears to be superior to others for certain subsets of people. Fears that insurers would no longer cover these services figured heavily in how the public responded.

The U.S. Preventive Services Task Force (USPSTF), created in 1984 under the Reagan Administration and authorized under Title IX of the Public Health Service Act, is an independent group of experts in preventive and evidence-based medicine that works to improve the health of Americans by making recommendations about clinical services that detect disease early (screening) or prevent it. Panel members, who are mostly practicing clinicians, are appointed by the Secretary of Health and Human Services but are not government employees. The panel conducts its analyses of the evidence for the value of a service according to public, state-of-the-science procedures, and publishes on its Web site the results of its reviews and the rationales for its recommendations, which are graded based on the strength of the underlying scientific evidence. The Task Force considers benefits and harms of a service; it does not consider costs.

In November 2009, during the most intense debates about health care reform in general and comparative effectiveness research in particular, the USPSTF released its updated guidelines for screening mammography. It replaced its previous recommendation for routine mammography in women beginning at age 40 with the following: "There is convincing evidence that screening with film mammography reduces breast cancer mortality, with a greater absolute reduction for women aged 50 to 74 years than for younger women," and, for women under age 50, recommended that doctors "individualize the decision to begin biennial screening according to the patient's context and values."

In May 2012, the USPSTF issued this statement regarding the use of the blood test for prostate-specific antigen (PSA) to screen for men for prostate cancer: "There is convincing evidence that PSA-based screening programs result in the detection of many cases of asymptomatic prostate cancer, and that a substantial percentage of men who have asymptomatic cancer detected by PSA screening have a tumor that either will not progress or will progress so slowly that it would have remained asymptomatic for the man's lifetime." The Panel recommended, "Do not use prostate-specific antigen-based screening for prostate cancer." The summary goes on to explain the harms of screening and the harms of treatment.

The release of the mammography and PSA recommendations caused firestorms with similar scripts. Women and men—including members of Congress, high-profile sports and entertainment figures, and ordinary people—who believed their lives had been saved by having the screening tests marshaled their personal testimonials as evidence the USPSTF recommendations were wrong. Some advocacy groups supported the findings of the Task Force and endorsed their recommendations; others deplored them. Some professional organizations went on the record saying that they supported the Task Force's recommendations in view of the current evidence, while others said they were not going to change what they recommended, regardless of what the Task Force found. Some of the latter are organizations of professionals whose income is derived in part from the interventions that are the subjects of revised recommendations. Members of Congress joined with other influentials to write editorials full of misinformation that inflamed the public's indignation.[27] Executive-branch government officials distanced themselves from the recommendations and reminded the public that the Task Force was not a government body and did not make health policy.

A careful reading of the criticisms and rebuttals captured in the media and comments posted in response to news articles shows that the backlashes to the mammography and PSA recommendations share similar features. First, critics infrequently attack the scientific evidence that is the basis for the recommendation or the process of evidence review and synthesis. Second, while critics occasionally, but not routinely, cast aspersion on the expertise of the Task Force panelists, they suspect or try to arouse suspicion that the panel is acting as the agent of the political party in power. Third, critics contend that the motivation behind the recommendations is not science, but rather to advance a political agenda or to disenfranchise certain segments of the population. Finally, the message that many critics hear or prompt the public to hear in the recommendations is that they will be used "to prevent me or someone I care about from getting something that I believe is important for my health and well-being."

The USPSTF makes recommendations based on current best evidence. It does not issue clinical practice guidelines or advise health insurers or health plans whether they should provide coverage or reimbursement for a particular health service. However, the evidence-based recommendations issued by the USPSTF are taken into account by entities that do issue practice guidelines, for example, some professional societies, and by third-party payers when they formulate coverage policies. Moreover, the Affordable Care Act has attached the lever of payment policy to the preventive health recommendations issued by the USPSTF. It mandates that health plans and health insurers "shall, at a minimum, provide coverage for and shall not impose any cost-sharing requirements for evidence-based items or services that have in effect a rating of 'A' or 'B' in the current recommendations of the USPSTF." (The USPSTF grade for screening mammography for women aged 40–49 is "C"; for women 50–74 is "B," and for PSA-based prostate cancer screening is "D.") The law goes on to say that insurers may provide coverage for services in addition to those recommended by the Task Force and are not prohibited from denying coverage for services not recommended by the Task Force.

Organized Medicine's Reaction to the Changed Recommendations

How did organized medicine respond to the updated USPSTF recommendations? Surely doctors would be better at handling new scientific evidence than patients. We will look at two groups: the American Medical Association and the American Urological Association.

The American Medical Association (AMA) is a 164-year old organization with over 225,000 physician-members (a little over a fourth of U.S. physicians belong) that says its mission is "to promote the art and science of medicine and the betterment of public health." On June 19, 2012, the AMA announced several new policies that the organization had adopted. The press release said, "Today, the AMA has adopted policy that starting at age 40, all women should be eligible for screening mammography. The policy also supports insurance coverage for this screening." Yet we saw that the comprehensive evidence review conducted by the U.S. Preventive Services Task Force in 2009 led the Task Force to conclude that the evidence indicates that "the additional benefit gained by starting screening at 40 years rather than at age 50 is small and that moderate harms from screening remain at any age." In coming to its conflicting assessment, did the AMA review scientific evidence that the Task Force did not have access to? Probably not. Does the AMA policy statement help it achieve its mission of bettering the public health? Or is it really about bettering the bottom line?[28]

The American Urological Association (AUA) is a professional organization of about 18,000 urologists. Its mission is "to promote the highest standards of urological clinical care through education, research, and the formulation of health care policy." The AUA has fought against the USPSTF recommendations on PSA testing since they were issued in draft form in October 2011. Their strategy included lobbying members of Congress, a body not known for its expertise in systematic reviews of medical scientific evidence. The organization congratulated the State of New Jersey for its "bold and decisive stand" when its legislature passed an act in January 2012 guaranteeing coverage for PSA testing in spite of the USPSTF recommendations. When the Task Force issued the final recommendations in May 2012, giving a grade of D to PSA-based screening programs for prostate cancer based on evidence showing that such testing leads to more harm than good, the AUA said it was "outraged and believes the Task Force is doing men a great disservice." Less PSA testing will cut into urologists' revenue from prostatectomy for prostate cancer, an operation that for many men does more harm than good.[29]

Both the AMA and AUA believe that insurance companies should cover screening mammography in women 40–49 and PSA testing for men. But should they be covered, given the current status of the evidence and ever-increasing health insurance costs? A sensible approach for items and services that have been demonstrated to be ineffective or of no net benefit might be to require individuals to pay for them out of pocket.

The American Public and the Concept of Scientific Evidence

Concerns about being able to access a personally valued (if unwarranted from an evidential standpoint) health service explains much of the outcry against the USPSTF recommendations on mammography and PSA testing, but another factor is at play: contemporary American views of experts. The American public has developed a deep suspicion of experts, especially experts who propound theories, frameworks, and recommendations that conflict with individuals' own personal anecdotal experiences of reality.

In the 1960s the view took hold that public policy decision making would be more rational if it were informed by systematic, data-based analysis and not just on history, intuition, and politics.[30] Schools of public policy began to be established to prepare individuals to produce and use data-based policy analyses. The Congress wanted data-based policy analyses, and two new agencies were established in the legislative branch: the Office of Technology Assessment in 1972 (eliminated by Congress in 1995) and the Congressional Budget Office in 1974. (Alice Rivlin, CBO's first director, called her office "the official purveyor of bad news to the Congress.") The planning, budgeting, and administration of federal social action programs, including health programs, became more systematic and data based. Systems analysts and policy analysts—experts— enjoyed a place at the table in the governmental decision-making process.

Over the past two decades the situation has changed. Analysts and experts in publicly funded programs have lost their cachet with a sizable segment of the American population, especially the political Right. On a daily basis attacks are made, for example, on climate change science, the science of evolutionary biology, economic analysis—not only on the science behind recommendations for preventive and therapeutic medicine.

While it is tempting to blame the political Right for the deposing of experts and what appears to be increasing anti-science attitudes in the United States, some of the problem may be with how we are educating members of our society. The American public has more formal education than ever. In 1970, only about half of Americans had graduated from high school, and just over 10% had graduated from college. In 2010, the corresponding percentages were 87% and

30%.[31] Despite having more formal education, the public's understanding of science is problematic. Surveys conducted by the National Science Foundation show that most Americans hold a favorable view of science and technology, but two-thirds (in 2001) do not have a firm grasp of what is meant by the scientific process. Moreover, sizable proportions hold beliefs in pseudoscience, for example, that the position of the sun and the stars can affect people's lives (25%) and in extrasensory perception (50%). People who do not understand the scientific process and cannot distinguish pseudoscience from science may be more susceptible than others to fear and suspicion mongering (e.g., "rationing" and "death panels") by individuals with certain political agendas. Those who do not understand the incremental nature of scientific advances may be frustrated and confused by evidence from one study that conflicts with that of another, and by what seems to be "flip-flopping" when recommendations change, based on emerging evidence, about the value of a particular test or treatment.

The American Public and Third-Party Payers for Health Care

Further compounding the problem is the fact that individuals often hear about the medical evidence for or against a certain health service first and most often from their health insurers. From financial as well as non-financial standpoints, Americans have a lot of what one of our informants called "skin in the game" that should ease the acceptance of payment policies that are based on scientific evidence of comparative effectiveness. Insured Americans pay for their medical care by paying insurance premiums; sharing the costs of covered items and services with health insurers through deductibles, co-payments, and coinsurance; and purchasing non-covered items and services out of pocket. In addition, Americans fund the public insurance programs of Medicare and Medicaid through a system of federal payroll taxes and state and local taxes.

But since the public backlash of the mid-1990s against managed care, Americans suspect that their health plans are more interested in the health of their bottom lines than the health of their beneficiaries. A 2008 poll of over 100,000 Americans revealed that consumers believe that health insurers keep 31% of the revenues they received as profit (employers thought it was 30%).[32] However, analyses of data from the Security and Exchange Commission indicate health plan profit margins are less than 5%.[33] The industry has an image problem. It is going to have to do better at educating consumers on how scientific evidence is used in coverage decisions and why evidence-based policies are in consumers' best interest.

While many Americans give good grades (A or B) to their health plans, half of people under age 65 report some type of problem with their health plan in the prior year, the most common being delays or denials of coverage or care (12% of all people; 28% of people with medical problems).[34] Denials of coverage

based on scientific evidence that the desired service is ineffective or less effective than an alternative hold little persuasive power for most consumers.

To be fair, the American public's concerns about individuals' access and coverage to health services are occurring against a backdrop of increasing health
care costs and intensifying problems paying medical bills. In 2012, one of four
Americans reported that they or a family member had problems paying medical bills in the past year, and three in ten postponed getting health care they
felt they needed.[35] This serious financial stress may seem paradoxical in view of
the fact that the proportion of personal health care expenditures paid for out
of pocket has been declining every year and in 2010 was 13.7% compared to
39.6% in 1970. However, percentages mislead. Total national health expenditures in 2010 were $2,186 billion, nearly 35 times what they were in 1970. The
share paid out of pocket in 2010 is 12 times greater than it was in 1970.

Why Third-Party Coverage Policies Based on Evidence of Comparative Effectiveness Are Better than the Alternative

We no longer have the luxury of paying for health care of no or marginal value.
In 2009, U.S. national health expenditures accounted for 17.6% of the Gross
Domestic Product, or an average of $8,086 per person. However, individuals do
not use "average" amounts of health services. For many years it has been noted
that medical care expenditures are concentrated in a small percentage of the
population. When members of the U.S. population are ranked by health expenditures, the top 5% of the population accounts for nearly 50% of expenditures,
with an annual mean expenditure of $40,682 (2009 data).[36] The lower 50% of
the population accounts for only 2.9% of health expenditures, with an annual
mean of $236. But while people vary widely in the amount of health care they
consume and the amount of costs they incur, our country's health insurance
patchwork levels significantly the amount any one of us pays for health care.
Putting this another way, people who are low users of services during a given
period help to pay for the services used by high users during that period. We
are paying for one another.

In 2010, 55.3% of Americans were covered by an employer-sponsored private plan, 14.5% by Medicare, and 15.9% by Medicaid.[37] The rest of the population was covered by directly purchased private health insurance (9.8%),
military health care (4.2%), or was uninsured. For Americans under age 65,
employer-sponsored insurance is the leading source of health insurance.[38] In
2011, 60% of U.S. firms offered health benefits to all or some of their workers;
among firms offering benefits, an average of 79% of their workers are covered.
Employees pay health insurance premiums regardless of whether the employee
or her family members use covered health services. In 2011, for all plan types

of employer-based insurance, the average annual premium was $5,429 for single coverage and $15,073 for family coverage, with the employee contributing, on average, 18% of the premium for single coverage (about $921) and 28% of the premium for family coverage ($4,129), and the employer paying the rest. If covered services are used, the employee faces additional costs that take the form of annual deductibles and/or paying part of the cost of the services used (co-payments or co-insurance). Most types of plans have annual deductibles; they are least common among HMOs, with 29% of HMO enrollees bound by an annual deductible. In 2011, depending on plan type, the average annual deductible for single coverage ranged from $675 to $1,908 and for family coverage from $1,487 to $3,666. Most workers also have to pay a part of the cost of the services they use (doctor visits, hospitalizations, prescription drugs, outpatient surgery), either a set amount called a co-payment, or a percentage, called coinsurance. Most plans limit the amount a covered worker must contribute for co-payments and coinsurance in a given year; the limits differ considerably.

Employers are shifting health care costs onto employees, further raising the stakes for a possible payoff of coverage policies based on evidence of comparative effectiveness. A sizable proportion of firms offering health benefits in 2011 took actions to control the costs of health coverage, such as reducing the scope of health benefits offered or increasing the amount of employee cost-sharing (22% of firms with 3–199 workers; 33% of firms with 200 or more workers), or increasing the worker's share of the insurance premium (19% and 46% of firms, respectively).[39]

Medicare is a federal health insurance program, tax-supported, that was established in 1965. Americans over age 65, younger people with certain disabilities, and people with end-stage renal disease are covered by Medicare, which consists of Part A (hospital insurance), Part B (physician and outpatient services insurance), Part C (Medicare Advantage), and Part D (prescription drug coverage, established in 2003). Medicare's original fee-for-service benefits consist of Part A and Part B. Beneficiaries may elect to enroll in Part A and B (and D), or in Part C, the Medicare Advantage program, which are plans offered by private companies approved by Medicare. Medicare Advantage plans must provide all Part A and Part B covered services; most include prescription drug coverage (Part D). In 2012, 27% of the nation's 42 million Medicare beneficiaries were enrolled in Medicare Advantage plans, and 73% in "original" Medicare.

Many people who are not covered by Medicare mistakenly believe that Medicare covers all health care costs. We give some figures here so that readers can form a truer impression of the impact that out-of-pocket costs exert on Medicare beneficiaries, many of whom have limited incomes and limited financial assets.

Medicare "original" beneficiaries incur out-of-pocket costs for their coverage and care. Regardless of whether they use any services, they pay monthly premiums. While most people do not have to pay a Part A premium because they paid taxes to Medicare during the years of their employment, for Part B, the standard premium in 2012 was $99.90 per month, with higher income individuals paying more. In addition to premiums, people who use services pay deductibles and pay part of the cost of services they use. The annual deductibles are $1,156 per hospital stay and $140 per year for physician and outpatient services. In addition to the out-of-pocket deductibles, enrollees in Part A and B pay co-payments for hospital stays exceeding 60 days ($289 per day) and 90 days ($578 per day), and coinsurance of 20% per visit of allowable costs for physician and outpatient services. Original Medicare has no annual limits on beneficiaries' out-of-pocket liabilities for co-payments and coinsurance. In 2012, enrollees in Part D had a $320 annual deductible and pay 20% coinsurance up to an initial coverage of limit of $2,930 in total drug costs; there is a gap in coverage between the amounts of $2,930 and $4,700; after that limit has been reached, enrollees pay 5% per drug.[40] Eight out of 10 Medicare beneficiaries pay for supplementary coverage[41] to help with deductibles and cost-sharing.

All enrollees in Medicare Advantage plans (Part C) must pay the standard monthly Part B Medicare premium, and nearly half of such plans charge an additional premium, which averaged $79.83 per month in 2012.[42] The federal government requires that Medicare Advantage plans cap out-of-pocket costs associated with using services at $6,700 (2012 level).

As the preceding paragraphs show, Medicare beneficiaries bear considerable out-of-pocket costs in a single year. A recent analysis showed that average cumulative out-of-pocket expenditures during the 5 years before death were $38,688 for individuals and $51,030 for couples in which one spouse dies.[43] For one of four people, their out-of-pocket expenditures for costs not covered by Medicare exceeded their baseline total household assets.

Our society in general and each of us as individuals are laboring under heavy burdens of costly health care. Knowledge from comparative effectiveness research will not only improve our health outcomes but will increase the value of the dollars we spend on health care.

Conclusions

As a society, we are all paying for each other's health care, not as obviously as in countries with tax-supported, full-access national health systems like the United Kingdom, but paying nonetheless, across generations, and through complex cost-shifting practices in which low users subsidize the costs incurred by high users, people who will never use certain services pay for others to use them, and in which providers shift costs across payers. It is in our best interests to pay for the medical services most likely to lead to desired health outcomes. Pre-existing trends in this direction in the health insurance sector will be accelerated by federally mandated comparative effectiveness research. However, if more and better comparative effectiveness research is to increase the value of the dollars we spend on health care, patients, providers, and third-party payers must become better students of medical evidence. Payment policies and the organization of health services will have to be reconfigured to increase the value of the health care dollars we are spending, while taking into account for some enduring aspects of the American psyche: our deep regard for innovation, the belief many of us hold that the newest technology is the best even when no evidence exists to support that belief, and the mistaken impression held by some of us that more health care is always better than less.

Notes

1. Data from 2005–2008. Between 1988 and 1994, the prevalence of uncontrolled blood pressure in Americans who had been told they had hypertension was 74%. Source: Health, United States 2010, p. 44. Accessed October 12, 2012, at http://www.cdc.gov/nchs/data/hus/hus10.pdf.
2. Stafford RS, Bartholomew LK, Cushman WC, et al. Impact of ALLHAT/JNC7 dissemination project on thiazide-type diuretic use. Arch Intern Med 2010;170:851–8.
3. Data from the Veterans Health Administration Pharmacy Benefits Management Strategic Healthcare Group. Accessed October 12, 2012 at http://www.pbm.va.gov/tig/felodipine.pdf.
4. Stranges E, Kowlessar N, Elixhauser A. Components of growth in inpatient hospital costs, 1997–2009: statistical brief #123. Accessed November 6, 2012, at http://www.hcup-us.ahrq.gov/reports/statbriefs/sb123.jsp.
5. Data are from the Stranges et al. paper cited earlier. Others have estimated that a hospital can "produce" a PTCA with stenting for about $4,000, well under the Medicare reimbursement rates.
6. Shahinian VB, Kuo YF, Gilbert SM. Reimbursement policy and androgen-deprivation therapy for prostate cancer. N Engl J Med 2010;363:1822–32.
7. And a good chance of harm; emerging research suggests an increase in risk for hip fracture, colon cancer, and other problems.
8. Holahan J, Chen V. Changes in health insurance coverage in the Great Recession, 2007–2010. The Urban Institute, December 2011. Accessed October 10, 2012, at http://www.kff.org/uninsured/8264.cfm.
9. Eibner C, Price CC. The effect of the Affordable Care Act on enrollment and premiums, with and without the individual mandate. RAND Health Technical Report TR-1221-CMF (2012). http://www.rand.org/content/dam/rand/pubs/technical_reports/2012/RAND_TR1221.pdf accessed June 13, 2012.
10. Data from the National Health Statistics Group, Office of the Actuary, Centers for Medicare and Medicaid Services. Accessed October 12, 2012, at http://www.cms.gov/NationalHealthExpendData/downloads/PieChartSourcesExpenditures2009.pdf.
11. U.S. Census Bureau, Statistical Abstract of the United States: 2012.
12. See, for example, Garber AM. Evidence-based coverage policy. Health Aff 2001;20:62–82.
13. Neumann PJ, Chambers JD. Medicare's enduring struggle to define "reasonable and necessary" care. N Engl J Med 2012;367:1775–7.

14. The MEDCAC, formerly known as the Medicare Coverage Advisory Committee, is a nongovernmental body of up to 100 experts charged to provide independent guidance and expert advice to CMS on specific topics related to items and services covered by Medicare or that may be eligible for coverage. Topic-specific panels of up to 15 members meet 4–8 times/year.

15. Accessed October 10, 2012, at http://www.cms.gov/Medicare/Coverage/DeterminationProcess/Downloads/8a.pdf

16. Council for Affordable Health Insurance. Trends in state-mandated benefits, 2010. October 2010. Accessed October 10, 2012, at http://www.cahi.org/cahI_contents/resources/pdf/PolicyTrendsMandatedBenefitsOct2010.pdf.

17. National Business Coalition on Health. Educating employers about the value–based purchasing of health care services, 2009. Accessed October 10, 2012, at http://www.nbch.org/vbpguide.

18. See Forward to: Consumer Financial Incentives: a decision guide for purchasers, by Dudley RA, Tseng CW, Bozic K, Smith WA, Luft HS. AHRQ Pub. No. 07(08)-0059, November 2007.

19. Choudry NK, Avorn J, Glynn RJ, et al. Full coverage for preventive medications after myocardial infarction. N Engl J Med 2011;365:2088–97.

20. Trivedi AN, Rakowski W, Ayanian JZ. Effect of cost sharing on screening mammography in Medicare health plans. N Engl J Med 2008;358:375–83.

21. For extensive information about trends in the pharmaceutical and biotechnology industry, see the numerous reports available online through Cutting Edge Information, available from http://www.cuttingedgeinfo.com/.

22. A recent example involves the cancer drug Zaltrap, made by Sanofi-Aventis. The drug, approved for marketing in August 2102, was priced at about $11,000 per month for a course of treatment. The drug maker provided discounts that halved the price after doctors at Memorial Sloan-Kettering Cancer Center said they were not going to prescribe it, because it did not work any better than Avastin (made by Genentech) and costs twice as much. Pollack A. Sanofi halves price of cancer drug Zaltrap after Sloan-Kettering rejection. New York Times 2012 Nov 8.

23. For an overview, see: Centers for Medicare and Medicaid Services, Roadmap for implementing value-driven healthcare in the traditional Medicare fee-for-service program, September 3, 2009. Accessed October 12, 2012, at http://www.cms.gov/Medicare/Quality-Initiatives-Patient-Assessment-Instruments/QualityInitiativesGenInfo/Downloads/VBPRoadmap_OEA_1–16_508.pdf.

24. Miller DC, Gust C, Dimick JB, Birkmeyer N, Skinner J, Birkmeyer JD. Large variations in Medicare payments for surgery highlight savings potential from bundled payment programs. Health Aff 2011;30:2107–15.

25. See: Ginsburg PS. Spending to save—ACOs and the Medicare Shared Savings Program. N Engl J Med 2011;364:2085–6, and Goldsmith J. Accountable Care Organizations: the case for flexible partnerships between health plans and providers. Health Aff 2011;30:32–40.

26. Murphy J, Geisen E, Olmstead MG, Williams J, Pitts A, Bell D, Morley M, Hill C. Methodology: U.S. News & World Report Best Hospitals 2011–12. Accessed June 26, 2012, at http://static.usnews.com/documents/health/best-hospitals-methodology.pdf.

27. For an egregious example see an editorial by Senator Kay Bailey Hutchison (R-TX) and Andrew von Eschenbach, the former head of the National Cancer Institute: "Lives saved by prostate test" published in the Houston Chronicle 2012 June 12.

28. According to the U.S. Centers for Disease Control and Prevention, 61.5% of American women aged 40–49 had a mammogram in 2008. A doctor's order is required for a mammogram, and results are provided to women by their doctors. Many doctors require office visits for test ordering and follow-up. Doctors also order and follow up on subsequent tests done to explore suspicious findings. A decline in mammography rates translates into a substantial loss in physician (and imaging center) revenue.

29. For example, see Wilt TJ, Brawer MK, Jones KM, et al. Radical prostatectomy versus observation for localized prostate cancer. N Engl J Med 2012;367:201–13.

30. See Rivlin A. Systematic thinking for social action. The Brookings Institution, 1971, Washington, DC.

31. Data from the Current Population Survey, reported by the U.S. Bureau of the Census. Accessed June 11, 2012, at http://www.census.gov/compendia/statab/2012/tables/12s0229.pdf.

32. WellPoint Institute of Health Care Knowledge. The facts about health insurer profits. November 2009. Accessed October 10, 2012, at http://www.wellpoint.com/prodcontrib/groups/wellpoint/@wp_news_research/documents/wlp_assets/pw_d014921.pdf.

33. America's Health Insurance Plans, a trade organization, found the average health plan profit margin for 2010 to be 4.4%. Accessed October 10, 2012, at http://www.ahipcoverage.com/2011/05/14/fact-check-health-plans-profits-accounted-for-12-of-1-of-total-health-care-spending-in-2010/.

34. Kaiser Family Foundation/Harvard School of Public Health. National survey on consumer experiences with and attitudes toward health plans. August 2001. Accessed October 10, 2012, at http://www.kff.org/insurance/loader.cfm?url=/commonspot/security/getfile.cfm&PageID=13858.

35. Kaiser Family Foundation. Health security watch, June 2012. Accessed October 10, 2012, at http://www.kff.org/healthpollreport/CurrentEdition/security/upload/8322.pdf.

36. Data from the Household Component of the Medical Expenditure Panel Survey. See Cohen SB. The concentration of health care expenditures and related expenses for costly medical conditions, 2009. AHRQ Statistical Brief #359, 2009. Accessed October 10, 2012, at http://meps.ahrq.gov/mepsweb/data_files/publications/st359/stat359.pdf.

37. Data from DeNavas-Walt C, Proctor BD, Smith JC. U.S. Census Bureau, Current Population Reports, P60–239, Income, poverty, and health insurance coverage in the United States: 2010. U.S. Government Printing Office, Washington, DC, 2011.

38. Kaiser Family Foundation and Health Research and Educational Trust. Employer Health Benefits, 2011 annual survey. Accessed October 10, 2012, at http://ehbs.kff.org/2011.html.

39. Ibid.

40. Kaiser Family Foundation. Fact Sheet: the Medicare prescription drug benefit, November 2011.

41. America's Health Insurance Plans: Medicare supplement (Medigap) insurance facts and myths. April 24, 2012. Accessed June 12, 2012, at http://www.ahip.org/Issues/Product-and-Market-Issues.aspx.

42. Kaiser Family Foundation. Medicare Advantage 2012 Data Spotlight: enrollment market update. Pub. No. 8323, 2012. Prepared by Gold M, Jacobson G, Damica A, and Neuman T.

43. Kelley AS, McGarry K, Fahle S, Marshall SM, Du Q, Skinner JS. Out-of-pocket spending in the last five years of life. J Gen Intern Med 2012 Sep 5 [epub ahead of print].

12

Dealing with Uncertainty

Payment Policy for the Generation of Evidence as Part of Clinical Practice

In the last chapter we discussed how payment policy is being used and might be used to bring medical practice into alignment with what the evidence shows works best in a given clinical scenario. Linking practice with evidence through payment policy will increase the value we get for the dollars we spend on medical care.

But how should we proceed when valid evidence about the benefits and harms of an intervention or course of action does not yet exist? As the truism goes, "Absence of evidence is not evidence of absence." If high-quality studies using bias-controlling design features have been conducted, and their findings indicate that an intervention is of no or marginal benefit, we have "evidence of absence" of effectiveness and can choose a more effective alternative. On the other hand, if the definitive studies evaluating the benefits and harms of an intervention have yet to be conducted, we cannot make a judgment that the intervention is of no or marginal value. We have a condition of uncertainty: "absence of evidence."

In fact, there are vast landscapes of uncertainty in medicine. We saw in Part I that great gaps exist in the current evidence base for many commonly used diagnostic and therapeutic interventions. The gaps are even worse for leading-edge technologies. And we cannot ignore the reality that medical science is incremental: even when we have good evidence for what works best today, how can we find out what will work best for tomorrow? In view of the realities of how the medical care system in the United States is organized and financed, what constructive options do we have for dealing with uncertainty? How are the justifiable interests of patients and payers best protected in situations of "absence of evidence"? Patients want the health services that will give them the best health outcomes. Purchasers and payers want to make financial outlays for services that lead to the best outcomes at the lowest cost.

Under conditions of uncertainty of the value of a health service, the best way to protect the interests of both parties is *to reduce the uncertainty*. Moreover, from the standpoint of medical ethics, acknowledging that uncertainty exists and working to reduce it is a course of action superior to simply treating the patient as if all answers are known.[1] Unfortunately, contemporary medical care in America is very far from this ideal.

To reduce uncertainty about what works best in medicine requires systematic inquiry and observation: in other words, research. If uncertainty in medicine is pervasive, and it is, then research should pervade clinical practice as well. But compared to the volume of clinical care delivered in the country, an infinitesimal amount of clinical research is conducted. At present, clinical practice and clinical research are endeavors that almost always occur in different "spaces." Patients, doctors, and other health professionals tend to believe that research into what works best is something done by someone else in some other setting.

In a given year, Americans make over 1.2 billion visits to physicians' offices and hospital outpatient and emergency departments. The roughly 5,000 non-federal community hospitals in the United States admit 35.7 million people annually and provide nearly 600 hospital days of care per 1,000 persons in the population. Each of these clinical encounters is an opportunity for learning what works best in medicine. Right now, most of them are missed opportunities.

Very few Americans participate in non-interventional epidemiology studies and in clinical trials. For example, only 2.3 million Americans—less than 1% of the U.S. population—enroll in the roughly 80,000 cancer clinical trials conducted each year.[2] To put this in a disease perspective, only 0.08% of men newly diagnosed with prostate cancer enroll in a National Institutes of Health (NIH)–funded prostate cancer trial, in the face of all the uncertainty about the best way to treat this common cancer. Perhaps due to the outstanding educational programs on clinical trials provided for lay people by the National Breast Cancer Coalition, the fraction of women with newly diagnosed breast cancer who enroll in trials is higher, but still only 3.2%.

Before we go further, we want the reader to note that our focus in this chapter is on the reduction of uncertainty in medicine by means of primary research, that is, research that requires interpersonal contact between the research participant and the investigator, rather than the secondary analysis of health care databases drawn from claims files or electronic health records. The latter has its place in reducing some kinds of uncertainty, as we saw in Chapter 1. However, fair tests of the comparative effects of clinical interventions almost always require primary research, specifically, clinical trials: clinical trials comparing interventions that have already obtained regulatory approval, or, in the case of surgical procedures, already entered routine use. (Clinical trials on not-yet-approved interventions that are conducted with regulatory intent and sponsored by the medical products industry do not concern us here.) What role can payment policy play to incentivize the reduction of uncertainty by means of such trials, and what else will be needed?

At present, coverage and reimbursement policies of third-party payers reward providers and patients for ignoring clinical uncertainty. Payers do not want to cover "investigational" interventions, and they do not, when they are called that. Drugs and devices come onto the market with some evidence of their effectiveness but very little if any evidence of how well they work compared to reasonable therapeutic alternatives, but patients and doctors have no other choice but to decide that one is somehow preferable (for whatever reason, including detailing by company representatives) and use that one. Regarding surgical procedures, as we saw in Chapter 4, because surgery is an unregulated medical technology, many invasive therapeutic procedures come into clinical use without having been put to fair tests of effectiveness compared to alternatives, and at best we might describe them as "promising but unvalidated." Yet insurers cover such procedures and reimburse providers for performing them. This state of affairs is reinforced by the belief held by many Americans that their doctor knows best (the same doctor who gets it right about half the time according to the McGlynn study described in the last chapter), beliefs that some doctors engender when they communicate with their patients. There is empirical evidence that when patients are appraised of the uncertainty around a clinical intervention, they make different choices for themselves. For example, presenting patients with standardized information about the risks, benefits, and uncertainties associated with preference-sensitive operations such as prostatectomy for obstructive urinary symptoms leads to substantial reductions in uptake of the operations,[7] indicating that the usual preoperative informed consent process may not be adequately disclosing clinical uncertainties.

Fortunately, a new framework is emerging for acknowledging uncertainty and using payment policy to incentivize its reduction.

Payment Policy and the Reduction of Uncertainty in Medicine

A payment model is being developed that incentivizes the acknowledgement of uncertainty in medicine and its reduction through participation in research. The Centers for Medicare and Medicaid Services (CMS) has taken the lead in this effort in the United States. Now "coverage only with study participation (coverage with evidence development)" is one of the four possible outcomes of Medicare's national coverage determination about a health care item or service (the other outcomes are non-coverage, coverage without special conditions, and conditional coverage). Coverage with evidence development models are emerging in other countries, for example, the "only in research" policies of the U.K.'s National Health Service[3] and a program of the province of Ontario, Canada that is called "conditional funding for field evaluation." These arrangements give the patient access to the item or service in return for contributing to an evidence base. They are more constructive than coverage denials or exclusions of promising but unvalidated technologies because they allow for an eventual scientific determination of effectiveness and relative effectiveness. This positions the insurer to make an evidence-based non-conditional policy decision about coverage. It also protects the patient by ensuring that the unproven technology is administered under circumstances that are more controlled.

Medicare's coverage with evidence development program had an interesting start. In Box 12.1 we provide an account told to us by one informant and confirmed by other interviewees. Agency officials had been struggling with coverage decisions pertaining to items and services for which the evidence base was insufficiently developed to meet Medicare's standard of "reasonable and necessary." In the early 2000s the landmark trial of lung volume reduction surgery for the treatment of emphysema became a paradigm for the constructive handling of clinical uncertainty.[4] Agency officials saw the value in having a means by which high-quality evidence could be generated about items and services that were high cost and/or high risk so that their coverage decisions would be informed. To resolve an appropriations standoff with Congress provoked by the agency's unwillingness to cover an expensive, unproven technology, CMS officials took the opportunity to try out such a policy of coverage with evidence development.

Box 12.1 **The Story behind Medicare's Coverage with Evidence Development Policy as Told to Us by a Former Medicare Official**

[Medicare's] formal explicit coverage process didn't come into being until 1999 or 2000 when we actually started doing decision memos. Prior to 1999, the only thing that existed was the final language that went into the Medicare manual that said, "We will pay for this x,y,z," no explanation at all. I was very intrigued by the lung volume reduction surgery model. That trial was then coming to a close. We actually got the coverage decision back to us with the data, and so we started looking for an opportunity to see if we could, what is the word, replicate the lung volume reduction surgery model using exactly the same regulatory language and legal arguments to tie it to the medical necessity language. We were just looking for kind of the proof of concept [*for coverage with evidence development, CED]* or a vehicle to do it with . . . The opportunity that arose was around PET [*positron emission tomography*] scanning for Alzheimer's disease. Senator Stevens [(R-AK). *Stevens chaired the Senate Appropriations Committee from 1997 to 2005 except for the 18 months when Democrats controlled the Senate*] was fairly passionate about the importance of PET coverage and had come back at Medicare on several occasions of reinforcing the seriousness of his interest, including one time, in 1999, that the entire HHS appropriations was held up over a PET coverage issue. It was only after Donna Shalala [*Secretary of HHS*] agreed to cover solitary pulmonary nodule as a PET indication that the HHS appropriations was able to go forward. So there was a track record of this being serious business.

So this whole issue was whether Medicare would pay for use of PET in diagnosis of Alzheimer's. We had a MEDCAC meeting on the topic, and we had Duke University do a decision model. We had a really robust platform to suggest there was not evidence of clinical utility. But the pressure was rather sustained, and so after we came out with a "no" decision we were encouraged to reopen the decision and have a NIH expert panel brought together. The NIH expert panel said, "We don't think the evidence is quite there, but it is very promising, and we would really encourage a future study on how it impacts care." It came to the point where it was pretty clear that maintaining a blanket Medicare non-coverage of PET for Alzheimer's was not going to be politically viable ... Sometime around then I just had the inspiration that maybe we could turn this lemon into lemonade, by using this as the vehicle to get the proof of concept for CED. So I made that as an offer to Senator Stevens through the intermediary of Mike Phelps [*a close friend of Senator Stevens*] that the evidence wasn't really there to support it, but there was probably enough evidence to support it in the context of the trial and maybe that would be a reasonable compromise. I would be willing to support it if they could convince Secretary Thompson that was something we ought to do.

That is what eventually happened. We put out a policy that said we will only pay for PET scanning for suspected dementia if and when there is an adequately designed pragmatic clinical trial, showing that it improved patient outcomes. Such a trial has been designed but it has never been funded . . . A group did submit a grant request to NIH but NIH turned it down and there was nobody else available to fund it. But the nice thing about it was that we now actually had a decision memo for the first time in the modern era that laid out the conceptual framework for CED.

While Medicare may require that the patient participate in a CMS-approved study in order to get coverage for the item or service in question, CMS itself does not sponsor, develop, or conduct such research. If no CMS-approved trial or registry is under way, there is no possibility of Medicare coverage for the item or service, even if the beneficiary would agree to participate in evidence development. This is a grave limitation to the value of Medicare's coverage with evidence development policies and one that will require resolution by cooperative agreements between CMS and the research agencies in the Department of Health and Human Services. The Patient-Centered Outcomes Research Institute (PCORI) could play a role here as well.

Medicare's coverage with evidence development policy generated controversy when it was started and some continue to find it objectionable from statutory and other viewpoints. The ethical foundations seem unassailable; first, that under conditions of decisional uncertainty due to a lack of scientific evidence, the standard for high-quality medical care is care that helps to reduce the uncertainty, namely participation in a clinical trial or observational study, and second, that individuals have no fundamental right to, and physicians have no obligation to prescribe, medical care that is of unproven benefit. Since the birth of the coverage with evidence development policy in 1999, CMS has expanded its use and continues to refine it, holding public comment periods and meetings to review how and when it is applied.[5]

Except in the Medicare program, coverage with evidence development is still in its infancy in the United States. However, important advances are being made in understanding the issues surrounding coverage with evidence development in the private sector and in developing organizational models suitable for purchasers and private insurers.[6] The increasing attention to comparative effectiveness research, and increased capacity for it, are likely to accelerate the development of these models. From a conceptual standpoint, coverage with evidence development policies would be relatively simple to develop and implement in integrated delivery systems. Provided regulatory and other barriers can be overcome, purchasers and insurers may develop partnerships, including partnerships between the public and private health care sectors, that use coverage with evidence development policies for rapid-cycle studies of comparative effectiveness of promising but unvalidated high-cost or high-risk treatments of mutual interest.

Risk-Sharing Arrangements between Product Makers and Payers

From the point of view of medical product makers, coverage with evidence development is a sort of conditional market entry. Another version of this is "risk-sharing." Pharmaceutical companies have entered into risk-sharing agreements with payers in order to gain market access for some of their products, in particular high-cost products that have received Food and Drug Administration approval and that appear promising, but have uncertain cost-effectiveness profiles. This model, which has been more commonly used in Europe than in the United States, involves tying the payment a drug maker gets for a drug to the outcomes of patients who use it. In return for a formulary listing for a trial period, or trial use in selected patients expected to benefit from the agent, a drug maker agrees to reimburse the insurer if expected outcomes are not attained.[7] While this arrangement is not a head-to-head comparative trial, it could provide some information about a product's clinical effectiveness relative to alternatives. However, there is no requirement that product makers must release valid and high-quality information about the results of risk-sharing arrangements on patients' health outcomes, and it is unlikely they will report unfavorable outcomes.

Payment Policy for the Reduction of Uncertainty: Necessary but Not Sufficient

Providing patients access to a health care item or service of uncertain value in return for their participation in the generation of evidence about it has great potential as a quid pro quo in the U.S. health care system. But establishing the formal policies governing coverage with evidence development is only the start. If the reduction of uncertainty through evidence generation is to become standard operating procedure in routine clinical care, we must understand and overcome the barriers that exist to participation in research. Some of these barriers are attitudinal and some are related to the infrastructure and prevailing logistics for clinical research. Moreover, new structures and processes must be established so that every clinician and every patient expects that evidence generation is part of all but the most mundane medical interactions. The structures and processes of evidence generation integrated with clinical practice must neutralize burdens on patients, maximize the benefits to them and their providers, minimize or compensate inconvenience, protect privacy, and avoid disrupting the relationship between the patient and his or her usual sources of care.

Clinical Trials: A Need for Simplification

Of particular interest (and intense need) is work to streamline randomized clinical trials, so that it is feasible to use the research design that yields the least biased and most valid estimates of an intervention's effects compared to one or several alternatives. Randomized evidence is needed to evaluate the magnitude and direction of the effects of interventions because evidence from nonrandomized studies is or uncertain validity.

Estimates are that, in clinical trials of new drugs conducted for regulatory purposes, the cost per participant is $5,000 to $10,000. At this level, not very many publicly funded comparative research trials can be conducted. While it is true that some research questions will always need exploration in the rarified atmosphere of the placebo-controlled efficacy trial conducted for regulatory purposes, most other research—even randomized trials—can and should be conducted in the messy world of routine practice. Over the past two decades, advances have been made in two types of clinical trials that have lower per-participant costs and seem very well suited for comparative effectiveness research incentivized by health insurers' payment policies: large, simple trials, first used in 1993 by Richard Peto and others of the Clinical Trial Service Unit at Oxford in the United Kingdom, and pragmatic clinical trials (also called practical or effectiveness trials), described in detail in multiple writings by David Sackett. In a large, simple trial, the entry criteria, the treatments, and the data requirements are kept to an absolute minimum. Though pragmatic clinical trials may not be large and may not be able to be called "simple," as a reading of examples will show,[8] the two kinds of trials share many features in common. Both are designed to detect modest treatment effects, not just large ones, and strive for maximal generalizability. Both pose questions relevant to practicing clinicians or health care managers and focus on outcomes that are relevant to patients. Both make individuals with the target disorder eligible for enrollment regardless of risk, likely responsiveness, record of compliance, or site of care; the trial participants are cared for by non-experts in routine clinical settings at routine frequencies. Both limit burdens on participants and investigators, and unobtrusively monitor compliance and adherence to the trial protocol. These conditions are very different from industry-sponsored trials conducted for regulatory purposes.

Much more developmental work needs to be done on the methods, logistics, and limitations of large simple trials and pragmatic trials, but these approaches have already shown great promise as robust tools for the generation of high-quality evidence in the setting of real-world clinical practice. This effort is being helped along by the fact that a major focus of the statute that established PCORI in 2010 is the development and periodic updating of comparative effectiveness research methodology. On July 23, 2012, PCORI's Methodology Committee published for public comment a draft of its first Methodology Report, "'Our questions, our decisions': standards for patient-centered outcomes research."[9] While PCORI's Methodology Committee will help advance the science of comparative effectiveness research, the increase in size and capability of the cadre of investigators conducting such research will be even

more important. Any time "critical mass" is achieved in a scientific field, great
advances are seen not only in topical but also methodological areas.

Hearts and Minds: Patients

Even if the trials have been designed and fielded, will patients enroll in them?
Very little systematic information exists on Americans' views of participating
in clinical research, and much groundwork remains to be done in this area.
However, people with cancer have been surveyed to determine the reasons
for the low rates of participation in cancer clinical trials.[10] Many people report
they were not made aware of the possibility of participating. Of those who are,
three-quarters forego enrolling for reasons such as fears of receiving a placebo,
beliefs that the standard treatment would be better than the one under testing,
fears of being treated like a guinea pig, and logistical issues such as unrealistic
travel requirements or uncertainty about insurance coverage. Regarding the
latter, the lack of national consensus about which parties (patients, insurers, or
research sponsors) are responsible for which trial-related costs has resulted in
uneven coverage and reimbursement policies across the country, which undermines desire and ability to enroll in a trial. The impact of payment policies on
trial participation rates may be greater for trials of already-approved therapies,
which are largely the topics with which comparative effectiveness research is
concerned.[11] While education and public information campaigns may allay
fears about clinical trials, it is clear that logistical and third-party coverage
problems will need to be solved if trial participation is to grow.

Americans are wary of the intentions behind the payment policies of their
health insurers, and insurers will have to develop and implement sound information strategies with their beneficiaries if they want to foster the reduction
of clinical uncertainty through coverage with evidence development policies.
Plans' communication strategies should use cultural cuing to change the culture around medical research and be tailored for specific groups of enrollees,
informed by considerations of health literacy and cultural competence. The key
message should be that, in order to improve the quality of care the plan can provide, enrollees need to help to gather information through research participation. Acknowledging consumers' concerns about their increasing out-of-pocket
health-care costs, health plans and insurers should explicitly communicate to
their beneficiaries that they intend to control average costs per beneficiary by
identifying and eliminating items and services (including invasive procedures)
for which there are more effective and safer alternatives. Plans and insurers
will have to deal constructively with consumers' justifiable concerns that this
strategy is simply intended to make the insurer or plan richer. Plans and insurers could offer to proactively notify their beneficiaries of health technologies
particularly in need of evidence generation as they arise and direct them to

opportunities to participate in evaluative studies. For example, an emerging technology is robotically assisted single-port (through the umbilicus) abdominal surgery, which is much more expensive than alternative approaches but is not yet known to confer incremental benefits.

When gaps exist in evidence for a promising but unvalidated new health technology, co-payments and coinsurance levels for participation in evidence development could be tiered to give patients choices about what kind of study they want to enroll in. In this approach, the consumer would pay the most for the item, service or procedure if they declined to participate in evidence generation about it, less for agreeing to participate in an observational (non-randomized) study, and the least or nothing for agreeing to participate in a randomized controlled trial.[13] This is similar to the idea behind value-based insurance designs in which interventions are classified into tiers based on their known effectiveness. Consumers would be assisted in their decision making about whether to participate in evidence generation in return for coverage if a respected source not associated with the insurance company was accessible that provided valid appraisals of the existing evidence on the technology's benefits, risks, uncertainties, and relative costs.

Hearts and Minds: Physicians

In 2009, there were 838,453 active physicians in the United States, about 58% of them office based.[12] Over the past decades the size and organization of physician practices have changed. The proportion of physicians working in solo or small (<5) practices has declined to just over 40% (2004–2005 data). The number of physicians working in multi-specialty practices has been decreasing and is now 27.5%,[13] while the number working in single-specialty practices has grown. The potential these physicians and practices have for evidence generation is enormous. It is difficult to see how much progress can be made without their participation.

We need a better understanding of physicians' barriers to participating in evidence development and enabling their patients to do so. The information we do have suggests that factors include lack of awareness about which trials are open and enrolling, lack of awareness about the uncertainty surrounding the comparative effectiveness of health care items and services, and fear the loss of income when a patient enrolls in a trial and transfers his or her care. Even more important, there are hassle and time factors for physicians to collaborate in clinical trials. One study estimated that it takes about 15 minutes to identify a patient who is suitable for a given protocol, and another 2.5 hours to take him or her through the informed consent and enrollment processes.[14] Subsequently there is the commitment for follow-up visits, reporting adverse events, and monthly trial-related administrative tasks. Reimbursement for time spent in research-related tasks is poorly worked out, and the incentives inherent in how physicians, especially surgeons, are paid discourage research and reward clinical volume. As one neurosurgeon told us when we interviewed him about his views on evidence generation as part of clinical practice, "I get paid to operate. I don't get paid to collect data." Few practicing physicians and surgeons will be able to be active members of the clinical research enterprise unless these barriers are removed.

U.S. Infrastructure for Clinical Research

The infrastructure for clinical research in America has undergone profound changes in the last decade. The infrastructure for industry-initiated and sponsored clinical trials has become vastly stronger than that for clinical research supported with public funds or by nonprofit entities. The nation's public, nonprofit infrastructure is not up to the task of accelerating high-quality comparative effectiveness research. Using payment policy to incentivize the reduction of uncertainty through evidence development will require the rejuvenation and reorganization of our public, nonprofit infrastructure for clinical research.

Over the past 30 years a major change has occurred in where industry-initiated and industry-sponsored research is conducted. While in the past most of it was conducted in academic medical centers by medical school faculty, now an estimated two-thirds of clinical trials are run by contract research organizations (CROs). CROs are for-profit companies to which the medical products industry outsources various elements of clinical trials, especially the recruitment of human subjects for trials,[15] which is the most time-consuming and costly element of clinical trials, and the monitoring of ongoing trials for regulatory compliance. CROs range from small niche companies to very large companies with a global reach. However, CROs even include for-profit research ethics review boards, which calls into question the degree to which ethics oversight to protect research subjects is independent of financial conflicts of interest. As the rosiglitazone story we told in Chapter 3 shows, it is all too easy to subvert good science.

The rise in the number and influence of CROs has been meteoric. According to the Association of Clinical Research Organizations, a trade association founded in 2002, CRO industry revenue was $20 billion in 2010, and the medical products industry routes a third of its research and development spending to CROs.

As industry-sponsored clinical trials have migrated to the CRO sector, the clinical trials infrastructure in academic medicine has deteriorated. Weak or nonexistent infrastructure wastes scarce human and financial resources for research and undermines the efficiency of systematic inquiry, including comparative effectiveness research incentivized by payment policy. Participants in a 2009 Institute of Medicine (IOM) workshop noted that most academic-sector clinical trials are "one-off" affairs, in which all the components (investigators, sites, staff, volunteers, procedures, and processes) of the trial are laboriously and at great expense put together de novo for the trial but are disbanded as soon as the trial is over.[16] This is exactly the opposite of the CRO model and explains why trials conducted by CROs are completed 30% more quickly and substantially less expensively than industry-sponsored trials in academic medical centers.

An alternative vision for public-sector clinical trials, which was put forth by the FDA's Janet Woodcock, a participant in the 2009 IOM workshop, is that of a permanent network of clinical trial resources supported by continuous federal funding via contracts instead of by one-off grants. In fact, this is the model of the highly successful VA Cooperative Studies Program. The NIH does support clinical research and clinical trials networks. One of the most illustrious is the 50-year old Clinical Trials Cooperative Group of the National Cancer Institute, in which 25,000 patients and thousands of clinical researchers participate every year.[17] And though the names of several hundred clinical research networks are listed in an inventory posted on the Clinical Trials Networks Best Practices Web site (the Duke Clinical Research Institute), many of these entities are not effective contributors to the nation's infrastructure for publicly funded clinical and comparative effectiveness research.

We need a publicly funded network of academic and practice-based organizations devoted to and accountable for the conduct of high-quality, rapid-cycle comparative effectiveness research, and capable of developing constructive partnerships with third-party payers interested in establishing payment policies for coverage with evidence development. Moreover, incentives to community-based physicians are needed in order to overcome their traditionally low rates of participation in the not-for-profit clinical research enterprise.

Conclusions

In the early 2000s the term "a learning health care system" began to be heard. The Institute of Medicine's Roundtable on Value and Science-Driven Health Care, convened in 2006 and still active in 2012, envisions a learning health care system as one in which "health care [is] improved through the systematic and routine capture and analysis of clinical data from point-of-care-learning, the seamless application of insights to improve the effectiveness and efficiency of care processes, and the outcomes and value optimized for each patient and the system as a whole."[18] We are decades away from building such a health care system. Nevertheless, the means and the end of comparative effectiveness research is learning through point-of-care observational or interventional research and then using it to optimize outcomes and value.

Innumerable challenges must be overcome to realize the vision of making evidence generation an inseparable part of the medical interactions that occur in routine clinical practice. Using payment policy to incentivize progress in this direction can be a major impetus. In this chapter, we have mentioned just a few of the other challenges. The Patient-Centered Outcomes Research Institute is positioned to encourage progress on many of them. PCORI may create considerable consumer demand for more opportunities to participate in clinical research. It has committed itself to involve consumers—patients—at every step of the research process, from setting PCORI's research priorities, to informing the design of individual studies, to serving as reviewers of grant applications, to serving on advisory committees for research studies in progress. It is impossible to say just how many consumers PCORI has involved in its operations to date, but it must number in the thousands by now. PCORI's activities are making it clear that patients are not just research subjects anymore. When patients begin to demand that their experiences with various health care items and services inform that of future patients, and have easy opportunities to make that happen, then we Americans will make progress toward the ethical requirement that all of us should share in the burdens of research just as we share in its benefits.

Notes

1. See, for example, Ashcroft R. Giving medicine a fair trial. BMJ 2000;320:1686.
2. Murthy VH, Krumholz HM, Gross CP. Participation in cancer clinical trials: race-, sex-, and age-based disparities. JAMA 2004;291:2720–6.
3. NICE Citizens Council. Only in research. January 2007. Available from http://www.nice. org.uk/media/129/29/OIRReport300407.pdf
4. Carino T, Sheingold S, Tunis S. Using clinical trials as a condition of coverage: lessons from the National Emphysema Treatment Trial. Clinical Trials 2004;1:108–21.
5. The public comments registered on coverage with evidence development from November 2011 to January 2012 can be found on the CMS Web site, accessed October 18, 2012 at http://www.cms.gov/medicare-coverage-database/details/mcd-view-public-comments. aspx?MCDId=8&ExpandComments=n&McdName=CED+Public+Solicitation&Searc hType=Advanced&CoverageSelection=National&NCSelection=NCA%7cNCD%7cME DCAC%7cTA%7cMCD&kq=true&bc=IAAAABAAAgAA&. In May 2012, the Medicare Evidence Development and Coverage Advisory Committee convened a meeting so that invited and public attendees could provide information and opinions on five questions pertaining to the evidential threshold that could be used to invoke a coverage with evidence development decision. The five questions are posted on the CMS Web site, accessed October 18, 2012, at http://www.cms.gov/medicare-coverage-database/details/ medcac-meeting-details.aspx?MEDCACId=63&bc=AAAIAAAAAAAA&.
6. This work is being led by Sean Tunis and others at the Center for Medical Technology Policy. See, for example, Center for Medical Technology Policy. Coverage with evidence development in the private sector: lessons in design and implementation [issue brief]. July 2012. Accessed October 17, 2012, at http://www.cmtpnet.org/wp-content/uploads/ downloads/2012/03/CED-in-the-Private-Sector.pdf.
7. Neumann PJ, Chambers JD, Simon F, Meckley LM. Risk-sharing arrangements that link payment for drugs to health outcomes are proving difficult to implement. Health Aff 2011;30:2329–7.

8. An example of large, simple trials is the ISIS-2: [No authors listed] Randomised trial of intravenous streptokinase, oral aspirin, both, or neither among 17,187 cases of suspected acute myocardial infarction: ISIS-2 (Second International Study of Infarct Survival) Collaborative Group. Lancet 1988;2(8607):349–60. An example of a pragmatic clinical trial is the CATIE: Lieberman JA, Stroup TS, McEvoy JP, et al. Effectiveness of antipsychotic drugs in patients with chronic schizophrenia. Clinical Antipsychotic Trials of Intervention Effectiveness (CATIE) Investigators. N Engl JMed 2005;353:1209–23.

9. Accessed October 17, 2012, at http://pcori.org/assets/MethodologyReport-Comment. pdf. See also Methodology Committee of the Patient-Centered Outcomes Research Institute (PCORI). Methodological standards and patient-centeredness in comparative effectiveness research: the PCORI perspective. JAMA 2012;307:1636–40.

10. Comis RL, Aldige CR, Stovall EL, Krebs LU, Risher PJ, Taylor HJ. A quantitative survey of public attitudes towards cancer clinical trials. Accessed October 18, 2012 at http://www.cancertrialshelp.org/CTHpdf/308-9.pdf.

11. For an excellent example, see Martin DF, Maguire MG, Fine SL. Identifying and eliminating the roadblocks to comparative effectiveness research. N Engl J Med 2012;363:105–7. Some third-party payers will cover the costs of routine services (care that they patient would have needed and gotten if he/she was not participating in a trial) while their insured patients are enrolled in a trial of an investigational, that is, not yet approved, drug or device (trial sponsors must pay for the services the trial participant received specifically for trial purposes only). However, payment polices are very unclear when the health care item or service that is the focus of the trial has already been FDA approved and/or is already in routine use.

12. Figures for the U.S. physician and hospital markets are from the U.S. Census Bureau, Statistical Abstract of the United States: 2012.

13. Liebhaber A, Grossman J. Physicians moving to mid-sized, single-specialty practices. Results from the Community Tracking Survey. Center for Studying Health System Change, No. 18, August 2007.

14. Dilts DM, Sandler AB, Cheng SK, et al. Steps and time to process clinical trials at the Cancer Therapy Evaluation Program. J Clin Oncol 2009;27:1761–6.

15. See Elliot C. What happens when profit margins drive clinical research? Mother Jones, September/October, 2010.

16. Institute of Medicine. Transforming clinical research in the United States: challenges and opportunities [workshop summary]. Washington, DC: National Academies Press, 2010.

17. Institute of Medicine. A national cancer clinical trials system for the 21st century: reinvigorating the NCI Cooperative Group Program [consensus report]. Washington, DC: National Academies Press, 2010.

18. Institute of Medicine. Engineering a Learning Healthcare System: A Look at the Future [workshop summary]. Washington, DC: National Academies Press, 2011:pg 4.

EPILOGUE

We began following legislative initiatives for comparative effectiveness research in early 2006. We were captivated by the possibility that legislative action might be taken to improve the state of the evidence supporting clinical decision making, ease the shortage of funding opportunities for comparative effectiveness research, make it possible to incorporate the evidence that does exist into actual clinical care, and create opportunities to make the generation of high-quality evidence a part of routine clinical practice. To be honest, we doubted that such action would be successful. In July 2008, when we received an Investigator Award in Health Policy Research from the Robert Wood Johnson Foundation to support the research for this book, we anticipated seeing the end of the legislative story sometime in 2009, after the presidential elections in November 2008, and that the end would be the death of any new federal mandate for comparative effectiveness research.

We were wrong on both counts. The story, and our research, lasted much longer, till the Affordable Care Act was signed into law in March 2010, and the ending was not what we expected but what we had hoped.

Along the way there was much high drama and several cliff-hangers. We did not anticipate the Democratic wins in the White House and Congress in 2008 that brought comprehensive health care reform within reach. We did not anticipate that a Great Recession would create the need for a massive economic stimulus package that would include down payments on health reform. Would the comparative effectiveness research provisions in the 2009 Recovery Act survive the conference committee? They did. Would the Affordable Care Act make it out of Congress, and which version—House or Senate—of the comparative effectiveness provisions would it include? The Affordable Care Act was signed into law in March 2010, and the Senate version prevailed. We have a Patient-Centered Outcomes Research Institute (PCORI) that is not a federal agency.

The story did not end even then. There were two additional challenges to the continued existence of the new PCORI. One was the challenge to the constitutionality of the Affordable Care Act's individual mandate and the Medicaid expansion provisions. If the Supreme Court held that the law or certain of its provisions were unconstitutional, the fate of PCORI was in doubt. However, in mid-2012, the Supreme Court upheld the law. The next challenge was the presidential and congressional elections of November 2012. During his campaign, Republican presidential contender Mitt Romney vowed that, if elected, he would "repeal Obamacare on Day 1." If Romney were elected, PCORI would likely be dismantled. But President Barack Obama was re-elected for a second term, the Democrats retained control of the Senate, and Republicans retained control of the House.

Having survived its two major challenges in 2012, the Affordable Care Act of 2010 and its comparative effectiveness research provisions will continue to be implemented as planned. Congressional Republicans have vowed to use their powers, especially the powers of the purse, to chip away at various provisions of the law. Because the PCORI is funded predominantly by fees on health insurers rather than by congressional appropriations, the Institute seems positioned to withstand incursions from that front, and the Institute's momentum got a boost from the November 2012 elections.

Indeed, PCORI has built considerable momentum over the 2.5 years of its existence.[1] It has become a well-functioning organization, thanks to its external governing bodies and internal operations staff. It has settled on a definition of "patient-centered outcomes research," established its initial research priorities (these were given in Chapter 10, Box 10.2), developed and begun to implement strategies for including patients in every step of the research process, and is actively educating researchers on how to bring the views of patients and other stakeholders into the research equation. It is beginning to advance the methods of patient-centered comparative effectiveness research. PCORI has engaged large segments of the health services and outcomes research community as advisors, contractors, applicants for grants, and reviewers of grant applications. It has begun to award peer-reviewed research grants. It is as yet too early to expect that PCORI's activities will have begun to ameliorate the nation's gaps in its knowledge base of the comparative effectiveness of alternative approaches to handling a given clinical or other health-related problem.

Now that it seems PCORI will survive, at least until 2019 when it must receive congressional reauthorization or phase out its operations, the question will be how well it fulfills its statutory mandate and the hopes of the proponents of federally mandated comparative effectiveness research. Several threats must be faced.

One threat is the realignment of the funding priorities of the National Institutes of Health (NIH) away from the sponsoring of comparative effectiveness research. In 2012, the NIH contributed $511 million of the $578 million the nation spent on comparative effectiveness research—88%. Amounts deposited to the PCOR Trust Fund and available for research support grow every year as fees are collected from public and private health insurers. Projections are that deposits will reach $613 million in 2015. However, if the NIH decides that the existence of PCORI means it can redirect elsewhere the funds it was allocating to comparative effectiveness research, we will find ourselves in the undesirable situation of having the same amount of public funds for this kind of research that we did pre-PCORI.

Another threat will arise from the fact that medical product makers see comparative effectiveness research as an endeavor that can make winners or losers of their products. Although product makers were unsuccessful in their efforts to keep mandates for comparative effectiveness research from becoming federal law, they did exert their influence in shaping the provisions, and they will not be relaxing their vigilance over PCORI's activities. As close observers of what was going on in Congress with regard to comparative effectiveness legislation, we were surprised when the name of the bill put forward by Senators Baucus and Conrad changed from the Comparative Effectiveness Research Act of 2008 (S. 3408) to the Patient-Centered Outcomes Research Act of 2009 (S. 1213). As we described in Chapter 9, it was the 2009 version of the Baucus Conrad bill that became law as part of the 2010 Affordable Care Act. We believe that the name change was made to satisfy the medical products industry, which had by that time created the Partnership to Improve Patient Care (PIPC), and was trying to ensure that any legislation on comparative effectiveness research would not hurt their financial interests. It was not only the name of the bill that changed. The 2009 version seems to reflect substantial concessions to the medical products industry, for example, increasing the limitations on how the findings of comparative effectiveness research might be used by the Secretary of Health and Human Services in the oversight of federal health insurance programs, not-so-subtle movements away from considering the costs of health care items and services as part of the effectiveness valuation, and the inclusion of public comment, disclosure, and response standards seemingly intended to slow the research process to a crawl, if not paralyze it completely.

Indeed, PCORI devoted substantial time, effort, and resources in its first months to defining "patient-centered outcomes research." As Box E.1 shows, the definitions of comparative effectiveness research (given in the statute) and patient-centered outcomes research (not given in the statute but created by the Institute) are not the same. Not all comparative effectiveness research need be "patient centered" (e.g., it could center on clinical decision making by doctors or nurses) and not all patient-centered outcomes research need evaluate the comparative effectiveness of alternative preventive, diagnostic, or treatment options. In a footnote to its definition, PCORI acknowledges that its definition "is intended to be broader" than that of comparative effectiveness research. One of the things to watch will be just how much comparative effectiveness research PCORI funds, versus what it calls "other focuses and other methodologies." The danger is that the nation's extensive needs for evidence on which clinical strategies work best will go unsatisfied, and that the "clinicians, purchasers, and policy makers" that the statute says PCORI is to assist, in addition to patients, are relatively neglected.

Box E.1 **Definitions of Comparative Effectiveness Research and the Purpose of the Patient-Centered Outcomes Research Institute**

From subsection (a)(2)(A&B): "'Comparative clinical effectiveness research' and 'research' mean research evaluating and comparing health outcomes and the clinical effectiveness, risks, and benefits of two or more medical treatments, services, and items... The medical treatments, services, and items ... are health care interventions, protocols for treatment, care management, and delivery, procedures, medical devices, diagnostic tools, pharmaceuticals (including drugs and biologicals), integrative health practices, and any other strategies or items being used in the treatment, management, and diagnosis of, or prevention of illness or injury in, individuals."

From subsection (c): "The purpose of the Institute is to assist patients, clinicians, purchasers, and policy-makers in making informed health decisions by advancing the quality and relevance of evidence concerning the manner in which diseases, disorders, and other health conditions can effectively and appropriately be prevented, diagnosed, treated, monitored, and managed through research and evidence synthesis that considers variations in patient subpopulations, and the dissemination of research findings with respect to the relative health outcomes, clinical effectiveness, and appropriateness of the medical treatments, services, and items described in subsection (a)(2)(B)."

Definition of patient-centered outcomes research:

"Patient-centered outcomes research helps people and their caregivers communicate and make informed health care decisions, allowing their voices to be heard in assessing the value of health care options... Patient-centered outcomes research:

1. Assesses the benefits and harms of preventive, diagnostic, therapeutic, palliative, or health delivery system interventions to inform decision-making, highlighting comparisons and outcomes that matter to people;

2. Is inclusive of an individual's preferences, autonomy, and needs, focusing on outcomes that people notice and care about such as survival, function, symptoms, and health-related quality of life;

3. Incorporates a wide variety of settings and diversity of participants to address individual differences and barriers to implementation and dissemination; and

4. Investigates (or may investigate) optimizing outcomes while addressing burden to individuals, availability of services, technology, and personnel, and other stakeholder perspectives."

(A footnote on the definition page states "This definition includes many components of comparative effectiveness research but is intended to be broader to also include other focuses and other research methodologies.")

Sources: Section 6301 of the Affordable Care Act; the definition of "patient-centered outcomes research" was developed by the Patient-Centered Outcomes Research Institute in March 2012.

The broad scope of research covered by PCORI's definition raises another question. What research does the Agency for Healthcare Research and Quality (AHRG) support, and how does it differ from PCORI's? Chronically beleaguered AHRQ must distinguish itself from PCORI, or lawmakers will view it as duplicative, unnecessary, and ripe for elimination. In fact, though most believed it was only political gamesmanship, the draft of the 2013 Department of Health and Human Services appropriations bill that was released by the Republican-led House Appropriations Committee on July 17, 2012 would have killed AHRQ by providing zero funding for it. (The issue was made moot because no regular appropriations bills were passed by the 112th Congress for fiscal year 2013; governmental operations were sustained by the enactment in September of a continuing resolution.) The Affordable Care Act linked PCORI and AHRQ in placing at AHRQ the dissemination and research-capacity building activities for patient-centered outcomes research,[2] but they might be easily moved back to PCORI or to the NIH.

The first research funding opportunity issued by PCORI, announced in September 2011, was for pilot projects focusing on PCORI's national research priorities, the collection of preliminary data, and research methodology. The announcement stated, "For the purposes of this PCORI funding announcement, PCORI is not interested in comparative effectiveness studies aimed at determining comparative efficacy for specific diseases or conditions" (PCORI received 856 applications by the December 1, 2011 deadline—many times what was expected—and announced in June 2012 that 50 would be funded). But now the hard part starts. In May 2102 and again in September 2012, PCORI announced that it was seeking applications "to support clinical comparative effectiveness research" to be funded at the $120 million mark. At least some of the research funded under these two announcements will be perceived by the medical product industry as winners-and-losers research. It will be interesting to see if and how the industry uses its resources to undermine the research process, intimidate researchers, tie up the statutory public comment periods on research methods and findings, and subtly and not so subtly threaten PCORI's leaders and existence. It is clear from the content of the Web site of the Partnership to Improve Care,[3] most of which focuses explicitly on PCORI, that it is watching every step PCORI takes and working to ensure it can influence the organization and what it does.

The interests of the federal government in high-quality evidence about medical therapy were based initially on protecting its citizens from harmful and subsequently from ineffective prescription drugs and medical devices. Now, with the provisions for comparative effectiveness research in the 2010 Affordable Care Act, the federal government has extended its interests past safety and effectiveness into the realm of "best value for money." Best value for money is a dicey proposition for the medical products industry. The industry is likely to use its ample resources to try to ensure that PCORI becomes nothing more than a paper tiger and to influence the public and the lawmakers to whose campaigns they contribute to believe that comparative effectiveness research is not in their best interests. But there are other stakeholders in comparative effectiveness research who gain when we know what works best in medicine. Will patients, physicians, other health professionals, purchasers, payers, and policy makers prevail?

Notes

1. Information from the PCORI Web site and PCORI's 2011 Annual Report, accessed November 14, 2012, at http://www.pcori.org/assets/AnnualReport.pdf.
2. This was a compromise negotiated between the Senate Finance Committee and the Senate HELP Committee. The former wanted all the functions—research, dissemination, and capacity building—to be housed outside government, and the latter all of them within government, at AHRQ.
3. Accessed November 13, 2012, at http://www.improvepatientcare.org/.

INDEX

Page numbers followed by *b* or *t* indicate boxes or tables, respectively. Page numbers followed by n indicate notes.